READING BETWEEN THE LINES

READING BETWEEN THE LINES

Advanced College Reading Skills

JoAnn Yaworski, Ph.D.
West Chester University

PEARSON
Longman

New York   San Francisco   Boston
London   Toronto   Sydney   Tokyo   Singapore   Madrid
Mexico City   Munich   Paris   Cape Town   Hong Kong   Montreal

Senior Acquisitions Editor: Susan Kunchandy
Development Manager: Janet Lanphier
Development Editor: Lai T. Moy
Senior Supplements Editor: Donna Campion
Senior Marketing Manager: Melanie Craig
Managing Editor: Bob Ginsberg
Production Manager: Joseph Vella
Project Coordination, Text Design, and Electronic Page Makeup: Electronic Publishing Services Inc., NYC
Cover Design Manager: John Callahan
Cover Designer: Maria Ilardi
Cover Illustration: Ben Johnson, *Through Marble Halls,* 1996. Acrylic on canvas. Used with permission
    by Ben Johnson.
Manufacturing Manager: Mary Fischer
Senior Manufacturing Buyer: Alfred C. Dorsey
Printer and Binder: R. R. Donnelly & Sons, Inc.
Cover Printer: Phoenix Color Corp.

For permission to use copyrighted material, grateful acknowledgment is made to the copyright holders on pp. 537-541, which are hereby made part of this copyright page.

Library of Congress Cataloging-in-Publication Data
Yaworski, JoAnn.
    Reading between the lines : advanced college reading skills / JoAnn Yaworski.— 1st ed.
        p. cm.
    Includes bibliographical references and index.
    ISBN 0-321-09971-0
 1. Reading (Higher education) I. Title.
LB2395.3.Y39 2004
428.4′071′1—dc22

Visit us at http://www.ablongman.com.

ISBN 0-321-09971-0

1 2 3 4 5 6 7 8 9 10—DOH—08 07 06 05

Contents

■ **CHAPTER 5**

Patterns of Organization—Simple Paragraphs **152**

■ **CHAPTER 6**

Text Patterns—Complex Paragraphs **192**

■ CHAPTER 10

Argument 376

PART III Learning and Studying Strategies 417

■ CHAPTER 11

Reading and Studying Textbooks 418

■ CHAPTER 12

Ensuring College Success   **460**

■ CHAPTER 13

Improving Your Reading Speed   **499**

Contents of Readings by Discipline

WORLD CULTURES

WORLD POLITICS

Preface

Many college professors who teach various disciplines believe that students need to be able to do much more than just read the words in a textbook. They feel strongly that students need to think critically and make judgments based on the information provided. These types of judgments and critical thought are what we call "reading between the lines." Says one Professor of English:

> I want students to come to some personal conclusions and personal judgments about whether they agree with what's in the text . . . They have to read it. Then they have to think about it. Then, they have to read it again.

Reading Between the Lines is a text that goes beyond the basics of reading and comprehending expository text. It is a tool for the college reading instructor to help students develop critical thinking skills. With this text, freshmen, first-generation college students, and adult college students develop critical reading, logical reasoning, and inferencing skills that will enable them to excel in college-level courses across the disciplines.

Along with these critical reading and reasoning skills, *Reading Between the Lines* offers strategies for learning new vocabulary, taking notes from both lectures and textbooks, preparing for essay exams, and establishing good general study skills. My hope is that students will hone and apply these critical thinking skills and strategies not only throughout their academic career, but into their professional lives as well.

THE TEXT

The Introduction discusses reading habits and the importance of developing critical reading skills.

Chapter 1 provides an overview for becoming an active reader, as well as a comprehensive discussion of the reading process and reading for meaning. Clear explanations of text patterns are also provided.

Chapter 2 provides reviews various vocabulary skills, including how to use a dictionary, context clues, word origins, and structural analysis (suffixes, prefixes, and roots). As a compliment to this chapter, students will receive a pre-packaged, text-specific supplement devoted to vocabulary. Such a supplement is ideal for instructors who do not wish their students to buy a separate vocabulary book.

Two chapters are devoted to helping students recognize the main idea: Chapter 3 emphasizes the five different relationships that can exist between the main idea and supporting: (1) the main idea as the first sentence, (2) the main idea as the last sentence, (3) the main idea split between the first and last sentences, (4) the main idea as the middle sentence, and (5) the main idea as an implied idea; Chapter 4 is devoted to the actual practice of recognizing these relationships in context. Chapters 5 and 6 present nine common textbook patterns, with the four simplest patterns explained and illustrated in Chapter 5: (1) term, definition, and example, (2) topics with lists, (3) process, (4) chronological order (time order), and the fire more complex patterns in Chapter 6: (1) description, (2) comparison/contrast, (3) cause/effect, (4) problem/solution, and (5) classification.

Chapter 7 introduces the concepts of making inferences, drawing conclusions, and using logical reasoning.

Chapter 8 emphasizes the author's purpose (to inform, to entertain, and to persuade) and tone of voice.

Chapter 9 introduces students to the concept of rhetorical argument. It discusses identifying the issues, identifying the argument, finding support for the argument, and understanding propaganda.

Chapter 10 goes into greater depth and practice in the area of argument. Detailed discussion focuses on support for good arguments (facts, statistics, common knowledge, personal experience, etc.) and provides identification of fallacies (begging the question, strawman, ad hominem, appeal to emotions, red herring, oversimplification, bandwagon, and so forth).

In Chapter 11, the PQ4R method for reading and study textbooks is presented. There are detailed explanations and practice exercises for each step. Exercises in text boxes encourage students to apply this method to textbook readings from their other disciplines.

Chapter 12 addresses note-taking from two perspectives: taking notes from textbooks and taking notes from lectures. The Cornell method is emphasized in both instances.

In Chapter 13, students are introduced to the concept of speed-reading. Myths are dispelled while reading speed is presented as the rate of processing information. Exercises for increasing thinking speed are presented with a gradual increase in difficulty and length. At the end of the chapter, three readings on the same topic are provided. The easiest reading provides background information while the progressively more difficult readings challenge a student's reading speed and comprehension.

Common to each chapter is the presentation of a skill with examples, short excerpts with comprehension questions; one-page excerpts with vocabulary and comprehension questions; and three-page excerpts with vocabulary and comprehension questions.

Also common to each chapter are "Reading Between the Lines" boxes that provide short practice exercises in critical thinking. Each box is intended to help a student develop his/her powers of inference.

Each chapter also features boxes called "Visual Literacy" boxes that focus on comprehension of visual aids. Included are exercises in reading pie charts, bar graphs, line graphs, Venn diagrams, and so forth.

In summary, throughout the book, students are given a demonstration of a reading skill along with practice exercises. The practice exercises cover readings that become progressively longer and more difficult. Scaffolding and progression strategies guide students from easy to more difficult readings. Readings feature high-interest topics to help students develop confidence in reading expository text information.

FEATURES

Reading Between the Lines offers a number of innovative features to enhance the learning experience:

- **More than 200 excerpts** from a large variety of college disciplines provide practice with reading biology, sociology, psychology, chemistry, communications, history, physical science, economics, geography, geology, English, and so on.

- **"Reading Between the Lines" boxes** that are connected to the chapter readings and/or chapter discussions provide critical thinking practice.

- **"Visual Literacy" boxes** that offer practice with reading and understanding maps, charts, graphs, diagrams, and so forth in context.

- **An emphasis on** inference and critical thinking skills.

- **Several chapters** devoted to note-taking and study skills.

- **One complete chapter** devoted to reading-speed.

ANCILLARY MATERIALS

For Instructors:

Instructor's Manual for *Reading Between the Lines* (Instructor ISBN: 0-321-09973-7): The IM includes suggestions for teaching the course, approaches for teaching each chapter of the test, and more.

Printed Test Bank for Developmental Reading (Instructor ISBN: 0-321-08596-5): Offers more than 3,000 questions in all areas of reading, including vocabulary, main idea, supporting details, patterns of organization, critical thinking, analytical reasoning, inference, point of view, visual aides, and textbook reading.

Electronic Test Bank for Developmental Reading (Instructor CD ISBN: 0-321-08179-X): Offers more than 3,000 questions in all areas of reading, including vocabulary, main idea, supporting details, patterns of organization, critical thinking, analytical reasoning, inference, point of view, visual aides, and textbook reading. Instructors simply choose questions, then print out the completed test for distribution OR offer the test online.

For Students

Critical Reading and Vocabulary Supplement to accompany *Reading Between the Lines:* This text-specific supplement cross-references to the complete chapter on vocabulary skills and reduces the need to purchase additional vocabulary supplements. Also included are ten additional readings of five expository and five narrative selections.

The Longman Textbook Reader, **Revised Edition (with answers Student ISBN: 0-321-11895-2 or without answers Student ISBN: 0-321-12223-2):** This supplement offers five complete chapters from our textbooks: computer science, biology, psychology, communications, and business. Each chapter includes additional comprehension quizzes, critical thinking questions, and group activities.

The Longman Reader's Portfolio and Student Planner: This unique new supplement provides students with a space to plan, think about, and present their work, as well as a 12-month calendar and student planner. The portfolio includes a diagnostic area (including a learning style questionnaire), a working area (including calendars, vocabulary logs, reading response sheets, book club tips, and other valuable materials), and a display area (including a progress chart, a final table of contents, and a final assessment).

The Longman Reader's Journal, **by Kathleen McWhorter (Student ISBN: 0-321-08843-3):** The first journal for readers, The Longman Reader's Journal offers a place for students to record their reactions to and questions about any reading.

Newsweek **Discount Subscription Coupon (12 weeks) (Student ISBN: 0-321-08895-6):** *Newsweek* gets students reading, writing, and thinking about what's going on in the world around them. The price of the subscription is added to the cost of the book. Instructors receive weekly lesson plans, quizzes, and curriculum guides as well as a complimentary *Newsweek* subscription. The price of the subscription is .59 cents per issue (a total of $7.08 for the subscription).

Interactive Guide to Newsweek (Student ISBN 0-321-05528-4): Available with the 12-week subscription to *Newsweek*, this guide serves as a workbook for students who are using the magazine.

MySkillsLab 2.0 (www.ablongman.com/myskillslab): MySkillsLab 2.0 offers the best online resources for developing readers and writers, all in one easy-to-use site. Here, students can improve their reading skills with the newly updated Reading Roadtrip 4.0 and sharpen their writing skills using Writing Voyage. Students will also find help with vocabulary, study skills, and research, and have access to a bank of more than 2,500 grammar exercises.

Reading Roadtrip 4.0 (www.ablongman.com/readingroadtrip): Reading Roadtrip 4.0 is part of MySkillsLab and is also available separately. Each of the 16 cities and landmarks on this tour throughout the United States corresponds to a reading or study skill (for example, finding a main idea, understanding patterns of organization, thinking critically, etc.). This new release of the most popular and exciting reading tool available offers even more practice exercises and test questions in all areas or reading skills. Students can now begin by taking a diagnostic test that helps them determine areas of weakness and offers feedback that directs them to key topics for skill improvement. An Instructor's Manual for Reading Roadtrip 4.0 is available. Please contact your Longman Sales representative for more information.

Penguin Discount Novel Program: In cooperation with Penguin Putnam, Inc., Longman is proud to offer a variety of Penguin paperbacks at a significant discount when packaged with any Longman title. Excellent additions to any Developmental Reading or English course, Penguin titles give students the opportunity to explore contemporary and classical fiction and drama. The available titles include works by authors as diverse as Toni Morrison, Julia Alvarez, Mary Shelley, and Shakespeare. To review the complete list of titles available, visit the Longman-Penguin-Putnam website: http://www.ablongman.com/penguin.

STATE-SPECIFIC SUPPLEMENTS

For Florida Adopters

Thinking Through the Test: A Study Guide for the Florida College Basic Skills Exit Test by D. J. Henry (Reading and writing combined student ISBN 0-321-27660-4; reading and writing combined with answers: ISBN 0-321-27756-2; reading ISBN 0-321-27746-5; reading with answers: ISBN 0-321-27751-1): FOR FLORIDA ADOPTIONS ONLY. This workbook helps students strengthen their reading skills in preparation for the Florida College Basic Skills Exit Test. It features both diagnostic tests to help assess areas that may need improvement and exit tests to help test skill mastery. Detailed explanatory answers have been provided for almost all of the questions.

For Texas Adopters

The Longman THEA Study Guide, **by Jeannette Harris (Student ISBN: 0-321-20271-6):** Created specifically for students in Texas, this study guide includes straightforward explanations and numerous practice exercises to help students prepare for the reading and writing sections of THEA Test.

For New York/CUNY Adopters

Preparing for the CUNY-ACT Reading and Writing Test, **edited by Patricia Licklider (Student ISBN: 0-321-19608-2):** This booklet, prepared by reading and writing faculty from across the CUNY system, is designed to help students prepare for the CUNY-ACT exit test. It includes test-taking tips, reading passages, typical exam questions, and sample writing prompts to help students become familiar with each portion of the test.

ACKNOWLEDGMENTS

I would like to thank Michael Yaworski, Cecilia Yaworski, and Glenn A. Usher for their love, friendship, and steadfast support during the writing of this text.

I have been very fortunate to work with Development Editor Lai T. Moy who went the extra miles to help me develop organization, clarity, and variation in the writing of the text.

I would also like to thank former Acquisition Editor, Steven Rigolosi for his belief in this book and current Acquisition Editor, Susan Kunchandy for her interest and input during the publication process.

Finally, thank-you to our reviewers across the country for their knowledgeable feedback: Edith Alderson, Joliet Junior College; Alison Devaney, El Camino College; Ava Drutman, Westchester Community College; Debra Herrera, Cisco Jr. College; Miriam Kinard, Trident Technical College; Joan Mauldin, San Jacinto College South; Janice McIntyre, Kansas City Kansas Community College; and Jose Rafael Trevino, Laredo Community College.

JOANN YAWORSKI , PH.D

READING BETWEEN THE LINES

PART I
Reading Skills

Achieving College Success

●●

The first course we take in each field of study—for example, biology, sociology, or psychology—is both exciting and challenging. Most instructors assign textbooks that provide us with general introductions to these subjects. Our textbooks act as *big dictionaries*; they define terms, provide examples, and offer interesting details to help us understand what we are reading. Our textbooks also act as *tour guides* to our college classrooms; they explain the major concepts from our professors' lectures so we can follow along and make sense of them. In addition to being dictionaries and tour guides, our textbooks are our *best friends*. They help us grow intellectually by challenging us to think in new ways. Over a period of two to four years, they help us to become experts in our chosen fields. However, in order for all of this to take place, we need to become expert readers.

RECOGNIZING READING HABITS

Let us consider the following statements made by college students. Although bright and capable, they were placed on academic probation for their low grades in college. Based on their comments, we can begin to see how important it is to upgrade our reading skills when we enter college.

ELINA: When I read a chapter in biology, I don't have a clue what is going on.
TONI: If I am not interested in a subject, I end up reading the whole page without learning anything.
MANUEL: Reading and note-taking are a waste of time.

NING: I read too slowly, and my concentration is terrible. The littlest thing will make me look away and set me off. Sometimes, I just read the first and last paragraphs and make up something in between.

Now compare these comments with those made by another group of college freshmen who managed to attain average to above-average grades:

RITA: Basically, I do it [read] by paragraphs. I try to summarize and write things in my notes and go on to the next paragraph.

KURIAN: Usually I look at headings and look for sentences that summarize things and the general topic, take things and just put things together. I usually read it all the way through and underline or highlight what's important.

FARAH: While I'm reading I will highlight the titles and then the subtitles, and then usually like right after the subtitles there's either a statement or a question that gets answered in the rest of the paragraph. So, I'll highlight the statement of the question and then I'll highlight the most important parts and then I'll just read the whole thing. And, I'll go back and either I'll reread it or, you know, I will just reiterate in my mind the part that I highlighted.

The students in the second group show a better understanding of *how* to read a textbook effectively. This is very important because two-thirds of the information we learn in college comes from our textbooks. Once we learn how to take from them the information we need, we are free to discover the new worlds they open up for us.

A college reading textbook is different from a subject-specific textbook because it is not a body of information to be memorized. Instead, it provides the directions or roadmap for learning how to read and study the textbooks for your other courses.

Reading Between the Lines is a reading textbook, and in a sense, it is the most important book that you will own in college. In it, you will find the keys that unlock the information to all of your other college texts. Each chapter presents a key strategy to help you increase your reading ability and efficiency so that it will become easier for you to understand your other courses' reading assignments.

Sometimes it is easier to understand written text if you can first see a picture of what the text is describing. For this reason, authors often provide visual representations of ideas and information in the form of tables, charts, graphs, and diagrams. To help you learn how to read and interpret the images in your college textbooks, each chapter of *Reading Between the Lines* includes Visual Literacy boxes that place these images within context.

For example, suppose you are reading a chapter from a book about different careers. The main topic discusses the elements that affect competition in the job market. To illustrate how one of these elements works to do this, the author may use tables such as the ones that appear in Visual Literacy Box I.1.

As you study Table 1, you can quickly deduce that competition for jobs is steep for those with a high school diploma because it is a common degree (obtained by more than 80% of both genders of the population in 1998). However, Table I.2 indicates that a college degree is not so common; only about 25%

of the population has this degree. Based on the information provided in the tables, we can conclude that individuals who hold a four-year degree are more qualified than 75% of the population for many jobs requiring a four-year degree. Although this conclusion is not explicitly written in the table, we have considered the statistics, thought about them logically, and as a result, were able to draw a reasonable conclusion from the information provided.

Knowledge of textbook reading and reasoning skills, along with an understanding of how to read images, can help you learn how to "read between the lines"—that is, to discover the meanings of a word or a passage that are not always directly stated on the page. As we said earlier, skill in reading textbooks is crucial to success in college. Therefore, in addition to Visual Literacy boxes, this book also presents Reading Between the Lines boxes. These boxes teach you how to dig deeply into language so that you can find the meanings beyond the literal definitions of words you see on the page.

Visual Literacy Box I.1

TABLES: EDUCATIONAL ATTAINMENT

A **table** is the easiest way to show an image of facts because it puts the information into neat columns and rows.

To read a table:

1. Study the title, subtitle, headings, and other labels to learn what type of information is in the table and how that information is arranged.

2. Then, study the column headings to learn what information is listed in each column.

3. To find information in the table, read down the column, then across that row to the correct column.

Visual literacy in practice: [Refer to Tables 1 and 2]

1. What percentage of males graduated from high school in 1990?

2. From 1940 to 1998, which gender had the larger percentage of high school graduates?

3. Which gender had the larger percentage of college graduates from 1940 to 1998?

4. In which year did the greatest gap occur between the genders with respect to graduation from college?

5. From 1940 to 1998, which gender had the larger percentage of college graduates?

(continued on next page)

(continued from previous page)

Table 1   Educational Attainment of U.S. Population Age 25 Years and Over, 1940–1998

	Completed Four Years of High School or More	
Year	*Male*	*Female*
1940	22.7%	26.3%
1950	32.6	36.0
1959	42.2	45.2
1970	55.0	55.4
1980	69.1	68.1
1990	77.7	77.5
1998	82.8	82.9

Table 2   Educational Attainment of U.S. Population Age 25 Years and Over, 1940–1998

	Completed Four Years of College or More	
Year	*Male*	*Female*
1940	5.5%	3.8%
1950	7.3	5.2
1959	10.3	6.0
1970	14.1	8.2
1980	20.8	13.5
1990	24.4	18.4
1998	26.5	22.4

Source: U.S. Bureau of the Census, *Current Population Reports*, P20–513.

CHAPTER

1

Becoming an Active Reader

In this chapter, "Becoming an Active Reader," we discuss how to
- recognize organizational patterns that signal the author's outline;
- recognize clues to the author's meaning;
- become an active reader.

RECOGNIZING ORGANIZATIONAL PATTERNS

Let's think about how authors help readers understand their works. An author writes to express ideas. For the reader to understand these ideas, she must create a mental picture of the information provided. Authors help a reader develop this mental picture by organizing their ideas and relating them to something that the reader already knows and can imagine.

Sometimes we don't have the knowledge to understand the author's clues. In that situation, we mistakenly arrive at a meaning different from what the author intends. Other times, we may direct our attention only to the things that interest us. In this case, we pay more attention to select parts of our reading and ignore others.

Clues to the Author's Outline

Why is it important for both the author and the reader to think in terms of organization? Think of a student, let's say Joe, who has packed all of his belongings at random into garbage bags and then unpacked them by dumping the contents of each garbage bag onto the middle of his dorm room floor. Now let's say that his roommate, Victor, needs a power cord so he can hook up his computer. Joe tells him, "Oh, sure, no problem. I have an extra power cord that you can borrow." How long do you think it would take Joe to find his extra power cord? It would probably take a long time or at least a much longer time than it would take if his belongings were all put away into their proper places.

This same organizational concept may be applied to reading. The author's writing has an outline. This outline makes it easier for the reader to understand how the **topics, main ideas,** and **details** are connected. The *topic* is a general idea of what a reading is about. The *main idea* is a general statement that explains the topic, and the *supporting details* are the statements that provide more information about the main idea.

For example, "Joe's Stuff" could be a topic. However, because Joe's belongings are mixed up in a huge pile on the floor, explaining what Joe brought to college by looking through the huge pile would be very frustrating. How could we make the search easier? Victor could help Joe organize his stuff. He might put his blankets, sheets, and towels on the bed and his clothes in the dresser. He could put his athletic equipment in the closet and his computer equipment and books on the desk. With all of Joe's belongings separated into specific groups, Victor now has a better chance of finding the power cord that he needs to borrow. What else can we say about Joe's belongings now that everything is organized?

Let us review. In our unpacking-for-college example, we said that our topic is "Joe's Stuff." Our main idea is "Joe brought clothing, bedding, athletic equipment, and computer equipment with him to college." Our supporting details, then, include sentences that describe the major groups of items that Joe brought.

Topic:	Joe's Stuff
Main Idea:	Joe brought clothing, bedding, athletic equipment, and computer equipment with him to college.
Detail:	We might mention that since this is the summer term, Joe's wardrobe mainly consisted of jeans, T-shirts, tennis clothes, and a bathing suit. [Here we are providing an observation or "supporting detail" about Joe's belongings.]
Detail:	Although Joe is not famous for making his bed, he did bring sheets, blankets, and a pillow.
Detail:	His love for sports led him to bring his golf clubs, tennis racket, lacrosse equipment, basketball, and Frisbee.
Detail:	Finally, wanting to be on the cutting edge of information technology, Joe brought his laptop, printer, scanner, and a bunch of extra power cords.

Just as it is easier to find a power cord among "Joe's stuff" after it is organized, so it is also easier for us to find the information we need when we recognize the author's organization or outline. (We will talk about topics, main ideas, and details more fully in Chapters 3 and 4.)

Paragraph Patterns

Good writers organize their thoughts into paragraphs. A **paragraph** is a group of sentences based on a certain topic. A good paragraph contains both the main idea and the supporting details. The term **paragraph patterns** refers to the various ways authors can arrange or organize the main idea and supporting details in a paragraph. The main idea and details can follow different patterns depending upon the author's purpose. The most common paragraph patterns found in textbooks include:

- topic and list
- term, definition, and examples
- process
- chronological order
- narration

Topic and List   The topic and list pattern is used when an author has a certain number of items to discuss and the order in which he presents them is unimportant. He organizes his paragraph by introducing the topic and then writing a sentence explaining the topic. This is usually the first sentence (which becomes the *topic sentence*). The author then lists the items that support the topic in random order (the items on the list are the *details*).

> In the beginning, <u>dating</u> < topic > was considered a form of recreation and only gradually assumed a direct relation to courtship or mate selection. Historically, there have been three approaches to mate selection < main idea about topic > and premarital heterosexual relationships: < items related to the topic > ①arranged, ②restricted-choice, and ③open-choice marriages (Adams, 1986). Arranged marriages are found in those societies dedicated to fostering and strengthening kinship groups and economic benefits. For most immigrants to the United States, arranged marriage was a custom left behind in the old countries. In the new land of individual opportunity, rarely did parents formally determine their children's future mates. In contrast, restricted- and open-choice marriages were based on individual decisions. (Davidson and Moore, 94)

A diagram of the Topic and List pattern looks like this:

Topic: Dating

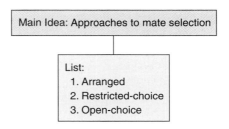

Term, Definition, and Examples   The term, definition, and examples pattern is the most common one found in introductory textbooks. The author highlights the new vocabulary word, usually by using **boldface** print, and then defines the term. He then includes one or several examples to clarify the term and to help the reader relate to its meaning.

> Changes in society from one generation to the next can affect the life course. Bernice Neigarten (1968, 1979) points out that an important cultural and generational influence on adult development is the **social clock**—age-graded expectations for life events, such as *beginning a first job, getting married, birth of the first child, buying a home, and retiring.* All societies have timetables for accomplishing major developmental tasks. Being on time or off time can profoundly affect self-esteem, since adults make social comparisons, measuring the progress of their lives against their friends', siblings', and colleagues'. Especially when evaluating family and occupational attainments, people often ask, "How am I doing for my age?" *(Berk, 459–60)*

A diagram of the term, definition, and examples pattern looks like this:

Topic: Changes in Society

Main Idea: Changes in society from one generation to the next can affect the life course.

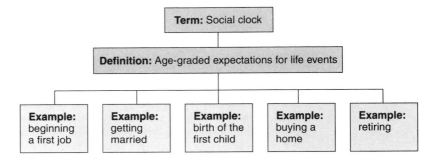

Process   Authors use the process pattern when they need to explain a series of events that must happen in a specific order. An explanation involving the steps that must be taken to complete a chemistry experiment or to follow a recipe would be a disaster if they were not followed in an exact order. The example below shows the stages in the process of dating.

> There are ***sequential stages in the dating process*** that determine the rules of the dating game: ①casual dating, ②steadily dating, ③seriously dating, and ④engaged-to-be-engaged. ***Parents may have defined casual dating*** in their day as "playing the field," in which the person was dating a number of different people at the same time. Today, this is often called "dating" or "hanging out." ***Steadily dating*** describes the stage in which persons date each other frequently and decrease their dating of other persons. An increase in interaction, affection, dependence, and control occurs at this stage. However, in this stage there is no agreement to date each other exclusively. The term ***seriously dating*** ("going out with" or "seeing someone") has, to a con-

siderable degree, replaced the term steady dating, particularly among college-age individuals. Seriously dating usually means a commitment to date each other exclusively as well as an emotional commitment in the relationship. The **engaged-to-be-engaged** status involves an understanding that the individuals will eventually marry each other, but there may be no public or formal declaration of this intent. (Davidson and Moore, 296)

A diagram of this process paragraph pattern looks like this:

Topic: The dating process

Main Idea: There are sequential stages in the dating process that determine the rules of the dating game.

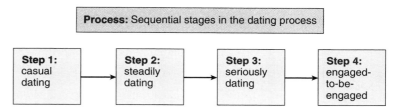

Chronological Order   Authors use the chronological order pattern when they need to report events in the order in which they happened (as in the case of historical text or a story) or should happen (as in the case of a recipe or directions to make something). This is also sometimes called the *time order pattern*. Below is an example of the history of dating in the United States.

In the twentieth century, a new social phenomenon arose called "dating," defined herein as a prearranged, planned social activity whose function is to allow people to meet and get acquainted with potential courtship partners. **Dating is thought to have begun among college students in the United States after World War I.** ①<u>During the 1920s and 1930s</u>, it became widespread on college campuses, eventually filtering down to high school and younger students ②<u>during 1940s and 1950s</u>. Decades of gradual change culminated ③<u>in the 1980s</u> in several new social trends in dating practices. ④<u>Dating in the 1990s is somewhat free-form.</u> Dating today has considerably less structured female/male behavior and fewer rules to follow. Rather than having a formal date, many young people gather in groups at different hangouts, such as their favorite restaurant or pizza parlor if they are younger or drinking establishments if they are older. (Davidson and Moore, 296)

A paragraph that follows a chronological order is often represented by a time line:

The History of Dating in the United States			
1920s/1930s	1940s/1950s	1980s	1990s
college students	high school students	fewer rules	free-form

Narration   Authors use the narration pattern when they want to tell a story. Events are told in the order in which they occur, and there is a beginning, middle, and end. Stories involve people, places, and *conflict* (opposition between characters). The conflict can be of three types: (1) human being against human being, (2) human being against nature, or (3) human being against self. (Conflict is discussed in more detail in Chapter 6.) The story below, about a conflict in the life of a former well-known football player who had been enormously popular, was taken from a history textbook.

> **On June 12, 1994,** his [O.J. Simpson's] estranged wife, **Nicole Brown Simpson, and another man were found stabbed to death** near the entry of her condominium in Brentwood, Los Angeles. ①Five days later, as police were about to arrest Simpson for her murder, he fled south on Freeway Five in a Ford Bronco driven by a former teammate. The police set off in pursuit. A bizarre, low-speed highway chase ensued, with Simpson's driver talking to police on a cell-phone ("Just back off. He's still alive. He's got a gun to his head"). Seven news helicopters swooped in to film the spectacle, crowds gathered on overpasses to witness it ("Go O.J., Go!"), and millions watched it live on TV. ②The chase ended quietly and Simpson was charged with murder. ③Several weeks later Simpson pleaded "absolutely, 100 percent not guilty." ④His trial lasted nine riveting months. (Garraty and Carnes 933–34)

A diagram of the narration pattern would look like the following story line:

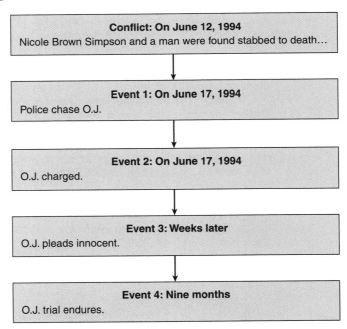

More challenging paragraph patterns include:

■ Description

■ Comparison/Contrast

- Cause/Effect
- Classification
- Problem/Solution

Description   Authors use the description pattern to either draw a picture in words (as with literature) or to give all of the characteristics of a term or subject. In the example below, the author describes the college experience.

> Many people view **the college years as formative**—more influential than any other period of adulthood. This is not surprising, since college serves as a "developmental testing ground," a time when full attention can be devoted to exploring alternative values, roles, and behaviors. To facilitate this exploration, college exposes young people to a form of "culture shock"—encounters with new ideas, new teachers and friends with varied beliefs, new freedoms and opportunities, and new academic and social demands (Pascarella & Terenzini, 1991). In the United States, 75 percent of high school graduates—more than any other nation in the world—enroll in an institution of higher education. Besides offering a route to a high-status career and its extrinsic rewards (salary and job security), Americans expect colleges and universities to have a transforming impact on the coming generation. (Berk 444–45)

A diagram of the description pattern looks like this:

Topic: The college years

Main Idea: Many people view the college years as formative—more influential than any other period of adulthood.

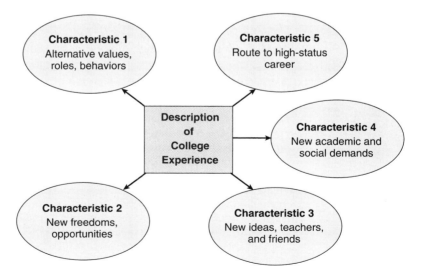

Comparison/Contrast   Authors use the comparison/contrast pattern when they want to show how two things are alike (comparison) and/or how they are different (contrast). In the example below, men and women are compared and contrasted.

They are alike in that they both construct dreams to help them make decisions about their futures, but they are different in the type of dreams they have.

> How do young adults cope with the opportunities and hazards of this period? Levison found that during the early adult transition (17 to 22 years), most construct a dream, an image of the self in the adult world that guides their decision making. The more specific the dream, the more purposeful the individual's structure building. **For men,** the dream usually emphasizes an ①independent achiever in an occupational role. In contrast, only **a minority of women** report dreams in which career dominates. Instead, most career-oriented women display ②"split dreams" in which both marriage and career are prominent. Also, women's dreams tend to ③define the self in terms of relationships with husband, children, and colleagues. Men's dreams are more ④individualistic: They view significant others, especially wives, as vital supporters of their goals. Less often do they see themselves as supporters of the goals of others. (Berk 458)

A diagram of the comparison/contrast pattern looks like this:
Topic: Men's and women's dreams about the future
Main Idea: Men's and women's dreams about the future differ.

	Construct a Dream	*Defining Self*
Men	① Emphasizes independence	④ Self as individual
Women	② Emphasizes both marriage and career	③ Self as relationship with husband, children, and colleagues

Cause/Effect   Authors use cause/effect patterns when they are writing about relationships between two things when one happened as a result of the other. The example below shows a cause/effect relationship between students and the college experience. In this case, there is only one cause—going to college. However, there are many effects.

> A comprehensive view of thousands of studies revealed broad psychological **changes from the freshmen to senior years of college** (Pascarella & Terenzini, 1991). In addition to knowledge of their major field of study, students gain in ways less obviously tied to their academic programs. [As Perry's theory of post-formal thought predicts], they become better at applying reason and evidence to problems for which there is no clear answer and identifying the strengths and weaknesses of different sides of complex issues. These cognitive changes are complemented by—revisions in attitudes and values—increased interest in literature, the performing arts, and philosophical and historical issues and greater tolerance for ethnic and cultural diversity. College also leaves its mark on moral reasoning by fostering concern with individual rights and human welfare. Finally, gains in reflective thought combined with exposure to multiple worldviews encourage young people to look more closely at themselves. During the college years, students develop greater self-understanding, enhances self-esteem, and a firmer sense of identity. *(Berk 444)*

A diagram of the cause/effect pattern looks like this:

Topic: College

Main Idea: A comprehensive view of thousands of studies revealed broad psychological changes from the freshmen to senior years of college.

Cause(s)	Effect(s)
Going to college	• Knowledge of major field of study
	• Increased ability to apply reason and evidence to problems
	• Increased ability to identify strengths and weaknesses of different sides of complex issues
	• Increased interest in literature, performing arts, and philosophical and historical issues
	• Greater tolerance for diversity
	• Increased concern with human rights
	• Greater self-understanding
	• Greater self-esteem
	• Firmer sense of identity

Classification   Authors use the classification pattern when they need to break down information into categories or classes. In other words, they organize people, places, things, or ideas into various groups or classify them. In the following example, people are put into two groups by classifying them as Type A or Type B. Read the following passage and determine which characteristics belong with the Type A personality and which belong with the Type B.

Psychology and medicine have sometimes found it useful to distinguish between two types of individuals identifiable largely in terms of the level of stress that seems to permeate their lives. These types are labeled Type A and Type B.

Type A individuals may be described as ①hard-driving, ②loud, ③aggressive, ④achievement-oriented, and ⑤impatient. These are individuals who drive themselves mercilessly, who sense most keenly the unrelenting pressures of time and the ⑥urgency of their lives. In contrast, **Type B** individuals are ①slow, ②relaxed, ③easygoing. ④They speak more softly, tend to ⑤impose few deadlines on themselves, and ⑥do not, in general, respond to life with the same sense of urgency that drives Type A's. *(Lefrancois 513)*

A diagram of the characteristics of Type A and Type B personalities would look like this:

Topic: Personality types

Main Idea: Psychology and medicine have sometimes found it useful to distinguish between two types of individuals identifiable largely in terms of the level of stress that seems to permeate their lives.

PERSONALITIES	
Type A	*Type B*
• hard-driving	• slow
• loud	• relaxed
• aggressive	• easygoing
• achievement-oriented	• speak softly
• impatient	• impose few deadlines on themselves
• driven by pressures of time and urgency	• no sense of urgency

Problem-Solution   Authors use the problem/solution pattern when their topic is about a problem. In this case, the reader must identify the problem and also look for ways the author might suggest to solve this problem. As with the comparison/contrast pattern, there can be more than one problem and more than one solution.

> A college degree channels people's post-college lives, affecting their interests and opportunities in enduring ways. Yet **40 percent of freshmen drop out,** most within the first year and many within the first 6 weeks. The price paid is high, in lifelong earnings and personal development. Factors involved in the decision to withdraw from college are usually not catastrophic; they are typical problems of early adulthood. Most dropouts either find it harder to deal with these difficulties or are unable to get assistance in doing so. <u>Reaching out to students, especially during the early weeks and throughout the first year, is crucial</u>. Young people who sense that they have entered a college community concerned about them as individuals are far more likely to persist to graduation. (Berk 444–45)

A diagram of the problem solution pattern looks like this:

Topic: College drop out rate

Main Idea: Yet 40 percent of freshmen drop out, most within the first year and many within the first 6 weeks.

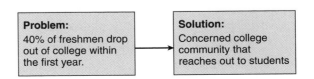

Problem:		**Solution:**
40% of freshmen drop out of college within the first year.	→	Concerned college community that reaches out to students

EXERCISE
1-1

Paragraph Patterns

Read the sentences below and determine which paragraph pattern they represent or introduce. The first question has been answered for you.

1. Generally, only 1 in every 4 students remains in college to receive a four-year degree. Many colleges and universities have developed freshmen experience and academic support programs in an attempt to address this problem.

   Problem/Solution

2. Rapid advances in technology from the early 1980s to the year 2000 radically changed the way information is processed in the business world.

   _____

3. There are many different types of educational institutions for high school graduates, including adult education, colleges, universities, community colleges, trade schools, technical schools, and apprenticeships.

   _____

4. When editing a paper, the writer should proofread for the following mistakes: run-on sentences, sentence fragments, and errors in punctuation and spelling.

   _____

5. A student's grade point average (GPA) is the average of all of his/her grades from the first semester until the last semester in school. For example, if Jamal went to college for one year and had 5 *A*s his first semester and 5 *B*s his second semester, his GPA would be a 3.5.

   _____

6. During their freshmen and sophomore years, all college students take the same basic requirements. Later, in their junior year, students are accepted into a specific course of study and take specialized classes. Finally, in their last year of college, students complete internships that provide practical experience.

   _____

7. Students who read their textbooks and attend all classes are more likely to succeed in college than those who don't buy their books and skip classes.

   _____

8. Changing the oil and filter of your car is an easy process once you have all of the necessary tools. First, you will need a pan to catch the oil.

   _____

9. Had she watched the news that morning, she would have taken the subway. All of the arteries in and out of New York City were blocked by the taxi strike, and she was already an hour and a half late for work.

---

10. The gaseous hot air from the city streets above swept through the open graffiti-decorated windows of the subway, making it both bearable and unbearable to breathe.

CLUES TO MEANING

Just as the organization of ideas helps the reader follow the author's train of thought, knowledge of the world helps the reader to interpret the meaning of the author's words. **World knowledge** refers to everything we have learned since we were born—all that we know about the world. When each new fact enters our brains, we immediately begin to classify it. We try to associate it with other information on that same topic—connect it to what we already know. Each time we do this, we create a network of information called a schema.

The process of putting the variables together is called **inference.** In other words, when we infer something, we draw a conclusion from information we already have or are given. Our knowledge of the world and the schemas that we have built greatly affect the inferences we make, what we pay attention to, and what we remember when we read. The following explanations and exercises will help you understand how we arrive at meaning instead of just pronouncing the words on the page.

World Knowledge

Every person has knowledge that is already stored in his memory. This *world knowledge* or *background knowledge* is everything you know about the world up to that point in time. Let us consider the case of Marissa. Marissa had just graduated from high school in Puerto Rico when her family moved to the United States. At first, she, her mother, and her younger brother lived in a cousin's basement. Her mother worked a menial job while going to night school to become an accountant. Marissa went to college without knowing English because her mother said to her, "You were bright in high school, you should go to college." Marissa decided to go because she had some previous experience—or background knowledge—about school. Even though she spoke a different language, she had some familiarity with the routine and expectations of school.

With each new experience, we increase our knowledge of the world. We gain new knowledge by reading, talking with other people, traveling, taking classes, and so forth. Our ability to add new information to the old in a way that makes sense allows us to understand that new information. Another word for this new understanding is *comprehension*. **Reading comprehension** is our ability to combine new information with what we already know when we read—and thus make sense of it.

Once at college, Marissa was exposed to a diverse student body. She made friends easily with bilingual students. They communicated frequently in both Spanish and English. This, along with what she was learning in both her English and reading classes, helped Marissa put her new knowledge together with what she already knew about language and school (the English language and the textbook information).

Schema

We process information in the following way: When a new piece of information enters our mind, we recognize that it is information we do not already know. We think about what this bit of knowledge means and then store it with other information related to it. When information on a certain topic accumulates and details connect in a meaningful way, we call the resulting network a **schema.** The road systems in our towns and cities are like schemas because they are made up of many meaningfully connected strips of land. Think of what it would be like to move around in a city in which a road ended suddenly at a river with no connecting bridge or if a road went around in a circle without leading anywhere. How many people would use a street that started and stopped without being connected to other roads, streets, or highways? The following diagram more clearly illustrates how a schema is like a road system.

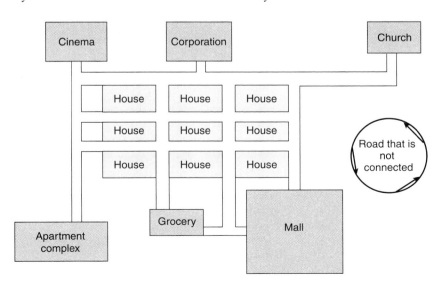

When we learn something new, it is like taking a new route home and figuring out how the unfamiliar street connects to the road or highway system we already know. New information relates to the old information already existing in our head. Let's see if we can identify a schema in Marissa's situation.

Remember, Marissa attended college without knowing English. However, while living in Puerto Rico, she went to high school and studied mathematics, psychology, government, literature, and so forth. When Marissa began to study government in college, she connected the new English vocabulary words that she learned with what she already knew about government. When she began to study psychology, she connected the new vocabulary with what she already knew about psychology, and so on.

(*Note:* Marissa is actually a real person who became bilingual, eventually graduated from college, and is now a teacher who owns her own real estate business. Marissa's ability to connect a new concept of one subject with a familiar concept of another shows that she can think schematically—that is, in a way that allows her to see how one thing can relate to another.)

Four things affect our ability to connect new information with what we already know: (1) inference, (2) variables, (3) attention, and (4) remembering.

Inference   Here is a good example of inference: We are reading a mystery novel in which a murder is committed. The author tells us that the butler was one of the two people who had access to the key of the wine cellar where the victim's body was found on Monday night. He also informs us that the butler was the only one in the house that night, and that the maid and the cook saw the butler leaving the wine cellar that same evening. The author never tells us straight out who the murderer is, but because she gives us clues, we are able to put these clues together and *guess* or *infer* that the murderer is the butler. These clues are called **variables.** We can put these variables together in a lot of different ways, but when we put them together in the way that the author intended, we can say that we understood what we read.

To better understand how we reached the conclusion that the butler is the murderer, let us break the scene down in parts and label them:

[CLUE]   The butler was one of two people who had a key to the wine cellar.

[CLUE]   The victim's body was found in the cellar on Monday night.

[CLUE]   The butler was the only one in the house on Monday night.

[CLUE]   The maid and the cook saw the butler leaving the wine cellar Monday night.

[INFER]   The butler is the murderer.

Keep in mind that as we read and are given new information, our inferences may change accordingly. For example, reading further, we find out that even though the body was found on Monday night, new evidence proves that the murder occurred Sunday night. We also learn that the maid was the other person who had a key to the wine cellar and that she was the only one on duty Sunday night. Now, we need to draw a new inference. Our first step would be to drop some of the old clues that no longer apply. Next, we need to replace them with the new clues. Finally, we need to think about the remaining clues and how they fit together.

[CLUE 1] The butler was one of two people who had a key to the wine cellar. (This means he may still be a suspect.)

[CLUE 2] The butler was the only one in the house on Monday night. (This no longer applies since the murder took place on Sunday night.)

[CLUE 3] The maid and the cook saw the butler leaving the wine cellar Monday night. (This is no longer applies since the murder took place on Sunday night.)

[CLUE 4] The maid was the other person who had a key to the wine cellar. (This means that the maid is a suspect.)

[CLUE 5] Only the maid was on duty Sunday night. (This means the maid is more likely a suspect than the butler.)

[INFER] The maid is the murderer.

EXERCISE 1-2

Inference

Read the following paragraphs and finish the quote with an inference. Then, based on the clues given, determine where each situation would most likely take place. The first question has been answered for you.

1. The four buffets were long and ran the whole length of the room: one was filled with cold seafood, one with hot seafood; one was covered with salads, and one with a variety of desserts. A man brought a bucket filled with ice and set it down at the next table. He began to pour white wine into the sparkling stemmed glasses. As we were reading the list of entrées, he came over to our table and asked,

Example: "Have you decided what you would like for dinner this evening?"

Where are they?: A restaurant

2. There were five minutes left. Donna knew she could remember more if only she was not so nervous. But everything depended on these scores. If she did not do well, her friends of twelve years would be moving on and she would be left behind without much of a future. A woman standing in front of a blackboard looked at her watch and said,

Example: " _____

_____ "

Where is Donna? _____

3. Jamal felt disappointed as he looked out of the small window and saw only clouds. He had hoped to see more of the landscape, but maybe it would clear up once they were on their way. When the cabin was full, a young woman in uniform began to give directions over the microphone. As he pressed a button for help in getting pills for motion sickness, a woman came by pushing a heavy food-laden cart on wheels and said,

Example: " _____

_____ "

Where is Jamal? _____

4. The popularity of the band had drawn a huge crowd. The dance floor was jammed. Everyone seemed to sway in unison to the strong, pounding beat. Every table was filled. Even the aisles were blocked by people holding beverages of various kinds. Clouds of blue smoke hung over the entire room. The song playing over the loudspeaker was about to end. Hurriedly, before the DJ had a chance to play a new song, Milo rushed over to him and asked,

Example: " _____

_____ "

Where was Milo? _____

5. The roar of the crowd thundered through the crisp air as thousands jumped up from their seats waving their banners. The bleachers trembled under the excitement. Mike, wearing the number 12 shirt, was the center of attention. He seemed to be invincible as he dodged his opponents and made his way toward the goalpost with the egg-shaped ball. As he crossed the line, an opponent tackled him from behind. It didn't matter; he was still holding the ball. The string of rosy-cheeked girls waved their pom-poms wildly as they began their chant. The crowd joined in, yelling,

Example: " _____

_____ "

Where was Mike? _____

Variables *Variables* are the pieces of knowledge that we have about a person, place, or event. They increase our ability to draw reasonable inferences. Often times, authors do not directly state information because they feel it can be inferred from the variables provided. Let's say we are reading a paragraph about a young man who is taking a young woman to a restaurant on a first date. The paragraph may not explicitly state the word *restaurant*. However, we can guess the setting is a restaurant because there are many variables associated with the word restaurant that provide us with clues. For example, let's read and break down the following paragraph:

> Since this was their first date, Sam decided to take Magali out for dinner. As the hostess showed them where to sit, Magali noticed piñatas hanging from the ceiling and that almost all of the tables in the dining room were filled. Once seated, a waiter handed them menus and took their drink orders. The menu was divided into four sections: (1) appetizers, (2) salads, (3) entrées, and (4) desserts. Since Sam didn't know Spanish, he couldn't read the menu. He peeked over at the next table to see what some other customers were eating. However, this didn't do him much good because these customers had already finished eating and were paying the bill.

[VAR 1]   People go to this place to eat dinner.

[VAR 2]   This place has a hostess who shows people where to sit.

[VAR 3]   People decide what they would like to eat from choices on a menu.

[VAR 4]   A waiter takes each customer's food and drink order.

[VAR 5]   People can make choices from four categories of food: appetizers, salads, entrées, and desserts.

[VAR 6]   People must pay for the food that they order.

[VAR 7]   There are piñatas hanging from the ceiling.

[VAR 8]   The menu is written in Spanish.

[INFER]   Sam and Magali are in a Spanish or Mexican restaurant.

If we were to draw a diagram of this paragraph, it would look like this:

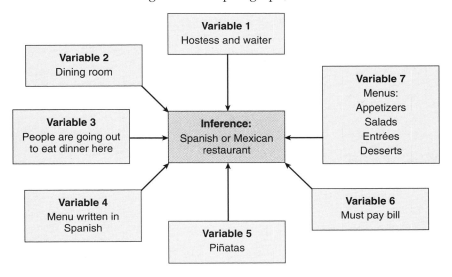

Sometimes the word that pulls together the entire scenario is missing, but all the other parts of the scene are described. In this case, the author gives us clues without coming right out to tell us what is happening. We can figure out (or infer) what is happening, though, by putting all of these clues together and applying our world knowledge to guess what is happening.

Let's consider the following paragraph:

> A lot of people are inside a large building. Some are looking up information on computers. Many are sitting in comfortable chairs and reading. Others are sitting at tables and writing. Still more are searching through long rows of books that cover the walls from ceiling to floor. It is very quiet, and only whispering can be heard.

A diagram of this scene would look something like this:

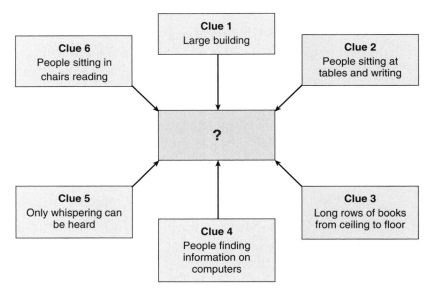

Note that only the clue (variable) boxes are filled in. If you add up all the clues (variables) together, what would you guess that these details are describing? The answer would be a library.

Variables

Because all people's life experiences are not the same, a writer's clues can be interpreted in various ways. In the following paragraph, two different inferences can be made. Read the paragraph carefully and explain what two conclusions can be reached. List the clues that led you to each conclusion.

> Rocky slowly got up from the mat, planning his escape. He hesitated a moment and thought. Things were not going well. What bothered him most was being held, especially since the charge against him had been weak. He considered his present

situation. The lock that held him was strong, but he thought he could break it. He knew, however, that his timing would have to be perfect. Rocky was aware that it was because of his early roughness that he had been penalized so severely—much too severely, from his point of view. The situation was becoming frustrating; the pressure had been grinding on him for too long. He was being ridden unmercifully. Rocky was getting angry now. He felt he was ready to make his move. He knew that his success or failure would depend on what he did in the next few seconds. (Anderson, Reynolds, Schallert, and Goetz p. 372)

Now that you have read the paragraph, write down the two different conclusions that can be reached.

Conclusion 1: _____

Conclusion 2: _____

List the clues that led you to each conclusion.

Conclusion 1	Conclusion 2
[CLUE 1]	[CLUE 1]
[CLUE 2]	[CLUE 2]
[CLUE 3]	[CLUE 3]
[CLUE 4]	[CLUE 4]
[INFERENCE]	[INFERENCE]

Attention In a research study, one group of students was asked to read a passage that described the inside of a home from a burglar's viewpoint. Another group was asked to read the same passage from a homebuyer's viewpoint. Afterward, all students were instructed to write down what they could remember about the passage. The students who read from the burglar's point of view remembered things that would be good to steal, such as a color TV, money in the den, and the places where the china and jewelry were kept. The students who read the passage from the point of view of the homebuyer, however, remembered such details as a crack in the foundation of the house, a damaged ceiling, and a leaky roof (Goetz, Schallert, Reynolds, & Radin, 1983). Depending on which point of view the students were reading from, one group would pay more attention to certain details than the other. This is known as **selective attention.** In other words, what we remember as we read is especially influenced by our viewpoint.

Viewpoints

Read the following passage from the viewpoint of a music major. Then answer the questions at the end of the passage.

> On Saturday night, four good friends got together. When Jerry, Mike, and Pat arrived, Karen was sitting in her living room writing some notes. She quickly gathered the cards and stood up to greet her friends at the door. They followed her into the living room but, as usual, they couldn't agree on exactly what to play. Jerry eventually took a stand and set things up. Finally, they began to play. Karen's recorder filled the room with soft and pleasant music. Early in the evening, Mike noticed Pat's hand and the many diamonds. As the night progressed the tempo of play increased. Finally, a lull in the activities occurred. Taking advantage of this, Jerry pondered the arrangement in front of him. Mike interrupted Jerry's reverie and said, "Let's hear the score." They listened carefully and commented on their performance. When the comments were all heard, exhausted but happy, Karen's friends went home. (Anderson, Reynolds, Schallert, and Goetz p. 372)

1. What was the purpose of the get-together?

   _____

   _____

2. List the clues that led you to that conclusion.

   [CLUE 1] _____

   [CLUE 2] _____

   [CLUE 3] _____

   [CLUE 4] _____

   [INFER] _____

3. Read the same passage again from the perspective of someone who spends his/her Saturday evenings playing cards. What was the purpose of the get-together?

   _____

   _____

4. List the clues that led you to that conclusion.

[CLUE 1] _____

[CLUE 2] _____

[CLUE 3] _____

[CLUE 4] _____

[INFER] _____

Remembering   When we try to remember information that we read but do not understand, two things can happen: we either ignore the information or we change it. We do this without realizing it! If we don't understand what we are reading, we tend to lose interest in it. We tune out the confusing details and focus our attention only on those points that keep our attention. On occasion, we attempt to use our background knowledge to explain what we don't understand. When we do this, however, we lose the author's intended meaning and replace it with our own. Again, we do this without realizing it.

In a psychology experiment, Sir Walter Bartlett (1932) used the following story to prove that when readers are faced with a detail or an event that they cannot explain, they invent their own explanations. When asked to read and then recall the story, the readers remembered and explained the confusing points of the story according to their own experiences and understanding of the world. To see how our knowledge influences our interpretations and memory, let's repeat a part of Bartlett's experiment by following the directions below.

A Reading in Educational Psychology

At a normal reading rate, read the North American Indian folk tale "The War of the Ghosts" twice through. Then complete the exercise that follows the story.

The War of the Ghosts

[1]   One night two young men from Egulac went down to the river to hunt seals, and while they were there it became foggy and calm. Then they heard war-cries, and they thought, "Maybe this is a war-party." They escaped to the shore, and hid behind a log. Now canoes came up, and

they heard the noise of paddles, and saw one canoe coming up to them. There were five men in the canoe, and they said:

[2]   "What do you think? We wish to take you along. We are going up the river to make war on the people."

[3]   One of the young men said, "I have no arrows."

[4]   "Arrows are in the canoe," they said.

[5]   "I will not go along. I might be killed. My relatives do not know where I have gone. But you," he said, turning to the other, "may go with them."

[6]   So one of the young men went, but the other returned home.

[7]   And the warriors went on up the river to a town on the other side of Kalama. The people came down to the water, and they began to fight, and many were killed. But presently the young man heard one of the warriors say: "Quick, let us go home: that Indian has been hit." Now he thought, "Oh, they are ghosts." He did not feel sick, but they said he had been shot.

[8]   So the canoes went back to Egulac, and the young man went ashore to his house, and made a fire. And he told everybody and said: "Behold I accompanied the ghosts, and we went to fight. Many of our fellows were killed, and many of those who attacked us were killed. They said I was hit, and I did not feel sick."

[9]   He told it all, and then he became quiet. When the sun rose he fell down. Something black came out of his mouth. His face became contorted. The people jumped up and cried.

[10]   He was dead.

(Bartlett)

Close your book for 15 minutes. Then, without looking back at the original, rewrite the story on a piece of paper using as much detail as you can remember.

_____

_____

_____

_____

Compare your retelling to the original story.

1. What, if any, parts of the story did you not understand?

_____

2. How did you explain the parts you did not understand?

_____

3. In what ways is your retelling different from the original story?

_____

4. What did you leave out?

_____

5. What did you add that was not in the original story?

_____

6. What do you do when you come to something in one of your textbooks that you do not understand?

_____

7. Based on this exercise, what do you think happens when you memorize information that you find confusing?

_____

8. Why is it a good idea to ask professors to explain information in your textbooks that is unclear to you?

_____

Reading Between the Lines Box 1.1

INFERENCE: "THE WAR OF THE GHOSTS"

Often times there are different ways that we can interpret the meaning of a word, such as the word "ghosts" in the American folk tale "The War of the Ghosts." We could interpret "ghosts," to mean the souls of dead people. Or we could interpret "ghosts" as the name of a war party (just as we might name a sports team "The Rams").

1. Reread "The War of the Ghosts" and look for clues that will help you determine who the "Ghosts" are.

2. Read the clues below.

3. Determine who you think the "ghosts" are by making an inference from the clues below.

[CLUE]   Then they heard war-cries, and they thought, "Maybe this is a _war-party._"

[CLUE]   They saw one canoe coming up to them. There were _five men_ in the canoe.

(continued on next page)

[CLUE]	We wish to take you along. We are *going up the river to make war* on the people.
[INFER]	<u>The war-party is made up of five men.</u>
[CLUE]	So one of *the young men went,* but the other returned home.
[CLUE]	And *the warriors went* on up the river to a town . . . and they began to fight.
[INFER]	_____
[CLUE]	The young man heard one of the warriors say, "Quick, let us go home: *that Indian has been hit,*" and he thought, "Oh, they are ghosts."
[CLUE]	When the young man went back to his home, he said, "Behold, *I accompanied the ghosts,* and we went to fight."
[CLUE]	"They said *I was hit,* and I did not feel sick."
[INFER]	_____
[CONCLUSION]	_____

A Reading in Short Story

Read the following short story and answer the questions at the end. Pay particular attention to the details that provide clues to the author's intended meaning. The first question has been answered for you.

The Getaway

[1]   Whenever I get sleepy at the wheel, I always stop for coffee. This time, I was going along in western Texas and I got sleepy. I saw a sign that said GAS, EAT, so I pulled off. It was long after midnight. What I expected was a place like a bunch of others, where the coffee tastes like copper and the flies never sleep.

[2]   What I found was something else. The tables were painted wood, and they looked as if nobody ever spilled the ketchup. The counter was spick-and-span. Even the smell was OK. I swear it.

[3]   Nobody was there, as far as customers. There was just this one old boy—really only about forty, getting gray above the ears—behind the counter. I sat down at the counter and ordered coffee and apple pie. Right away he got me started feeling sad.

[4]   I have a habit: I divide people up. Winners and losers. This old boy behind the counter was the kind that MEAN well; they can't do enough for you, but their eyes have this gentle, far-away look, and they can't win.

You know: With their clean shirt and their little bow tie? It makes you feel sad just to look at them. Only take my tip: Don't feel too sad.

[5]   He brought the coffee steaming hot, and it tasted like coffee. "Care for cream and sugar?" he asked. I said, "Please," and the cream was fresh and cold and thick. The pie was good too.

[6]   A car pulled up outside. The old boy glanced out to see if they wanted gas, but they didn't. They came right in. The tall one said, "Two coffees. Do you have a road map we could look at?"

[7]   "I think so," the old boy said. He got their coffee first, and then started rooting through a pile of papers by the telephone, looking for a map. It was easy to see he was the type nothin's too much trouble for. Tickled to be of service.

[8]   I'm the same type myself, if you want to know. I watched the old boy hunting for his map, and I felt like I was looking in a mirror.

[9]   After a minute or two, he came up with the map. "This one's a little out of date, but . . ." He put it on the counter, beside their coffee.

[10]   The two men spread out the map and leaned over it. They were well dressed, like a couple of feed <u>merchants</u>. The tall one ran his finger along the Rio Grande and shook his head. "I guess there's no place to get across, this side of El Paso."

[11]   He said it to his pal, but the old boy behind the counter heard him and lit up like a light bulb. "You trying to find the best way south? I might be able to help you with that."

[12]   "How?"

[13]   "Just a minute." He spent a lot of time going through the papers by the telephone again. "Thought I might have a newer map," he said. "Anything recent would show the Hackett Bridge. Anyway, I can tell you how to find it."

[14]   "Here's a town called Hackett," the tall one said, still looking at the map. "It's on the river, just at the end of a road. Looks like a pretty small place."

[15]   "Not any more. It's just about doubled since they built the bridge."

[16]   "What happens on the other side?" The short one asked the question, but both of the feed-merchant types were paying close attention.

[17]   "Pretty fair road, clear to Chihuahua. It joins up there with the highway out of El Paso and <u>Juarez</u>."

[18]   The tall man finished his coffee, folded the map, put it in his pocket, and stood up. "We'll take your map with us," he said.

[19]   The old boy seemed startled, like a new kid at school when somebody pokes him in the nose to show him who's boss. However, he just shrugged and said, "Glad to let you have it."

[20]   The feed merchants had a little conference on the way out, talking in whispers. Then they stopped in the middle of the floor, turned around, reached inside their jackets, and pulled guns on us. Automatic pistols, I think they were. "You sit where you are and don't move," the tall one said to me, "And you, get against the wall."

[21] Both of us did exactly what they wanted. I told you we were a lot alike.

[22] The short man walked over and pushed one of the keys of the cash register. "Every little bit helps," he said, and he scooped the money out of the drawer. The tall man set the telephone on the floor, put his foot on it, and jerked the wires out. Then they ran to their car and got in. The short man leaned out the window and shot out one of my tires. Then they took off fast.

[23] I looked at the old boy behind the counter. He seemed a little pale, but he didn't waste any time. He took a screw-driver out of a drawer and squatted down beside the telephone, I said, "It doesn't always pay to be nice to people."

[24] He laughed and said, "Well, it doesn't usually cost anything," and went on taking the base plate off the telephone. He was a fast worker, actually. His tongue was sticking out of the corner of his mouth. In about five minutes he had a dial tone coming out of the receiver. He dialed a number and told the Rangers about the men and their car. "They did?" he said. "Well, well, well. No, not El Paso. They took the Hackett turnoff." After he hung up, he said, "It turns out those guys robbed a supermarket in Wichita Falls."

[25] I shook my head. "They sure had me fooled. I thought they looked perfectly all right."

[26] The old boy got me another cup of coffee, and opened himself a bottle of <u>pop</u>. "They fooled me, too, at first." He wiped his mouth. "Then I got a load of their shoulder <u>holsters</u> when they leaned on the counter to look at the map. Anyway, they had mean eyes, I thought. Didn't you?"

[27] "Well, I didn't at the time."

[28] We drank without talking for a while, getting our nerves back in shape. A pair of patrol cars went roaring by outside and squealed their tires around the Hackett turnoff.

[29] I got to thinking, and I thought of the saddest thing yet. "You knew there was something wrong with those guys, but you still couldn't keep from helping them on their way."

[30] He laughed. "Well, the world's a tough sort of place at best, is how I look at it."

[31] "I can understand showing them the map," I said, "but I'm damned if I'd have told about the bridge. Now there's not a snowball's chance in hell of catching them. If you'd kept your mouth shut, there'd at least be some hope."

[32] "There isn't any—"

[33] "Not a shred," I went on. "Not with a car as fast as they've got."

[34] The way the old boy smiled made me feel better about him and me. "I don't mean there isn't any hope," he said. "I mean there isn't any bridge."

(Savage)

Vocabulary Questions: Multiple Choice

_____c_____ **1.** The narrator refers to the owner of the gas station/restaurant as an "old boy" because
  a. the owner is elderly.
  b. the owner is a young boy.
  c. "old boy" is a nickname given to males who live in the rural south.
  d. the owner's son usually works there and the narrator confused the owner with his son.

_____ **2.** The word *merchant* refers to
  a. someone who buys and sells goods.
  b. someone who is an agricultural specialist.
  c. someone who is a farmer.
  d. someone who rents property.

_____ **3.** Juarez is a city in:
  a. Mexico.   c. Arizona.
  b. Texas.   d. Canada.

_____ **4.** As used in this selection, the word *pop* means:
  a. father.   c. soda.
  b. a loud noise. d. popcorn.

_____ **5.** A *holster* is a:
  a. gun.   c. holder for a gun.
  b. belt.   d. wallet.

Questions for Thought: Multiple Choice:

_____d_____ **1.** Why did the author think the restaurant owner was a loser?
  a. The restaurant owner was mean-spirited.
  b. The owner did not take care of the restaurant.
  c. The owner wore dirty clothes and looked poor.
  d. The owner was too willing to please others.

_____ **2.** This story took place in:
  a. Northern Texas.   c. Western Texas.
  b. Southern Texas.   d. Nevada.

_____ **3.** When does the author give the reader the first clue that the restaurant owner might not be such a loser after all?
  a. When the author said he felt he was looking in the mirror at himself as he watched the restaurant owner.

       b. When the author said "Only take my tip: Don't feel too sad."
       c. When the owner gave the gunmen directions.
       d. When the author told the owner there was not a chance the gunmen could be caught.

_____ **4.** The gunmen were trying to get across the border to
       a. Mexico.   c. Texas.
       b. Canada.   d. The United States.

_____ **5.** The restaurant owner gave the gunmen
       a. an accurate map.
       b. an outdated map.
       c. a map that showed the Hackett Bridge.
       d. passes to get across the bridge.

Questions for Discussion

Write out the answers to the following questions. By doing this, you will be prepared for a group or class discussion.

1. At first, what was the narrator's opinion of the restaurant owner? What line in the story led you to think that is the case?

    _____

2. In the beginning of the story, was there any indication that the narrator might have been too hasty in his judgment? What clue did the author provide?

    _____

3. In the end, did the robbers get away by crossing Hackett Bridge?

    _____

4. Do you think the narrator's opinion of the restaurant owner changed? Why or why not?

    _____

5. Is "being nice" a good quality or a bad quality? Why do you think someone might be called a loser by appearing to be "too nice"?

    _____

Reading Between the Lines Box 1.2

INFERENCE: "THE GETAWAY"

In the story "The Getaway," the narrator does not come right out and tell us how he feels about himself, but we can interpret his feelings through the things that he says about himself and about others.

1. Reread "The Getaway" and look for clues that will help you determine how the narrator felt about himself.

2. Read the clues below.

3. At the beginning of the story, does the narrator think that he is a winner or a loser?

4. How does the narrator feel about himself at the end of the story?

Beginning:

[CLUE]	Right away he got me started feeling sad. I have a habit: I divide people up. Winners and losers. *This old boy* behind the counter was the kind that . . . *can't win*.
[CLUE]	*I'm the same type* myself, if you want to know. I watched the old boy hunting for his map, and *I felt like I was looking in a mirror*.
[CLUE]	Both of us did exactly what they wanted. I told you we were a lot alike.
[CLUE]	I got to thinking, and I thought of the saddest thing yet. "You knew there was something wrong with those guys, but you still couldn't keep from helping them on their way."
[INFER]	_____ _____

End:

[CLUE]	*"They fooled me, too, at first."* He wiped his mouth. *"Then* I got a load of their shoulder *holsters* when they leaned on the counter to look at the map. Anyway, *they had mean eyes, I thought*. Didn't you?"
[CLUE]	The way the old boy smiled made me *feel better about* him and *me*.
[INFER]	_____ _____

THE IMPORTANCE OF BECOMING ACTIVE READERS

In this chapter, we have discussed how to become an active reader by developing the ability to think logically and reason as we read. We will continue to focus and build on these skills in the following chapters because they are crucial to success in college and especially in today's workplace. According to Zunker, employers in the twenty-first century will require six "workplace competencies," including learning skills, basic reading and cognitive reasoning skills, and problem-solving skills. Learning skills are ranked the highest because employees must be able to keep up with the rapid pace of change that most organizations are experiencing. Future employment will also require more than basic reading skills. "Basic skills are a minimum requirement, but they are not narrowly defined as an ability to read . . . employees must be able to apply information they read . . . into action on a job." (519). And so, in today's job market, we cannot just read; we must also be able to think, reason, and learn as we "read between the lines."

Vocabulary Development

* *

Vocabulary knowledge is very important to reading comprehension. Without a good sense of vocabulary, we would not be able to read as well or as critically. In this chapter, we

- learn the basics of vocabulary and recognize context clues;
- understand how context clues work;
- understand how word history and origins can help us define words;
- learn how to use a dictionary effectively;
- learn about other types of vocabulary references;
- learn about various types of word puzzles;
- understand how one word can be confused with another.

VOCABULARY BASICS AND CONTEXT CLUES

INSTRUCTOR: What do you do when you come to a word that you don't know while reading?

LUCY: Truthfully, I skip it and don't even go back. I pretend it is not even there.

Let us examine Lucy's comment above. If we use the same strategy as she does whenever we come across a word we do not know while reading, we will not grasp the full meaning of what we read. Each word in a text adds an element of meaning. Sometimes even one letter of one word can make all the difference between our understanding or not understanding an entire passage. For example, look at the sentence below:

They took the Florida *intrastate* highway to a remote part of the *county*.

Let's say that we did not know what the word "intrastate" meant, but we did know that "interstate" highways were roads that went across the country. So we decided that an "intrastate" highway could be the same thing, since the two words have *almost* the same spelling. At this point, we could easily mistake the word "county" for "country" because we have decided that an "intrastate" highway goes across the "country." And so, as we read, we may wonder why the characters in our novel never seem to leave the state of Florida or get started on their trip across the country.

However, if we take the time to look up the word *intrastate* in the dictionary, we would learn that it is a highway within one state's boundaries that does not go into any other states. As we reread the sentence, "They took the Florida *intrastate* highway to a remote part of the *county*," we would realize that our characters are not going across the *country* but rather traveling to another *county* within the state.

Context Clues

While having a dictionary by our side as we read is recommended, there are times when referring to one is not necessary. In many cases, an author may give the definition of a word right in the same sentence. In other cases, the author may give clues to the definition instead. Thus, we can learn many new words simply by paying attention to the other words in the sentence. These other words are called **context clues** because they surround the unfamiliar words with hints toward their meaning within the sentence or paragraph.

Definitions An author may help us out by directly defining a word in the same sentence or in the surrounding paragraph in which it is used. For example, in the sentence below the author actually states that he is defining the word *hypertension*. (The example and those following are from Campbell, Mitchell, and Reese.)

Hypertension is defined as a persistent blood pressure of 140/90 or higher; the higher the values, the greater the risk of serious cardiovascular disease. (474)

Usually the author of a textbook will **boldface**, *italicize*, or highlight a word that is being defined. From the clues in this sentence, we know that *hypertension* is the word being defined because it appears in boldface print. We also know the definition of *hypertension* is "having a continuous blood pressure of 140/90 or above" because the words "is defined as" indicate this.

Sometimes an author will define a term by using the words *is*, *are*, or *is/are called*. Look at the following sentence and determine the term being defined and its definition:

Memory, which is essential for learning, is the ability to store and retrieve information related to previous experiences. (581)

Although no words are in bold or highlighted, the word *is* acts as an equal sign:

Memory = the ability to store and retrieve information related to previous experiences.

We can tell from the word *is* that *memory* is the word being defined and that "the ability to store and retrieve information related to previous experiences" is the definition of *memory*.

Other times, an author may define a word by simply placing the word or the definition in between commas or hyphens. In the sentence below, *diabetes mellitus* is the term being defined. Can you tell what the definition is?

Diabetes mellitus, a serious hormonal disease in which the body cells are unable to absorb glucose from the blood, affects as many as five out of every 100 people in the United States. (527)

In this case, the definition of *diabetes mellitus* is "a serious hormonal disease in which the body cells are unable to absorb glucose from the blood." This sentence would still make sense without the definition: "Diabetes mellitus affects as many as five out of every 100 people in the United States." It is up to us to look for the definition of a word when we come across sentences constructed in these ways.

Signals to Definitions	
is	are
is called	are called
is defined as	are defined as
commas [,]	hyphens [-]
boldface	*italics*
highlights	

<table>
<tr><td>EXERCISE
2-1</td><td>

Definitions
</td></tr>
</table>

Read the following sentences selected from a biology textbook. In each, identify the word that is being defined along with its definition. The first word and its definition have been supplied for you.

1. Animals rely on many kinds of chemical signals to regulate their body activities. A **hormone** is a regulatory chemical that travels in the blood from its

production site and affects other sites in the body, often at some distance. (518)

Term: _hormone_

Definition: _a regulatory chemical that travels in the blood from its production_

site and affects other sites in the body.

2. Collectively, all hormone-secreting cells constitute the **endocrine system**, the body's main chemical-regulating system. (518)

Term: _____

Definition: _____

3. The **endorphins**, a kind of anterior pituitary hormone, are sometimes called the body's natural painkillers. (523)

Term: _____

Definition: _____

4. **Insulin** is a protein hormone produced by clusters of specialized pancreatic cells. (526)

Term: _____

Definition: _____

5. **Neurotransmitters** are chemicals that carry information from one nerve cell to another, or from a nerve cell to another kind of cell that will react, such as a muscle cell or an endocrine cell. (518)

Term: _____

Definition: _____

Details   Sometimes it takes more than a simple definition to help readers understand a concept. In this case, an author will define a word by including *details* that illustrate the meaning of the word. Details may include:

■ physical descriptions

■ places of origin

■ names

■ functions

It is up to the reader to choose the most important details and to create from those details a definition. Read the following excerpt about a county government. Which details would you use to define or would you choose to include in your definition of county government? (This and following excerpts are from Edwards, Wattenberg, and Lineberry 711–12.)

> The largest geographic unit of government at the local level is the *county* government. County governments are administrative arms of state government. Typically, counties are responsible for keeping records of births, deaths, and marriages; establishing a system of justice and law enforcement; maintaining roads and bridges; collecting taxes; conducting voter registration and elections; and providing for public welfare and education.

Before going into the details of the term *county government*, you should first recognize its basic definition: a county government is "the largest unit of local government." But what does this mean, exactly? The definition alone does not tell us much about its purpose or what it does. This is where details are necessary. For example, to understand how a county government functions and why it is important, we can explain that the county government is responsible for record keeping, law and order, roadways, taxes, voting, education, and public welfare. Thus, a more complete definition might look like this:

> *County government*—the largest unit of local government; responsible for recordkeeping, law and order, roadways, taxes, voting, education, and public welfare.

EXERCISE 2-2   **Using Details**

Read the following sentences selected from a government textbook. In each, identify the word being defined and create a definition from the details provided. The first one has been done for you.

1. *Township* governments primarily assist with county services. Township officers oversee public highways and local law enforcement, keep records of vital statistics and tax collections, and administer elections.

Term: _Townships_

Definition: _The level of government that assists with county services such as_

public highways, local law enforcement, keep records of vital statistics and tax

collections, and administer elections.

2. Cities are more formally known as municipal governments or _municipalities._ They typically provide police and fire protection, street maintenance, solid waste collection, water and sewer works, park and recreation services, and public planning. Some larger cities also run public hospitals and health programs, administer public welfare services, operate public transit and utilities, manage housing and urban development programs, and even run universities.

Term: _____

Definition: _____

3. Originally, many municipalities in the United States were run with a special form of direct democracy—**the town meeting.** Under this system, all voting-age adults in a community gathered once a year to make public policy, such as passing new local laws, approving a town budget, and electing a small number of local residents to serve as town officials.

Term: _____

Definition: _____

4. _Council-manager government._ In this form of municipal government, voters elect a city council, and sometimes a mayor who often acts as both presiding officer and voting member of the council. The council is responsible for setting policy for the city.

Term: _____

Definition: _____

5. In _commission government_, voters elect a panel of city commissioners, each of whom serves as both legislator and executive. Each member is also

elected as a commissioner of a functional area of city government such as public safety.

Term: _____

Definition: _____

EXAMPLES

Often times an author defines a word and then provides an example to further illustrate its meaning. Some phrases that help us recognize examples include: "for example"; "such as"; "to illustrate this"; and "as shown by." Read the paragraph below and identify the new term, the definition, and the example(s) that further explain the definition.

> Do infants come into the world with the ability to express **basic emotions**— those that can be directly inferred from facial expressions, such as happiness, interest, surprise, fear, anger, sadness, and disgust? Most researchers agree that signs of almost all these emotions are present in early infancy. Over time, they become well-organized signals. (Berk 180)

In this case, the new term is _basic emotions_ and the definition is "emotions that can be directly inferred from facial expressions." The author further defines basic emotions by listing examples: happiness, interest, surprise, fear, anger, sadness, and disgust. We can tell these are examples of basic emotions because they are introduced with the phrase "such as."

Signals to Examples	
for example	to illustrate
such as	as shown by
for instance	include/including
em-dash [—]	

EXERCISE
2-3

Using Examples

Read the following sentences taken from a child development textbook (Berk 190–91). In each, identify the term being defined and find examples that support the meaning of the term. The first term and examples have been identified for you.

1. A variety of *built-in signals*—grasping, smiling, crying, and gazing into the adult's eyes—help bring newborn babies into close contact with other humans.

   Term: <u>Built-in signals</u>

   Example(s): <u>grasping, smiling, crying, gazing into the adult's eyes</u>

2. The *"attachment in-the-making"* phase (6 weeks to 6–8 months). During this phase, infants start to respond differently to a familiar caregiver than to a stranger. For example, at 4 months, Byron smiled, laughed, and babbled more freely when interacting with his mother and quieted more quickly when she picked him up. But even though they can recognize the parent, babies do not yet protest when separated from her. The attachment is underway but not yet established.

   Term: _____

   Example(s): _____

3. *The phase of "clear-cut" attachment* (6–8 months to 18 months–2 years). Now attachment to the familiar caregiver is clearly evident. Babies display **separation anxiety,** becoming upset when the adult whom they have come to rely on leaves. For example, as Rachael reached 8 months of age, she became more wary of strangers and displayed a strong desire to remain close to familiar adults. Separation anxiety appears universally around the world after 6 months of age, increasing until about 15 months.

   Term: _____

   Example(s): _____

4. Besides protesting the parent's departure, older infants and toddlers try hard to maintain her presence. Crawling and walking babies approach, follow, and climb on her in preference to others. And they use her as a **secure base** from which to explore, venturing into the environment and then returning for emotional support.

   Term: _____

   Example(s): _____

5. *Formation of a reciprocal relationship* (18 months–2 years and on). By the end of the second year, rapid growth in representation and language permits toddlers to begin to understand the parent's coming and going and to predict her return. As a result, separation protest declines. Now children start to negotiate with the caregiver, using requests and persuasion rather than crawling after and clinging to her. For example, at age 2, April asked Felicia to read a story before leaving her with a baby-sitter. The extra time spent with her mother, along with a better understanding of where Felicia was going ("to a movie with Daddy") and when she would be back ("right after you go to sleep"), helped April tolerate her mother's absence.

Term: _____

Example(s): _____

Compare/Contrast   Authors compare two or more persons, places, or things, to show how they are alike, and they contrast them to show how they are different. Sometimes an author defines a new word by telling how it is alike or different from something that he thinks is familiar to his readers. He can show similarity by using words such as *like, just as, similar to, the same as.* Can you tell from the information provided in the following sentence what the word *scholarly* means?

> Tien excels in mathematics, computer science, and English literature, and his brother is *just as* **scholarly**.

You can tell the word *scholarly* means "academic" because the sentence tells us that Tien and his brother are very good at mathematics, computer science, and English—all academic subjects.

When a contrast clue is present, the meaning of the new word is shown to be different than an idea that is familiar to us. Some word clues that show differences include *in contrast, different from this, on the other hand, however,* and *although.* Look at the following excerpt.

> When water stirs everything it comes into contact with on its way downstream, the flow is turbulent. *However,* when water flows *more* steadily downstream with no mixing of sediment, the flow is **laminar**. (Hewitt, Suchoki, and Hewitt 600)

The first sentence describes rough, turbulent water. In the second sentence, the word *however* tells us to switch our thinking away from this idea—that *laminar* has a different or opposite meaning from *turbulent.*

Signals to Compare	Signals to Contrast
like	in contrast
just as	different from this
similar to	on the other hand
the same as	however
	although

Compare and Contrast

Read the following sentences. In each, identify the word clue and the definition of the italicized word. The first clue and definition have been identified for you.

1. Like the term rookie, the term *freshmen* is used to describe first-year students who are new to college and/or university life.

   Word clue: <u>like</u>

   Word meaning: <u>first-year students who are new to college and/or university life</u>

2. Aaron found *The Occupational Outlook Handbook* and other similar *tomes* to be a great help in deciding what major to choose.

   Word clue: _____

   Word meaning: _____

3. In contrast to "on-the-job training," college students pay *tuition* in exchange for educational training that qualifies them for a professional career.

   Word clue: _____

   Word meaning: _____

4. Some people believe the best way to earn a Bachelor's Degree is to attend college every semester for four years. However, others like *alternating* work and school by enrolling in cooperative employment programs. Participating corporations offer students paid full-time work in their field one semester and time off to go to school the next.

Word clue: _____

Word meaning: _____

5. Although Information from career centers and placement offices indicates that college-level *credentials* are important, it is difficult to get a job without work experience.

Word clue: _____

Word meaning: _____

Multiple Meanings   All fields have their own specialized terminology or vocabulary. As we read the textbooks for each new field, we recognize many familiar terms. However, we quickly realize that many of the terms that we know and use in our everyday conversations have taken on a new meaning—one particular to that subject. For example, we know what a *chair* is—a piece of furniture having four legs and a back. Usually, a chair is intended for one person. We have a lot of experience sitting on chairs—at the breakfast table, in classrooms, in our living rooms, and so forth. But, as we open our political science textbook, we see our familiar word used in a new way:

> The *chair* appointed a subcommittee to appropriate funds for the projects Congress had approved.

As this sentence illustrates, in political science terms, our familiar word *chair* means a position of authority, such as a congressional committee leader. In terms of academia, however, a *chair*—or, more commonly, a *university chair*—often refers to a professor who holds the position as head of a department. In the field of music, the *chair* represents the position of a player in an orchestra or a band, as in the sentence "In the horns section, Daniel was *first chair* because he was the best player."

Party is another good example of a word with multiple meanings among which you must choose depending on the context in which it appears. Most people associate the word *party* with some type of celebration. However, in political science or in business law, this word does not mean "a social gathering." Look at the sentences below. In which sentence does the word *party* refer to a group of people involved in politics and government? In which sentence does the word *party* refer to a person or group involved in a legal debate?

1. The Republican *Party* presented its platform at the convention in Philadelphia.

2. The judge listened intently to the opposing *party's* closing statement.

Words with Multiple Meanings

Each sentence contains an italicized word that has multiple meanings. Read through the list of possible meanings and choose the one that makes the most sense. The first meaning has been chosen for you.

_____b_____ **1.** California recently had a *recall* election.
    a. a memory
    b. a calling back of defective merchandise
    c. a special election called in an attempt to overthrow an elected official

_____ **2.** The members of the *House* were expected to vote differently than those in the Senate on the environmental issue.
    a. a building in which a family lives
    b. an audience in a performing arts facility
    c. a law-making group

_____ **3.** The *bill* was approved by the House but rejected by the Senate.
    a. the statement of cost for goods sold
    b. paper money
    c. the proposal of a law

_____ **4.** The news reporter had been working the same *beat* since the beginning of his career.
    a. a specific location from which news is reported
    b. rhythm or tempo
    c. driving force

_____ **5.** During the crisis, the president sought advice from his *cabinet*.
    a. a cupboard
    b. a collection of biology specimens
    c. a group of advisors appointed by the president or head of state

WORD HISTORIES AND ORIGINS

Etymology is the study of word histories. The history of a word often helps us understand the meaning of a term. Do you know why New York City is often referred to as the "Big Apple"?

The term the Big Apple was first used by in the early '20s by stable hands to refer to the New Orleans race track, then the king of race tracks. The name was later borrowed by traveling jazz musicians to refer to Harlem, then the jazz capital of the world. The dance "The Big Apple" was all the rage in

Reading Between the Lines Box 2.1

WORD PARTS: AN INTRODUCTION TO PREFIXES, ROOTS, AND SUFFIXES

An understanding of word parts can greatly increase your ability to learn new words without even opening your dictionary. A **word part** is a letter combination that carries a specific meaning when it appears at the *beginning, middle,* or *end* of a word. Take, for example, the **prefix** *trans,* which means "across." The **suffix** *port* is from the Latin **root** *portare,* which means "to carry." Thus, the word *transport* means "to carry across" (**trans** + **port** = **transport**). Try your luck with the following Greek and Latin roots. The first one has been done for you.

1. *bio* (Greek root meaning "life") + *logy* (suffix meaning "the study of") =

   the study of life or biology

2. *geo* (Greek root meaning "earth") + *logy* (suffix meaning "the study of")

   = _____

3. *thermo* (Greek root meaning "heat") + *meter* (Greek root meaning

   "measure") = _____

4. *con* (prefix meaning "together") + *gregare* (Latin root meaning "collect or

   gather") = _____

5. *ex* (prefix meaning "out") + *trahere* (Latin root meaning "pull") =

   _____

Harlem nightclubs in the '20s and '30s. In 1971, the term "The Big Apple" was revived as part of a publicity campaign to upgrade New York's image and promote tourism. (*Etymologically Speaking*)

You don't have to be a historian to learn the history of a word; you can find it in a regular dictionary. The origin of the word is either labeled *Etymology*, or it is found immediately before the definition between two brackets [word origin].

The most common word origins are Old English (OE), Middle English (ME), Old Norse (ON), Old High German (OHG), Middle French (MF), Latin (L), Greek (Gk), or Sanskrit (Skt). When reading an explanation of word origins, the word *from* (fr.), shows that the word came from an older language. Related words are marked by the phrase *akin to.* For example, the word *candidate* came from the Latin word *candidus,* which refers to the white toga worn by candidates for office in ancient Rome. Information about the word's origin would look like this: [fr. L.

candidus, the white toga worn by candidates for office in ancient Rome]. The dictionary entry looks like this:

> **Candidate** \'kan-(d)ə‚dāt \ *n*, **[L** *candidatus*, fr. *candidatus* clothed in white, fr. candidus white; fr. the white toga worn by candidates for office in ancient Rome] (1600) **1:** one that aspires to or is nominated or qualified for an office, membership, or award **2:** a student in the process of meeting final requirements for a degree
>
> *Source: Reprinted with permission from* Merriam-Webster's New Collegiate Dictionary, *Ninth Edition.* ©1989 by Merriam-Webster, Incorporated.

Complete the exercise below to gain a better understanding of word origins. A study of Greek and Latin word parts also provides clues to the original meanings of words. (See Reading Between the Lines Box 2.1 on page 49.)

EXERCISE 2-6   Etymologies

Use the dictionary to find the etymologies of the lettered words. Then match these terms with their word histories. The first term has been matched for you.

Part a

___b___	**1.** Gothic for "letter"	a. career
_____	**2.** From Latin meaning "road for vehicles"	b. book
_____	**3.** From Latin meaning "salt"	c. biscuit
_____	**4.** From Middle French meaning "twice-cooked bread"	d. carpenter
_____	**5.** From Latin meaning "carriage maker"	e. salary

Part b

_____	**1.** From Old English meaning "ninth hour from sunrise"	a. couch
_____	**2.** From Latin meaning "to cook"	b. kitchen
_____	**3.** From Latin meaning "to drive off by clapping"	c. noon
_____	**4.** From Latin meaning "to set in place"	d. woman
_____	**5.** Old English for "wife + man"	e. explosion

USING THE DICTIONARY

The dictionary is one of the most useful tools available for learning new words. For each entry, it provides the

- pronunciation,
- part of speech,
- etymology (word history),
- definitions, with examples.

Online dictionaries are becoming quite popular because of their speed and auditory benefits. It is much faster and easier to use an online dictionary than a traditional one. A popular online dictionary, for example, is the *Merriam-Webster Collegiate Dictionary*, located at *http://www.m-w.com*.

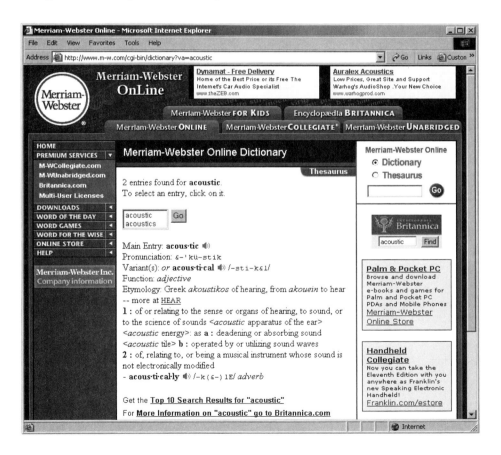

The entry below shows the various types of information you will find when you look up a word online. In this case, the word is *acoustic*. Notice the speaker symbol next to the main entry in the online version. If your computer has a speaker, you will be able to click on this symbol and hear a voice pronounce the word.

The same information can be found in a hard copy of a dictionary. You can see that the pronunciation is followed by the word's part of speech, etymology, and meanings.

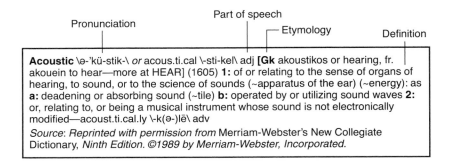

Part of speech

Pronunciation

Etymology

Definition

Acoustic \ə-'kü-stik-\ *or* acous.ti.cal \-sti-kel\ adj **[Gk** akoustikos or hearing, fr. akouein to hear—more at HEAR] (1605) **1:** of or relating to the sense of organs of hearing, to sound, or to the science of sounds (~apparatus of the ear) (~energy): as **a:** deadening or absorbing sound (~tile) **b:** operated by or utilizing sound waves **2:** or, relating to, or being a musical instrument whose sound is not electronically modified—acoust.ti.cal.ly \-k(ə-)lē\ adv

Source: Reprinted with permission from Merriam-Webster's New Collegiate Dictionary, *Ninth Edition. ©1989 by Merriam-Webster, Incorporated.*

Pronunciation

If your computer does not have speakers, look for a pronunciation guide such as the one below. If you are using a traditional dictionary, look for the pronunciation guide at the bottom of the page.

Pronunciation Symbols		
\ə\ as **a** and **u** in ab**u**t	\e\ as **e** in b**e**t	\o\ as **aw** in l**aw**
\ə\ as **e** in kitt**e**n	\ē\ as **ea/y** in **ea**s**y**	\oi\ as **oy** in b**oy**
\ər\ as **ur/er** in f**ur**th**er**	\g\ as **g** in **g**o	\th\ as **th** in **th**in
\a\ as **a** in **a**sh	\i\ as **i** in h**i**t	\th\ as **th** in **th**e
\ā\ as **a** in **a**ce	\ī\ as **i** in **i**ce	\ü\ as **oo** in l**oo**t
\ä\ as **o** in m**o**p	\j\ as **j** in **j**ob	\u\ as **oo** in f**ooo**t
\au\ as **ou** in **ou**t	\[ng]\ as **ng** in si**ng**	\y\ as **y** in **y**et
\ch\ as **ch** in **ch**in	\O\ as **o** in g**o**	\zh\ as **si** in vi**si**on

After the main entry, you will see the word again, but it will look different because it is spelled *phonetically*, or as it sounds. For example, the word *acoustic* is spelled with symbols and letters (ə-'kü-stik) and broken into three parts. The stress mark (©) tells you to emphasize the middle part of the word when you say it. Looking at the pronunciation symbols, you can see that the symbol (ə) stands for a short ă, as in <u>about</u>. From the chart, we can tell that the middle part of the word ('kü) is pronounced as "koo" because the \ü\ has the <u>oo</u> sound, as in <u>loot</u>. The last part of the word is pronounced "stick" because the \i\has the *i* sound, as in the word <u>hit</u>. Put the three parts together and you have the pronunciation for *acoustic*.

Word Meaning

Most words have more than one meaning and several shades of the same meaning. When you look up a word in the dictionary, read through all of the definitions and choose one. Then reread the sentence or passage with the meaning in mind to see if it makes sense. For example, after reading the sentence below, you will quickly recognize that the meaning of *acoustic* lies in the first entry, not the second.

> The primary sense of the dolphin is acoustic, for vision is not a very useful sense in the often murky and dark depths of the ocean.

> **1:** of or relating to the sense or organs of hearing, to sound, or to the science of sounds <*acoustic* apparatus of the ear> <*acoustic* energy>
> **2:** of, relating to, or being a musical instrument whose sound is not electronically modified

The word *acoustic*, in this sentence, refers to the dolphin's hearing and not to a musical instrument.

For many words in the dictionary, a **synonym** (a word that has the same or a similar meaning) follows the definition. For the word *acoustic*, no synonym is provided. However, if you look up the word *passive*, you will find a synonym at the end of the definition entries. It will read like this: *syn* see **inactive**. The "syn" stands for *synonym* and tells us that *passive* means the same thing as *inactive*. Sometimes an **antonym** of the word is provided; its symbol is *ant*. In this case, you need to remember that *antonym* means "opposite in meaning."

Word Endings

Dictionaries also provide a word's **variants** and **inflections**. To understand what a variant is, let's take another look at the word *acoustic*. In the sentence "The primary sense of the dolphin is acoustic," we could replace *acoustic* with its variant *acoustical* without changing the meaning of the sentence. The primary sense of the dolphin is *acoustic* or *acoustical*. A guitar may be an *acoustic* guitar or an *acoustical* guitar. In this case, the different endings have no effect on the meaning or use of the word.

Inflections are word endings that slightly change the meaning of the word. Such changes are (1) making a word plural (plant, plant<u>s</u>); (2) making a word show ownership (Celcilia'<u>s</u> car); (3) making a word show that the action took place in the present or the past (communicate<u>s</u>, communicat<u>ing</u>, communicat<u>ed</u>); and (4) making the word show a comparison (fast, fast<u>er</u>, fast<u>est</u>).

For example, let's look at the word *murky* in the sentence "Vision is not a very useful sense in the often <u>murky</u> and dark depths of the ocean." The inflectional endings given in the dictionary are *murkier* and *murkiest*.

Parts of Speech

The dictionary also identifies the function a word has in a sentence—noun, verb, adjective, adverb, etc. For example, if you look up the word *perceive*, you will find out that it is a verb. You will also find that it has other forms; it can be an adjective (*perceivable*), an adverb (*perceivably*), and a noun (*perceiver*). Some dictionaries spell out the part of speech; others abbreviate it: *n.* for noun; *adj.* for adjective; *adv.* for adverb, *v.* for verb, etc. All dictionaries have an abbreviation guide or key either at the beginning or the end of the book.

Spelling

Two **guide words** are provided at the top of every page in a hard-copy dictionary to help you find specific words more easily. The guide word on the top left refers to the first word on the page and the guide word on the top right refers to the last word on the page. Since words in the dictionary are listed alphabetically, you can tell by the guide words on which page you will find your target word. For example, the word *acoustic* can be found on the page with the guide words *achromatic lens* and *acquitting* because the *aco* in *acoustic* comes after the *ach* in *achromatic lens* (first word on the page) and before the *acq* in *acquitting* (the last word on the page).

The dictionary can be frustrating if you do not know the correct spelling of a word. Using the traditional dictionary, you will have to think of every possible way to spell the word and then look up every possibility until you find the right entry. Two electronic resources can speed this process. You could open a word processing program (such as Microsoft Word or WordPerfect) and type the word the way you think it is spelled. Then, you could run the *spell-checker* under the Tools menu. The spell-checker lists words spelled similarly to the one you typed, the spelling you need may be among them. The other way to speed the process is to use an electronic dictionary. You must still think of all the possible spellings, but it is much quicker to type in your guesses than it is to look up each possibility in a traditional dictionary.

EXERCISE 2-7	**Using the Dictionary**

Read the passage below about dolphins and communication from a physical science textbook. Then use what you have learned about the dictionary to answer the questions that follow. The first question has been answered for you.

> The primary sense of the dolphin is <u>acoustic,</u> for vision is not a very useful sense in the often <u>murky</u> and dark depths of the ocean. Whereas sound is a <u>passive</u> sense for us, it is an active sense for dolphins, which send out sounds and then <u>perceive</u> their surroundings on the basis of the echoes that come back. The <u>ultrasonic</u> waves <u>emitted</u> by a dolphin enables it to "see" through the bodies of other animals and people.

Because skin, muscle, and fat are almost <u>transparent</u> to dolphins, they "see" only a thin outline of the body, but the bones, teeth, and gas-filled <u>cavities</u> are clearly <u>apparent.</u> Physical evidence of cancers, tumors, and heart attacks can all be "seen" by dolphins—as humans have only recently been able to do with <u>ultrasound</u>.

What's more interesting, a dolphin can reproduce the sonic signals that paint the mental image of its surroundings; thus the dolphin probably communicates its experience to other dolphins by communicating the full acoustic image of what is "seen," placing the image directly in the minds of other dolphins. It needs no word or symbol for "fish," for example, but communicates an image of the real thing—perhaps with <u>emphasis</u> highlighted by selective <u>filtering</u>, as we similarly communicate a musical concert to others via various means of sound reproduction. Small wonder that the language of the dolphin is very unlike our own! (Hewitt, Suchocki, and Hewitt 241)

Use the pronunciation key and entries below to answer the following questions.

Pronunciation Symbols		
\ə\ as **a** and **u** in abut	\e\ as **e** in bet	\o\ as **aw** in law
\ə\ as **e** in kitten	\ē\ as **ea/y** in easy	\oi\ as **oy** in boy
\ər\ as **ur/er** in further	\g\ as **g** in go	\th\ as **th** in thin
\a\ as **a** in ash	\i\ as **i** in hit	\t͟h\ as **th** in the
\ā\ as **a** in ace	\ī\ as **i** in ice	\ü\ as **oo** in loot
\ä\ as **o** in mop	\j\ as **j** in job	\u\ as **oo** in foot
\au\ as **ou** in out	\[ng]\ as **ng** in sing	\y\ as **y** in yet
\ch\ as **ch** in chin	\O\ as **o** in go	\zh\ as **si** in vision

> Main Entry: **murky**
> Pronunciation: \' mər - kE\
> Function: *adjective*
> Inflected Form(s): **murk•i•er; -est**
> Date: 14th century
> **1:** characterized by a heavy dimness or obscurity caused by or like that caused by overhanging fog or smoke
> **2:** characterized by thickness and heaviness of air : **<u>FOGGY</u>, <u>MISTY</u>**
> **3:** darkly vague or obscure <*murky* official rhetoric>
> - **murk•i•ly**   \ - kə - 1ē\ *adverb*
> - **murk•i•ness**   \ - kə - nəs\ *noun*

_____a_____ **1.** As used in the passage, the best meaning for the work *murky* is:
     a. Entry 1.
     b. Entry 2.
     c. Entry 3.

_____ **2.** The adverb of _murky_ is:
    a. murkily.
    b. murkiness.
    c. murkiest.

_____ **3.** When you pronounce the word _murky_, you would put the emphasis on:
    a. the first syllable (first part of the word).
    b. the second syllable (second part of the word).
    c. both syllables (both parts of the word).

_____ **4.** When you look at the pronunciation of _murky_ (Pronunciation: 'm&r-kE), the "E" in the second syllable is pronounced as:
    a. \e\ as **e** in b**e**t.
    b. \E\ as **ea** in **ea**sy.
    c. \i\ as **i** in h**i**t.

_____ **5.** The word _murky_ is:
    a. a noun.
    b. an adjective.
    c. an adverb.

Main Entry: **trans•par•ent**
Pronunciation: - 2nt
Function: _adjective_
Etymology: Middle English, from Medieval Latin _transparent-_, _transparens_, present participle of _transparEre_ to show through, from Latin _trans-_ + _parEre_ to show oneself
Date: 15th century
1a(1)**:** having the property of transmitting light without appreciable scattering so that bodies lying beyond are seen clearly **: PELLUCID** (2)**:** allowing the passage of a specified form of radiation (as X-rays or ultraviolet light) **b:** fine or sheer enough to be seen through **: DIAPHANOUS**
2 a: free from pretense or deceit **: FRANK b:** easily detected or seen through **: OBVIOUS c:** readily understood
synonym see CLEAR
- **trans•par•ent•ly** _adverb_
- **trans•par•ent•ness** _noun_

_____ **6.** As used in the passage, the word _transparent_ means:
    a. Entry 1a.
    b. Entry 1b.
    c. Entry 2a.

_____ **7.** The synonym for the word _transparent_ is:
    a. transmitting.
    b. obvious.
    c. clear.

_____ **8.** Originally, the word *transparent* meant:
   a. to show oneself.
   b. obvious.
   c. clear.

_____ **9.** The word *transparent* came from:
   a. Latin.
   b. Greek.
   c. French.

_____ **10.** The word *transparently* is:
   a. a noun.
   b. a verb.
   c. an adverb.

BEYOND DICTIONARIES

The Thesaurus

The **thesaurus** is like a dictionary. For each entry it provides a definition, the part of speech, an example of the word used in a sentence or phrase, a list of synonyms (words with similar meanings), and a list of related words. This tool can help you with both reading and writing. When you come to an unfamiliar word while reading, you can look it up in a thesaurus and substitute a synonym to make sense of the passage.

| EXERCISE 2-8 | **Using a Thesaurus** |

Use a thesaurus and the passage about dolphins from Exercise 2-7 to answer the following questions. The first one has been answered for you.

___a___ **1.** A synonym for the word *passive* is:
   a. inactive.   c. acoustic
   b. active.

_____ **2.** A synonym for the word *apparent* is:
   a. deceptive.
   b. evident.
   c. emphasis.

_____ **3.** The meaning of the word *cavity*, as used in the passage, is:
   a. the area of decay in a tooth.
   b. vibrations of sound.
   c. a hollowed-out space.

_____ **4.** The meaning of the word *emitted*, as used in the passage, is:

    a. to throw or give off.

    b. to speak or say out loud.

    c. to publish.

_____ **5.** In this passage, the word *ultrasound* means:

    a. vibrations above the range of human hearing.

    b. technique used to examine internal body structures.

    c. a filtering device.

Glossaries

Most textbooks have a glossary at the end of the book, but some also have one running along the outside margin to help the reader as she goes through the text. A **glossary** is like a dictionary, but only the terms used in that particular book are included. The terms are listed in alphabetical order (or, if it's a running glossary, in the order that they appear) followed by their definitions. Below is an excerpt from a glossary in a physical science textbook.

Water table	The upper boundary of the zone of saturation, the area where every pore space is filled with water.
Wave	A disturbance or vibration propagated from point to point in a medium or in space.
Wave speed	The speed with which waves pass a particular point: Wave speed = frequency × wavelength
Wavelength	The distance between successive crests, troughs, or identical parts of a wave.
Weight	The gravitational force exerted on an object by the nearest most-massive body (locally, by the Earth).
White dwarf	A dying star that has collapsed to the size of the Earth and is slowly cooling off; located at lower left of the H-R diagram.
Work	The product of the force and the distance through which the force moves: $W = Fd$
Work-energy theorem	The work done on an object is equal to the energy gained by the object: Work = ΔE (Hewitt, Suchocki, and Hewitt 772)

Look through the above section of a glossary and find the definition of *work*. As you can see, *work* is defined as "the product of the force and the distance through which the force moves." The formula for *work* is also provided: $W = Fd$.

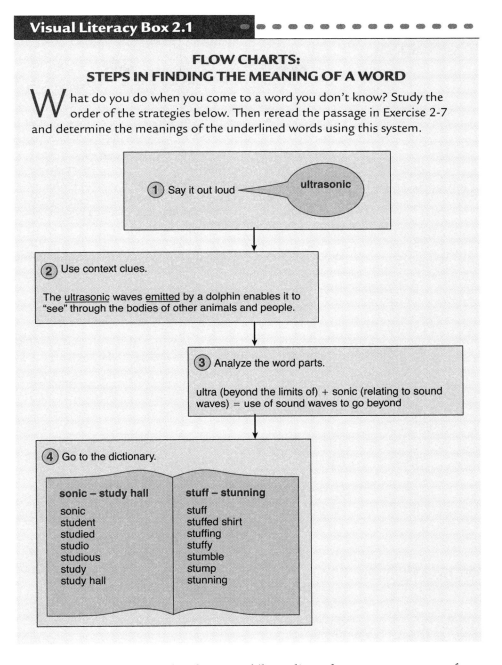

Visual Literacy Box 2.1

FLOW CHARTS:
STEPS IN FINDING THE MEANING OF A WORD

What do you do when you come to a word you don't know? Study the order of the strategies below. Then reread the passage in Exercise 2-7 and determine the meanings of the underlined words using this system.

1 Say it out loud — **ultrasonic**

2 Use context clues.

The <u>ultrasonic</u> waves <u>emitted</u> by a dolphin enables it to "see" through the bodies of other animals and people.

3 Analyze the word parts.

ultra (beyond the limits of) + sonic (relating to sound waves) = use of sound waves to go beyond

4 Go to the dictionary.

sonic – study hall	stuff – stunning
sonic	stuff
student	stuffed shirt
studied	stuffing
studio	stuffy
studious	stumble
study	stump
study hall	stunning

It is important to use the glossary *while* reading when you are unsure of any terms used. If you do not take the time to understand terms as you read, your understanding of the reading will be far less than if you knew the meanings of all the terms.

Using a Glossary

Read the following excerpt from a physical science textbook and answer the questions that follow. The first response has been provided for you.

> [1]Because the nuclear fires of a white dwarf have burned out, it is not actually a star anymore. [2]It's more accurate to call it a stellar remnant. [3]It may continue to radiate energy and change from white to yellow and then to red, until it slowly but ultimately fades to a cold, black lump of matter—a **black dwarf**. [4]The density of a black dwarf is enormous. [5]Into a volume no more than that of an average-size planet is concentrated a mass hundreds of thousands times greater than that of the Earth. [6]The black dwarf has a density comparable to that of a battleship squeezed into a pint jar! (Hewitt, Suchocki, and Hewitt 712)

1. What is a white dwarf? If you cannot tell from the paragraph, look it up in the glossary.

   A dying star that has collapsed to the size of the Earth and is slowly cooling off.

2. From what the passage tells you and from what you found in the glossary, explain how a white dwarf becomes a black dwarf.

3. How large is a black dwarf?

4. What does the word *comparable* mean?

5. Which sentences show that a black dwarf's density is greater than its volume?

WORD PUZZLES

An **analogy** is a form of logical reasoning in which the thinker draws a comparison between two unlike objects or ideas to understand a new concept. You can practice this type of logical thinking through analogy word puzzles.

Synonym Word Puzzles

Synonyms are words that have nearly the same meaning. An example of a word puzzle using a synonym looks like this:

automobile : car :: tome : book

The analogy is read in the following manner: automobile *is to* car *AS* tome *is to* book. Another way to read this puzzle is as follows: *automobile* is another word for *car*, just as *tome* is another word for *book*.

Antonym Word Puzzles

Antonyms are words that have opposite meanings. An example of a word puzzle using an antonym looks like this:

white : black :: inhale : exhale

The way we read this puzzle is as follows: *white* is the opposite of *black*, just as *inhale* is the opposite of *exhale*.

Classification Word Puzzles

Classification refers to the way items or ideas can be divided into groups. All of the items within the group have something in common that makes them a part of the group or class. An example of a word puzzle using classification looks like this:

oak : tree :: rose : flower

The way we read this puzzle is as follows: an *oak* is a type of *tree*, just as a *rose* is a type of *flower*.

Part-to-Whole Word Puzzles

Part-to-whole puzzles show the relationship between the items that make up a larger system. An example of a word puzzle using the part-to-whole pattern looks like this:

arm : body :: California : United States

The way we read this puzzle is as follows: the *arm* is part of the *body*, just as *California* is part of the *United States*.

Cause-and-Effect Word Puzzles

Cause-and-effect word puzzles show the relationship between an event and the happenings that caused the event. An example of a word puzzle using a cause-and-effect relationship looks like this:

infection : disease :: hurricane : devastation

The way we read this puzzle is as follows: an *infection* causes *disease*, just as a *hurricane* causes *devastation*.

Word Puzzles

Finish each word puzzle by supplying the correct word. The first has been done for you. If you do not know the meaning of any of the words in this exercise, look them up in a dictionary before you make your choice. If you have access to a computer, you can use the online dictionary (*http://www.m-w.com*).

1. occur: happen   ::   abundant: <u>many</u> (few, many)

2. spend: save   ::   anterior: _____ (interior, posterior)

3. beetle: insect   ::   angiosperm: _____ (animal, plant)

4. spoke: wheel   ::   cornea: _____ (eye, ear)

5. terrorism: fear   ::   unemployment: _____ (wealth, poverty)

COMMONLY CONFUSED WORDS

Words that are similar in sound or in spelling can often be confused. For example, the words *to, too,* and *two* all sound the same but have different spellings and different meanings. *To* is a preposition that shows movement and direction, as in the sentence "We are going *to* the university." *Too* is an adverb that means "in addition to" or "also," as in the sentence "Not only will Ezekiel compete, but Joaquin will enter the race *too*." Finally, *two* is an adjective that describes a number that is greater than one and less than three, as in "There were *two* dolphins swimming along the coastal waters." Study the list of often-confused words below and complete the exercise that follows.

> **COMMONLY CONFUSED WORDS**
>
> **1. affect**—to influence or change. Tamaqua's home was not *affected* by the tornado.
> **effect**—the change that was brought about by an influencing force. The *effects* of the tornado could be seen for miles around; uprooted trees and demolished buildings were everywhere.
>
> **2. accept**—to agree to receive. Olga *accepted* the gift without hesitation.
> **except**—to leave out, exclude. Everyone received a gift *except* Myron.
>
> **3. cite**—an observation. Ziomara *cited* the article in her reference list.
> **site**—a particular place, either physical or virtual. Go to this Web *site* for more information about the news show.

sight—the ability to see; vision. Tamara's eye*sight* has improved since she stopped watching television.

4. **its**—the possessive for the pronoun *it*. The storm ran *its* course, and the weather calmed down.
it's—the contraction of *it is*. *It's* terribly hot outside.

5. **your**—possessive pronoun for *you*. Bring *your* books with you to the study session.
you're—contraction of *you are*. *You're* the leader of this study session.

6. **than**—conjunction used to compare. The lab is more fun *than* the lecture.
then—adverb indicating time. Read the textbook first; *then* complete the experiment.

7. **their**—possessive of the pronoun *them*. Tell them to bring *their* cell phones.
there—adverb that shows place. We can go *there* to buy a cell phone.
they're—contraction of *they are*. *They're* going to buy another cell phone.

8. **right**—adjective that means "correct." Shannon had a 100% on the final exam; all of her answers were *right*.
write—verb for symbolic communication on paper. *Write* your lecture notes into a summary.

9. **here**—adverb that shows place. "We came *here* to listen to the concert."
hear—to listen. "I cannot *hear* you because the music is too loud."

10. **fewer**—refers to items that can be counted. We have *fewer* books to buy this semester.
less—refers to general amounts. We have *less* work to do this semester.

EXERCISE
2-11

Commonly Confused Words

Read the following sentences and fill in the blank with the correct word. The first has been filled in for you.

_____b_____ **1.** The flu shot had a terrible _____effect_____. I was dizzy and nauseous all day.
  a. affect
  b. effect

_____ **2.** I took all of the requirements for the biology major _____organic chemistry.
  a. accept
  b. except

_____ **3.** You need to _____at least three references in your
English paper.
   a. cite
   b. site
   c. sight

_____ **4.** Julio's research paper is not long enough; _____only
two pages long.
   a. its
   b. it's

_____ **5.** Because of the holiday, we will not have class on Friday.
_____next class meeting will be on Monday.
   a. Your
   b. You're

_____ **6.** Celina is taller_____her boyfriend only when she
wears heels.
   a. than
   b. then

_____ **7.** _____leaving at 7:00 AM; you can either ride with
them or take the shuttle.
   a. Their
   b. There
   c. They're

_____ **8.** Please_____ this in your notes.
   a. right
   b. write

_____ **9.** I did not_____what the professor said because I was
late for class.
   a. here
   b. hear

_____ **10.** I have_____assignments this semester than last
semester.
   a. fewer
   b. less

ACRONYMS

Some titles or names are too long, cumbersome, or technical to use repeatedly.
Therefore, nicknames, or acronyms, are created. An acronym is an abbreviation
formed from the first letter of each word in a title or name. For example, it is
quicker and easier to say "FBI" rather than "Federal Bureau of Investigation." The
rule of thumb in writing concerning **acronyms** is as follows: (1) The first time a
name or formal title is introduced, the author is expected to give its acronym

immediately afterward in parentheses. (2) After that, the author may refer to the name or title by its acronym only. Examples of common acronyms are listed below.

1. USA—United States of America
2. NASA—National Aeronautics and Space Administration
3. SCUBA—Self-contained Underwater Breathing Apparatus
4. LAN—Local Area Network
5. GPA—Grade Point Average

EXERCISE
2-12

Practice with Acronyms

Can you guess what the following acronyms stand for? In the exercise below, match the acronyms with the corresponding terms. Check your answers by looking them up in the dictionary. The first one has been done for you.

Part a

___e___	1. NASCAR	a. United Nations
_____	2. CIA	b. Central Intelligence Agency
_____	3. NBA	c. National Broadcasting Company
_____	4. UN	d. National Basketball Association
_____	5. NBC	e. National Association of Stock Car Auto Racing

Part b

_____	1. ABC	a. National Public Radio
_____	2. PTA	b. American Broadcasting Company
_____	3. CBS	c. Public Broadcasting Service
_____	4. PBS	d. Parent-Teacher Association
_____	5. NPR	e. Columbia Broadcasting System

TRANSITIONAL WORDS

Authors use **transitional words** to move from one idea to another. These words help the reader follow the author's train of thought. For example, think of a writer describing a baseball game. He would use words indicating direction, such as *over there, to the left, to the right, beyond, above,* and *near.*

Near the stadium stood the catcher. *To the right* was first base, *to the left* was third base, and *beyond* the catcher stood the pitcher.

Below is a list of transitions along with the words that signal them. Study the chart and complete the exercise that follows.

Transition	Author's Purpose	Signal Words
Topic with a list	To explain more about a topic	also, in addition, moreover, furthermore
Cause/Effect	To explain what caused something to happen	as a result, consequently, therefore
Time order	To state in a specific order	first, second, next, then, after that, finally, first of all
Example	To explain through example	for example, to illustrate this, to demonstrate this
Summary	To briefly restate	in summary; in conclusion; to sum up

EXERCISE
2-13

Practice with Signals

Read the following sentences and choose the correct signal words for the context. The first has been chosen for you.

1. Russian literature is often difficult to read because the authors generally introduce numerous characters into their novels. _____Also_____, they refer to each character by his nickname, confusing the reader even more. (Also; To sum up)

2. No matter where we are on the Earth, the part of our atmosphere in which we are able to breathe is only two miles high. _____, if you can imagine walking twenty city blocks straight up, you can imagine where our atmosphere ends. (As a result; For example)

3. Studying a foreign language is not difficult. First, listen to conversations to get a feel for the sound and rhythm of the new language. Then, listen to and imitate the pronunciation of new vocabulary words. _____, learn the translations for the words you are studying. (That is; Finally)

4. Many scholars believe that human nature does not change and that history actually repeats itself. _____, they believe we should study the past. (Therefore; Moreover)

5. There are several steps in solving a mathematics problem._____,
examine every step in the example. If you do not understand any of the steps,
ask your instructor for an explanation. Finally, begin to work out the practice problems. (First of all; In conclusion)

―――

TEN PRACTICE EXERCISES

| EXERCISE 2-14 | **Terms and Definitions** |

Read the following passage from Campbell, Mitchell, and Reese (137). Then
identify the new terms along with their definitions. The first one has been done
for you.

1. Cancer, which currently claims the life of one out of every five people in the
United States and other developed nations, is a disease of the cell cycle.
Unlike normal cells of the body, **cancer cells** do not have a properly functioning cell-cycle control system; they divide excessively and can invade
other tissues of the body.

Term: _cancer_____

Definition: _a disease of the cell cycle._____

2. This excessive growth can result in an abnormal mass of cells called a **tumor**.

Term: _____

Definition: _____

3. Not all tumors are cancerous, however. A **benign tumor** is an abnormal
mass of essentially normal cells. Benign tumors can cause problems if they
grow in certain organs, such as the brain, but usually they can be completely removed by surgery. They always remain at their original site in
the body.

Term: _____

Definition: _____

4. In contrast to a benign tumor, a **malignant tumor** is cancerous. It is a mass of cancer cells, which are capable of spreading into neighboring tissues and often to other parts of the body. Arising from a single cancer cell, a malignant tumor displaces normal tissue as it grows. If the tumor is not killed or removed, some of the cancer cells spread into surrounding tissues, enlarging the tumor.

Term: _____

Definition: _____

5. Cells may also split off from the tumor, invade the **circulatory system** (lymph vessels and blood vessels) and travel to new locations, where they can form new tumors.

Term: _____

Definition: _____

6. The spread of cancer cells beyond their original site is called **metastasis.**

Term: _____

Definition: _____

7. Cancers are named according to the organ or tissue in which they originate. For simplicity, they are grouped into four categories. **Carcinomas** are cancers that originate in the external or internal coverings of the body, such as the skin or the lining of the intestine.

Term: _____

Definition: _____

8. Sarcomas arise in tissues that support the body, such as bone and muscle.

Term: _____

Definition: _____

9. Cancers of blood-forming tissues, such as bone marrow, spleen, and lymph nodes, are called **leukemias.**

Term: _____

Definition: _____

Words with Multiple Meanings

Each sentence contains an italicized word from the field of sociology. Each term has multiple meanings. Choose the meaning that makes the most sense within the sentences provided. The first meaning has been chosen for you.

____b____ **1.** According to the study conducted by Thomas J. Stanley and William D. Danko, many millionaires live in middle- or working-*class* neighborhoods.
    a. a group of students led by a teacher
    b. economic position of individuals within a society
    c. sophistication

_____ **2.** According to the famous psychiatrist Sigmund Freud, our personalities are made up of the *id*, the ego, and the superego.
    a. abbreviation of the word *identification*
    b. an unconscious part of the personality
    c. dictionary abbreviation for the word *idiom*

_____ **3.** The official was elected to the government, although he was not supported by the *masses*.
    a. religious ceremonies usually held on Sundays
    b. scientific measurements of matter
    c. a large body of people who do not have political power

_____ **4.** The governor declared the northern counties of Georgia to be in a *state* of emergency after the tornado struck.
    a. a condition of being
    b. the political organization of a group of people who occupy and govern a specific territory
    c. to say or tell the specifics of an idea

_____ **5.** The United States is an unusual country because its population comes from a variety of ethnic backgrounds. Its people are a mixture of many *races* and nationalities.
    a. running competitions
    b. industrial watercourses
    c. classifications of people based on ethnic, cultural, or genetic background

EXERCISE 2-16	**Practice with Word Parts**

Study the word parts below and use them to figure out the meanings of the words. The first has been done for you.

mal = wrong or bad	**mis** = wrong	**re** = again
a = not	**ab** = not or away	

1. mislead (mis + lead) = <u>lead in the wrong direction</u>

2. malformed (mal + formed) = _____

3. review (re + view) = _____

4. atypical (a + typical) = _____

5. abnormal (ab + normal) = _____

EXERCISE 2-17	**Finding Etymologies**

Use the dictionary to find the etymologies of the lettered words. Then match these terms with their word histories. The first term has been matched for you.

__e__	1. From Old French, meaning "to weave"	a. cancer
_____	2. From Greek, meaning "to change"	b. metastasis
_____	3. From Greek, meaning "to grow flesh"	c. sarcoma
_____	4. From Greek, meaning "cancer"	d. carcinoma
_____	5. From Greek and Latin, meaning "crab"	e. tissue

EXERCISE 2-18	**Using the Dictionary**

Use the sentence below to answer the following questions. Use the dictionary as a reference when necessary. The first question has been answered for you.

> Carcinomas are cancers that originate in the external or internal coverings of the body, such as the skin or the lining of the intestine.

_____a_____ **1.** The word *external* means:
  a. outside.
  b. pertaining to relationships with foreign countries.
  c. not essential.

_____ **2.** The word *external* is:
  a. a noun.
  b. a verb.
  c. an adjective.

_____ **3.** The word *external* came from:
  a. Latin.
  b. Greek.
  c. French.

_____ **4.** As used in the sentence, the word *internal* means:
  a. existing within the mind.
  b. occurring within an organization.
  c. inside.

_____ **5.** The word *internal* is:
  a. a noun.
  b. an adjective.
  c. an adverb.

EXERCISE 2-19

Practice with Acronyms

Spell out the following acronyms. You will probably not be able to guess them because they come from a specialized area of science, astronomy. Check (or obtain) your answers by looking them up in the dictionary. The first one has been done for you.

1. AU   astronomical unit _____

2. CCD   _____

3. GPS   _____

4. RA   _____

5. UT   _____

A Reading in Physical Science

Use the passage below from Hewitt, Suchocki, and Hewitt (536) to complete the comprehension quesions that follow and the remaining exercises in the rest of this chapter.

Asbestos: Friend and Foe

[1]   When the word <u>asbestos</u> is mentioned, people tend to think of lung disease and/or removal problems, but it hasn't always been that way. The first known reference to asbestos goes back to the time of <u>Aristotle</u>, when this material was discovered to have fireproof qualities. Since then, the <u>incombustibility</u> and low heat <u>conductivity</u> of asbestos, plus its <u>fibrous</u>, flexible nature, have prompted humans to use it in many ways. It has been woven into fabrics (as theater curtains and fireproof suits) and utilized in building materials (fireproof insulation) and as a flame retardant in plaster, ceiling, and floor tile. It has also been used in automobile brake shoes and clutch facings, air and water filters, cigarette tips, military gas masks, and toothpaste! In the 1970s, the commercial use of asbestos reached an all-time high, but then it was found to be linked to lung disease. The fibrous nature that makes asbestos so flexible also allows easy penetration into bodily tissues, particularly the lungs. The history of asbestos is one of bitter paradox because the unique qualities that allowed it to save lives have also been found to endanger lives.

[2]   Asbestos is not a single mineral but rather a family of silicate minerals known for their fibrous structure. There are six types of asbestos minerals, but only two are of commercial importance—chrysotile and crocidolite. The asbestos mineral crysotile accounts for 95 percent of asbestos production worldwide, and crocidolite accounts for the remaining 5 percent. Chrysotile has a sheet silicate structure that makes it soft and flexible. Because of its softness, chrysotile is easily broken down in the body, producing no apparent damage. This form of asbestos, leached from the ground, is present in many reservoirs of quite-safe drinking water. Recent scientific medical evidence indicates that people exposed for long periods to moderate amounts of chrysotile show no lung ailments.

[3]   Crocidolite is a different story, however, for this type of asbestos has a double-chain silicate structure that makes it strong and stiff, and thus more dangerous in the body. People exposed either to high levels of crocidolite or to moderate levels over a prolonged period of time have been found to develop lung disease. Thus it is crocidolite that is the principal culprit in asbestos-related lung diseases. Despite this knowledge, many reports on asbestos health hazards fail to make a distinction between the various types.

[4]   This failure to distinguish between harmless and dangerous asbestos has contributed to a public view that any asbestos mineral is fatal. The widely embraced and emotionally volatile premise that "one fiber can kill" has made asbestos the most feared contaminant on the Earth. It is by far the most expensive pollutant in terms of regulation and removal. The removal of asbestos-containing materials from schools, hospitals, and other public buildings has cost billions of dollars over the past 20 years. With only 5 percent of asbestos minerals posing a health problem, however, many scientists question the practice of eliminating all forms of asbestos, proposing that a more responsible method of remediation would distinguish among the different types. As with electricity in the 1800s, gasoline-powered vehicles in the early 1900s, and radioactivity in the late 1900s, public fears about asbestos will likely persist for some time before informed common sense prevails. Then we may view asbestos as both friend (chrysotile) and foe (crocidolite).

_____c_____ **1.** Which of the following is NOT a synonym for the word *fibrous*?
        a. stringy
        b. wiry
        c. heavy

_____ **2.** The best meaning for the word *asbestos* is:
        a. minerals used as fireproof insulating materials.
        b. plaster used in high-rise buildings.
        c. floor tile used in schools and hospitals.

_____ **3.** Who was Aristotle?
        a. a Greek philosopher who lived from 384 to 322 B.C.
        b. a famous nineteenth-century chemist.
        c. a twentieth-century manufacturer of asbestos.

_____ **4.** The meaning of the word *incombustibility* is:
        a. not capable of being burned.
        b. capable of being burned.
        c. manufacture.

_____ **5.** In this passage, the word *conductivity* means:
        a. ability to transmit.
        b. ability to burn.
        c. inability to burn.

EXERCISE 2-20

Practice with Word Puzzles

Finish each word puzzle by supplying the correct word. If you do not know the meaning of a word in this exercise, look it up in a dictionary before you make your choice. If you have access to a computer, you can use the online dictionary (*http://www.m-w.com*). The first has been done for you.

1. crocidolite: dangerous   ::   chrysotile: _____safe_____ (, safe)

2. leach: remove   ::   indicate: _____ (show, eliminate)

3. asbestos: mineral   ::   lung: _____ (organ, silicate)

4. silicate: salt   ::   chrocidolite: _____ (crysotile, mineral)

5. crocidolite: soft   ::   crocidolite: _____ (stiff, flexible)

EXERCISE
2-21

Practice with Commonly Confused Words

Read the following sentences and fill in the blank with the correct word. The first blank is filled for you.

___b___   **1.** In the 1970s, the commercial use of asbestos reached an all-time high, but ___then___ it was found to be linked to lung disease.
  a. than
  b. then

_____   **2.** _____ are six types of asbestos minerals, but only two are of commercial importance—chrysotile and crocidolite.
  a. Their
  b. There

_____   **3.** None of the six types of asbestos minerals are of commercial importance _____ chrysotile and crocidolite.
  a. accept
  b. except

_____   **4.** Chrysotile has no _____ on the body because its chemical components are easily broken down.
  a. effect
  b. affect

_____   **5.** Public fears about asbestos will likely persist for some time before informed common sense prevails. _____ we may view asbestos as both friend (chrysotile) and foe (crocidolite).
  a. Then
  b. Than

EXERCISE 2-22	**Practice with Transitions**

Study the list below. Then read the following sentences and choose the correct transitional words for the context. The first one has been completed for you.

Transition	Author's Purpose	Signal Words
Addition	To explain more about a topic	also, in addition, moreover, furthermore
Summary	To briefly restate	in summary, in conclusion, to sum up
Sequence	To state in a specific order	first, first of all, second, next, since then, after that, finally
Comparison	To show similarities and differences	like, just as, similar to; unlike, different from
Causation	To explain what caused something to happen	as a result, consequently, therefore, thus

_____a_____ **1.** [Asbestos] has been woven into fabrics (as theater curtains and fireproof suits), and utilized in building materials (fireproof insulation) and as a flame retardant in plaster, ceiling, and floor tile. It has___also___ been used in automobile brake shoes and clutch facings, air and water filters, cigarette tips, military gas masks, and toothpaste!
   a. also
   b. to sum up

_____ **2.** The first known reference to asbestos goes back to the time of Aristotle, when this material was discovered to have fireproof qualities. _____, the incombustibility and low heat conductivity of asbestos, plus its fibrous, flexible nature, have prompted humans to use it in many ways.
   a. As a result
   b. Since then

_____ **3.** Recent scientific medical evidence indicates that people exposed
for long periods to moderate amounts of chrysotile show no
lung ailments. Crocidolite is a different story, _____, for
this type of asbestos has a double-chain silicate structure that
makes it strong and stiff, and thus more dangerous in the body.
a. finally
b. however

_____ **4.** People exposed either to high levels of crocidolite or to moderate
levels over a prolonged period of time have been found to
develop lung disease. _____ it is crocidolite that is the
principal culprit in asbestos-related lung diseases.
a. Thus
b. Moreover

_____ **5.** _____ this knowledge, many reports on asbestos health
hazards fail to make a distinction between the various types.
a. Despite
b. First of all

Topic, Main Idea, and Supporting Details

In Chapter 2 we learned that in order to improve our reading comprehension, we need to improve our vocabulary skills. One important way to help us do this is to keep a dictionary by our side at all times so that we can refer to it whenever we come across a word we do not know, and another is to rely on context clues. Improving our vocabulary is not the only factor to improving our reading comprehension, however. In this chapter we review other major factors, including:

- the common problems students have while reading and how to deal with them;
- the topic of a paragraph and how to identify it;
- the main idea of a paragraph and how to distinguish it from a topic;
- major and minor supporting details and how to use them to help locate the main idea;
- paragraphs that include a topic, a main idea, and supporting details, and how to connect those paragraphs into an essay.

COMMON PROBLEMS IN READING

When interviewed, professors of various disciplines at a small private college in New England talked about problems their students had reading college textbooks. They said the most common problem students have is finding the **main idea.** (This term is also known as the **central point,** but we use the term *main idea* in this chapter and throughout.)

Professor of English: I'm often surprised when I give a small [reading] selection of only a page and a half and ask, "What is the key thing the author wanted to tell us?" and the vast majority cannot tell me.

Professor of English: Students skim through [their readings], and I don't think they follow trains of thought; they read isolated sentences. They don't see how they connect up. When I say, "Give the major idea. What do you remember?" most cannot tell me.

Professor of Economics: Students pay attention to the wrong thing! If a paragraph starts "Man has always been in love with the machine," that is what they underline. Throw that away because the next sentence says, "In the global economy of robotics, the following is true. Japan has 20% fewer employees than America." That is what they should have highlighted, but they underline "Man is in love with the machine!" They have no idea what is important in what they read. Therefore, they have trouble answering essay questions. (Yaworski 167–69)

If you are not exactly sure how to go about finding the main idea as you read college-level textbooks, don't worry. You have a lot of company! If you did not spend 20 to 30 hours per week reading your textbooks in high school, you probably did not develop this ability. Now is the time to make up for that.

Ask yourself these three questions when you are looking for the main idea:

1. What is the topic of the paragraph?
2. What is common to all of the sentences of the paragraph?
3. Which sentences have specific facts that are not common to the other sentences?

The **topic** tells us the general idea of a paragraph or selection in one word or phrase. The **main idea,** which should always be stated as a sentence, is a general statement that relates to all of the sentences in the paragraph; in other words, each sentence in the paragraph gives more information about the main idea. The **supporting details** include all of the sentences that are not the main idea yet offer specific facts that give more information about it. The most important details are called **major details.** Details that help to explain the major details and the main idea are called the **minor details.** Once you have located the main idea, you can usually locate the supporting details. For example:

Coffee <**TOPIC**> has become more than just a morning pick-me-up. <**MAIN IDEA**> Most people, especially students, drink up to three or four cups of coffee throughout the day. <**MAJOR DETAIL**> In New York City, Starbuck's Cafés can be seen on practically every street corner. <**MINOR DETAIL**> Some coffee shops are open and filled with customers until late evening. <**MAJOR DETAIL**> No one who lives in New York City will ever be threatened by a coffee shortage.

TOPICS

A reading can be about anything in the world—people, places, events, and ideas. It is important to have a specific focus before we start reading or we will feel lost among the millions of possibilities. The topic provides this focus for us; the **topic** tells us who or what a paragraph is about.

Knowledge of the topic enables us to select the appropriate schema that will help us make sense of the reading. As we learned in chapter 1; *schemata* are an accumulation of details about a certain topic that we can connect in a meaningful way.

The topic directs our attention. Without knowledge of the topic or an appropriate schema, reading is like walking into a room full of people who have already started a conversation. We don't know how to contribute to this conversation because we don't know what it is about. How can we figure out the topic of the conversation if no one turns to us and says, "We are talking about the problems with parking on Campus X"? We need to listen carefully for clues.

For example, one individual recounts the inconveniences he went through when his car was towed. Someone else explains the procedure she had to go through to pay a parking fine. Another person adds that Campus X is always crowded during the evenings. It might take us a while to piece together all of this information, but eventually we would correctly guess that the conversation is about parking on Campus X. As this example illustrates, having knowledge of the topic beforehand is extremely important because it tells us what details to expect and how to focus our attention on them.

How Do We Detect Topics?

Identifying a topic is much like playing *Jeopardy*. The player looks at a series of clues about an item within a *category*, which is the name for a group of related items. A *category* is the general name for a group of more specific items. For example, if we saw a basket filled with apples, bananas, oranges, peaches, and pears, instead of naming every item, we could simply refer to it as a basket of "fruit." When people look into the basket, they know what to expect. In other words, *fruit* is the name of the category and *apples, bananas, oranges, peaches,* and *pears* are the items in that category.

To help us picture this idea, let's review the following organization chart:

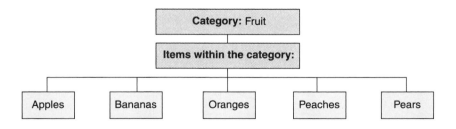

The word *fruit* is written in the top box to name the general category. The different types of fruit that are written in the boxes below it represent specific members of this category. Thus, a category is essentially the topic and the items within the category are essentially the details that are related to the topic.

Another example of a topic is "country." If the word *country* represents a nonspecific, general idea, then Canada, China, and Russia are names that represent specific ideas—that is, countries. These names cannot be used to represent the general idea "country." For example, Japan, China, and Russia (specific countries) cannot be listed as details of the United States because it is another specific country. The diagram below helps us to visualize this concept.

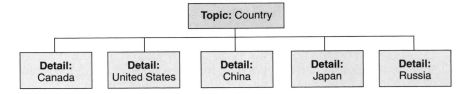

Identifying the Topic

Look at the items in each list and ask yourself what all these items have in common. Then, identify the topic from the list of items and circle it. The first one has been done for you.

1. (inventions)
   telegraphs
   computers
   telephones
   radios

2. Bill Clinton
   Jimmy Carter
   Gerald Ford
   former presidents
   George Bush

3. Vermont
   New Hampshire
   Massachusetts
   New England States
   Maine

4. classical
   music
   jazz
   rock
   big band

5. novels
   textbooks
   magazines
   newspapers
   reading materials

Identifying the Major Category or Detail

Look at the items listed below and identify the major category or topic. The first one has been done for you.

____fish____ **1.** trout, salmon, halibut, fish, flounder, haddock, blue, carp

_____ **2.** Atlantic, Pacific, Arctic, Indian, oceans, Antarctic

_____ **3.** maple, trees, oak, hickory, chestnut, pine, birch

_____ **4.** peas, carrots, tomatoes, beans, celery, vegetables, lettuce, beets

_____ **5.** Oldsmobile, Ford, Cadillac, Toyota, Chevrolet, Dodge, cars

_____ **6.** hats, gloves, winter clothes, scarves, coats, boots

_____ **7.** insects, spiders, grasshoppers, mosquitoes, flies, butterflies

_____ **8.** football, baseball, tennis, sports, golf, basketball, soccer

_____ **9.** Trenton, Los Angeles, New York, cities, Atlanta, Austin

_____ **10.** Erie, lakes, Superior, Huron, Michigan, Ontario

_____ **11.** Caribbean, Caspian, Mediterranean, Adriatic, seas

_____ **12.** _Time, Newsweek, Life, People,_ magazines, _Business Week_

_____ **13.** train, bus, transportation, airplane, automobile, subway

_____ **14.** psychology, mathematics, academic disciplines, biology, sociology, history, business management

_____ **15.** dormitory, dining hall, faculty offices, classrooms, college campus, infirmary

MAIN IDEA

Every paragraph has a **main idea** that is always stated as a sentence and is usually the first sentence in a paragraph. The sentence containing the main idea identifies the topic by telling the reader who and/or what the paragraph is about.

Have you ever listened to someone ramble on about a certain topic and wanted to ask her the following questions?

■ So, what's your point in all of this?

■ Where are you going with this?

■ Just what are you getting at?

■ What exactly are you trying to say?

Just as we try to sum up the point of a conversation, we should try to find the author's main idea in each paragraph we read. As the professors who were interviewed stated earlier in this chapter, finding the main idea is finding the most important information. Once we find the main idea, we know the author's main reason or point for writing.

How Do We Detect Main Ideas?

How do we know which idea is the main one? The main idea is presented in a general statement that relates to every other sentence in the paragraph. For example, the main idea sentence of a paragraph describing the topic "apples" might look like this:

There are many varieties of apples to choose from when making fruit baskets.

The sentences that follow are called the supporting details because they are related to and give the reader more specific information about the different varieties of apples. One related sentence may describe the Macintosh apple. Another related sentence might provide information about the Red Delicious apple. Other sentences may give specific details about Cortland, Gala, and, Yellow Delicious apples. The diagram below shows the relationship between the main idea statement with the other sentences (that show the supporting details) in a paragraph.

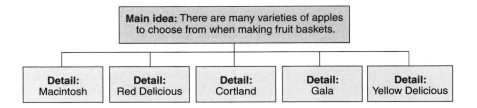

The sentences in our paragraph on apples might look something like this:

■ **[MI] There are many varieties of apples to choose from when making fruit baskets.**

■ **[SD]** The Macintosh is multicolored and tart.

■ **[SD]** The Red Delicious and the Yellow Delicious apples are both sweet, differing only in appearance.

■ **[SD]** Cortland apples are good for snacking, while Gala apples are perfect for baking.

The first sentence states the main idea. It tells us the paragraph is about the different types of apples that appear in fruit baskets. The remaining sentences are related to the topic and specifically identify those apple types as well as describe what those types might look like or how they might taste. In the following passage, try to determine what the supporting details illustrate.

> [1]Beauty influences first impressions. [2]First of all, a physically attractive person has more influence in job interviews. [3]Beauty can also affect courtroom decisions. [4]The outcome of a blind date is especially vulnerable to appearance. [5]Finally, students' grades can be either positively or negatively affected by physical appearance. (Barker and Gaut 65)

If you chose the first sentence as the one that states the main idea, you are right! The first sentence introduces the topic "beauty and first impressions" and makes a general statement concerning the influence that beauty has on first impressions. The remaining sentences provide details—in this case, examples of how beauty affects first impressions.

Visual Literacy Box 3.1

CHARTS: MAIN IDEA

Common Variations in Family Organization and Structure

Instructions

Study the chart below and answer the main idea quesions that follow.

Family Type	Composition of Family Unit
Nuclear family	Wife, husband, and children, if any
Extended family	Nuclear family plus grandparents, aunts, uncles, or other kin
Blended family	Wife, husband, plus children from previous marriage(s)
Single-parent family	Household led by one parent (woman or man) due to divorce, death, desertion, or never having married
Commune family	Women, men, and children who live together, share rights and responsibilities, and collectively own and/or use property; may abandon traditional monogamous marriage
Serial family	Woman or man having a succession of marriages, thus acquiring several spouses and different families over a lifetime but only one nuclear family at a time
Cohabitation	More or less permanent, sexually intimate relationship between two unmarried persons of the opposite sex who share a household
Lesbian or gay couple	Two persons of the same sex who develop and maintain a homosexual relationship and living arrangement

Source: (Davidson and Moore 23)

If we were going to write a paragraph on the above information,

____c____ 1. What would be the topic?

     a. The nuclear family

     b. Cohabitation

     c. Family types

_____ 2. Which sentence would make a good main idea statement?

     a. A blended family consists of a husband, a wife, and children from previous marriages.

     b. There are many common types of family units.

     c. The nuclear family has only a husband, a wife, and children (if any).

_____ 3. Which sentence would provide good support for the main idea?

     a. The are many common variations in the organization of a family.

     b. Families can be structured in a variety of ways.

     c. One type of family arrangement, cohabitation, refers to a relationship between two unmarried persons of the opposite sex who share a household.

The second sentence is *not* the main idea because it is the only sentence that mentions job interviews. The other sentences do not add more information about job interviews.

The third sentence is not the main idea because it mentions blind dates. None of the other sentences in the paragraph provides more information concerning blind dates.

The last sentence is not the main idea because it mentions students' grades. No other sentence expands on the point that students' grades are affected by physical appearance.

Only the first sentence can be related to every other sentence in this paragraph. It makes the connection between "beauty" and "first impressions." The remaining sentences provide more detailed information and explain this connection. This careful reading of the paragraph has revealed to us the author's main idea.

Often, authors organize the main idea and supporting details as a visual display. See, for example, the chart in Visual Literacy Box 3.1 on page 83. In general, the heading or title indicates the topic and/or main idea while the items on the chart show the supporting details.

EXERCISE
3-3

Distinguishing Between the Topic and the Main Idea

Read each of the paragraphs below. Write the topic of the paragraph in the space provided. Then, determine which sentence contains the main idea and write it out on the space below the topic. The first one has been done for you.

1. People generally respond favorably to high immediacy. The communicator who demonstrates high immediacy conveys a sense of interest and attention, a liking for and an attraction to the other person. "High immediacy" refers to extreme closeness and connection, while "low immediacy" refers to distance and a lack of togetherness. *Immediacy* refers to the degree to which the speaker and listener are connected or joined. (DeVito 163)

Topic: Immediacy in conversation

Main Idea: Immediacy refers to the degree to which the speaker and listener

are connected or joined.

2. Whereas mutations in the human population offer new hope in combating AIDS, the virus is mutating as well, making it that much harder to control. At the twelfth International AIDS Conference in Geneva in 1998, scientists presented evidence of a new HIV/AIDS "superbug" that is "potentially untouchable" by new drugs and that can be readily transmitted from person to person (Krieger, 1998; Schultz, 1998). As one observer noted regarding the "Inventive AIDS virus," "It dodges. It hides. When cornered, it simply re-creates itself" (Krieger, 1998). (Bryjak and Soroka 281)

Topic: _____

Main Idea: _____

3. If these arteries become clogged, the heart muscle dies from lack of oxygen. Cardiac muscle cells are nourished and supplied with oxygen by blood vessels called coronary arteries. A heart attack is the death of cardiac muscle cells and the resulting failure of the heart to deliver enough blood to the rest of the body. The coronary arteries branch from the aorta just as it emerges from the heart. (Campbell, Mitchell, and Reece 472)

Topic: _____

Main Idea: _____

4. Chemistry is the practice of thinking carefully about matter, where matter includes anything you can touch, taste, smell, see, or hear. When you wonder about what the earth, sky, and oceans are made of, you're thinking chemistry. When you wonder how a puddle of water disappears in the sunlight, how a car gets its energy from gasoline, or how your body gets its energy from the food you eat, you're again within the realm of chemistry. By definition, chemistry is the study of matter and the transformations it can undergo. (Hewitt, Suchocki, and Hewitt 363)

Topic: _____

Main Idea:_____

5. People who feel powerless in areas of their lives tend to feel insecure, unhappy, and stressed. Those who have some control feel happier and confident. An understanding of power is critical in understanding relationships. If the power balance between two partners in an intimate relationship is uneven, the less powerful one may feel unloved, depressed, and resentful. The one with the more power may feel critical, unsympathetic, and tied down by the one with less power. (Manis 161)

Topic: _____

Main Idea: _____

Locating the Main Ideas

All of the sentences in a paragraph are related to each other through a single topic. The topic is usually introduced in the first sentence and refers to a general category or idea. The main idea may discuss or describe a certain aspect of the topic and is often stated in the first sentence as well. Sometimes, however, the paragraph may be structured differently, and the main idea statement may be put in a number of other positions within the paragraph.

For example, instead of being in the first sentence, the main idea may be found in the last sentence, a middle sentence, split between the first and last sentence, or implied (understood, but not stated in words). There are five places in a paragraph where we can find the main idea, with the fifth being understood, but not stated—in other words, **implied.** (In chapter 4, we focus on main idea statements that are implied.) Study each paragraph below and note the relationship between the main idea statement and the sentences that explain it.

Main Idea in the First Sentence.

> <u>The causes of relationship deterioration are many.</u> One obvious cause is that the reasons for establishing the relationship have diminished. For instance, when loneliness is no longer lessened, the relationship may suffer. If stimulation weakens, one or both parties may begin to look elsewhere for stimulation. When attractiveness fades, an important reason for establishing the relationship in the first place may be lost. We know, for example, that when relationships break up, it is the more attractive partner who initiates the breakup. *(DeVito 199)*

Notice here that the main idea is in the first sentence: "The causes of relationship deterioration are many." The sentences that follow explain the main idea by giving reasons why relationships deteriorate: (1) loneliness, (2) lack of stimulation, and (3) loss of attraction. The structure of the paragraph resembles an upside-down triangle, with the most important idea presented first and the details following.

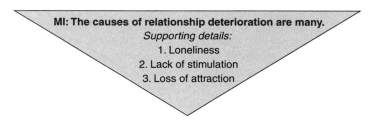

> **MI: The causes of relationship deterioration are many.**
> *Supporting details:*
> 1. Loneliness
> 2. Lack of stimulation
> 3. Loss of attraction

Main Idea in the Last Sentence.

> Should you decide that you want to repair the relationship, you might discuss this with your partner at the interpersonal repair phase. You might at

this stage consider changing your behaviors or perhaps changing your expectations. Here you might discuss the problems in the relationship, the corrections you would want to see, and perhaps what you would be willing to do and what you would want the other person to do. <u>In the interpersonal repair phase, you would analyze what went wrong and consider ways of resolving your differences.</u> (DeVito 200)

In this case, the main idea is found in the last sentence. All of the changes that could repair the relationship are listed. The last sentence pulls this information together and draws a conclusion. In this case, the conclusion is that people analyze their problems and consider solutions in the interpersonal repair phase. The structure of this paragraph resembles a triangle right-side up, where the (supporting) details lead into a final (main idea) sentence that pulls them all together.

Supporting details:
1. Change behaviors
2. Change expectations
3. Discuss problem and corrections
MI: In the repair phase, we analyze problems and consider solutions.

Main Idea in the Middle Sentence.

Rewards are those things that fulfill your needs for security: social approval, love, financial gain, status, sex, and so on. Rewards also involve some cost or "payback." <u>Social exchange theory claims that you develop relationships that you think will provide more rewards than costs</u> (Thibaut & Kelly, 1959; Kelly & Thibaut, 1978). In order to acquire the reward of financial gain, for example, you must take a job and thus give up some freedom (a cost). *(DeVito 207)*

As this passage illustrates, sometimes the main idea is found in the middle of a paragraph. Several details lead up to the main point, and then several more clarifying details or examples follow. In this case, since the term *reward* is critical to understanding the paragraph and its main idea, *reward* needs to be defined first. Once this crucial term is defined, we can then establish that the main idea is *people look for relationships that offer more rewards than costs.* To further emphasize *reward* as necessary to the main idea, "financial gain" is given as an example of a reward. The structure of this paragraph, then, resembles a diamond. Supporting details precede the main idea statement, which ties together the first set of details, and then that statement is followed by yet another supporting detail that clarifies it.

```
1. Rewards fulfill needs.
2. Rewards involve cost.
3. MI: Relationships having more rewards than costs are attractive.
4. Financial gain involves loss of freedom.
```

Main Idea Split Between the First and Last Sentence.

Children are often brought into the world to save a relationship. In some cases they do. The parents stay together because they feel, rightly or wrongly, that it is in the best interests of the children. In other cases, the children provide a socially acceptable excuse to mask that real reason—convenience, financial advantage, a fear of being alone, and so on. In childless relationships, both parties can be more independent and can make life choices based more on individual needs and wants. These individuals, therefore, are less likely to remain in relationships they find unpleasant or uncomfortable. When children are involved, even a souring relationship is often maintained. (DeVito 203)

Notice how the main idea is split between the first and last sentences. The idea that people maintain a relationship when children are involved (from the first sentence) is repeated in the last sentence. The structure of this paragraph resembles a box, where the main idea encloses the supporting details.

```
1. MI: Children are used to save relationships.

    2. Staying together is best for children.

    3. Children provide an excuse to stay together.

    4. Unpleasant childless relationships are not maintained.

5. MI: Relationships are often maintained when there are children.
```

Main Idea Supplied by the Reader (Implied).

The individuals may fear the outside world; they may fear being alone and of facing others as "singles." As a result they may feel that their current relationship is a better alternative. Sometimes the fear may be of social criticism and of what others will think of them if the relationship ends. Sometimes that fear concerns the consequences for violating some religious or parental tenet that tells you to stay together, no matter what happens. (DeVito 203–04)

In this case, there is no main idea statement. Each sentence contains details that lead to a common idea, but this idea is not stated in writing. In order to arrive at the main idea, we have to compare every sentence and figure out what they have in common. We discover that what they all have in common is *fear*. Therefore, we can state the main idea as "Fear motivates many couples to stay together."

The structure of this type of paragraph resembles a house, where each stated supporting detail is like a room and together all of the rooms make up the house. Just as there is no particular room name (e.g., dining room, living room, bedroom, kitchen) for the entire house, we know it is a house because it is made up all of the various rooms. Likewise, the implied main idea is not actually stated, but we can guess what the implied main idea is based on the details provided.

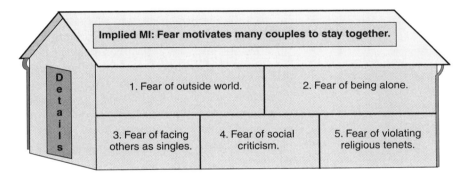

EXERCISE
3-4

Locating the Main Idea

Note that the main idea may be located in the first, last, or middle part of the paragraph. It may be split between the first and last sentence. Or, it may not be stated at all; it may be implied. Each sentence in the following paragraphs is numbered. Read each paragraph and write the number of the sentence that contains the main idea. If the main idea is implied, write "0." If the main idea is split between the first and last sentence, write the number of both sentences. The first one has been done for you.

___2___ 1. [1]It is often said that clothes make a person, but it may be more true to say that clothes *are* the person. [2]Your clothes provide visual clues to your interests, age, personality, and attitudes. [3]Even status information is gained from the clothes' age, condition, and fashion. [4]Some of us are interested in clothing as a means of keeping up with the latest social changes. [5]Others use clothing as a form of decoration and self-expression. [6]T-shirts designs, for example, are a communication channel between the wearer and the world.

_____ 2. [1]In her book, *Letitia Baldrige's New Complete Guide to Executive Manners,* Ms. Baldrige (1993) emphasizes the importance of clothing in the business community. [2]She suggests that clothing determines a person's job success. [3]Thus, dress is an influential variable in the total system of nonverbal communication. [4]It can fulfill functions ranging from protection, sexual attraction and self-assertion to self-denial, concealment, group identification, and the display of status and role. [5]To illustrate, have you ever thought of the impact that clothing can have on evaluations of job performance?

_____ 3. [1]Numerous studies have shown that clothing indeed affects how people perceive us. [2]One team of researchers interested particularly in "fashion in the classroom" included Tracy Morris, Joan Gorham, Stanley Cohen, and Drew Huffman (1996). [3]Focusing on the effects of clothing worn by male and female graduate teaching assistants (GTAs), the researchers asked students to rate GTAs on five dimensions of source credibility: competence, character, sociability, composure, and extroversion. [4]The three types of clothing that the GTAs wore were *formal* (dark business suits, dress shoes), *casual professional* (casual slacks/skirt, sports shirt/sweater, leather shoes/pumps), or *casual dress* (faded, worn blue jeans, T-shirt or flannel shirt, sport/athletic shoes).

_____ 4. [1]Results of the study revealed that formal dress was associated with higher levels of competence, particularly for female students evaluating female GTAs. [2]A close second was casual professional attire, with the lowest ratings of competence reserved for casual attire. [3]Male GTAs wearing casual professional attire were rated higher in competence than female GTAs in similar attire. [4]In contrast, students' ratings of GTA sociability and extroversion were most positive in the casual dress condition, followed by casual professional, then business professional. [5]In other words, students rated GTAs in very casual dress as far more sociable, extroverted, and interesting presenters than GTAs dressed in the other two types of attire.

_____ 5. [1]Although we must be careful generalizing these results to other situations, they do support what we have known for some time. [2]Dress up and you will be perceived as higher in competence, status, power, poise, and success.[3] Dress down and you will be perceived as more friendly, likable, sociable, and enthusiastic. (Barker and Gaut 66–67)

SUPPORTING DETAILS

After locating the main idea, we may sometimes think that it is not necessary to read further—that is, we know all that we need to know. This kind of thinking is only acceptable if all we need to do is get the gist of an article or if we are mainly reading for pleasure and are not concerned with detailed description. However, textbook reading requires much more work on our part. To get a good understanding of new terms and concepts, we also need to focus our attention on the supporting details.

We call the sentences that add more information about the topic and the main idea the **supporting details.** These sentences are the support or backup to the topic and main idea because they provide information that increases our understanding of both. As stated earlier in the chapter, there are two types of supporting details: **major** and **minor.** The details are important because they illustrate, explain, or clarify what we do not know about the main idea. Noticing and studying the details can help especially when concepts are introduced and then explained through examples.

How Do We Detect Supporting Details?

To find the supporting details, we have to read each paragraph looking for words that describe or support the main idea. In the case of our fruit example, the main idea of the paragraph tells us that we are reading about varieties of apples:

> There are many varieties of apples.

The other sentences in this paragraph give the reader more specific information about the different types of apples. These different types represent our major details because they describe the main idea—apples. For instance, one sentence describes the Yellow Delicious apples. Another sentence presents the Macintosh apples. Still another sentence gives information about the Red Delicious apples, and yet another explains the uses of the Gala apple. In other words, the supporting details give us specific information about each variety of apple. The specific information of each variety of apple represents our minor details because they describe the major details—the different apple varieties. For example:

> There are many varieties of apples to choose from when making fruit baskets. The "Macintosh" is multicolored and tart. The "Red Delicious" and the "Yellow Delicious" apples are both sweet, differing only in appearance. "Cortland" apples are good for snacking while "Gala" apples are perfect for baking.

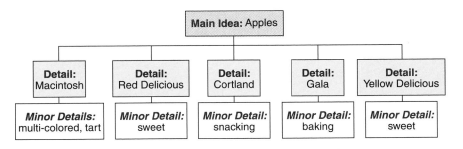

The sentences in our paragraph on apples might look something like this:

■ **[MI] There are many varieties of apples to choose from when making fruit baskets.**

■ [MajD] The Macintosh is [MinD] multicolored and tart.

■ [MajD] The Red Delicious and the Yellow Delicious apples are both [MinD] sweet, differing only in appearance.

■ [MajD] Cortland apples are good for [MinD] snacking, while [MajD] Gala apples are perfect for [MinD] baking.

In addition to providing specific information, details are extremely helpful when a new term is introduced. Details, in the form of examples, can illustrate a new term and help us understand the author's main point. Read the paragraph below. What details help us understand the meaning of "personality traits?" Which details are major and which are minor?

Topic: Perceptual Contact

A relationship may be seen as beginning when you first make perceptual contact: you see, hear, and perhaps even smell the other person. According to some researchers (Zunin, 1972), it's during this stage—within the first 4 minutes of interaction—that you decide whether or not to pursue the relationship. At this stage, physical appearance is especially important because this is what is seen most quickly. Yet, personality traits such as friendliness, warmth, openness, and dynamism are also revealed at this stage. If you decide you like the individual and want to pursue the relationship, you proceed to the later, interactional contact, where you would begin to communicate. (Devito 194)

At first, we may be unsure as to what the author means when he uses the term *personality traits*. However, when we look at the examples of personality traits— "friendliness, warmth, openness, and dynamism"—the meaning becomes clear. Complete the reading and exercises below to practice recognizing the details as support for the main idea, then refer to Visual Literacy Box 3.2 on page 94 for how details can be more easily understood when set up as a chart.

A Reading in Biology

Read the paragraphs below and answer the questions that follow on facts and supporting details.

Topic: AIDS Leaves the Body Defenseless

[1]   In the past two decades, AIDS has killed more than 11 million people worldwide, and more than 33 million people are now infected with the AIDS virus, HIV. At present rates of infection, this number will double in the next few years.

[2]   HIV is deadly because it destroys the immune system, leaving the body defenseless against most invaders. HIV can infect a variety of cells, but it has a preference for helper T cells—the cells that activate other T cells and B cells as well. When HIV depletes the body of helper T cells, the immune system cannot carry out either the cell-mediated or the humoral response. Death usually results, not from AIDS itself but from another infectious agent or from cancer.

[3]   Time is a big problem in the fight against AIDS. Drugs and vaccines must be thoroughly tested for efficacy and for toxic side effects before they can be released for general use. While hearing the outcry of AIDS patients and activists, some experts predict that it may take decades to develop effective vaccines and affordable drugs. At present, education remains our best weapon against AIDS. The World Health Organization concurs with Magic Johnson's campaign for practicing safer sex. Reducing promiscuity and increasing the use of condoms could save millions of lives. (Campbell, Mitchell, and Reece 500)

_____b_____ **1.** How many millions of people are infected with the AIDS virus now?
     a. 11 million
     b. 33 million
     c. 66 million
     d. 311 million

_____a_____ **2.** HIV affects the
     a. helper T cells.
     b. T cells.
     c. B cells.
     d. D cells.

_____b_____ **3.** A person with HIV can die from
     a. AIDS.
     b. cancer.
     c. too many T cells.
     d. too many B cells.

_____c_____ **4.** Before the AIDS vaccines can be released for the general public, they must
     a. be tested for a decade.
     b. be tested for several decades.
     c. be tested for toxic side effects.
     d. be tested for T cells.

_____d_____ **5.** The best weapon against AIDS is
     a. vaccines.
     b. drug therapy.
     c. promiscuity.
     d. practicing safe sex.

Visual Literacy Box 3.2

CHARTS: SUPPORTING DETAILS

AIDS Cases by Race or Ethnicity in the United States

Race or Ethnicity	# of AIDS Cases	% of AIDS Cases
White, not Hispanic	288,541	45.00
Black, not Hispanic	230,029	35.90
Hispanic	115,354	18.00
Asian/Pacific Islander	4,589	.01
American Indian/Alaska Native	1,783	.007
Race/ethnicity unknown	790	.001
Total	641,086	99.0

Source: Centers for Disease Control, 1998. Cited in Bryjak and Soroka 280.

As we read information in our textbooks, details—especially statistics—are often presented in charts. Use the details in the chart above to answer the following questions. The first one has been done for you.

Overview: As of December 1998, 1 in every 300 Americans was reported to be HIV positive. The chart above indicates the number and percentages of people who have AIDS according to their race or ethnicity.

___c___ **1.** Which group was reported as having almost half of the AIDS cases in the United States?

      a. Black, not Hispanic
      b. Asian
      c. White, not Hispanic

___b___ **2.** Which group living in the United States was reported as having the fewest number of AIDS cases?

      a. Asians
      b. American Indians
      c. Hispanic

___b___ **3.** Which group was reported as having almost 20 percent of the AIDS cases in the United States?

      a. Black, not Hispanic
      b. Hispanic
      c. White, not Hispanic

(continued on next page)

___A___ **4.** Which group was reported as having just over a *quarter of a million* AIDS cases?

    a. Black, not Hispanic
    b. White, not Hispanic
    c. Hispanic

___b___ **5.** Which group was reported as having almost 2,000 AIDS cases?
    a. Hispanic
    b. Alaska Native
    c. Pacific Islander

Details can be arranged in a number of ways. These arrangements can be seen over and over again in academic writing. Once we are familiar with these arrangements of details or **patterns of organization,** we can grasp the meaning of the paragraphs more quickly.

One pattern common to textbook writing is the **process pattern.** When a reader recognizes a process pattern, he knows to look for more than just a list of items that occur in a specific order. For example, in the exercise below, the main idea statement tells us there are five stages in small group interaction. These stages must occur in the order in which they are introduced for this paragraph to make sense. In other words, you cannot have the closing stage occur before the opening stage. There is a certain process that happens in a specific order. To see how this process looks when diagrammed, see Visual Literacy Box 3.3 on page 97. (Organizational patterns are discussed in greater detail in chapters 5 and 6.) Complete the reading and exercise below to practice recognizing details by looking at the way the information is arranged.

A Reading in Communications

Read the paragraphs below and answer the questions that follow on facts and supporting details.

Topic: Small Group Stages

As in conversation, **there are five stages in small group interaction: opening, feedforward, business, feedback, and closing.** The **opening** period is usually a getting-acquainted time where members introduce themselves. . . . ("How was your weekend?" "Does anyone want coffee?"). After this preliminary get-together, there is usually some **feedforward,** some attempt to identify what needs to be done, who will do it, and so on. In a more formal group, the agenda (which is a perfect example of feedforward) might be reviewed and the tasks of the group meeting identified. The **business** portion is the actual discussion of the tasks—the problem solving, the sharing of information, or whatever goal the group needs to achieve. At the **feedback** stage, the group might reflect on what it has done and perhaps what remains to be done. Some groups may even evaluate their performance at this stage. At the **closing** stage the group members again return to their focus on individuals and will perhaps exchange closing comments—"It was good seeing you" or "Let's get together again next week." (DeVito 246)

_____b_____ **1.** Members introduce themselves during the
   a. feedforward stage.
   b. opening stage.
   c. business stage.
   d. feedback stage.

_____c_____ **2.** During the feedback stage, members of a small group
   a. solve problems.
   b. share information.
   c. reflect on their accomplishments.
   d. get acquainted.

_____a_____ **3.** During the closing stage, group members exchange comments such as
   a. "Let's get together again next week."
   b. "How was your weekend?"
   c. "Does anyone want coffee?"
   d. "Let's go over what we talked about at the last meeting."

_____b_____ **4.** During the business stage members of a small group
   a. introduce themselves.
   b. solve problems.
   c. talk about what has been done.
   d. evaluate their performance.

_____d_____ **5.** The agenda is reviewed during the
   a. opening stage.
   b. closing stage.
   c. business stage.
   d. feedforward stage.

Visual Literacy Box 3.3

FLOW CHARTS: MAIN IDEAS AND SUPPORTING DETAILS

Flow charts show steps in a process. Each step is placed in a box with an arrow connecting it to the next step. The main idea is usually stated in the title, with each step representing a supporting detail. With this in mind, reread the paragraph "Small Group Stages" and fill in the missing details in the flow chart below.

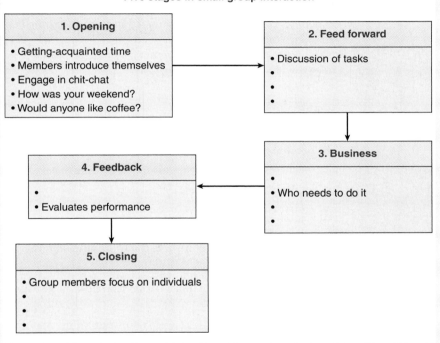

Five stages in small group interaction

1. Opening
- Getting-acquainted time
- Members introduce themselves
- Engage in chit-chat
- How was your weekend?
- Would anyone like coffee?

2. Feed forward
- Discussion of tasks
- •
- •
- •

3. Business
- •
- Who needs to do it
- •
- •

4. Feedback
- •
- Evaluates performance

5. Closing
- Group members focus on individuals
- •
- •
- •

MAIN IDEAS WITH SUPPORTING DETAILS

The supporting details are all of the sentences except the main idea. The main idea is the one statement that does not contain any details. Therefore, once you have identified the main idea, you have also found the supporting details. To see how main ideas and supporting details work together, see Visual Literacy Box 3.3 above.

In our apple paragraph below, if we know that the first sentence is the main idea, then we know the remaining sentences are the details.

There are many varieties of apples. The Yellow Delicious apple is sweet and brightens up a fruit basket with its bright yellow color. The Red Delicious apple is also sweet but dark red in appearance. Although tart, the Macintosh apple is a great favorite for many. The Cortland and Gala apples make wonderful pies.

A Reading in Political Science

Sometimes people become discouraged from participating in government because they feel their voice does not matter. Read the following selection from a political science textbook to see how one woman made a huge difference in people's lives through her determination to participate. Complete the vocabulary section before reading to learn the new terms.

Vocabulary in Context

   a. inundated—flooded; overwhelmed

   b. presumably—assumed or accepted as true without evidence

   c. incentive—something that motivates people to take action

   d. legislate—to make a law

   e. construed—understood or seen in a certain way

Use the terms above to complete the following statements. The first one has been done for you.

    _____d_____   **1.** Each state has a different drinking age because only the state governments can _____ them.

    _____   **2.** _____ we can say that none of the senators wanted to be known as someone who would encourage teenage drunken driving.

    _____   **3.** The senators wanted to give the states an _____ to raise the drinking age since they could not force them to do so through federal law.

    _____   **4.** President Reagan and the senators did not want, in the public's eyes, to be _____ as being in favor of drunk driving.

    _____   **5.** Lightner and her many supporters _____ the state capitals, lobbying to get the drinking age raised.

After reading, go through the selection again and study the boldfaced sections. Decide if each highlighted section is (a) the topic, (b) the main idea, or (c) the supporting details. Explain the reasoning behind your choice. The first question has been done for you.

_____c_____ 1. **Candy Lightner was no politician.** She was a California real estate broker and, more important, a mother suffering from a tragedy: her 13-year-old daughter Cari was killed by a drunk driver. The agony associated with children's deaths caused by drunk drivers is real. When the drunk driver is a teenager, inexperienced at both drinking and driving, passions heat further. Ms. Lightner was not content to grieve the loss of her child. She decided to do something about it.
     a. topic
     b. main idea
     c. supporting detail

_____a_____ 2. Her first step was to form **Mothers Against Drunk Driving (MADD).** This group was the seed from which sprouted hundreds of local MADD chapters, as well as offshoots like Students Against Drunk Driving (SADD). MADD had no trouble rousing support against the carnage of deaths caused by drunk drivers. No politician wants to be accused of supporting drunks on the road aiming two-ton vehicles at defenseless children. Lightner's lobbyists **inundated** state capitals to get the drinking age raised. Between 1976 and 1983, 19 states raised their drinking age, typically to age 21.
     a. topic = subject
     b. main idea
     c. supporting detail

_____b_____ 3. There were still 31 states that allowed people under 21 to drink, however. Ms. Lightner and her MADD supporters had to become *main idea* political strategists. **They realized that it was much easier to get a national law passed once than to lobby each of 50 state legislatures separately.** Therefore, in 1983, at a press conference on the steps of the Capitol, Lightner and then Secretary of Transportation Elizabeth Dole, Senator John Danforth (R-MO), Senator Richard Lugar (R-IN), and Senator Frank Lautenberg (D-NJ) announced their intention to support a national standard drinking age. Because they could not pass a bill directly setting the drinking age in the states, however, they proposed using federal highway funds as an **incentive** for the states to pass their bills.
     a. topic
     b. main idea
     c. supporting detail

4. The legislation stemming from the Lightner-Dole-Lautenberg-Lugar press conference was an amendment to the Surface Transportation Act of 1982. The federal government could not **legislate** drinking ages, so it relied on a carrot-and-stick strategy: Congress would withhold 10 percent of all federal highway aid from states that did not raise their legal drinking age to 21 by 1988. The legislation sailed through Congress (the Senate passed it by a vote of 81 to 16, few Senators **presumably** wanting their votes **construed** as tolerating teenage drunken driving). President Reagan—a staunch opponent of federal regulations—signed the legislation in October 1984. **By the end of 1989, every state had a legal drinking age of 21. Candy Lightner had made a difference.** (Edwards, Wattenberg, and Lineberry 76)
   a. topic
   b. main idea
   c. supporting detail

    5. States still retain the power to decide who is legally drunk, however. In 1998, Mothers Against Drunk Driving pressured members of Congress to adopt a national blood alcohol level of .98 to indicate drunkenness, but that effort failed. Thus, the blood alcohol content required for determining legal intoxication varies dramatically, from a low of .05 in Colorado to a high of .1 in several states. (O'Connor and Sabato 96)
   a. topic
   b. main idea
   c. supporting detail

A Reading in Communications

Where do you choose to sit in the classroom or at the dinner table? Read the following selection from a communications book to find out what our choice of seating tells others about us. Complete the vocabulary exercise first to familiarize yourself with the new terms.

Vocabulary in Context

   a. **designated**—assigned; selected
   b. **spatial**—having to do with space or layout
   c. **modular**—made up of standardized units that can be used in a variety of ways
   d. **horticulture**—the science of growing plants
   e. **dissemination**—the spreading of information, knowledge, goods, etc.

Use the terms above to complete the following statements. The first one has been done for you.

_____a_____ **1.** Did you know that you could be _____ the leader of a group simply because of your choice in a seating arrangement?

_____ **2.** Many libraries choose a _____ seating arrangement so that the space can be used in a lot of different ways.

_____ **3.** A seating arrangement can be referred to as a _____ arrangement because it refers to the way things are organized in their surrounding space.

_____ **4.** We use newspapers, magazines, lectures, and other media for the _____ of information.

_____ **5.** She majored in _____ because she wanted to own a greenhouse and sell plants for landscaping.

Comprehension

Each sentence in the following paragraphs is numbered. Read each paragraph of the selection and write the number of the sentence that contains the main idea on the line provided. If the main idea is implied, write "0." Then, write a sentence that expresses the main idea. The first one has been done for you.

_____4_____ **1.** [1]Did your father always sit at the head of the table in your house? [2]The person who sits at the head of a table will usually be **designated** the "leader," whether or not that designation is appropriate. [3]Have you ever avoided taking a chair at the head of a table for this very reason? [4]The two ends of a table and the middle seats on the sides are "hot seats" in which people either do, or at least are expected to, talk more.

_____

_____

_____1_____ **2.** [1]These examples illustrate the effects of seating arrangements on interpersonal interactions. [2]Some **spatial** arrangements, such as a round table, encourage us to face each other and to communicate. [3]Other arrangements—for example, a row of chairs in a theater or classroom—force us to face away from one another. [4]These arrangements naturally produce less interaction.

Seating arangmnts.

_____

_____   **3.** [1]Thus, different seating arrangements are desirable for different types of interactions. [2]If two people are having a friendly conversation, they might prefer seats at the corner of a rectangular table. [3]When working together on a task, they might sit side by side. [4]During competition (playing cards, for example) they would prefer to sit across from one another, thereby making it more difficult to see each other's hand and easier to establish strong eye contact.

different seating arrngmnt
& interaction

_____   **4.** [1]Similarly, spatial relationships in the classroom can influence student-teacher interactions. [2]The three most popular ways to arrange classrooms are in rectangular, horseshoe, and **modular** arrangements (see Figures 3.2, 3.3, and 3.4). [3]Most classrooms in North America are rectangular, with desks arranged in straight rows. [4]This arrangement is best for information **dissemination** or straight lectures. [5]Horseshoe and modular arrangements are frequently used with smaller classes. [6]Courses in disciplines such as home economics, architecture, **horticulture,** and speech communication would be likely to use these arrangements. [7]Both the horseshoe and modular arrangements increase student participation. [8]The grouping of the modular design allows for maximum interaction and is especially effective for teachers who need to work with groups and individual students.

Spatial arrangements

_____   **5.** [1]Most of us also have preferences about where we sit in classes. [2]Have you ever been disappointed, on the first day of class, to find that you couldn't sit in the back row, in front of the teacher, or by the blackboard? [3]A variety of factors, such as wanting to sit by the best-looking student, or wanting to be able to see the board, determine seating preferences. [4]Investigations of seating arrangement and interactions in classrooms indicate that students who sit in front rows may actually receive higher grades than those who sit farther back (Holliman & Anderson, 1986). [5]Additionally, proximity or closeness to the teacher is related to student enjoyment, motivation, interest, and feelings of inclusion (Millard & Stimpson, 1980). (Barker and Gaut 69–72)

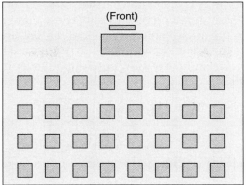

FIGURE 3.2 Rectangular seating arrangement

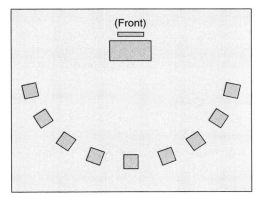

FIGURE 3.3 Horseshoe seating arrangement

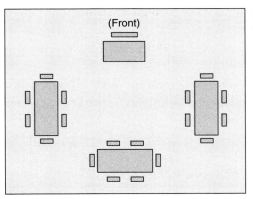

FIGURE 3.4 Modular seating arrangement

Earlier in this chapter we discussed how some main ideas are not stated but simply understood or implied. These main ideas require a closer reading of the supporting details. Take a look at Reading Between the Lines Box 3.1. Complete the accompanying practice exercises. Then, with implied main ideas fresh in your mind, carefully read and answer the questions to the final reading selection.

A Reading in Sociology

When you study sociology, world cultures, and anthropology, you will find that all groups of people on earth develop a culture. Read the following selection to learn what makes up a culture and how people's actions may differ from one culture to the next. Complete the vocabulary exercise first to familiarize yourself with the new terms.

Vocabulary in Context

  a. components—parts of a whole

  b. material culture—human technology; man-made products and changes to the earth

  c. nonmaterial culture—knowledge, beliefs, values, and rules for behavior

  d. norms—rules of acceptable behavior for a culture

  e. mores—norms (rules) that a culture develops about what is right and wrong

  f. folkways—a culture's norms (rules) that are largely left up to individual interpretation

  g. ideal norm—expectation of what people should do under perfect conditions

  h. cognitive culture—shared beliefs of people within a culture about what the world is like

  i. values—a culture's idea of what is good and bad and what is desirable and undesirable

  j. real norm—rule that allows for differences in individual behavior

Use the above terms to complete the following statements. The first one has been done for you.

_____c_____ **1.** Every society has a _____, which consists of everything we know, our beliefs, our values, and the rules we make up that govern our behavior.

Reading Between the Lines Box 3.1

INFERENCE AND APPLICATION

You can better understand what you read, and even become more interested, if you relate what you are reading to your own lives and experiences. This is part of what one does in the reflection stage of reading. After rereading the article on seating arrangements (page 101), answer the following application questions.

1. How often do you sit at the head of a table? In which situations do you sit at the head of a table? Do you like to talk more or less than other people?

_____

_____

_____

2. Think of the seating arrangements in the places you go. Where and in which situations do you sit at a round table? in a row of chairs?

_____

_____

_____

3. In which situations do you sit next to or beside another person? In which situations do you prefer to sit facing another person? Why do you think this is so?

_____

_____

_____

4. Which of your classes use the rectangular seating arrangement? the horseshoe seating arrangement? the modular arrangement? Why do you think your professors arrange the desks as they do?

_____

_____

_____

5. Where do you prefer to sit in each of your classes? Why?

_____

_____

_____

_____ **2.** If you violate a society's _____, you may have to deal with the law.

_____ **3.** In American society, we believe that marriage should last a lifetime. However, we call this an _____ because life is not always perfect and people often times divorce.

_____ **4.** Every culture has _____ because they define "normal" expected behavior and help people achieve predictability in their lives.

_____ **5.** Wearing a baseball cap to a formal dinner dance is a violation of a culture's _____. People may think you are a little odd, but you will not be in trouble with the law for this behavior.

_____ **6.** Even though the rule is to always stop for a red light, in reality, many drivers see no harm in going through a red light at 3:00 A.M. if no other drivers are on the road. We would call this a _____ because it allows for differences in behavior according to individual circumstances.

_____ **7.** People have created _____ in order to live and survive in harsh conditions on the earth.

_____ **8.** If work is believed to be a highly desirable activity in a particular culture, we could say that their _____ include the work ethic.

_____ **9.** Our _____ includes everything we know about the world and what we believe to be true.

_____ **10.** Material culture, nonmaterial culture, and cognitive culture are three _____ of culture.

As you read, determine the main idea of each paragraph. Write the number of the sentence that contains the main idea or central point (main point of entire passage) on the line provided. If the main idea is split between two sentences, write both numbers. If the main idea is implied, write "0" and create a sentence that expresses the main idea.

At the end of the reading selection, review and complete the exercise on organization in Visual Literacy Box 3.4 on page 112.

Components of Culture

[1] [1]The concept of culture is not easy to understand, perhaps because every aspect of our social lives is an expression of it and also because familiarity produces a kind of nearsightedness toward our own culture, making it difficult for us to take an analytical perspective toward our everyday social lives. [2]**Sociologists find it helpful to break down culture into separate components: material culture (objects), nonmaterial culture (rules), cognitive culture (shared beliefs), and language** (Hall, 1990).

Material Culture

[2] [1]**Material culture** consists of *human technology—all the things human beings make and use, from small hand-held tools to skyscrapers.* [2]Without material culture our species could not long survive, for material culture provides a buffer between humans and their environment. [3]Using it, human beings can protect themselves from environmental stresses, as when they build shelters and wear clothing to protect themselves from the cold or from strong sunlight. [4]Even more important, humans use material culture to modify and exploit the environment. [5]They build dams and irrigation canals, plant fields and forests, convert coal and oil into energy, and transform ores into versatile metals. [6]Using material culture, our species has learned to cope with the most extreme environments and to survive and even to thrive on all continents and in all climates. [7]Human beings have walked on the floor of the ocean and on the surface of the moon. [8]No other creature can do this: None has our flexibility. [9]Material culture has made human beings the dominant life form on earth.

Nonmaterial Culture

[3] [1]Every society also has a **nonmaterial culture,** which consists of *the totality of knowledge, beliefs, values, and rules for appropriate behavior.* [2]The nonmaterial culture is structured by such institutions as the family, religion, education, economy, and government. [3]While material culture is made up of things that have a physical existence (they can be seen, touched, and so on), the elements of nonmaterial culture are the ideas associated with their use. [4]Although engagement rings and birthday flowers have a material existence, they also reflect attitudes, beliefs, and values that are part of our culture. [5]There are rules for their appropriate use in specified situations.

[4] [1]**Norms** *are central elements of nonmaterial culture.* [2]*Norms are the rules of behavior that are agreed upon and shared within a culture and that prescribe limits of acceptable behavior.* [3]They define "normal" expected behavior and help people achieve predictability in their lives. [4]For example,

Edward T. Hall (1966) has found that Americans follow many unwritten rules concerning public behavior. [5]As soon as an individual stops or is seated in a public place, a small, invisible sphere of privacy that should not be violated develops around the person. [6]The size will vary with the degree of crowding, the age, sex, and importance of the person, and the general surroundings. [7]Anyone who enters this zone and stays there is intruding. [8]In order to overcome this personal-space barrier, a person who intrudes for a specific purpose will usually acknowledge the intrusion by beginning with a phrase like, "Pardon me, but can you tell me . . . ?"

_____

_____

[5] [1]In contrast, pushing and shoving in public places is a characteristic of Middle Eastern culture, a characteristic that, unlike the attitude in Western cultures, is not considered rude behavior. [2]For the Arab, there is no such thing as an intrusion of space in public. [3]Occupying a given spot does not give you any special rights to that area at all. [4]If, for example, person A is standing on a street corner and person B wants that spot, it is perfectly all right for person B to try to make person A uncomfortable enough to move.

_____

_____

[6] [1]Arabs also have a completely different set of assumptions regarding the body and the rights associated with it than do Westerners. [2]Arabs do not have any concept of a private zone outside the body. [3]In the Western world, the person is synonymous with the individual inside the skin, and you usually need permission to touch the body and even the clothes if you are a stranger. [4]For the Arab, however, the location of the person in relation to the body is quite different. [5]The person exists somewhere down inside the body, protected from touch. [6]Touching the outside of the body—skin and clothes—is not really touching the person. [7]Arabs also believe that sharing smells is an act of friendship and to deny the smell of your breath to your friends is interpreted as an act of shame. [8]So it is that Americans, trained as they are not to breathe in people's faces, automatically communicate shame to the Arabs (Hall, 1966).

_____

_____

[7] [1]**Mores** *(pronounced more-ays) are strongly held norms that usually have a moral connotation and are based on the central values of the culture.* [2]Violations of mores produce strong negative reactions, which are often supported by the law. [3]Desecration of a church or temple, sexual molestation of a child, rape, murder, incest, and child beating all are violations of American mores.

---

[8] [1]Not all norms command such absolute conformity. [2]Much of day-to-day life is governed by traditions, or **folkways,** *which are norms that permit a wide degree of individual interpretation as long as certain limits are not overstepped.* [3]People who violate folkways are seen as peculiar or possibly eccentric, but rarely do they elicit strong public response. [4]For example, a wide range of dress is now acceptable in most theaters and restaurants. [5]Men and women may wear clothes ranging from business attire to jeans, an open-necked shirt, or sweater. [6]However, extremes in either direction will cause a reaction. [7]Many establishments limit the extent of informal dress: Signs may specify that no one with bare feet or without a shirt may enter. [8]On the other hand, a person in extremely formal attire might well attract attention and elicit amused comments in a fast-food restaurant.

---

[9] [1]Good manners in our culture also show a range of acceptable behavior. [2]A man may or may not open a door or hold a coat for a woman, who may also choose to open a door or hold a coat for a man—all four options are acceptable behavior and cause neither comment nor negative reactions from people. [3]These two examples illustrate another aspect of folkways: They change with time. [4]Not too long ago a man was *always* expected to hold a door open for a woman, and a woman was never expected to hold a coat for a man.

---

[10] [1]Folkways also vary from one culture to another. [2]In the United States, for example, it is customary to thank someone for a gift. [3]To fail to do so is to be ungrateful and ill-mannered. [4]Subtle cultural differences can make international gift giving, however, a source of anxiety or embarrassment to well-meaning business travelers. [5]For example, if you give a

gift on first meeting an Arab businessman, it may be interpreted as a bribe. [6]If you give a clock in China, it is considered bad luck. [7]In Latin America you will have a problem if you give knives or handkerchiefs. [8]The former connotes the end of a friendship; the latter is associated with sadness (*New York Times*, December 6, 1981).

$\boxed{1}$ _____

_____

[11] [1]Norms are specific expectations about social behavior, but it is important to add that they are not absolute. [2]Even though we learn what is expected in our culture, there is room for variation in individual interpretations of these norms that deviate from the ideal norm. [3]**Ideal norms** *are expectations of what people should do under perfect conditions.* [4]These are the norms we first teach our children. [5]They tend to be simple, making few distinctions and allowing for no exceptions. [6]That drivers should "stop at red lights" is an ideal norm in American society. [7]So is the norm that a marriage will last "until death do us part."

_____

_____

[12] [1]In reality, however, nothing about human beings is ever that dependable. [2]For example, if you interviewed Americans about how drivers respond to red lights, you would get answers like: Ideally, drivers should stop at red lights. [3]In actual fact, however, drivers sometimes run red lights. [4]So even though you can pretty much count on a driver stopping for a red light, it pays to be careful. [5]Also, if it looks like a driver is not going to stop for a light, you had better play it safe and slow down. [6]In other words, people recognize that drivers usually do feel they should stop when a traffic light is red, but they also acknowledge that there are times when a driver will not stop for a red light. [7]The driver may be in a hurry, drunk, upset, or simply not paying attention. [8]**Real norms** *are norms that are expressed with qualifications and allowances for differences in individual behavior.* [9]They specify how people actually behave. [10]They [real norms] reflect the fact that a person's behavior is a function not only of norm guidance but also of situational elements, as exemplified by the driver who does not always stop at a red light if no car appears to be coming from the other direction.

_____

_____

[13] [1]The concepts of ideal and real norms are useful for distinguishing between mores and folkways. [2]For mores, the ideal and the real norms tend to be very close, whereas folkways can be much more loosely connected: Our mores say *thou shalt not kill* and really mean it, but we might violate a folkway by neglecting to say thank you, for example, without provoking general outrage. [3]More important, the very fact that a culture legitimizes the difference between ideal and real expectations allows us room to interpret norms to a greater or lesser degree according to our own personal dispositions.

3
_____

_____

Cognitive Culture

[14] [1]**Cognitive culture** is *the thinking component of culture, which consists of shared beliefs and knowledge of what the world is like—what is real and what is not, what is important and what is trivial.* [2]The beliefs need not even be true or testable as long as they are shared by a majority of people. [3]Cognitive culture is like a map that guides us through society. [4]Think of a scout troop on a hike in the wilderness. [5]The troop finds its way by studying a map showing many of the important features of the terrain. [6]The scouts who use the map share a mental image of the area represented by the map. [7]Yet just as maps differ, each perhaps emphasizing different details of the terrain or using different symbols to represent them, so do cultures differ in the ways in which they represent the world. [8]It is important not to confuse any culture's representation of reality with what ultimately is real—just as a map is not the actual terrain it charts.

_____

_____

[15] [1]**Values** are *a culture's general orientations toward life—its notions of what is good and bad, what is desirable and undesirable.* [2]Values themselves are abstractions. [3]They [values] can best be found by looking for the recurring patterns of behavior that express them. (Tischler 73–77)

_____

_____

Visual Literacy Box 3.4

ORGANIZATION CHARTS:
COMPONENTS OF CULTURE

Study the selection "Components of Culture" and make a visual diagram to show the relationship among the ideas. Use the following terms to finish the organization chart.

values   folkways

cognitive culture   components of culture

real norms   material culture

mores   ideal norms

norms

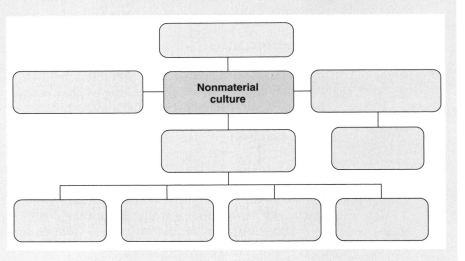

4

Implied Main Ideas and Central Point

- -

In this chapter, we:

- review your knowledge of main idea patterns;
- apply those patterns to help distinguish between a stated and an implied main idea;
- locate the main idea and distinguish it from the central point.

What do you look for when you read a textbook? Review the comments made by students who earned average to above-average grades and compare them to the comments made by students on academic probation. What do you think is the difference in the way that they read?

Comments made by students with average to above-average GPA:

ROSE: When I'm reading a chapter, I read every word and *I highlight the important information that the teacher has gone over in class.* So, I know exactly where it is.

ROSS: Usually I'd *look at headings and look for sentences that summarize things and the general topic;* I just put things together. I'll go through and highlight sometimes and just read those over. If I want to review for a test, I usually read it all the way through and underline or *highlight what's important, or what is told to me is going to be important.* And then I'll go through it a second time and I'll just concentrate on that!

ERIC: I read it three times. First I read it once completely. Second, *I read it again completely and highlight.* The third time I read it and copy the highlights into study notes.

Copyright © 2006 by Pearson Education, Inc.

Comments made by students on academic probation:

TONI: I *skim* and study notes.

LYNN: Sometimes I go back and skim and go on from there.

JODY: I take a big fat highlighter and I sit down and pretty much *skim* the textbook. I really do. There's no story to it, so I really *skim* hard and I *skim* them twice to get anything out of them. (Yaworski)

The first group of students is actually involved in a process called *finding the main idea,* while the probation group is relying on another process called *skimming.* Both processes are useful, but they have different purposes.

MAIN IDEA PATTERNS

When reading textbooks, we really need to read *all* of the information first and then determine how it fits together. We do this by looking for the author's main points and connecting them with the more specific points or examples. We call the main points the *main ideas* and the specific points or examples the *supporting details.* As discussed in chapter 3, the supporting details can be divided into major and minor details.

The process of **skimming** simply involves looking for the main ideas without reading the other sentences. This is a useful strategy *when we have already learned the information* and we are just trying to locate it in a book. However, it is difficult and sometimes impossible to understand main ideas without reading the information (that is, the supporting details) that explains them.

When we are learning new information, we need to compare all of the sentences in a paragraph to determine which one is the main idea. If we skip this process and just guess at one, we will probably not understand what we are reading. Thus, students who only skim their textbooks are not really learning the information and, as a result, are not likely to do as well as they could academically.

Where Is the Main Idea Located?

In chapter 3, we looked at various main idea patterns. Some paragraphs stated the main idea in *the first sentence.* These general statements were followed by sentences that explained or gave more information about them. We called these sentences that followed the *supporting details* because they contained specific information that backed up the first sentence.

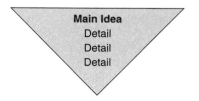

We also looked at paragraphs in which the supporting details came first. Each sentence provided a chain of reasoning that led the author to draw a conclusion in the final sentence. Thus, the *last sentence* was the main point or main idea.

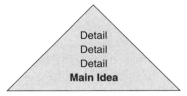

There were also paragraphs in which the main idea was stated *in the middle.* Some details were given at the beginning of the paragraph, and other details provided more support for the main idea in the final sentences.

Finally, we looked at paragraphs in which the main idea was *split between the first and last sentences.* We noticed that the first sentence did not include enough information to cover all of the ideas mentioned in the paragraph, nor did the last sentence. But, when combined, the first and last sentences created a general statement that could be related to all of the details in the paragraph.

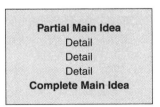

THE IMPLIED MAIN IDEA

Once we locate the sentence with the main idea, the remaining sentences must contain the supporting details. Thus, once we have identified all of the supporting details, the main idea is easier to spot.

In this chapter, however, we will look at paragraphs that contain *only* sentences with supporting details. Does that mean these paragraphs lack a main idea? No. It means that *we* must figure out the main idea in our minds based on the details we are given. To do this, follow these four steps:

Step 1: Look at the individual facts in each sentence.

Step 2: Decide what they have in common.

Step 3: Make up a general statement that includes the common points. In other words, establish a main idea.

Step 4: Check the facts in each sentence against the main idea you have just established. Check to see if the facts in each sentence provide more information about the general statement.

If all of the sentences in the paragraph support our main idea, we can say that we understand the author's unstated or implied main idea. Let's follow these steps to create an **implied main idea** for the paragraph below. Consider the following example and think about how the above four steps can help us determine the unstated main idea of the paragraph.

Example:

Many insects, for example, swim the way we do, using their legs as oars to push against the water. Squids and some jellies are jet-propelled, taking in water and squirting it out in bursts. Fishes swim by moving their body and tail from side to side. Whales and other aquatic mammals move their body and tail from top to bottom. *(Campbell, Mitchell, and Reece 602)*

Step 1: What are the individual facts in the each sentence?

- Insects use their legs to swim.
- Squids and jellies take in water and squirt it out to swim.
- Fishes move from side to side to swim.
- Aquatic mammals move from top to bottom to swim.

Step 2: What does each sentence have in common?

- All of the sentences in this paragraph are about swimming.
- Each sentence is about a different type of animal.

Step 3: Which sentence includes the common parts?

- Many ways of swimming have evolved among animal types.

Step 4: Do the facts from step 1 give more information about the statement made in step 3?

- Does the statement "Insects use their legs to swim" provide information about animals having different ways of swimming?
- Does the statement "Squids and jellies take in water and squirt it out to swim" give us more information about animals having different ways of swimming?

- Does the statement "Fishes move from side to side to swim" give us more information about animals having different ways of swimming?
- Does the statement "Aquatic mammals move from top to bottom to swim" give us more information about animals having different ways of swimming?

Now that we've completed all four steps, what general statement can we make about the supporting details? One possible observation could be: "Many different ways of swimming have evolved among animal types." This statement expresses the point the author is trying to make. We can safely say, therefore, that this statement contains the implied main idea.

EXERCISE 4-1

Stating the Implied Main Idea

The following paragraphs do not have a stated main idea. After reading each paragraph, decide which sentence among the choices provided would make a good main idea statement. The first one has been done for you.

___a___ **1.** Geologists call the forces within Earth that cause movements of the crust plate tectonics. These forces affect life in many ways. Not only do they move continents and cause mountain ranges to rise, they also produce volcanoes and earthquakes. The boundaries of crustal plates are hotspots of geological activity. California's frequent earthquakes result from movement along the infamous San Andreas fault, which is part of the border where the Pacific plate and the American plate grind together and gradually slide past each other. (Campbell, Mitchell, and Reece 300)

    a. Plate tectonics affect life in many ways.
    b. The San Andreas fault causes frequent earthquakes in California.
    c. The study of movements in the Earth's crust is called plate tectonics.

___B___ **2.** One of the most important contributions parents can make to the children is to let them know they are loved, valued, cared for, and accepted. Parents who demonstrate these attitudes through praise, encouragement, and showing interest help children develop self-esteem and confidence. Parents who reject or overly criticize their children can contribute to feelings of ill-worth or dependence that may show up as anger or clinginess in later relationships. (Manis 27)

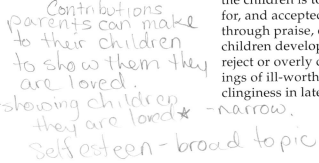
Contributions parents can make to their children to show them they are loved.
showing children they are loved ★ – narrow.
self esteem – broad topic

a. Parents need to let children know that they are loved, valued, cared for, and accepted.
b. Through their actions, parents can either help children develop self-esteem and confidence or dependence, anger, and clinginess.
c. Children can become angry, clingy, and dependent if their parents reject or overly criticize them.

_____C_____ 3. How is diabetes detected? The early signs of either type of diabetes are a lack of energy, a craving for sweets, frequent urination, and persistent thirst. A combination of these symptoms and a family history of diabetes indicate that a person should be tested for the disease. The diagnostic test for diabetes is a glucose-tolerance test: The person swallows a sugar solution and then has blood drawn at prescribed time intervals. Each blood sample is tested for glucose. (Campbell, Mitchell, and Reece 527)

diagnosis-detecting of [diabetes]

a. Diabetes can be detected through a glucose-tolerance test.
b. A person should be tested for diabetes if there is a family history of this illness.
c. A person should take a glucose-tolerance test if there are early signs of diabetes and if there is a family history of diabetes.

_____b_____ 4. Through the cultural changes from scavenging-gathering-hunting to high-tech societies, humans have not changed biologically in any significant way. We are probably no more intelligent than our forebears who lived in caves. The same toolmaker who chipped away at stones now fashions microchips for computers. The know-how to build computers and spaceships is stored not in our genes but in what is passed along by parents, teachers, and books. We are presently the most numerous and widespread of all large animals, and everywhere we go, we bring change. There is nothing new about environmental change. What is new is the speed of change, for cultural changes outpace biological evolution by orders of magnitude. We are changing the world so quickly that many species cannot adapt; in fact, we may be jeopardizing our own existence as well. (Campbell, Mitchell, and Reece 300)

Cultural change Human evolution

a. Humans are no more intelligent than their ancestors.
b. Although humans have not changed biologically, they are changing the environment so quickly that many species, including the human population, may not survive.
c. The know-how to build computers and spaceships is stored not in our genes but in what is passed along by parents, teachers, and books.

_____ **a** **5.** When you put your ideas into speech, you're putting them into a code, hence encoding. When you translate the sound waves (the speech signals) that impinge on your ears into ideas, you take them out of the code they're in, hence decoding. Thus, speakers or writers are referred to as encoders, and listeners or readers as decoders. (DeVito 10)

— encoding, decoding
— Communication

  a. Speakers and writers are referred to as encoders because they put their ideas into a code, while listeners are referred to as decoders because they are taking ideas that they hear out of a code.
  b. When you put your ideas into speech, you're putting them into a code.
  c. When you hear speech signals, you are taking ideas out of a code.

A Reading in Communications

How much space do you need to feel comfortable around other people? Read this excerpt, taken from *Communication*, by Larry L. Barker and Deborah Roach Gaut, to find out how you claim your personal territory. Stop after each paragraph and make a list of the ideas that are common to all or most of the sentences in the paragraph. Then write a main idea statement that includes these common ideas. (The first one has been done for you.) Complete the vocabulary exercise before reading the passage to become familiar with some of the terms used in the reading.

Vocabulary in context:

  a. **vital**—necessary to continue living
  b. **proxemics**—the study of how much personal space people need when they communicate with others, depending on their culture
  c. **comprise**—contain; be made up of
  d. **conversely**—on the other hand; opposite from this
  e. **infringe**—to impose or go beyond another's personal or legal boundaries

Use the terms above to complete the following statements. The first one has been done for you.

_____a_____ 1. Without physical contact, children may later experience physical and psychological problems. Therefore, physical contact is _____ to healthy development.

_____ 2. Children who are brought up in families that did not hug each other will probably not be overly willing to give hugs. _____, if parents teach their children to hug, their children will probably be more apt to display this type of affection.

_____ 3. The study of these spatial factors is called _____; it focuses on how you react to space around us, how you use that space, and how our use of space communicates certain information.

_____ 4. Nuclear families generally _____ a mother, a father, and two children.

_____ 5. When you put your belongings on a chair to mark your territory, you are telling others not to _____ on this space.

Touching

[1]   Do you often reach out to touch other people? Although ours is not a "high-contact" culture, touching is nonetheless the most basic form of nonverbal communication. We all use touch at times. To emphasize a point or to interrupt another person, for instance, we may grab the speaker's elbow and interrupt with, "But you don't understand." Touching can be used as a calming gesture, too. We frequently try to comfort someone with a pat on the back and an "I know." In other situations, touching provides reassurance. Not only do we reach out to reassure ourselves of the presence of people we are fond of, but we sometimes do the same with objects— stroking the smooth leather of our gloves, for instance.

   a. What do all or most sentences have in common?
      touching; communication; non verbal information
   b. What is the main idea?
      We all use touching in many ways to communicate nonverbal information.

[2]   These behaviors suggest the importance of touching to human beings. In fact, physical contact with other humans is **vital** to healthy development. Lack of such contact in childhood may contribute to physical and psychological problems later in life. To understand the significance of this statement, consider how parents touch and teach their children about touch. A child who is reared in a high-contact family will have a high touch orientation. As a result, he or she generally will see and share touch in different ways than a child who is reared in a low-contact family. If parents teach their children through words or deeds that touch is something to be given

generously, in turn, their children will see and give touch in this way. **Conversely,** children who are taught that touch is "dirty"—or, at best, should be minimized—will grow up to view touch as their parents did.A A

a. What do all or most sentences have in common?

touching: teaching children: healthy development

b. What is the main idea?

touching should be taught to children because it is vital to healthy developme.

[3]   Just as we communicate with words, gestures, and facial expressions, we also can send messages by placing ourselves in certain spatial relationships with other people and objects. The study of these spatial factors is called **proxemics;** it focuses on how we react to space around us, how we use that space, and how our use of space communicates certain information. For example, the amount of space in which a person must live or work communicates a message about the status of that individual. Consider a North American family that **comprises** a single parent and three sons, but whose house has only two bedrooms for the children. In recognition of the eldest son's status, chances are that he will have a room to himself, while the two younger children share the second bedroom.

a. What do all or most sentences have in common?

Spacial relationships: Communication

b. What is the main idea?

The study of spacial factors called proxemics; the reaction to space around us. affects the social status

[4]   Scientists have long observed the territorial habits of animals but have only recently begun to understand that humans exhibit similar territorial needs and controls. In fact, all of us carry our own personal space around with us. This territoriality—the need to call space our space—is another facet of proxemics.

a. What do all or most sentences have in common?

territorial, personal space: human needs.

b. What is the main idea?

Everyone carries needs their own personal space. with them

[5]   Territoriality implies a desire to possess or give up space or objects around us. For example, different body parts permit us to claim temporary possession of an object. Thus, we often use our hands to reach out and grab an object (as in straightening someone's tie or holding another person's hand). Or, we employ our whole bodies as spatial indicators. Standing with hands on hips and elbows extended, for instance, claims all the space around our bodies and says, "Don't come any closer to me than my elbows, or else!" On the other hand, when we are kissing, we close our eyes, perhaps to break down spatial barriers. "It's okay," you imply. "Your closeness is not **infringing** on my territory." We also use objects to define our territory. Have you ever used books, paper, pencils, sweaters, and other objects to stake out your space at a library table? Such markers say, "This area is mine." (Barker and Gant 67)

a. What do all or most sentences have in common?

territorial space; possession, spacial body language. barriers

b. What is the main idea?

People use body language and/or objects to claim a spacial territory

A Reading in Biology

Is it possible to get all of the nutrients you need from a vegetarian diet? Read the paragraphs below, selected from *Biology: Concepts and Connections* by Neil A. Campbell, Lawrence G. Mitchell, and Jane B. Reece, to find out what is missing from a vegetarian diet and how that can be corrected. After reading the selection, determine if the main idea of each paragraph is stated or implied. If it is stated, underline the sentence that contains the main idea. If it is implied, write what you think the main idea is on the line below the paragraph. Complete the vocabulary exercise before reading the passage to become familiar with some of the terms used in the reading.

Vocabulary in Context

a. **amino acids**—the main parts of a protein that are either made by the body or obtained from the diet

b. **deficiency**—lack of; not having enough

c. **lipids**—combine with proteins and carbohydrates to form living cells

d. **correlate**—show a relationship between two things

e. **susceptible**—vulnerable to or unable to resist an outside force

Use the terms above to complete the following statements. The first one has been done for you.

_____b_____ 1. If we do not eat the types of foods that our bodies need to stay healthy, we can develop a _____ in vitamins or proteins.

_____ 2. Vegetarians are able to get all of the essential _____ by eating a combination of whole grains and beans or whole grains and dairy products.

_____ 3. Three essential components of the human body are proteins, _____, and carbohydrates.

_____ 4. We become _____ to diseases and cancers when our bodies do not get proper nutrition.

_____ 5. Vegetarian diets sometimes _____ with protein deficiencies when people are not eating the correct combination of foods.

A Healthful Diet

[1]   Is it possible for a person to be a true vegetarian—that is, obtain all necessary nutrients by eating only plant material, without animal products of any kind, including eggs, milk, or cheese? The answer is yes, and many people do so, but they have to know how to get all the essential nutrients.

Implied: It is possible for true vegetarians to get all the essential nutrients from

plant material.

[2]   The simplest way to get all the essential **amino acids** is to eat meat and animal by-products such as eggs, milk, and cheese. The proteins in these products are said to be complete, meaning they provide all the essential amino acids in the proportions needed by the human body. In contrast, most plant proteins are incomplete, or deficient in one or more essential amino acids. People may become vegetarians by choice or, more commonly, because they simply cannot afford animal protein. Animal protein is more expensive to produce, and usually to buy, than plant protein, and most of the human population is primarily vegetarian. Nutritional problems can result when people have to rely on a single type of plant food—just corn, rice, or wheat, for instance. When they do, they stand a good chance of becoming protein-deficient.

beneficial amino acids

protein alternat sources

Amino-acids from meat & animal by-products are necessary so one does not become protein-deficient.

[3]   The key to being a healthy vegetarian is to eat a variety of plant foods that together supply sufficient quantities of all the essential amino acids. Simply by eating a combination of beans and corn, for example, vegetarians can get all nine essential amino acids. Most societies have, by trial and error, developed balanced diets that prevent protein **deficiency.** The Mexican staple diet of corn tortillas and beans is one example.

[handwritten left margin: Sufficient quantities of essential amino acids]

[handwritten: A vegetarian's need to eat all the essential amino acids to keep a balanced diet]

[4]   In our culture, excess body fat is considered unattractive. In contrast, some other cultures tend to equate a well-rounded or plump body with beauty and prosperity. Whatever our cultural perspective, fats and related **lipids** are essential components of the human body. For instance, body fat helps insulate us against cold, and, in moderate amounts, it seems to **correlate** with a healthy immune system. Extremely thin people tend to have lower levels of vitamin A and beta-carotene in their blood, which may make them more **susceptible** to certain forms of cancer. Healthy women may have as much as 20–25% of their body weight in fat; for healthy men, the amount is typically 15–19%. When we are too fat, our body fat may be 20% or more above these amounts. Being too fat, or obese, can increase our chances of developing certain diseases (such as heart disease) and decrease our life span.

[handwritten left margin: good & bad effects of Body Fat / Body Fat]

[handwritten: The body's percentage of fat and related lipids are essential components to good or bad health/effects.]

[5]   Fad diets are designed to take pounds off fast, but they rarely succeed. Whatever weight is lost in fad dieting is usually quickly regained once the diet ends and we return to our usual eating habits. Fad diets are not only ineffective in the long run but also they can be harmful. (Campbell, Mitchell, and Reece 444)

[handwritten left margin: Fad diets / Fad diets are harmful]

[handwritten: Fad diets are used to take of weight quickly, we return to our usual eating habits, making it harmful to our bodies]

A Reading in Biology

Have you ever wondered if animals could think? Read the passage below to find out how researchers are proving that chimpanzees can not only learn sign language but also can think and reason. Complete the vocabulary exercise before reading the passage to become familiar with some of the terms used in the reading. Then read the passage. After that, answer the questions that follow to determine the central point, the stated main ideas, and the implied main ideas.

Vocabulary in Context

   a. **extensively**—thoroughly

   b. **exhibt**—show

   c. **biochemical**—chemical make up of living organisms

   d. **acutely**—with extreme or intense perception

   e. **entrenched**—firmly established

Use the terms above to complete the following statements. The first one has been done for you.

_____a_____ **1.** Chimpanzees have been studied _____, and many aspects of their behavior resemble human behavior.

_____ **2.** It was once believed that only humans are capable of making and using simple tools and raiding other groups. However, scientists found that chimpanzees _____ these same behaviors.

_____ **3.** The way that chimpanzees act in front of mirrors challenges one of our most _____ beliefs—that humans are the only beings that can think.

_____ **4.** Through _____ evidence, scientists have found that humans are more closely related to chimpanzees than to any other animals.

_____ **5.** These research findings are _____ affecting people's perceptions of animals and of themselves.

Apes Are Our Closest Relatives

[1]   [1]Chimpanzees have been studied **extensively,** and many aspects of their behavior resemble human behavior. [2]For example, chimpanzees make and use simple tools. [3]Chimpanzees also raid other social groups of their own species, **exhibiting** behavior formerly believed to be uniquely human. [4]Researchers have demonstrated repeatedly that chimpanzees can learn human sign language. [5]However, we do not yet know what role symbolic communication plays in the behavior of wild chimpanzees.

[2]   [1]One of our most **entrenched** beliefs is that humans are the only thinking, self-aware beings. [2]The behavior of chimpanzees in front of mirrors, however, challenges this belief. [3]When first introduced to a mirror, a chimpanzee responds the way most other animals do—as if it were seeing another individual of its species. [4]After several days, though, a chimp will begin using a mirror in ways that indicate it has a concept of self. [5]It will inspect its face and other parts of its body that it cannot see without the mirror. [6]It will also make faces at the mirror, using expressions different from those used in communicating with others.

[3]   [1]Recent **biochemical** evidence indicates that the chimpanzee and the gorilla are more closely related to humans than they are to other apes. [2]Humans and chimpanzees are especially closely related; human DNA differs from chimpanzee DNA by less than 3%. [3]Primate researchers are **acutely** aware of the special significance of the great apes to us. [4]In the words of chimpanzee authority Jane Goodall, "The most important spin-off of the chimp research is probably the humbling effect it has on us who do the research. [5]You are not, after all, the only aware, reasoning beings on this planet." (Campbell, Mitchell, and Reece 402–03)

Questions for Thought

_____e_____ **1.** The topic of this passage is:
a. chimpanzees and self-awareness.
b. biochemical evidence.
c. human behavior.
d. Jane Goodall.
e. chimpanzees' self-awareness and human behavior.

_____c_____ **2.** The central thought of this passage is:
a. Chimpanzees have been studied extensively.
b. Researchers have demonstrated repeatedly that chimpanzees can learn human sign language.
c. Research on chimpanzees' behavior and biochemical evidence show that chimpanzees and humans are closely related.
d. Human DNA differs from chimpanzee DNA by less than 3%.
e. A chimp will begin using a mirror in ways that indicate it has a concept of self.

_____a_____ **3.** The main idea of paragraph 1 is stated in:
a. Sentence 1.
b. Sentence 2.
c. Sentence 3.
d. Sentence 4.
e. Sentence 5.

_____a_____ **4.** The implied main idea from paragraph 2 is:
  a. Humans are the only thinking, self-aware beings.
  b. A chimp will begin using a mirror in ways that indicate it has a concept of self.
  c. A chimp will make faces in a mirror, using expressions different from those used in communicating with others.
  d. The behavior of chimpanzees in front of mirrors challenges the beliefs that humans are the only thinking, self-aware beings.
  e. When first introduced to a mirror, a chimpanzee responds as if it were seeing another individual of its species.

_____a_____ **5.** The main idea of the third paragraph is:
  a. Sentence 1.
  b. Sentence 2.
  c. Sentence 3.
  d. Sentence 4.
  e. Sentence 5.

A Reading in Sociology

According to psychologist Robert Manis, men and women have different ways of communicating. Read the selection below to see how an understanding of these differences can improve relationships. Complete the vocabulary exercise before reading the passage. Then answer the discussion and main idea questions that follow. Finally, complete the exercise detailed in Reading Between the Lines Box 4.1.

Vocabulary in Context

  a. self-segregated—having separated oneself from others

  b. formative—characterized by growth and development

  c. agenda—an outline or plan of things that need to be completed

  d. hierarchical—relating to the categorization of people according to their abilities or financial and social status

  e. negotiate—an agreement made through compromise

Use the terms above to complete the following statements. The first one has been done for you.

_____b_____ **1.** During their _____ years, children rapidly learn about their environment.

_____ **2.** Men's and women's soccer teams are often _____ to provide equal playing fields for equal abilities.

_____ **3.** The success of a relationship depends on how well men and women can accept their differences and _____ a solution.

_____ **4.** In everyday conversation, men and women both have a plan or list of certain things they would like to talk about. If they don't understand each others' underlying _____, they will probably fail in their ability to communicate with each other.

_____ **5.** In public conversation, men compete with each other for recognition. They are constantly trying to win a higher position in a _____ social order.

What Planet Are You from Anyway?

[1]   [1]Not only are sex role stereotypes promoted by parents, teachers, storybooks, movies, and television, but often most strongly by children themselves. [2]Most children are raised in almost completely **self-segregated** environments, where boys do boy things and girls do girl things.

[2]   [1]According to linguist Deborah Tannen, boys and girls are in effect raised in two separate cultures, two different worlds for most of their early and most **formative** parts of their lives. [2]When they try to get together as adults in marriages and relationships, the result is often misunderstandings and conflict. [3]Tannen studied men's and women's conversations and interactions both separately and together and found out that quite often each sex had quite a different **agenda** from what the other thought was going on.

[3]   [1]According to Tannen, most men are socialized through games and male play into competition. [2]They often come to think of themselves as part of a somewhat **hierarchical** social order, where they are either, in her terms, "one-up" or "one-down." [3]Conversations are **negotiations** in which they either playfully or for real try to achieve or maintain the upper hand, or at least protect themselves from others' attempts to put them down. [4]For men, life is a struggle to preserve independence.

[4]   [1]Women, on the other hand, tend to see themselves in a network of connections. [2]They are socialized through girls' games and helping around the house to value connectedness. [3]Conversations for them are negotiations for closeness and support. [4]Women try to protect themselves from others' attempts to push them away. [5]For women, life is a struggle to preserve intimacy and avoid isolation. [6]While not all men and women fit neatly into these categories, these themes showed up repeatedly in Tannen's research.

Two Examples:

[5] [1]*"Put down that paper and talk to me."* [2]In public, men tend to dominate conversations. [3]They speak often, and at greater length. [4]They tend to interrupt more often than women. [5]Yet many women complain that at home, men become silent, burying their heads in newspapers or watching television. [6]Why is it that men dominate in public and disappear at home? [7]Tannen suggests that for both men and women, home is a place to be offstage. [8]But that offstage feeling has a different meaning for men and women. [9]For men, getting home means freedom from having to prove and defend themselves through talking. [10]They are free to remain silent and just "be together." [11]For women, however, home is a place where they are free to talk—unlike in public, where they may be somewhat intimidated, and where they feel the greatest desire to talk—with those they feel closest to. [12]For them, being home means the freedom to talk without being judged.

[6] [1]*"What do you want from me anyway?"* [2]Many men are mystified by women's "troubles talk." [3]They offer helpful advice, often only to get rejected, sometimes with anger. [4]Tannen gives the example of a woman who had minor breast surgery and was disturbed by the scar. [5]When she talked to her friends, they offered support by saying things like, "I know, I was upset too, when it happened," and "I know, it's like having your body violated." [6]But when she told her husband, he responded, "You could have plastic surgery to cover up the scar." [7]While she found her friends' comments comforting, her husband's comments upset her. [8]Not only did she not hear what she wanted—that he understood her feelings—but, worse, she felt that he wanted her to undergo more surgery. [9]"I'm not having any more surgery, and I'm sorry you don't like the way it looks." [10]He, in turn, was puzzled by her anger at his response. [11]Like many women, she wanted the gift of understanding, and like many men, he responded with a gift of what he felt was helpful advice. [12]Men are socialized to take action, to solve problems, while women are more socialized to nurture and comfort. [13]Tannen feels that by knowing these gender differences, couples can begin a process of communication that leads to greater understanding by recognizing the effects of socialization. (Manis 52–53)

Questions for Discussion

1. What does the title suggest about men and women?

_____

_____

2. Why do misunderstandings and conflicts sometimes arise in adult relationships and marriages?

_____

_____

3. How can recognizing the effects that socialization has had on communication lead to greater understanding between men and women?

_____

_____

4. How do men and women differ in their thinking about communication in public and private?

_____

_____

5. From your experiences, do you think men and women have different ways of communicating?

_____

_____

Questions for Thought

_____e_____ 1. The topic of this passage is:
   a. planets.
   b. marriages and relationships.
   c. human communication.
   d. sex role stereotypes.
   e. sex role stereotypes and communication.

_____c_____ 2. The central thought of this passage is:
   a. Sex role stereotypes are promoted by parents, teachers, storybooks, movies, and television.
   b. Misunderstandings and conflict arise in marriages and adult relationships because men and women are raised differently.

      c. By recognizing the effects of socialization, couples can under-
stand gender differences and communicate more effectively.

      d. Men tend to dominate conversations.

      e. Women feel that men don't listen to them.

_____ **3.** The second sentence in paragraph 1 contains:

      a. the topic.

      b. the central thought.

      c. the main idea.

      d. an implied main idea.

      e. a supporting detail.

_____ **4.** The implied main idea from paragraph 2 is:

      a. Deborah Tannen is a linguist who has studied men's and
women's conversations.

      b. When they try to get together as adults, men and women
have trouble communicating.

      c. Men and women have different agendas when they talk.

      d. Men and women often do not understand each others' agen-
das in their conversations and interactions because they
have been raised in two separate cultures.

      e. Boys and girls are raised in two separate cultures for the for-
mative parts of their lives.

_____ **5.** The main idea of paragraph 3 is:

      a. Sentence 1.

      b. Sentence 2.

      c. Sentence 3.

      d. Sentence 4.

      e. Sentence 5.

_____ **6.** The main idea of paragraph 4 is:

      a. Sentence 1.

      b. Sentence 2.

      c. Sentence 3.

      d. Sentence 4.

      e. Sentence 5.

_____ **7.** The implied main idea for paragraph 5 is:

      a. "Put down that paper and talk to me."

      b. In public, men tend to dominate conversations and interrupt
more often than women.

      c. Men and women have different agendas for talking in public
and private places.

      d. When at home, women feel they have freedom to talk with-
out being judged.

      e. When at home, men feel they are free from proving and
defending themselves through talking.

_C_ **8.** All of the following are true *except:*
   a. Home is a place to be offstage for both men and women.
   b. Women don't understand why men become silent once they are home.
   c. Women feel comfortable expressing their feelings in public.
   d. Men feel that home is a place where they can be free from talk and just "be together."
   e. Women feel the greatest desire to talk at home.

_e_ **9.** The main idea of paragraph 6 is:
   a. Sentence 1.
   b. Sentence 5.
   c. Sentence 9.
   d. Sentence 11.
   e. Sentence 13.

_d_ **10.** All of the following are true *except:*
   a. Women would rather have someone understand their problem instead of someone giving them advice for solving the problem.
   b. Women give other women reassurance instead of advice.
   c. Men are socialized to take action and to solve problems.
   d. Men understand women's "troubles talk," and women appreciate their advice.
   e. Although helpful, men's advice is often rejected.

Reading Between the Lines Box 4.1

PSYCHOLOGY: WHAT PLANET ARE YOU FROM ANYWAY?

Consider the second sentence from paragraph 1 of the reading:

> Most children are raised in almost completely self-segregated environments, where boys do boy things and girls do girl things.

Notice that the author never defines "boy things" and "girl things." You might think of little girls playing house with dolls or playing with make up. On the other hand, you may think of little boys playing with cars and trucks or playing cowboys and Indians. In this way, you read between the lines by adding the information that the author left out.

Read the following statements from the passage. Make a list of specific examples the author could use to further support her points. The first one has been done for you.

(continued on next page)

1. "Not only are sex role stereotypes promoted by parents, teachers, story-books, movies, and television, but often most strongly by children themselves."

Brainstorm and list the ways that sex role stereotypes are promoted by:

a. parents <u>clothe girls in dresses and boys in slacks</u>

b. teachers _____

c. storybooks _____

d. movies _____

e. television _____

2. "Men are socialized to take action, to solve problems, while women are more socialized to nurture and comfort."

Brainstorm and list examples that show how men are taught to "take action and solve problems." The first one has been done for you.

a. _____

_____

b. _____

List examples from your own experience that show how women are taught to "nurture and comfort" people. The first one has been done for you.

a. _____

_____

b. _____

Implied Ideas in Literature

When reading literature, you will notice that some ideas are directly stated, while others are implied. To understand implied ideas in literature, you must look for clues in: (1) what the narrator says about the character, (2) what the character says about herself/himself, (3) what other characters say about the character, and (4) what characters say *to* each other. In his short story "Tain't So," the African American author, Langston Hughes, uses all of these techniques to get his ideas across to the reader without stating them. For example, read the sentence below and determine Hughes' implied idea.

> Miss Lucy Cannon was a right nice old white woman, so Uncle Joe always stated, except that she really did not like colored folks, not even after she come out West to California.

The author does not say outright that prejudice against African Americans existed at the time of the story, but uses the character Uncle Joe to tell us this. You gain further evidence of prejudice from what the main character says about herself.

> Said Miss Lucy to herself, "I'll never in the world get used to the North. . . . Why, down in Alabama a Negro patient wouldn't dare come in here and sit down with white people like this!"

In the exercise below, look for Langston Hughes's implied ideas by noting what is said about the characters and what they say about themselves. Practice with Reading Between the Lines Box 4.2 on page 135 before going ahead with the reading.

A Reading in Short Story

Before reading the following short story, study the vocabulary words and complete the accompanying exercises. Then read the excerpt below and respond to the discussion questions. Finally, refer to Reading Between the Lines Box 4.3 (page 140) to put what you've learned about the characters into practice.

Vocabulary in Context

a. **ailing**—suffering from bad health

b. **infirmities**—disabling physical conditions

c. **spry**—alert and quick mentally or physically

d. **condescending**—having an attitude of superiority

e. **impudence**—overly confident, cocky, or bold

Use the words above to complete the following statements. The first one has been done for you.

    b   **1.** Many elderly people are unable to function as they did when they were younger because of _____ that have developed over the years.

Reading Between the Lines Box 4.2

ANALYZING LITERATURE

Analyzing Characters

Authors express their thoughts, feelings, perceptions, and opinions about the world through literature. An author's character might remind you of someone you know, a situation might seem similar to one you've experienced, or an entire new segment of life might be introduced to you.

Authors often create characters with weaknesses or flaws to illustrate a point. Your job as reader is to recognize the underlying message the author is giving through these character flaws. Read the story "Tain't So" by Langston Hughes and describe the flaw in the main character, Miss Lucy Cannon. Then read the section below and answer the questions that follow.

Drawing Information from Other Sources

In order to understand characters, you may need to look up information from sources in the humanities. Suppose you suspect that the flaw in Miss Lucy's character is prejudice. Henry L. Tischler, in his textbook *Introduction to Sociology*, describes prejudice as:

> . . . being down on something you are not up on, the implication being that prejudice results from inadequate knowledge of, or familiarity with, the subject. People, particularly those with a strong sense of identity, often have feelings of prejudice towards others who are not like themselves. Literally, prejudice means a "prejudgment." According to Wirth (1944), prejudice is "an attitude with an emotional bias." . . . For our purposes, you shall define prejudice as an irrationally based negative, or occasionally positive, attitude toward certain groups and their members.

Analyzing Character Flaws

1. What is Miss Lucy Cannon's character flaw?

2. In the above excerpt defining prejudice, the author lists three causes of prejudice. Which one best explains why Miss Lucy Cannon is prejudiced?

3. From the way the story ends, do you think Miss Lucy changes her beliefs, or do you think she remains prejudiced? What does she say or do that makes you think so?

4. Why do you think Langston Hughes chose to portray his main character in this way?

5. What do you think he wants the reader to consider after reading this story?

_____ **2.** The senior citizen was unusually _____ for his age, running or swimming a mile every day.

_____ **3.** Miss Lucy Cannon had a _____ attitude toward people from cultures different than her own.

_____ **4.** Miss Lucy Cannon often tried to convince others that she was _____ from a heart condition and therefore deserved special attention.

_____ **5.** Miss Lucy Cannon sincerely believed that she had many serious health conditions and felt that the faith healer had a lot of _____ for telling her that this was not so.

Tain't So

[1]   Miss Lucy Cannon was a right nice old white woman, so Uncle Joe always stated, except that she really did *not* like colored folks, not even after she come out West to California. She could never get over certain little southern ways she had, and long as she knowed my Uncle Joe, who hauled her ashes for her, she never would call him *Mister*—nor any other colored man *Mister* neither, for that matter not even the minister of the Baptist Church who was a graduate of San Jose State College. Miss Lucy Cannon just wouldn't call colored folks *Mister* nor *Missus*, no matter who they was, neither in Alabama nor in California.

[2]   She was always **ailing** around, too, sick with first one thing and then another, delicate, and ever so often she would have a fainting spell, like all good southern white ladies. Looks like the older she got, the more she would be sick and couldn't hardly get around—that is, until she went to a healer and got cured.

[3]   And that is one of the funniest stories Uncle Joe ever told me, how old Miss Cannon got cured of her heart and hip in just one cure at the healer's.

[4]   Seems like for three years or more she could scarcely walk—even with a cane—had a terrible bad pain in her right leg from her knee up. And on her left side her heart was always just about to give out. She was in bad shape, that old southern lady, to be as **spry** as she was, always giving teas and dinners and working her colored help to death.

[5]   Well, Uncle Joe says, one New Year's Day in Pasadena a friend of hers, a northern lady who was kinda old and retired also and had come out to California to spend her last days, too, and get rid of some parts of her big bank full of money—this old lady told Miss Cannon, "Darling, you just seem to suffer so all the time, and you say you've tried all the doctors and all kinds of baths and medicines. Why don't you try my way of overcoming? Why don't you try faith?"

[6]   "Faith, honey?" says old Miss Lucy Cannon, sipping her jasmine tea.

[7]   "Yes, my dear," says the northern white lady. "Faith! I have one of the best faith healers in the world."

[8]   "Who is he?" asked Miss Lucy Cannon.

[9]   "She's a woman, dear," said old Miss Northern White Lady. "And she heals by power. She lives in Hollywood."

[10]   "Give me her address," said Miss Lucy, "and I'll go to see her. How much do her treatments cost?"

[11] Miss Lucy warn't so rich as some folks thought she was.

[12]   "Only ten dollars, dearest," said the other lady. "Ten dollars a treatment. Go, and you'll come away cured."

[13]   "I have never believed in such things," said Miss Lucy, "nor disbelieved, either. But I will go and see." And before she could learn any more about the healer, some other friends came in and interrupted the conversation.

[14]   A few days later, however, Miss Lucy took herself all the way from Pasadena to Hollywood, put up for the weekend with a friend of hers, and thought she would go to see the healer, which she did, come Monday morning early.

[15]   Using her customary cane and hobbling on her left leg, feeling a bit bad around the heart, and suffering terribly in her mind, she managed to walk slowly but with dignity a half-dozen blocks through the sunshine to the rather humble street in which was located the office and home of the healer.

[16]   In spite of the bright morning air and the good breakfast she had had, Miss Lucy (according to herself) felt pretty bad, racked with pains and crippled to the use of a cane.

[17]   When she got to the house she was seeking, a large frame dwelling, newly painted, she saw a sign thereon:

[18]   MISS PAULINE JONES

[19]   "So that's her name," thought Miss Lucy, "Pauline Jones, Miss Jones."

[20]   *Ring and Enter* said a little card above the bell. So Miss Lucy entered. But the first thing that set her back a bit was that nobody received her, so she just sat down to await Miss Jones, the healer who had, she heard, an enormous following in Hollywood. In fact, that's why she had come early, so she wouldn't have to wait long. Now, it was only nine o'clock. The office was open—but empty. So Miss Lucy simply waited. Ten minutes passed. Fifteen. Twenty. Finally she became all nervous and fluttery. Heart and limb! Pain, pain, pain! Not even a magazine to read.

[21]   "Oh, me!" she said impatiently. "What is this? Why, I never!"

[22]   There was a sign on the wall that read:

[23]   BELIEVE

[24]   "I will wait just ten minutes more," said Miss Lucy, glancing at her watch of platinum and pearls.

[25]   But before the ten minutes were up another woman entered the front door and sat down. To Miss Lucy's horror she was a colored woman! In fact, a big black colored woman!

[26]   Said Miss Lucy to herself, "I'll never in the world get used it in the North. Now here's a great—my friend says great—faith healer treating

darkies! Why, down in Alabama a Negro patient wouldn't dare come in here and sit down with white people like this!"

[27]   But, womanlike (and having still five minutes to wait), Miss Lucy couldn't keep her mouth shut that long. She just had to talk, albeit to a Negro, so she began on her favorite subject—herself.

[28]   I certainly feel bad this morning," she said to the colored woman, **condescending** to open the conversation.

[29]   "'Tain't so," answered the Negro woman placidly, which sort of took Miss Lucy back a bit. She lifted her chin.

[30]   "Indeed, it is so," said she indignantly. "My heart is just about to give out. My breath is short."

[31]   "'Tain't so a-tall," commented the colored woman.

[32]   "Why!" gasped Miss Lucy. "Such **impudence!** I tell you *it is so!* I could hardly get down here this morning."

[33]   "'Tain't so," said the woman calmly.

[34]   "Besides my heart," went on Miss Lucy, "my right hip pains me so I can hardly sit here."

[35]   "I say, 'tain't so."

[36]   "I tell you it *is* so," screamed Miss Lucy. "Where is the healer? I won't sit here and suffer this—this impudence. I can't! It'll kill me! It's outrageous."

[37]   "'Tain't so," said the large black woman serenely, whereupon Miss Lucy rose. Her pale face flushed a violent red.

[38]   "Where is the healer?" she cried, looking around the room.

[39]   "Right here," said the colored woman.

[40]   "What?" cried Miss Lucy. "You're the—why—you?"

[41]   "I'm Miss Jones."

[42]   "Why, I never heard the like," gasped Miss Lucy. "A *colored* woman as famous as you? Why, you must be lying!"

[43]   "'Tain't so," said the woman calmly.

[44]   "Well, I shan't stay another minute," cried Miss Lucy.

[45]   "Ten dollars, then," said the colored woman. "You've had your treatment, anyhow."

[46]   "Ten dollars! That's entirely too much!"

[47]   "'Tain't so."

[48]   Angrily Miss Lucy opened her pocketbook, threw a ten-dollar bill on the table, took a deep breath, and bounced out. She went three blocks up Sunset Boulevard, walking like the wind, conversing with herself.

[49]   "'Tain't so," she muttered. "'Tain't so!' I tell her I'm sick and she says, "'Tain't so!"

[50]   On she went at a rapid gait, stepping like a young girl—so mad she had forgotten all about her **infirmities,** even her heart—when suddenly she cried, "Lord, have mercy, my cane! For the first time in three years I'm *without* a cane!"

[51]   Then she realized that her breath was giving her no trouble at all. Neither was her leg. Her temper mellowed. The sunshine was sweet and warm. She felt good.

[52] "Colored folks do have some funny kind of supernatural conjuring powers, I reckon," she said, smiling to herself. Immediately her face went grim again. "But the impudence of 'em! Soon's they get up North—calling herself *Miss* Pauline Jones. The idea! Putting on airs and charging me ten dollars for a handful of "*tain't so's!*"

[53] In her mind she clearly heard, "'Tain't so!" (Hughes)

Questions for Discussion

1. Why did Miss Lucy seek out a faith healer?

_____

_____

2. What are Miss Lucy's feelings toward African American people? How can you tell?

_____

_____

3. What are the narrator's feelings toward caucasion people? How can you tell?

_____

_____

4. As Miss Lucy was leaving, Miss Pauline Jones said "You've had your treatment, anyhow." What was the treatment?

_____

_____

5. The words "'Tain't so" helped Miss Lucy overcome her health problems. Do you think these same words will help her overcome prejudice? Why or why not?

_____

_____

Questions for Thought

Determine if the statement is true or false and then write T for true or F for false on the line in front of the statement. The first one has been done for you.

___T___ **1.** You can tell that Miss Lucy feels superior to African Americans because the narrator tells us that she refuses to address men of this race as "Mister."

_____ **2.** Miss Lucy believed she had a bad heart and needed a cane to walk.

_____ **3.** Miss Lucy felt sure the faith healer was white because the sign on the door said "Miss Pauline Jones."

_____ **4.** The faith healer used supernatural powers to heal Miss Lucy's heart and hip.

_____ **5.** The narrator leads us to believe that Miss Lucy's problems may be more cultural than physical when he describes her as "Delicate, and ever so often she would have a fainting spell, like all good southern white ladies."

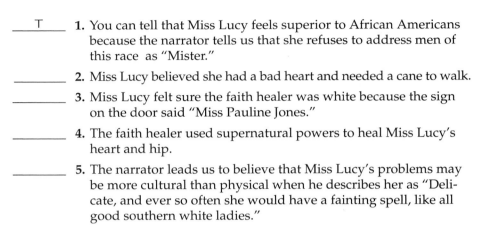

Reading Between the Lines Box 4.3

INFERENCE THROUGH CHARACTER SKETCH

Authors create a character through descriptions of the character's physical appearance, personality, and relationships with other people. They may use the comments of the narrator or other characters to provide additional information about a character.

In order to get to "know" a character, the reader must put all of these descriptions together and make inferences concerning the character's nature. As we read, we look for further evidence to support our impressions of the character. We call this a *character* sketch. Below is a sketch of Langston Hughes' character, Miss Pauline Jones from the story "Tain't So." Study this model step by step and then write a character sketch of Miss Lucy. Include both physical traits and personality traits and provide reasons for the inferences that you draw.

Model Character Sketch of Miss Pauline Jones

1. Think of three adjectives that describe Miss Jones and write them in a **topic sentence.**

2. Find three reasons why Miss Jones is "adjective 1" and write about it.

3. Find three reasons why Miss Jones is "adjective 2" and write about it.

4. Find three reasons why Miss Jones is "adjective 3" and write about it.

5. Make **an inference** about the type of character Miss Pauline is.

(continued on next page)

Topic Sentence: Miss Pauline Jones is a [1]wise, [2]well liked, [3]African American woman.

Information from #2: Miss Jones is very wise because [1]she stayed calm while she told Miss Lucy that her ailments were imagined. [2]Also, she is wise because she stayed calm when Miss Lucy called her a liar. [3]She was also wise to take Miss Lucy's ten dollars.

Information from #3: It is obvious that Miss Jones is well liked because [1]she had a large following of clients in Hollywood. [2]Also, Miss Jones was recommened by Miss Lucy's northern friend as being "one of the best faith healers in the world." [3]Even Miss Lucy begins to warm up to her by the end of the story.

Information from #4: We can see that Miss Jones is an African Amercian woman because she was described by Miss Lucy several times as being [1]"a colored woman," [2]"a Negro," and [3]a "black colored woman."

Inference: Miss Pauline Jones Is a wise and likable African American woman who understands people and cares about them.

Character sketch of Miss Lucy Cannon

1. Think of three adjectives that describe Miss Lucy Cannon and write them into a topic sentence.

2. Find three reasons why Miss Lucy is "adjective 1" and write that into a sentence.

3. Find three reasons why Miss Lucy is "adjective 2" and write that into a sentence.

4. Find three reasons why Miss Lucy is "adjective 3" and write that into a sentence.

5. Make an inference about the type of person Miss Lucy Cannon is.

   Topic Sentence: Miss Lucy Cannon is *adjective 1, adjective 2,* and *adjective 3.*

   Sentence 1: She is adjective 1 because (a) _____, (b) _____, and (c) _____.

   Sentence 2: She is adjective 2 because (a) _____, (b) _____, and (c) _____.

   Sentence 3: She is adjective 3 because (a) _____, (b) _____, and (c) _____.

   Inference: Miss Lucy Cannon is: _____.

CENTRAL POINT

So far, you have learned that every paragraph has a topic that centers our focus on a particular subject. You know that the main idea is a statement that explains the topic by telling the reader who and/or what the paragraph is about. And you know that the supporting details provide more specific information about the topic and main idea.

Now let's think about what happens when you read a section of an article or a section of a book chapter. Most articles or chapters are broken into sections that are related to a particular topic. You would call this a **passage.** Just as a paragraph has a main idea, a passage has a central point. The **central point** tells us the main idea of the entire passage. It is generally located in the first paragraph.

The central point is important because it tells us who or what the entire section is about and the main thought the author has about the topic. The main idea of each paragraph can be related to the central point.

How Do You Detect the Central Point?

In order to find the central point, you must first look at the topic of the passage and then at the main ideas of each paragraph in the passage. Each main idea expands on, or provides more information about, the central point. Therefore, the central point is the main thought of the passage and all of the main ideas that support it.

In our fruit basket example below, you know that our topic is *fruit.* If each paragraph introduces a different kind of fruit, such as apples, bananas, oranges, peaches, and pears, then these are the topics for the paragraphs in our passage. Each paragraph also has a main idea that explains why each fruit is included in the fruit basket.

Our supporting details, then, consist of even more specific fruit types. For example, the first paragraph is about apples. The supporting details might include several varieties of apple, such as Macintosh, Red Delicious, Cortland, Gala, and Golden Delicious. Our second paragraph is about bananas. The supporting details are the various types of bananas—Red, Baby, Baking, and Dessert.

• What details support a main idea statement about oranges?
• What details support a main idea statement about peaches?
• What details support a main idea statement about pears?

The following diagram shows us how the main idea and details are organized.

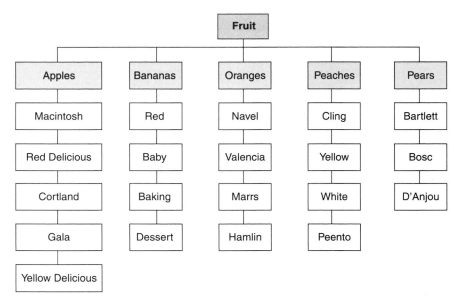

Let's look at an entire passage on *fruit* and note the various roles each sentence plays. Notice that the first sentence of each paragraph contains the main idea. Also notice that each main idea introduces a different type of fruit and that the supporting details describe them. In the following passage,

- **CT** stands for central thought
- **T** stands for topic
- **MI** stands for main idea
- **SD** stands for supporting detail

Fruit baskets that include apples, bananas, oranges, peaches, and pears make great gifts because these fruits vary greatly in taste, color, and use. **(CT)** Although sweet and delicious, each type of fruit contributes a taste of its own. **(SD)** There are also differences in color among the varieties. **(SD)** These differences make the fruit baskets more interesting and festive. **(SD)**

There are many varieties of apples. **(MI)** The Yellow Delicious apple is sweet and brightens up a fruit basket with its bright yellow color. **(SD)** The Red Delicious apple is also sweet but dark ed in appearance **(SD).** Although tart. the Macintosh apple is a great favorite for many. **(SD)** The Cortland and Gala make wonderful pies. **(SD)**

There are also many types of bananas from which to choose. **(MI)** Dessert bananas, as their name suggests, are used in making desserts. **(SD)** Baking bananas, of course, are used for making baked goods such as banana bread. **(SD)** Baby bananas, because of their size, can be very useful in making smaller fruit baskets. **(SD)** Red bananas, known for their red color can be very decorative. **(SD)**

Different kinds of oranges can also be found in fruit baskets. **(MI)** The flesh of the Hamlin orange is pulpy, so this type is better for juicing than for eating. **(SD)** The Valencia orange can be eaten whole or squeezed for juice. **(SD)** Navels are excellent eating oranges because they have thick skins, no seeds, distinct segments, and sweet flavors. **(SD)**

A fruit basket is not complete without several varieties of peaches. **(MI)** Cling peaches are often used for canning. **(SD)** The Yellow peach is named for its yellow-colored flesh. **(SD)** The White peach has a light or white flesh, with red or pink near the pit. **(SD)** Peento peaches add interest to a fruit basket because they are flat or doughnut shaped. **(SD)**

Various types of pears also mix well in a fruit basket. **(MI)** Bartlett pears are good for cooking, canning, and just plain eating. **(SD)** The Moonglow makes a wonderful dessert pear. **(SD)** The Kieffer is poor to fair for dessert but good for canning and baking. **(SD)**

As we learned earlier, the central point tells us what the passage is about. Each paragraph combines the main idea and the details that support it. We can tell what each individual paragraph is about by locating its main idea and recognizing its supporting details.

A Reading in Biology

Do you smoke or have friends who smoke? Read the passage below to find out why smoking is not a good thing to do. Complete the vocabulary exercises first to become familiar with the terms, then read the selection below and then decide whether the highlighted portion of each paragraph is a (a) topic, (b) main idea, (c) supporting detail, or (4) central thought.

Vocabulary in Context

   a. adapted—adjusted to new circumstances or surroundings

   b. bronchi—area of the body that leads into the lungs

   c. cilia—small hairs that line the nose, throat, and lungs; their function is to move fluid or mucus out of the body

   d. macrophages—cell tissues that protects the body against infection

   e. alveoli—the part of the lungs that contains air

Use the terms above to complete the following statements. The first one has been done for you.

____e____ **1.** If the _____ fill up with fluid, the person will have difficulty breathing or may not be able to breathe at all.

_____ **2.** If the _____ are destroyed by toxic particles and tobacco smoke, the body will not be able to protect itself again infection.

_____ **3.** When tobacco smoke destroys the _____, the body loses its ability to move fluid or mucus out of the lungs.

_____ **4.** When toxic air travels through the _____, it may do a lot of damage before reaching the alveoli.

_____ **5.** Our lungs are not _____ to tolerate tobacco smoke and other types of toxic air pollution.

Smoking Is One of the Deadliest Assaults on Our Respiratory System

____d____ **1.** Virtually everywhere today, the air you breathe exposes the cells in your respiratory system to chemicals that they are not **adapted** to tolerate. Air pollutants such as sulfur dioxide, carbon monoxide, and ozone are associated with serious respiratory diseases. One of the worst sources of toxic air pollutants is tobacco smoke. A single drag on a cigarette exposes a person to over

40,000 different chemicals, many of which are known to be harmful and potentially deadly.
   a. topic
   b. main idea
   c. supporting detail
   d. central thought

_____C_____ 2. The visible smoke from a cigarette, cigar, or pipe is mainly microscopic particles of carbon. Sticking to the carbon particles are many different kinds of toxic chemicals. Tobacco smoke irritates the cells lining the **bronchi,** inhibiting or destroying their **cilia** and **macrophages.** This interferes with the normal cleansing mechanism of the respiratory system and allows more toxin-laden smoke particles in the inhaled air to reach the lung's delicate **alveoli.** Frequent coughing—common in heavy smokers—then becomes the system's attempt to clean itself.
   a. topic
   b. main idea
   c. supporting detail
   d. central thought

_____b_____ 3. Every year in the United States, smoking kills about 350,000 people, more than all the deaths caused by traffic accidents or illegal drug abuse. Some of the toxins in tobacco smoke cause lung cancer, which nearly always kills its victims.
   a. topic
   b. main idea
   c. supporting detail
   d. central thought

_____c_____ 4. Smokers also have a markedly greater risk than nonsmokers of developing cancers of the bladder, pancreas, mouth, throat, and several other organs. Another disease, called emphysema, can develop as cigarette smoke makes the thin-walled alveoli brittle. Many of the alveoli eventually rupture, reducing the lungs' capacity for gas exchange. Breathlessness and constant fatigue result, as the body is forced to spend more and more energy just breathing. The heart is also forced to work harder, and emphysema often leads to heart disease. Probably every cigarette a person smokes takes about five minutes away from his or her life expectancy. Moreover, some studies indicate that nonsmokers exposed to secondary cigarette smoke are also at risk.
   a. topic
   b. main idea
   c. supporting detail
   d. central thought

_____ 5. Clearly, efforts to reduce smoking and secondary exposure to smoke can have positive effects on personal and public health. For former smokers, it is encouraging that after about 10 years of not smoking, the chances of developing lung cancer and heart disease seem to drop to levels similar to those of people who have never smoked. (Campbell, Mitchell, and Reece 457)

    a. topic
    b. main idea
    c. supporting detail
    d. central thought

A Reading in Health Sciences

Did you know that you could die from drinking alcohol? Read the following selection to find out what happens to your body when you drink. Complete the vocabulary exercise before you begin reading to familiarize yourself with the new terms. Then read the following passage and decide which sentence contains the central thought. Determine the main idea for each paragraph. Finally, use Visual Literacy Box 4.1 to help you organize everything you've learned about the effects of alcohol on your body.

Vocabulary in Context

  a. depressant—substance that reduces the body's ability to function

  b. sedation—use of a substance to force a relaxed state

  c. assaying—measuring

  d. sobriety—state of being sober (not drunk)

  e. introspective—reflecting inward on thoughts or feelings

  f. inhibitions—inner agents that stop one from joining in an activity

  g. repressed—use of self-control to keep from joining in an activity

  h. avail—bring about a desired result

  i. accumulate—to gather or acquire little by little

  j. scatological—obscene

Use the terms above to complete the following statements. The first one has been done for you.

_____j_____ 1. You can often expect _____ conduct from those who have exceeded the one-drink-per-hour rule for social drinking.

_____ 2. Alcohol slows the body's natural functions and is therefore a
_____.

_____ 3. At first, alcohol makes the drinker feel a sense of well-being. During the next stage, _____, the drinker feels relaxed. In the final stages, he becomes intoxicated, and if he does not stop drinking, he may die.

_____ 4. The police use sobriety tests for _____ the amount of alcohol that is in the bloodstream.

_____ 5. Before taking his first alcoholic drink, a person is considered to be in a state of _____; at that point he is completely sober.

_____ 6. Between the third and fourth drinks, the drinker may become _____ and involved with his own thoughts rather than joining the party.

_____ 7. After three or four drinks, the drinker may lose his _____ and become the life of the party.

_____ 8. Later the drinker may regret his actions and wish he had _____ the urge to say what was on his mind.

_____ 9. Time is the only thing that can bring back a drinker from drunkenness to a sober state. Coffee is of no _____.

_____ 10. If a person has more than one drink an hour, the alcohol will _____ and he will become drunk.

What Happens When I Drink?

[1]   Alcohol is a drug. It acts on the central nervous system as a **depressant** (not as a stimulant). Normally, it first produces euphoria or a feeling of well-being, then a certain amount of **sedation** interpreted as relaxation, then intoxication, and, finally, death. Each of these stages is governed by the amount and rate of alcohol entering the bloodstream of the drinker. There is no hocus-pocus involved here. The amount of alcohol in the system can be precisely determined at any time by means of a common blood test. However, the degree of effect of alcohol upon any given person is determined by many factors: your weight, amount of food in the stomach at the time alcohol is ingested, the emotional outlook of the person at the time he is drinking, previous drinking history, and overall tolerance to the drug. These factors, and others, can alter the absorption rate of alcohol into the system. Still, the level of alcohol in the blood is the final determinant for **assaying** states through **sobriety** into full-fledged drunkenness. As the alcohol level rises, specific physiological and psychological changes can be safely predicted.

Central Thought: As the alcohol level rises, specific physiological and
psychological changes can be safely predicted.

[2]   The formula works this way: One shot of liquor (one and one-half ounces) will place the alcohol concentration in the blood at approximately 0.030 percent, or 0.03 grams of alcohol for every 100cc of blood. These figures are based on an average adult male of about 150 pounds; the concentration would be higher for most women and children, of course. Now, at this level, it is virtually impossible to label anyone as intoxicated. However, the second drink, if taken within an hour of the first, will raise the alcohol in the blood to a little more than 0.05 percent, and we begin to experience alcohol's first plateau: we feel relaxed, more talkative. Our problems don't seem quite as pressing, and the company around us suddenly seems more pleasant, more "fun to be with." We are still not drunk in any legal sense, and our judgment and physical coordination is virtually unimpaired. So far, so good.

a person

Main Idea: A person's gender, body weight and
consumption per hour
impairment is based on from alcohol

[3]   Somewhere between the third and fourth drink, things begin to happen rapidly. With the fourth drink, our alcohol concentration has reached 0.10 percent, or more, and we can at last be classified as legally drunk. The people we are with may still be "fun," but we're not noticing them as much as we did earlier. We are really becoming more **introspective,** although we may be the "life of the party" since our normal **inhibitions** against outrageous or **scatological** conduct have been **repressed.** It is at this point that we make the pass at the cocktail waitress or guffaw too loudly at a dirty joke. Our brain is reacting to the soporific effects of alcohol, and our motor functions are becoming "loose" and uncoordinated. It is at this level that we are a definite hazard on the highway, and most states now consider a blood-alcohol analysis of 0.10 percent as legal evidence for drunkenness.

Main Idea: People whom hav consumed .10
percent of alcohol are considered a hazard
on the road.

[4]   But it's New Year's, or Armistice Day, or the boss-just-fired-me day, or the mother-in-law-is-here-to-stay day, so we have a few more. The sixth drink jumps our alcohol level to between 0.15 and 0.20 percent. At this level, we are almost unrecognizable, both to ourselves and others. If sleep doesn't overtake us, we are likely to undergo violent changes in our mood

and behavior. We may laugh one minute, cry the next. We may pick a fight or take our clothes off on Main Street. We are no longer in control of our actions, and our behavior is completely unpredictable. If we drive in this state, we stand a high chance of killing ourselves and others.

Main Idea: *A person is unpredictable and out of control because of excessive drinking from lot drinks.*

[5]   But let's really tie one on, okay? It's very easy to do. The only requirement is that we stay awake long enough to keep pouring back the hooch. At about the eighth continuous drink, the alcohol level in our blood will rise to somewhere around 0.35 percent. Most of us can't walk at this level, so we had better just stay at the bar, provided we can still get service. Better still, we can check into a hotel with a bottle and there'll be no one to bother us. The company we were with lost their charm a long time ago, and it's better to be by ourselves.

Main Idea: *Drinking too much pushes other people away.*

[6]   Somewhere between the eleventh and thirteenth drink, our alcohol level jumps to 0.50 percent and we suddenly can't drink another drop. Reason: We have passed out. However, if we drink very quickly, we might be able to down two or three more before the curtain descends. By doing this, we can pretty well assure ourselves that we may hit the alcohol bull's eye with a blood concentration of 0.55 to 0.60 percent. At this point, we will die in an acute alcoholic coma, and our little drinking bout comes to a sudden close. *Alcohol level 0.50%*

Main Idea: *Drinking till a person renders themselfe unconscious could result in death*

[7]   We are talking here of facts, not fiction. While tolerance to alcohol, and other factors, may allow one person to drink more than another, the alcohol concentrations mentioned above will produce the effects exactly as described, plus hundreds of others not mentioned. Alcohol is a drug. It cannot be played with without endangering life itself. It can be consumed safely, and that is the whole purpose of sane drinking practices.

Main Idea: *Drink resposibly because alcohol is not a substance that should be abused*

I'm drunk. What do I do now?

[8]   When we become drunk, the only cure is to stop drinking. Coffee will not sober us up. Steam baths will do nothing. Exercise is of no **avail.** Only time can bring us back to a sober state.

[9]   The body's system must oxidize all the alcohol that is ingested. It does this at a rate of approximately .015 percent an hour. The rule of thumb is to allow about one hour of sobering up time for each drink consumed. It takes this long for alcohol to be eliminated within the system. Beyond the one drink an hour limit, alcohol **accumulates** in the bloodstream and only time (and the liver) can remove it. There are no shortcuts.

[10]   There are, however, ways in which the absorption rate can be slowed. The principal method is by food. It is always better to drink with food in the stomach than to drink on an empty stomach. While this will not save us from overindulgence, it will provide some moderate protection against the first couple of drinks. Similarly, sipping a drink over a long period of time will reduce its net effect.

[11]   And that's about it. Anything else we may have heard is probably an old wives' tale. If we drink, alcohol will enter your bloodstream. If we continue to drink, it will accumulate in your bloodstream. That's the pure fact, and anything else is myth. (Halegood)

Central Point: _Alcohol consumption, responsible drinking. Time can only bring you to a sober state_

Visual Literacy Box 4.1

CHARTS: THE ANATOMY OF ALCOHOL

It is important to know how to read charts because a visual display is often easier to understand than a written explanation. It is equally important to be able to create a chart from the details provided in a reading. Practice this skill by making a chart from the article "What Happens When I Drink." The headings and the first row of information have been provided. Find and fill in the missing information.

Number of Drinks	Alcohol Concentration in Blood	Effects on Body
1 drink	0.03	not intoxicated
2 drinks		
4 drinks		

(continued on next page)

Number of Drinks	Alcohol Concentration in Blood	Effects on Body
6 drinks		
8 drinks		
11–13 drinks		
14 + drinks		

Alcohol can be oxidized at a rate of approximately 0.15 percent an hour. The rule of thumb is to allow about one hour of sobering-up time for each drink consumed. These figures are based on an average adult male of about 150 pounds.

5

Patterns of Organization—
Simple Paragraphs

In this chapter, we learn how to

- recognize organizational patterns in writing;
- identify the different patterns;
- recognize and understand mixed patterns.

INTERVIEWER: How do you determine the author's train of thought?

BINIAM: I don't. I just read it and hope I understand it.

JULIE: I read slowly if it's a textbook. I'll read slowly . . . like wordy sentences, because sometimes you read over and over and you don't understand the words, like right away . . . I'll reread them until they sink in.

INTERVIEWER: How do you think your students determine the author's train of thought?

PROFESSOR WILLIAMS: Students look upon reading material as a series of individual items, which should be committed to memory . . . rather than look for larger structures.

What are these larger structures that Professor Williams' students should be looking for? A good author, when he writes, organizes his ideas and information so that others can follow his train of thought and understand what he is saying. When we write essays and papers, we try to do the same thing to make it easier for others to understand our thoughts.

PATTERNS OF ORGANIZATION

The organization of ideas in writing is called the **text pattern.** If you do *not* look for the organizational pattern of the text while you read, some major clues to understanding the author's point will escape you.

The text is the written or printed information and the pattern refers to how the writing is organized or arranged. There are more than 100 different kinds of text patterns but Chapters 5 and 6, however, focus specifically on the most commonly found patterns in college textbooks. In this chapter we cover the following patterns:

- term, definition, and example
- topics with lists
- process
- chronological order (time order)
- narration

Term, Definition, and Example

Before we begin studying a particular subject or discipline, we must first master its basic vocabulary and major concepts. Each subject (business, sociology, psychology, anthropology, political science, biology, philosophy, etc.) has its own. Basic information is presented in textbooks that are usually called "introductory" or "elementary" because they are used in the first (or prerequisite) courses taken in a given field. The following are some examples of introductory course textbooks:

- *Introduction to Business Management*
- *Introduction to Psychology*
- *Introduction to Sociology*
- *Elementary Algebra*
- *Biology: Concepts and Connections*

Freshman textbooks introduce us to the terminology (vocabulary) and concepts used in subjects such as business management, psychology, and so forth. They are organized like dictionaries with examples that explain the terms.

The most common pattern found in freshman texts is called the **term, definition, and example** pattern. First, a new term is introduced. Then, it is highlighted, underlined, *italicized,* or placed in **boldface** print to make it stand out from the other information. Next, this new term is defined somewhere in the same paragraph in which it is introduced. Finally, one or more examples are given to further define and explain the new term or concept.

Let's look at an example from psychology:

The theory of **possible selves** *is the overall focus of what people want their lives to be like in the future.* Based on past experiences, the person develops expectations for either the "hoped-for self" that he could become or the "dreaded self" that he fears of becoming. For example, a college student's "hoped-for self" might be a person on the Dean's List at the end of the semester. His "dreaded self" might be a person on academic probation when classes are over. The student's expectation for becoming either possible self gives him motivation to take action towards a goal that he wants or to avoid actions that would lead to the undesired future.

The term being defined is *possible selves*. It appears in **boldface print**. The definition of *possible selves* is "the overall focus of what people want their lives to be like in the future." The author has placed this definition in italics to help the reader connect the term with the definition. Then, examples are given to help us understand and remember the concept of possible selves: the "hoped-for possible self" (Dean's List) and the "dreaded possible self" (academic probation).

An introductory textbook is laid out in this way so that we can learn the terms related to a particular field of study. These terms *will not* be defined again in upper-level textbooks; the authors assume that we read the introductory text and know the language of the field.

Oftentimes, freshmen try to cut corners by skipping the examples and reading only the terms and definitions. They may even try to memorize the terms and definitions from study sheets and old exams instead of reading the textbook. This "cutting corners" strategy doesn't work very well, and students usually end up failing their exams. Below is an excerpt from an interview with a student who, as a junior in college, was still trying to cut corners in reading.

INSTRUCTOR: Do you read the whole chapter?
GENE: No.
INSTRUCTOR: Then how do you study?
GENE: For my test on Human Biology on Monday, I'll take all my quizzes and all my study sheets that we had to fill out previously before every class and review them and get the past tests in the library and just review; but I'd probably still fail . . .
INSTRUCTOR: Do you go back and read the chapter?
GENE: No.

Gene already knows he will fail the exam using this tactic. But what he doesn't know is why his strategy is not a good one. The "cutting-corners" strategy is ineffective because it eliminates the examples, which are just as important as the terms and definitions. Until we have seen one or several examples illustrating a concept or a term that we can relate to our own experiences, we may not fully understand what a definition means.

Without this extra information, we are just memorizing the term. When the time comes to take the exam, two things happen. Either we don't remember the information because we didn't understand it in the first place, or we don't understand the question because it is worded differently from the words that we memorized.

Signals   As noted earlier, new words that are being defined are normally highlighted, boldfaced, italicized, or underlined. In addition, some authors use signals or transitions to help us determine the definition of a term without us having to refer to a dictionary. **Signals** or **transitions** are clue words such as *is*,

are, is defined as, and means. Punctuation symbols such as dashes, parentheses, and commas can also be used to signal a term that is about to be defined. For example,

```
        term to be defined set in boldface                    definition
                        |                                         |
    The theory of possible selves is the overall focus of what people want their lives to
    ─────────────────────────────        |
    be like in the future.              Signal
```

Reading Between the Lines Box 5.1

SIGNALS IN SCIENCE

In the excerpt below, we know the term being defined is "light-years" because it appears in boldfaced print. Read the following passage from a college-level astronomy textbook and answer the questions that follow.

> We study the universe by studying light from distant stars and galaxies. Light travels extremely fast by earthly standards: The speed of light is 300,000 kilometers per second, a speed at which it would be possible to circle the Earth nearly eight times in just 1 second! Nevertheless, even light takes substantial amounts of time to travel the vast distances in space. For example, light takes about 1 second to travel from the Moon to the Earth.
>
> Light from the stars takes many years to reach us, and distances to the stars are measured in units called **light-years**. One light-year is the distance that light can travel in 1 year, which is about 10 trillion kilometers, or 6 trillion miles. Note that a light-year is a unit of distance, not of time.

Common Misconceptions: Light-Years

> A recent advertisement illustrated a common misconception by claiming, "It will be light-years before anyone builds a better product." This advertisement makes no sense, because light-years are a unit of distance, not a unit of time. If you are unsure whether the term *light-years* is being used correctly, try testing the statement by remembering that 1 light-year is approximately 10 trillion kilometers, or 6 trillion miles. The advertisement then reads, "It will be 6 trillion miles before anyone builds a better product," which clearly does not make sense. (Bennett, Donahue Schneider, and Voit 7)

1. What is the definition of light-years?

2. What signal word helped you to recognize the definition?

3. What example does the author use to explain how the term *light-years* can be misunderstood?

4. In the last paragraph, the author indicates that people often have a common misconception about the term *light-years*. What is sometimes misunderstood about this term?

5. How can you test a statement to determine if *light-years* is being used correctly?

- The theory of **possible selves**—*the overall focus of what people want their lives to be like in the future*—is based on past experiences.
- The theory of possible selves (*the overall focus of what people want their lives to be like in the future*) is based on past experiences.
- The theory of possible selves, *the overall focus of what people want their lives to be like in the future,* is based on past experiences.

The author may also introduce special terms by using phrases like *for example, such as, to illustrate this,* and *for instance:*

- **For example,** a college student's "hoped-for self" might be to become a person on the Dean's List at the end of the semester. His "dreaded self" might be to become a person on academic probation when classes are over.

Once you have read a paragraph and understand the term, definition, and example, you should mark the textbook so that this relationship clearly stands out. Circle the term, underline its definition, and highlight the examples.

> The theory of **possible selves** *is the overall focus on what people want their lives to be like in the future.* Based on past experiences, the person develops expectations for either the "hoped-for self" that he could become or the "dreaded self" that he fears of becoming. For example, a college student's "hoped-for self" might be a person on the Dean's List at the end of the semester. His "dreaded self" might be a person on academic probation when classes are over. The student's expectation for becoming either possible self gives him motivation to take action towards a goal that he wants or to avoid actions that would lead to the undesired future. (Yaworski)

EXERCISE 5-1   Identifying the Term, Definition, and Example

Read the following paragraphs and find the term, definition, and examples. Then circle the term, underline the definition, and highlight the examples. The first one has been done for you.

1. Revolutionaries

A revolutionary is a person who desires to overthrow the existing political order and to replace it with a quite different one, using political violence if necessary. Some revolutionaries, such as Mao Zedong (China), Fidel Castro (Cuba), and Nelson Mandela (South Africa), eventually achieved leadership roles in their political system, after years or even decades of struggle. (Danziger 50)

Term(s): ___Revolutionary_____

Definition(s): <u>a person who desires to overthrow the existing political order</u>

<u>and replace it with quite a different one, using political violence if necessary</u>

Example(s):   Mao Zedong (China), Fidel Castro (Cuba). and Nelson Mandela

(South Africa)

2. Socialization

Socialization is the process by which knowledge, beliefs, and values are taught to members of society. In all societies, the family is the first and most influential source of socialization. Parents teach their children many of the skills and attitudes which will help them fit into society. Of course, the socialization process continues in other ways throughout life, but the socialization received in the family setting is a powerful and basic influence that may be felt for the rest of one's life. (Manis 1)

Term(s): _____

Definition(s): _____

_____

Example(s): <u>Families , Parents ,skills. &</u>

<u>attitudes.</u>

3. Caffeine

Caffeine is the most widely used stimulant in almost all countries in the world. Acting on our central nervous system, it keeps us awake by increasing our heart and breathing rates. Some examples of food that have caffeine in them are coffee, tea, green tea, milk chocolate candy, some colas, and many over-the-counter drugs. Coffee has roughly 50–200 milligrams of caffeine. Tea and colas have 30–60 milligrams, while cocoa, milk chocolate candy, and decaffeinated coffee have much less, 1–15 milligrams. Most of us cannot drink more than one or two cups of coffee with a meal before we become nervous and fidgety. Researchers have found that people who take in more than 600 milligrams of caffeine per day develop stomach problems, depression, and sleeplessness. (Campbell, Mitchell, and Reece 571)

Term(s): _____

Definition(s): _____

_____

Example(s): *Increase heart rate* coffee, tea, green tea, milk chocolate, colas & over the counter drugs

nervous fidgety

4. Nuclear Families

The nuclear family is a family composed of two parents and two children. For example, former president John F. Kennedy had a nuclear family. It consisted of himself, his wife, Jackie, and their children, John Jr. and Caroline. This family structure, however, is changing in composition as well as quality. Divorce has decreased the size of the family by creating single-parent households. Even when families stay together, the increasing cost of living has forced both parents to work, leaving children without much parental supervision or attention. (Bryjak and Soroka 81)

Term(s): _____

Definition(s): _____

_____

Example(s): John F. Kennedy / divorce structure change, single parents

5. Plea Bargaining

A man is charged with murder and he pleads guilty, but he is not punished for murder. Why? Because during a process called plea bargaining, he pleads guilty to robbery, theft, and drunk driving, and is in fact punished only for those crimes. Does this sound fair? Most cases in American courts are settled through this process. The prosecutor and the defendant's lawyer agree that the state will not hold the guilty party accountable for the more serious crime if he pleads guilty to one or more lesser crimes. (Edwards, Wattenberg, and Lineberry 129)

Term(s): _____

Definition(s): _____

_____

Example(s): _____

_____

6. Reference Groups

Peers are people who are in the same age group and hold the same social position as we do. Same-age classmates, neighbors, and co-workers who have the same socioeconomic status or social position would be considered peers. Often times our peers become a part of our reference group—the people we use as a standard to measure our progress. For example, if you went to a social function once a week and your peers only went to social functions once a month, you would feel that you had a good social life. But, if most of your friends and classmates went to social functions every night, then your feelings about your social life would change. (Bryjak and Soroka 81)

Term(s): _____

Definition(s): _____

_____

Example(s): _____

_____

7. Terrorism

Perhaps the most troublesome issue in the national security area is the spread of terrorism—the use of violence to demoralize and frighten a country's population or government. Terrorism takes many forms, including the bombing of buildings (such as the American embassy in Kenya in 1998), the assassinations of political leaders (as when Iraq attempted to kill former president George Bush in 1993), and the kidnappings of diplomats and civilians (as when Iranians took Americans hostage in 1979). (Edwards, Wattenberg, and Lineberry 669)

Term(s): _____

Definition(s): _____

_____

Example(s): _____

_____

8. Weight Control

The best approach to weight control is a combination of exercise and a restricted but balanced diet. As indicated in the table, a balanced diet provides at least 1200 kcal (kilocalories or "Calories" listed on food labels) per day and adequate amounts of all essential nutrients. Such diets meet the Recommended Dietary Allowances (RDAs), minimal standards established by nutritionists for preventing nutrient deficiencies. A restricted, balanced diet, along with regular aerobic exercise, can trim the body gradually and keep extra fat off without harmful side effects. (Campbell, Mitchell, and Reece 443)

Term(s): _____

Definition(s): _____

_____

Example(s): _Recommended Dietary Allowances_
(RDA's)

9. Self-Concept

Your self-concept is your image of who you are. It's how you perceive yourself: your feelings and thoughts about your strengths and weaknesses, your abilities and limitations. Self-concept develops from the image that others have of you; the comparisons between yourself and others, your cultural teachings; and your evaluation of your own thoughts and behaviors.

If you wished to see the way your hair looked, you'd probably look in a mirror. What would you do if you wanted to see how friendly or how assertive you are? According to the concept of the *looking-glass self* (Cooley, 1922), you would look at the image of yourself that others reveal to you through their behaviors and especially through the way they treat you and react to you.

You would look to those who are most significant in your life—to your *significant others*. As a child you would look to your parents and then to your elementary school teachers, for example. As an adult you might look to your friends, romantic partners, or children. If these significant others think highly of you, you will see a positive self-image reflected in their behaviors; if they think little of you, you will see a more negative image. (DeVito 32)

Term(s): _____

Definition(s): _____

_____

Example(s): *Looking glass self, cooley '22*
friends, romantic, partners, parents,
Balanced diet, Percieve yourself.
a bit

10. Types of Classrooms

Teachers and students are grouped in several ways in the elementary school and in one dominant pattern in junior and senior high school. At the elementary school level, the self-contained classroom is the most traditional and prevalent arrangement. In this type of classroom, one teacher teaches all or nearly all subjects to a group of about twenty-five children, with the teacher and students remaining in the same classroom for the entire day. Often art, music, physical education, and computer skills are taught in other parts of the school, so students may leave the classroom for scheduled periods. Individual students may also attend special classes for remedial or advanced instruction, speech therapy, or instrumental music and band lessons.

In open-space schools, students are free to move among various activities and learning centers. Instead of self-contained classrooms, open-space schools have large instructional areas with movable walls and furniture that can be rearranged easily. Grouping for instruction is much more fluid and varied. Students do much of their work independently, with a number of teachers providing individual guidance as needed.

In middle schools and junior and senior high schools, students typically study four or five academic subjects taught by teachers who specialize in them. In this organizational arrangement, called departmentalization, students move from classroom to classroom for their lessons. High school teachers often share their classrooms with other teachers and use their rooms only during scheduled class periods. (Parkay and Stanford 135–36)

Term(s): _____

Definition(s): _____

_____

Example(s): _____

_____

Topic and List

Another common pattern of organization is called the **topic and list** or **simple listing** pattern. You will see this pattern quite often in political science, business law, sociology, and psychology texts. It is the easiest to recognize because oftentimes the items listed are actually numbered or bulleted. The topic sentence tells you to look for a list by using phrases such as:

■ There are many kinds of . . .

■ There are many reasons why . . .

■ A number of factors contributed to . . .

■ Three problems related to the . . .

■ There are various types of . . .

■ Five types of . . . are . . .

Look at the passage below. What is the topic? How many items are in the list? What do all of the items on the list have in common? Keep in mind that certain words act as signals, including first, second, third, next, finally, also, in addition, and moreover. Still more signals come from the structure of the sentence, paragraph, or passage. Commas separate words in a series when the author makes a list within a sentence. Or, the list may be spread throughout the passage, with each item on the list taking its own paragraph. It is not unusual for authors to use combinations of these two techniques.

The Universal Culture Pattern

Six needs, common to people at all times and in all places, form the basis of a "universal culture pattern":

1. *The need to survive.* Men and women must have shelter, clothing, and the means to provide for their offspring's survival.

2. *The need for social organization.* For people to make a living, raise families, and maintain order, a social structure is essential. Views about the relative importance of the group and the individuals within it may vary with any such social structure.

3. *The need for stability and protection.* From earliest times, communities have had to keep peace among their members, defend themselves against external attack, and protect community assets.

4. *The need for knowledge and learning.* Since earliest times, humankind has transmitted knowledge acquired through experience, first orally, then by means of writing systems, and now by electronic means as well. As societies grow more complex, there is increasing need to preserve knowledge and transmit it through education to as many people as possible.

5. *The need for self-expression.* People responded creatively to their environment even before the days when they decorated the walls of Paleolithic caves with paintings of animals they hunted. The art appears to have a lineage as old as human experience.

6. *The need for religious expression.* Equally old is humanity's attempt to answer the "why" of its existence. What early peoples considered supernatural in their environment could often, at a later time, be explained by science in terms of natural phenomena. Yet today, no less than in archaic times, men and women continue to search for answers to the ultimate questions of existence. (Brummett et al. xxix)

The topic is "The Universal Culture Pattern." The first sentence tells us that there are six items on the list. It also tells us about the topic—that all people have the same needs. As we skim through the passage, we can see the author has organized the six items by numbering them and has provided additional information about each item on the list. Now take a look at Reading Between the Lines Box 5.2. As you can see, the simple-listing pattern also applies to the arts.

Reading Between the Lines Box 5.2

SIGNALS IN THE ARTS

Read the excerpt below from a book on acting, and follow the directions beneath it to identify the author's lists and the signals that we use to identify them. The first one has been done for you.

. . . [T]here are certain basic things that all good actors must do.

First, every good actor creates a performance that is entertaining. We can be entertained in many ways: we can enjoy watching a good actor even when this person is making us feel sad, angry, or frightened, because we appreciate the quality of the performance . . . a good actor entertains us by creating a performance that is both *skillful* and *truthful*.

A good actor is also *compelling*; we sometimes say that we "can't take our eyes off" him or her. This doesn't mean that the actor is "showing off" or trying to get our attention in inappropriate ways. What attracts us to some actors are the same things that make us watch star athletes: their effortless skill, their total concentration of the job at hand, their tremendous sense of aliveness.

Good actors also create performances that are *believable*. They make us feel that we can recognize their characters as real human beings within the particular worlds of their stories. Notice that believability doesn't always mean "true to everyday life." Not all stories take place in everyday life; they may be set in a historical period, some other culture, or a fantasy world. It is the world of the story that establishes what is "real." Therefore the actor's performance has to be believable within that world.

Finally, it is not enough for an actor to be entertaining, truthful, compelling, and believable. A truly good performance must also *contribute to the particular story being told*. Every character in a story has been created by the writer to fulfill a certain job within the world of that story. Characters are created for many reasons: they may move the plot forward, provide an obstacle to some other character, provide information, represent some value or idea, provide comic relief, and so on. Whatever the character was created to do, the actor must above all create a

(continued on next page)

(continued from previous page)

performance that successfully fulfills that particular job. This constitutes the character's dramatic function. Fulfilling the *dramatic function* of the role is the most important responsibility of a good actor. (Benedetti 3–4)

1. In the first paragraph, the author lists three media in which actors can perform. What are they?

    a. _____

    What signals did the author use to indicate a list?

    b. _____

2. The author tells us "there are certain basic things that all good actors must do." Make a list of these things along with their signal words.

    a. _____

    b. _____

    c. _____

    d. _____

3. The author lists the reasons for which characters are created. What are they?

    a. _____

    b. What signals did the author use to indicate a list?

    _____

Signals   Since the details in the simple-listing pattern are equally important, they can be listed in any order. If the list is not obvious through numbering, bulleting, and so forth, then as with the term, definition, and example pattern, the reader must look for signals—clue words or clue phrases—to find the list. These clue words and phrases include the following:

first	second	third	next
finally	also	in addition	moreover

Some paragraphs written in this pattern introduce a clue word at the beginning of each sentence. Others may use just one clue word throughout the entire paragraph. Read the paragraph on the next page and look for clues that signal the list pattern.

> There are three elements of a **crime:** the act, the capacity, and the intent. The *act* is a social wrong against the state (federal, state, or district) that can be either civil or criminal. *Capacity* refers to the ability to distinguish between right and wrong and to be able to adhere to that which is right. Finally, *intent* refers to the desire to commit a crime. Intent can also be defined as behavior that is so reckless that it will probably endanger someone else. (Maxwell "Three Elements")

We know we are looking for a list of three items because the first sentence tells us "there are three elements of a crime." We also know from the first sentence that these three elements are the *act,* the *capacity,* and the *intent.* As we read further, we can see that the author uses the remainder of the paragraph to define these items.

The word *finally* is another clue to the topic and list pattern; it signals that "intent" is the last item on the list. In addition to using signal words, the author also uses *italics* to help us recognize the items that are listed.

Once again, mark your textbook after you have identified the organizational pattern of the reading. First <u>underline</u> the topic and then number the list. Take notes from the passage by simply writing down the items that you have marked and by making a topic and a list. Add key words that will help you remember the definitions. Once marked, you will not need to spend time later rereading the passage to recognize the main points. Furthermore, you will be able to see the author's organization at a glance.

> There are <u>three elements of a **crime**</u>: the act, the capacity, and the intent. The [1]<u>act</u> is a social wrong against the state (federal, state, or district) that can be either civil or criminal. [2]<u>Capacity</u> refers to the ability to distinguish between right and wrong and to be able to adhere to that which is right. Finally, [3]<u>intent</u> refers to the desire to commit a crime. Intent can also be defined as behavior that is so reckless that it will probably endanger someone else.

Topic: Three elements of a crime

1. act (civil or criminal)
2. capacity (right and wrong)
3. intent (desire or reckless behavior)

EXERCISE 5-2	**Identifying the Topic and List**

Following the examples above, find the topic and list in each of the following paragraphs below. Annotate each paragraph and take notes. The first paragraph has been done for you.

1. Controlling Fertility

Population growth in developing nations is the result of rapidly declining mortality (death) in the years after World War II. The three ways in which this growth can be slowed are to decrease fertility, increase mortality, or employ some combination of these. Since increasing mortality is not realistic for a number of moral, religious, and practical reasons, the second and third alternatives can be dismissed. This leaves us with controlling fertility as the only acceptable way of reducing the rate of population increase. (Bryjak and Soroka 294)

Signal Words: three ways; second; third

Topic: Fertility control

List:

1. decrease fertility

2. increase mortality

3. employ some combination of decreasing fertility and increasing mortality

2. Street Gangs

Street gangs are numerous in large cities, especially New York City, Los Angeles, and Philadelphia. Chicago alone is reputed to have as many as 100,000 gang members (Painter and Weisel, 1997). Malcolm Klein (in "Gangs in the Heartland," 1997) estimates that whereas 100 cities and towns had active gangs in 1970, that number had climbed to almost 800 locales in the mid-1990s. The rapid proliferation (increase) of gangs is a function of family members of gangs relocating, the emergence (arrival) of local gangs, and members of "supergangs" attempting to extend their territory. (Bryjak and Soroka 182)

Signal Words: _____

Topic: Street gangs.

List:

1. _____

2. _____

3. _____

3. Understanding Power Plays

Power is often used unfairly in conversations at home and at the office. Here are three examples of the unfair use of power—called power plays, consistent patterns of behavior designed to control another person (Steiner, 1981).

In **Nobody Upstairs,** the person refuses to acknowledge your request. Sometimes the "nobody upstairs" player ignores socially and commonly accepted (but spoken) rules such as not opening your mail or not going through your computer files. The power play takes the form of expressing ignorance of the rules: "I didn't know we weren't supposed to have access to each other's E-mail accounts."

In **You Owe Me,** a person, often a friend or co-worker, does something nice for you but then asks for something in return: "But, I lent you money when you needed it."

In **Thought Stoppers,** someone literally stops you from thinking and expressing your thoughts. The interruption is probably the most common thought-stopper. Before you can finish expressing your thought, the other person interrupts and either completes it or goes off on another topic. Other thought-stoppers include using profanity and raising one's voice to drown you out. (DeVito 159)

Signal Words: _____

Topic: _____

List:

1. _____

2. _____

3. _____

4. Fad Diets

Fad diets almost never work. In the beginning weight is lost quickly. However, once the diet ends, most people return to their usual eating patterns and regain the weight they just lost. Along with not working very well, fad diets can also do harm to the body.

- **Low-carbohydrate diets,** or diets with less than 100g of carbohydrates per day, may cause muscle loss, fatigue, and headaches.

- **Low-fat diets** are those with less than 20% of the kilocalories coming from fat. On this diet, a person does not eat animal protein, fats, nuts, or seeds. This diet may cause irregular menstrual cycles in women. It may also decrease the body's ability to absorb fat-soluble vitamins such as vitamin A and vitamin D.

- **Formula diets** are commercial diets that are prepackaged. These are harmful because they are very low in kilocalories. Eating fewer than 1200 calories per day can cause body protein loss, hair loss, dry skin, constipation, and salt imbalance.
- **Balanced diets of 1200kcal or more** can provide a safe way to lose weight if they include all nutrient needs. Dieters can expect to lose 1–2 pounds per week on this routine. (Campbell, Mitchell, and Reece 443)

Signal Words: _Low carb, Low fat, formula, Balanced_

Topic: _Fad diets - almost never work_

List:

1. _weight lose quickly_

2. _go back to reg. eat habits_

3. _harm body_

5. Wealth

How do you become rich? We often think of doctors and lawyers as being rich and plumbers and secretaries as being poor because the doctors and lawyers make more money. However, if you make a lot of money and spend it all, or spend more than you make on a credit card, you cannot get rich, you will just live high. Wealth is the money that you keep, not how much money you spend. Those who become wealthy do so through hard work, sacrifice, self-discipline, planning, and determination. Hardly ever does someone become rich simply by being intelligent, getting a Ph.D., or having money given to them. Seven things wealthy people have in common are:

1. They learn to live on less money than they make.
2. They spend their time, energy, and money in ways that will help them make more money.
3. They believe it is better to save money and look like an average person than to spend money and look rich.
4. Their parents did not continue giving them money after they became adults.
5. Their own children are able to support themselves.
6. They are good at finding opportunities in the stock market.
7. They chose the right occupation. (Stanley and Danko 3–4)

Signal Words: _____

Topic: _____

List:

1. _____

2. _____

3. _____

Process

Another text pattern found in introductory course textbooks and in much of our everyday print is called the **process pattern**. Authors use this pattern to describe the steps in a process. It is used in almost every type of textbook, from biology to computer science.

The process pattern looks a lot like our topic and list pattern. Even when we take notes, we write the steps of a process in a list. However, the difference between the two patterns is that the steps in the listing pattern can be written in any order. The steps in the process pattern, however, must follow a specific order.

We see this pattern in recipes, directions, and instructions. This writing pattern allows an author to explain the step-by-step procedure for processes such as:

- building a Web site
- changing a flat tire
- making a bill into a law
- cloning an embryo
- introducing a guest speaker
- taking notes from a lecture

The steps in most processes must be followed in a specific order or the process will not work. For example, to put a new tire on your car, you have to take the old tire off first. Or, you cannot bake an apple pie until you have made the crust and cut up the apples.

Signals To help us identify the steps in a process pattern, authors usually list the steps in the order they should occur. They may also number, letter, or bullet them. In addition to carefully arranging the steps in a specific order, authors often provide signal words to help us locate the steps. You'll note that some of these clues are the same as those used to signal a topic with a list.

The first step is	Second	Third	Next
During the next step	At this point	Then	Now
Once that is finished	After that	Once	Finally

Look at the paragraph below. Can you identify the signals the author uses to help us locate the steps in the process?

To make a submarine sandwich, you must *first* cut an Italian roll in half and toast it in the oven. *Once* it is toasted, spread mayonnaise on the roll. *Then*, place ham, salami, and pepperoni onto the roll as the first layer. *Next*, place a layer of provolone cheese on top of the meat. *After this*, put shredded lettuce, tomatoes, and onion on top of the cheese. Top this off with some hot peppers and olive oil mixed with spices. Fold the sandwich together, and place it in the oven for two minutes to melt the cheese. *Finally*, take your sandwich out of the oven, cut it in half, and enjoy!

Would you buy a submarine sandwich if any of the above steps in the process were left out? You would probably say something to the cook if the ham, salami, and pepperoni were left out. Would you be pleased if the lettuce were on the bottom with the meat on the top? What if the mayonnaise were spread on the meat instead of the roll?

EXERCISE 5-3	**Identifying the Process**

Read the following paragraphs. For each, find the topic, and write it on the space provided. Then identify the process and record the steps in the correct order below each passage. The first one has been done for you.

1. The Art of Cloning

Robert Lanza, Michael West, and Jose Cibelli are working on human therapeutic cloning. This procedure is hoped to replace any worn out or diseased cells in a patient's body. In other words, it will provide a patient with a fresh supply of cells that has his genetic code by using cloning to reproduce his own cells. Lanza, West, and Cibelli are hoping this process will eventually eliminate diseases such as Parkinson's, Alzheimer's, cancer, heart disease, and diabetes.

While working at a small biotech company in Massachusetts called Advanced Cell Technology, these scientists were the first to clone a human embryo. The process goes like this: (1) Remove the DNA from several human eggs. (2) Replace them with DNA from a body cell. (3) Trick the eggs into thinking they have been fertilized so they will begin multiplying. (4) Gather the stem cells. (5) Make the stem cells specialize. (Fischer 57)

Process: cloning a human embryo _____

Steps in the Process:

1. Remove the DNA from several human eggs. _____

2. Replace them with DNA from a body cell. _____

3. Trick the eggs into thinking they have been fertilized so they will begin

   multiplying. _____

4. Gather the stem cells. _____

5. Make the stem cells specialize. _____

2. **Criminal Procedure** *[Main Idea]* *[Topic]*

There are nine elements in our court system's criminal procedure. First, a crime is committed. Second, the suspect is arrested if there is evidence of probable cause. Third, the police tell the suspect that he has the right to remain silent. Next, the suspect is turned over to either a grand jury or a public prosecutor for a trial. Then, the suspect is asked to answer to the court. He must decide whether to plead guilty, not guilty, or "No Contest." When he pleads "No Contest," he is not admitting to guilt, but he is not saying that he is innocent either. During the next step in the criminal procedure, the judge decides whether or not to allow the suspect to be released on bail. After that, either a trial will occur or it will be avoided through plea-bargaining. Finally, a verdict is given. If the person is sentenced, he may then appeal the decision. (Maxwell)

[handwritten margin note: Identify topic Main idea Signal words.]

Process: *steps in the criminal pocedure*

Steps in the Process:

1. *crime committed*
2. *arrested if probable cause.*
3. *rights are read.*
4. *assigned a prosecutor/trial*
5. *makes his plea*
6. *bail or no bail*
7. *trail or plea Bargan*
8. *verdict*
9. *may be appealed.*

3. Creating a Presentation

PowerPoint is fun to learn and easy to use. Each slide will help you organize your thoughts by providing a place to insert your main points and supporting information. Before you start, make an outline of your presentation. Then, go to your computer and choose "Start," "Programs," "PowerPoint," "AutoContent Wizard," and "Next." After that, choose "Recommending a Strategy," "Presentation," "Next," "On-Screen," and "Next." Now, enter the title of your presentation in the first box and then enter your name in the second box. Choose "Finish."

You should now be in the mode to create your presentation. First, replace the generic information with the information from your outline. Then, choose "Format" and "Apply Design." A list of backgrounds will appear. Next, choose a background for your presentation and click on "Apply." Finally, look at the bottom left-hand corner to preview your presentation. There are five modes from which to view your presentation. The first view puts you in the edit mode. The second view provides an outline of your presentation. The third view shows a miniature layout of all the slides in your presentation. The fourth view provides a place to take notes underneath each slide. The last view gives you a slide show of your presentation. (Yaworski 14–21)

Process: _____

Steps in the Process:

1. _____

2. _____

3. _____

4. _____

5. _____

6. _____

7. _____

8. _____

9. _____

10. _____

4. Thanking a Guest Speaker

We often have guest speakers in class, at work, and at club functions. Whatever the situation, it is extremely important to let the guest know that his or her message was heard and that it was appreciated, especially if you would like the speaker to return at a later date. Below are some tips to help you make your best impression and feel confident when in this situation. First, listen very carefully to the speaker's presentation and take notes on his main points. Then, write down two or three things that you found interesting about the talk. After the speaker has finished his presentation, stand up, face the speaker, and thank him or her for taking the time to speak at the function. Then, tell the speaker that he or she has given the audience valuable information and specifically mention two or three interesting points the speaker has made (these are the items that you took notes on). Next, say something such as "I am sure we will all find this information very useful as we continue with our studies at this university (as we continue our work at corporation X). Finally, turn to your audience and say something like "Please help me in thanking our guest speaker, Mr. Y, for taking time out of his busy schedule to give us this information." Finally, lead the audience in clapping for the guest speaker.

Process: _____

Steps in the Process:

1. _____

2. _____

3. _____

4. _____

5. _____

6. _____

7. _____

8. _____

5. Sending an E-mail Attachment

In order to send an e-mail attachment, first place your file on the desktop. Then open your Netscape mail. Next, choose "New Message" and type in the e-mail address of the recipient (person you are sending the attachment to).

Then, from the second menu bar, choose "Attach." After that, drag the cursor down and choose "File." A new box will appear asking you to enter the file you would like to attach. At this point, choose "Desktop" and click on this file. Then, choose "Open." And, finally, choose "Send." Your attachment should be in the mail!

Process: _____

Steps in the Process:

1. _____

2. _____

3. _____

4. _____

5. _____

6. _____

7. _____

8. _____

Earlier, we discussed how patterns of organization in a text are sometimes easier to recognize when visually displayed; this is especially the case in computer science books, whose text patterns are very process-oriented. To see a visual display of the steps in creating a Web Site, go to Visual Literacy Box 5.1 on page 175.

Chronological Patterns

When events need to be introduced in the order in which they occurred, this pattern is known as **chronological order,** or **time order.** This pattern is especially common in history texts where events are documented in the order in which they occurred. It can also be found in most other textbooks when the history or background of a topic is being presented. In addition to documenting time, authors use this pattern when they provide situations as examples to explain new concepts. For instance, business law textbooks present story like situations called *cases* that wouldn't make sense if the events were not arranged in the order in which they happened. Authors of sociology and psychology textbooks generally use time order patterns to show trends or the changes that take place over a period of time. Look at the example on page 176. What trend does this information show?

STEPS IN CREATING A WEB SITE USING NETSCAPE

The process pattern is especially important when reading textbooks on computer science. Signal words help us to follow an author's directions or sequence. Choose signal words from the list below that would make sense of each stage of creating a Web Site and place them in the boxes:

| first of all | second | now | once that is finished | finally |
| during the next step | at this point | then | after that | third |

Open a blank page
(1) Open Netscape Navigator
    File
       New
          Blank page
Type information into page just as you would into a word processor page in Netscape.

(7) **Send it to the server**

(2) **Choose a background**
    Format
       Page colors and Properties
       Choose colors for:
          Normal text
          Link text
          Active link text
          Followed link text
          Background

(6) **Link email address**
    Highlight word that will link to file
       Click on "Link" button on the
       Composition Toolbar
          In the box to the right of
          the words "Link to a
          page location or file,"
          type:
    mail to "Your email address"
          Click on OK
          Save

(3) **Link files**
    Highlight a word that will link to file
       Click on "Link" button on the
       Composition Toolbar
          Click on "Choose File"
          Desktop
          Click on File to be linked
          Open
          OK
          Save

(5) **Link images**
    Place mouse pointer on image
       Right click and drag down to
       "Save Image As"
          Save in: Desktop
          Save
          Follow directions for
          linking to files

(4) **Link Internet web pages**
    Highlight word that will link to file
       Click on "Link" button on the
       Composition Toolbar
          Type URL in the box to the right of
          the words "Link to a page location
          or file"
          Click on OK
          Save

Divorce and Children

Divorce affects not only the men and women who terminate their marriages, but hundreds of thousands of children as well. Since 1900, approximately 25 to 30 percent of all children in the United States have experienced divorce, and by the 1980s, 40 to 50 percent were so affected. Of the almost one million children who have witnessed their parents divorce annually over the past few years, almost 50 percent are between 2.5 and 6 years of age. (Bryjak and Soroka 202)

We can see from the order in which the details were given that there has been a steady increase in divorce since the year 1900. This information becomes clearer when we lay it out on a time line.

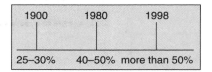

So, far we have looked at time order as being *linear,* where the events occur one after another and can be diagrammed in a straight line, as our time line above. But time order can also be *cyclical* where the events occur in cycles and can be diagrammed in a circle because the last event leads into the first. Study the following paragraph and the diagram beneath it. At what point does the cycle end?

The heat from the sun causes the water from an ocean to evaporate. As this water vapor enters the atmosphere, it clings to small particles such as salt from the sea spray and begins to condense (form water droplets) to form clouds. The water droplets join together to form larger droplets and eventually fall from the sky back into the ocean as rain. The process begins again as the heat from the sun causes water to evaporate.

As we can see from reading the above paragraph, the cycle never ends. We can diagram such a cycle by using a circle instead of a straight line, marking points on the circle to show the order of the events and their repetitive nature.

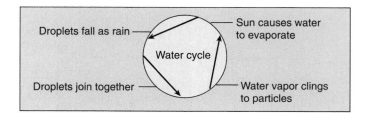

Signals.   Clue words that signal time order patterns include:

since	first	next	then
after	during	later	finally
previously	prior to	follow a cycle	at the beginning of the cycle

Visual Literacy Box 5.2 ● ● ● ● ● ● ● ● ● ● ● ● ● ● ●

PIE CHARTS: THE DIVORCE RATE

A pie chart shows the entire amount of something. Like a pie, it is sliced into pieces that represent parts of the whole; it represents fractions and percentages of the entire amount. Below is a pie chart that represents the living arrangements of children under age 18 in 1998. We can see that out of all the children in the United States the largest number of children (68.1%) were living with two parents. The next largest part shows us that 23.3% of the children were living with only their mother, while 4.4% were living only with their father. The smallest piece of the pie shows that 4.2% were not living with either parent. Label the pie chart for the year 1970 using the following statistics: Two parents—85.2%; Mother only—10.8%; Father only—1.1%; Neither parent—2.9%. Compare the two charts. What changes can you see since 1970?

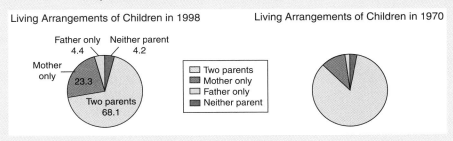

Living Arrangements of Children in 1998   Living Arrangements of Children in 1970

Father only — 4.4   Neither parent — 4.2
Mother only — 23.3
Two parents — 68.1

☐ Two parents
■ Mother only
☐ Father only
■ Neither parent

EXERCISE
5-4

Identifying the Topic

Read each paragraph below and identify the topic. Next, list the events or stages along with the period of time in which they occurred. Then, draw a time line to show the relationship between the time periods and the events. The first one has been done for you.

1. According to Piaget, there are four stages of cognitive development. The sensorimotor stage occurs from birth to age two. During this stage, infants use their eyes, ears, and hands to learn about the world. The preoperational stage takes place when the child is from two to seven years old. During this time, children develop their ability for language and symbolic thinking. From ages seven to eleven, children go through the concrete operational phase, in which their reasoning becomes more logical and they are able to organize thought into categories and subcategories. The formal operational stage begins at age eleven and continues throughout adulthood. At this point, adolescents begin to refine their ability to think in abstract terms. (Berk 21)

write topic list events in order #3 #5

Topic: Stages of cognitive development

Events:

1. sensorimotor stage—birth to age two

2. preoperational stage—two to seven years old

3. concrete operational phase—ages seven to eleven

4. formal operational stage—age eleven throughout adulthood

TIME LINE:

2. By about 1650, approximately 500 million people inhabited the world. Between 1650 and 1850, the population doubled to 1 billion; it doubled again to 2 billion between 1850 and 1930, and doubled still again by 1975 to more than 4 billion. In 1998, the population numbered about 5.9 billion people. At the current rate of increase, it takes less than three years for world population to add the equivalent of another United States (about 270 million). If the present growth persists, scientists estimate that there will be about 8 billion people on Earth by the year 2025. (Campbell, Mitchell, and Reece 708)

Topic: _____

Events:

1. _____

2. _____

3. _____

4. _____

5. _____

6. _____

TIME LINE:

3. The crack-cocaine epidemic that began in the mid-1980s and started to wane in the early to mid-1990s is but the latest drug crisis to occur in the United States. These epidemics follow a cycle of predictable events that play themselves out over a number of years. The recent "crack crisis," therefore, is similar to an earlier cocaine era that began in the 1880s and the marijuana-hallucinogen years of the 1960s.

In the initial phase of the cycle, one or more drugs are "discovered" and considered harmless (if not beneficial) by responsible people. In the absence of proof to the contrary from medical experts, the drugs are generally accepted and used by a significant portion of the population. As a result of deaths and a rising crime rate, health officials re-evaluate the harmful effect of drugs. The weight of changing public opinion and accumulated scientific evidence begins to stem the use of drugs. At this point in the cycle, people start to associate drug use with the lower classes as well as racial and ethnic minorities, regardless of the truth of this association. (Bryjak and Soroka 185)

Topic: _____

Events:

1. _____

2. _____

3. _____

4. _____

5. _____

6. _____

TIME LINE:

4. The modernization of many Asian nations can be traced to the end of World War II, when Japan lay in ruins, partially as a result of the destruction of Tokyo, Hiroshima, and Nagasaki (the latter two cities being leveled by atomic bombs). The country was in shambles and its economy was virtually nonexistent. In the late 1940s and early 1950s, the Japanese produced a variety of inexpensive items (plastic toys, cheap tools, kitchen utensils, etc.) of such poor quality that the phrase "Made in Japan" was synonymous with junk (synonymous means the same as). However, the country's businessmen quickly realized that if they were to be successful in the global marketplace, they would have to improve the reliability and durability of their products dramatically. And improve they did. Optical equipment and cameras soon rivaled those made in Switzerland and Germany, and the "Japanese miracle" was underway. Automobiles and electronic equipment rolled off assembly lines and were shipped around the world. . . . By 1990, Japan's economy was the second largest in the world. (Bryjak and Soroka 250–51)

Topic: _____

Events:

1. _____

2. _____

3. _____

4. _____

5. _____

TIME LINE:

5. Bill Gates and Paul Allen met in 1967 at an elite private school. That year their school acquired a digital training terminal that was connected by

phone to a mainframe computer. The boys' lives revolved around the computer. Gates taught himself how to write programs and began to design computerized machines to count and analyze data. In 1975, while attending Harvard, Gates and Allen told the president of MITS, a company that manufactured an early desktop computer, that they had written software for this computer. Although Gates and Allen had not invented the program yet, they agreed to bring it to MITS within two months. Meeting the deadline within hours, Gates and Allen stunned company executives with the first program capable of typing letters and computing numbers.

Gates dropped out of Harvard to start a new company with Allen. They named their company Microsoft. In 1980, IBM asked Gates to write the operating software for its new personal computer. IBM did not want other computer companies to copy its design. However, Gates persuaded IBM to make its specifications public, arguing that it would make IBM the leader in manufacturing printers, monitors, keyboards, and applications. This also meant that Gates's software MS-DOS (Microsoft–Disk Operating System) would run on every personal computer, thus allowing Gates to "monopolize the market for PC operating software." "Microsoft's sales jumped from $7.5 million in 1980 to $140 in 1985 and by 1991, Gates was the wealthiest man in the world." (909) (Garraty and Carnes 908–09)

Topic: _____

Events:

1. _____

2. _____

3. _____

4. _____

5. _____

TIME LINE:

MIXED PATTERNS

In more complex writings, an author may use several textbook patterns on the same page or even in the same paragraph. Because introductory college textbooks introduce a great many new words, the term, definition, and example pattern is commonly found within all of the other patterns. A new term may be introduced (highlighted, underlined, *italicized*, or placed in **boldface** print) within a numbered or bulleted list of items, or it may be introduced within one of the steps in a process pattern.

A list of items may be found within a process pattern. Let's say that we are reading the directions for baking a cake. We are following a step-by-step process that must follow a specific order, but within this process we find a list of ingredients. The ingredients may even be listed in two or more different groups, as in wet ingredients (water, milk, vanilla) and dry ingredients (flour, oatmeal, sugar).

Authors may define words, list important points, and explain procedures within a selection that introduces events in the order they occur. Thus, there is no limit to the combinations of patterns that authors may use in their textbooks. The following exercise tests your ability to recognize the pattern when combinations of definition, time order, process, and simple listing are used in textbooks.

| EXERCISE 5-5 | **Identifying Paragraph Patterns** |

#2-5
Identify

Read the paragraphs below and decide which paragraph pattern applies. Choose from the following patterns: (a) term, definition, and example, (b) topic with a list, (c) process, (d) chronological order, and (e) narration. The first one is done for you.

___d___ 1. In 1950, New York City was the world's only megacity. By 2000, 12 of the 15 cities with 10 million plus residents were located in the developing world. The United Nations estimates that of 26 megacities in the year 2015, only 4 will be in the rich nations. Eighteen of these giants will be Asian cities, including 2 in Japan. (Bryjak and Soroka 322)

_____ 2. Have you ever become so interested in working on a task that you became unaware of everything around you? In the field of acting, the ability to become so completely focused on your role that you forget others are watching is called **public solitude.** For example, when an Olympic athlete performs in front of millions of people as though he were practicing in private, he is in the state of public solitude. He has become unaware that people are watching because he has forgotten that he is in public. (Benedetti 25)

_____ **3.** Cities in the developing world face many problems. One problem is the shortage of housing. Another problem that city dwellers face is high rates of unemployment. Water and noise pollution are also common problems. In addition to pollution, there are often water, food, and power shortages. Along with these obstacles, developing countries rarely have enough schools and hospitals. (Bryjak and Soroka 322)

_____ **4.** Elton Mayo was a Harvard University professor of business who is credited with discovering the Hawthorne effect, the (now generally recognized) fact that work productivity increases when workers are given attention as human beings. Mayo and his team of researchers drew this conclusion while conducting a series of experiments at Western Electric Company's Hawthorne plant near Chicago, Illinois. Prior to Mayo's arrival, Western Electric had been attempting to determine the best lighting levels for optimum performance in their plant. Management was perplexed. They couldn't figure out why productivity increased whether the lighting was increased, decreased, or remained constant. So they invited Mayo and his Harvard colleagues to investigate the matter further. After conducting a number of experiments on their own, Mayo and his research drew a surprising conclusion: the workers were more productive because of the attention they were receiving from the researchers. Mayo was the first to discover that human factors are related to work behavior. (Barker and Gaut 174)

_____ **5.** You can make vocabulary flash cards to study terms for any subject. First, make a list of all of the terms you would like to learn. Write your first term or vocabulary word on one side of a note card. Next, write its definition on the back of the same note card. Also, write an example of the definition on the back of the note card. Finally, repeat this process for all of the terms you need to study.

A Reading in Psychology

Have you ever lived in an area that was torn apart by war? Read the following selection to find out what it is like for children to grow up in areas of the world that are involved in military conflict. First complete the vocabulary exercise to familiarize yourself with the new terms. After reading the selection, follow the directions to answer the comprehension questions.

Vocabulary in Context

   a. chronic—continuing, constant

   b. impaired—worsened

   c. pessimistic—negative; gloomy, distrustful

   d. maladjusted—not well-adjusted; disturbed; unstable

   e. cohesive—unified; connected

Use the terms above to complete the following statements. The first one has been done for you.

    _____b_____ **1.** Children's psychological function can be seriously
           _____ when they lose parents to war and continue to live in frightening circumstances.

    _____ **2.** The closer children are to wartime activities, the greater their chances are of becoming _____.

    _____ **3.** When children are constantly surrounded by war and have nothing but terrifying memories of violence, they begin to hold a _____ view of the world.

    _____ **4.** International organizations must step in and help because the neverending danger and _____ conditions of lasting war take their toll on the children.

    _____ **5.** Organizations such as the United Nations must encourage nations to build _____ communities instead of communities where hatred turns into civil war.

Children of War

[1]   On May 27, 1992, Zlata Filipovic, a 10-year-old Bosnian girl, recorded the following reactions to the intensifying Serb attack on the city of Sarajevo in her diary:

> SLAUGHTER! MASSACRE! HORROR! CRIME! BLOOD! SCREAMS! TEARS! DESPAIR!
>
> That's what Vaso Miskin Street looks like today. Two shells exploded in the street and one in the market. Mommy was nearby at the time . . . Daddy and I were beside ourselves because she hadn't come home. I saw some of it on TV but I still can't believe what I actually saw . . . I've got a lump in my throat and a knot in my tummy. HORRIBLE. They're taking the wounded to the hospital. It's a madhouse. We kept going to the window hoping to see Mommy, but she wasn't back . . . Daddy and I were tearing our hair out . . . I looked out the window one more time and . . . I SAW MOMMY RUNNING ACROSS THE BRIDGE. As she came into the house she started shaking and crying. Through her tears she told us how she had seen dismembered bodies . . . Thank God, Mommy is with us, Thank God. (Filipovic, 1994, p. 55).

[2]   Violence stemming from ethnic and political tensions is increasingly being felt around the world. Today, nearly all armed conflicts are internal civil wars in which well-established ways of life are threatened or destroyed and children are frequently victims (Mays et al., 1998).

[3]   Children's experiences under conditions of armed conflict are diverse. Some may participate in the fighting, either because they are forced or because they want to please adults. Others are kidnapped, terrorized, or tortured. Those who are bystanders often come under direct fire and may be killed or physically maimed for life. And as Zlata's diary entry illustrates, many children of war watch in horror as family members, friends, and neighbors flee, are wounded, or die (Ladd & Cairns, 1996).

[4]   When war and social crises are temporary, most children are comforted by caregivers' reassuring messages and do not show long-term emotional difficulties. But **chronic** danger requires children to make substantial adjustments, and their psychological functioning can be seriously **impaired.** Many children of war lose their sense of safety, become desensitized to violence, are haunted by terrifying memories, become suspicious of others, and build a **pessimistic** view of the future (Cairns, 1996).

[5]   The extent to which children are negatively affected by war depends on other factors. Closeness to wartime events increases the chances of

maladjustment. For example, an estimated 50 percent of traumatized 6- to 12-year-old Cambodian war refugees continued to show intense stress reactions when they reached young adulthood (Kinzie et al., 1998). The support and affection of parents is the best safeguard against lasting problems. Unfortunately, many children of war are separated from family members. Sometimes, the child's community can offer protection. For example, Israeli children who lost a parent in battle fared best when they lived in kibbutzim, **cohesive** agricultural settlements where many adults knew the child well and felt responsible for his or her welfare (Lifschitz et al., 1977).

[6]   When wartime drains families and communities of resources, international organizations must step in and help children. Until we know how to prevent war, efforts to preserve children's physical, psychological, and educational well-being may be the best way to stop transmission of violence to the next generation in many parts of the world. (Berk 340)

Comprehension:

Choose the letter of the correct answer and write it in the blank provided. The following questions pertain to all of the skills that you have learned so far. The first one has been done for you.

_____b_____ 1. The topic of this passage is:
    a. today's civil wars.
    b. the psychological effects of war on children.
    c. a family's escape from civil war.

_____ 2. The main point of this selection is:
    a. Children's experiences under conditions of armed conflict are diverse.
    b. Nearly all armed conflicts stem from internal civil wars.
    c. When children of war are separated from family members and live in chronic danger, they experience serious psychological trauma.

_____ 3. Which of the following text patterns is used in paragraph 1?
    a. term, definition, and example
    b. narration
    c. process

_____ 4. The text pattern used in paragraph 3 is:
    a. topic with a list.
    b. term, definition, and example.
    c. chronological order.

_____ 5. The text pattern used in the last sentence of paragraph 4 is:
    a. topic with a list.
    b. term, definition, and example.
    c. chronological order.

A Reading in Interpersonal Communications

We all know what we think about others, but what do you think about yourself? Read the selection below to learn about self-esteem and how we can create positive thoughts about ourselves. First complete the vocabulary exercise to become familiar with the new terms. After reading the selection, complete the comprehension exercises that follow it.

Vocabulary in Context

a. interpersonal—between two or more people

b. illogical—not logical; does not make sense based on logic

c. impels—strongly encourages; forces forward

d. imperfections—things that are not perfect

e. internalized—when we consciously or subconsiously use outside information as guidelines for making decisions

Use the terms above to complete these statements. The first one has been done for you.

_____b_____ 1. If we do not identify beliefs that are _____, they will cause us to make self-defeating decisions because they are not based on logic.

_____ 2. If we expect everything to be perfect, we will find it difficult to deal with the daily _____ in our lives.

_____ 3. The level of our self-esteem affects all of our _____ relationships and our motivation to succeed at given tasks.

_____ 4. If we have subconsciously _____ any self-destructive beliefs, we may not be aware that our decisions are based on negative thoughts.

_____ 5. Unrealistically high expectations to achieve _____ some students to try to obtain perfect scores on every exam.

Creating Positive Self-Esteem

[1]   How much do you like yourself? How valuable a person do you think you are? How competent do you think you are? The answers to these questions reflect your self-esteem, the value you place on yourself. People who have high self-esteem, for example, are going to communicate this throughout

Read
2-10
Identify pattern

their verbal and nonverbal messages. The ways they phrase their ideas and questions or the way they hold their head and maintain eye contact are likely to differ greatly from the way the person with low self-esteem would communicate. Similarly, people with different views of themselves will develop and maintain relationships with friends, lovers, and family differently. As you read this unit, think about your own relationships and how the way you see yourself influences them.

[2]   Self-esteem is very important because success breeds success. When you feel good about yourself—about who you are and what you are capable of doing—you will perform better. When you think like a success, you are more likely to act like a success. When you think you're a failure, you're more likely to act like a failure. Increasing self-esteem will, therefore, help you to function more effectively in school, in **interpersonal** relationships, and in careers. Here are a few suggestions for increasing self-esteem.

Attack Your Self-Destructive Beliefs

[3]   Self-destructive beliefs are those that damage your self-esteem and prevent you from building meaningful and productive relationships. They may be about yourself ("I'm not creative"; "I'm boring"), your world ("The world is an unhappy place"; "People are out to get me"), and your relationships ("All the good people are already in relationships"; "If I ever fall in love, I know I'll be hurt"). Identifying these beliefs will help you to examine them critically and to see that they are both **illogical** and self-defeating.

[4]   Another way of looking at self-destructive beliefs is to identify what Pamela Butler (1981) calls "drivers"—unrealistic beliefs that may motivate you to act in ways that are self-defeating. For example, the drive to be perfect **impels** you to try to perform at unrealistically high levels in just about everything you do. Whether it is directed toward work, school, athletics, or appearance, this drive tells you that anything short of perfection is unacceptable and that you are to blame for any **imperfections.** The drive to be strong tells you that weakness and any of the more vulnerable emotions, such as sadness, compassion, loneliness, are wrong. Instead of helping you become successful, these drivers almost ensure your failure. Are you motivated by these unrealistic drivers?

[5]   Recognizing that you may have **internalized** self-destructive beliefs is a first step toward eliminating them. A second step involves recognizing that these beliefs are unrealistic and self-defeating. Psychotherapist Albert Ellis *(1988; Ellis and Harper 1975)* and other cognitive therapists *(Beck 1988)* would argue that you can accomplish this by understanding why these beliefs are unrealistic and substituting more realistic ones. For example, following Ellis, you might try replacing an unrealistic desire to please everyone in everything you do with a more realistic belief that it would be nice if others were pleased with you but it certainly is not essential. A third step is giving yourself permission to fail, to be less than perfect, to be normal.

[6]   Do recognize that it is the unrealistic nature of these drivers that creates problems. Certainly, trying hard and being strong are not unhealthy when they are realistic. It is only when they become absolute—when you try to be everything to everyone—that they become impossible to achieve, and create problems.

Engage in Self-Affirmation

[7]   Remind yourself of your successes. There are enough people around who will remind you of your failures. Focus, too, on your good acts, your good deeds. Focus on your positive qualities, your strengths, your virtues. Focus on the good relationships you have with friends and relatives.

[8]   The way you talk to yourself about yourself influences what you think of yourself. If you talk positively about yourself, you will come to feel more positive about yourself. If you tell yourself that you are a success, that others like you, that you will succeed on the next test, and that you will be welcomed when asking [someone] for a date, you will soon come to feel positive about yourself.

Seek Out Nourishing People

[9]   Psychologist Carl Rogers drew a distinction between noxious and nourishing people. Noxious people criticize and find fault with just about everything. Nourishing people, on the other hand, are positive. They are optimists. They reward you, they stroke you, they make you feel good about yourself. Seek out these people.

Work on Projects That Will Result in Success

[10]   Some people want to fail, or so it seems. Often, they select projects that will result in failure. Perhaps the projects are too large or too difficult. In any event, they are impossible. Instead, select projects that will result in success. Each success helps build self-esteem. Each success makes the next success a little easier.

[11]   When a project does fail, recognize that this does not mean that you are a failure. Everyone fails somewhere along the line. Failure is something that happens; it is not something inside you. Further, your failing once does not mean that you will fail the next time. So put failure in perspective. Do not make it an excuse for not trying again. (Devito 75–77)

Questions for Thought

Choose the letter of the correct answer and write it in the blank provided. The following questions pertain to all of the skills that you have learned so far. The first one has been done for you.

_____c_____   1. The topic of this passage is:
            a. nourishing versus noxious people.

      b. self-destructive beliefs.

      c. building self-esteem.

_____ **2.** The main point of this selection is:

      a. Self-destructive beliefs are those that damage your self-esteem and prevent you from building meaningful and productive relationships.

      b. Each success makes the next a little easier.

      c. We can increase our self-esteem by becoming aware of any self-destructive thoughts and by using self-esteem–building techniques.

_____ **3.** The overall text pattern for this selection is:

      a. term, definition, and example.

      b. topic with a list.

      c. chronological order.

_____ **4.** The text pattern used in paragraph 3 is:

      a. topic with a list.

      b. term, definition, and example.

      c. chronological order.

_____ **5.** The text pattern used in paragraph 1 is:

      a. topic with a list.

      b. term, definition, and example.

      c. chronological order.

_____ **6.** In paragraph 4:

      a. the term *driver* is defined and several examples are given.

      b. the term *driver* is defined but no examples of drivers are provided.

      c. several examples of drivers are provided, but the term is not defined.

_____ **7.** The text pattern used in paragraph 5 is:

      a. topic with a list.

      b. process.

      c. both "process" and "topic with a list."

_____ **8.** In paragraph 7, the heading "Engage in Self-Affirmation" is:

      a. the *term* that is defined within the paragraph.

      b. the *topic* that is followed by a list of items in the paragraph.

      c. the *signal* words that indicate a chronological order pattern.

_____ **9.** The text pattern used in the last sentence of paragraph 8 is:

      a. topic with a list.

      b. term, definition, and example.

      c. chronological order.

_____ **10.** In paragraph 11, the author presents a list of three items:
1. Everyone fails somewhere along the line.
2. Failure is something that happens; it is not something inside you.
3. Failing once does not mean that you will fail the next time.

Which topic goes with this list?
a. Reasons supporting the statement "you are not a failure if a project fails"
b. Ways to prevent a project from failing
c. Excuses for not trying again

CHAPTER

6

Text Patterns—
Complex Paragraphs

• •

In Chapter 5 we looked at several basic textbook patterns. In this chapter we familiarize ourselves with the more complex textbook patterns. These include:

- description;
- comparison/contrast;
- cause/effect;
- problem solution;
- classification.

INSTRUCTOR: How do you determine the author's train of thought?

TYRONE: In my business book, there are little things on the side that's supposed to be important. I'll look at those . . . I'll read that area.

INSTRUCTOR: How do you link the ideas presented in a chapter?

TYRONE: Hopefully, they keep in order.

INSTRUCTOR: What if they're not in order?

TYRONE: Sometimes you just get really lost trying to figure out where and what the point is.

INSTRUCTOR: What strategies do you use to read college textbooks?

LIDIA: I kind of only read the first couple of sentences, like a paragraph and then I skip . . . to the end.

INSTRUCTOR: If you did a second reading, would you read the entire chapter? Or just read the first sentences in each paragraph?

LIDIA: I would probably read just the first sentences.

INSTRUCTOR: When you're reading, do you look for patterns or relationships between the ideas?

LIDIA: No, I just simply read.

Many students, when they read, do not understand the importance of identifying the **text pattern**. As a result, they may miss the most obvious clues to what they should understand and take away from a reading. The text pattern is the author's *outline*. For example, if the reader does not realize that the author is presenting a series of ideas in the form of a topic and list, the reader may not realize the connection between each idea. If the reader has not caught on that the order of ideas is written in a chronological pattern, he may not know that the events being described had to happen in a specific time order.

DESCRIPTION

The **descriptive pattern** is popular in literature and narratives, but it is used in all disciplines when writers want their readers to imagine concrete images (things that we can see, hear, touch, taste, or smell). The following sentences illustrate how the use of descriptive terms can make a reading come alive:

Sight: With standing room only, the crowded gymnasium was filled with fans wearing *brightly colored* sports jackets—*red and gold* for the home team and *blue and green* for the visitors.

Sound: *Shouts* of victory *thundered* through the air as the home team's ball *swooped* through the basket.

Touch: The bleachers *shook* as the fans jumped up in unison and rebounded to their seats.

Taste: The *sweet,* syrupy *taste* of the cola fizzled down his parched throat.

Smell: The *smell of fresh-baked pretzels* filtered into the crowded, closed-in space from the snack bar.

When authors write description, they paint a picture with words. They want us, through our imagination, to experience what they have experienced. Their aim is to make the people, places, or things they know about seem very real to us.

Authors do this by including words that relate to the five senses: sight, sound, taste, touch, and smell. Compare the two paragraphs below. Which one is better at helping you "experience" rather than merely "observe" the situation? Why?

Paragraph 1

My friend and I went down to the beach. It was a hot day. We walked across the sand and then jumped into the ocean. We felt cooler than we did before we jumped into the water.

Paragraph 2

The coconut smell of the suntan lotion made me nauseous as it melted, holding the gritty sand against my body like glue. The sweltering sun beat down, making the sand as hot as a griddle on the bottom of our feet as we made our way toward the salty spray of crashing waves. We felt relief as we stepped into the churning white foam. The cool, sunlit mist mixed with the beads of sweat at our hairlines, and the water put out the fire in our feet.

The second paragraph appeals to all our five senses and makes us feel as though we are the ones experiencing the heat. Therefore, it is descriptively more effective than the first.

Reread the second paragraph. Underline all of the words that pertain to sight, sound, taste, touch, and smell. Then, list the words or phrases that appeal to your five senses below:

Sight: _____

Sound: _____

Taste: _____

Touch: _____

Smell: _____

If you have ever eaten a coconut, then you know exactly what coconuts smell like. The smell of coconut, by itself, doesn't usually make people sick to their stomach, but extreme heat can. So, the description "the coconut smell of the suntan lotion made me nauseous," indicates the intensity of the heat. Other descriptive words confirm this. We can "see" that it is hot because the two characters have "beads of sweat" on their faces. We can tell the characters feel the heat because the sand is described as being "hot as a griddle" and the sun is described as being "sweltering." We can imagine the characters' feelings of discomfort from the heat because the suntan lotion is described as "melted" and as acting "like glue." We know that it is an intensely hot day (as opposed to just a warm day) because the characters' feet are described as being "on fire."

We can guess that the characters can probably smell or taste salt because they were walking into a "salty mist." We can also guess that they hear the sound of water hitting the sand because of the words "crashing waves."

EXERCISE 6-1	**Using Descriptive Words**

Read the paragraph below. It lacks descriptive words and so appears less interesting than it might be.

The amusement park was crowded, and many people were waiting in line to get onto the roller coaster. We were a little nervous as it pulled up and people got off. We were first in line.

Make a list of words that could add more life to this paragraph. Draw on each of the five senses (at least two descriptive words for each sense). Then rewrite the paragraph by adding your descriptions to it.

Sight: _____

Sound: _____

Taste: _____

Touch: _____

Smell: _____

Visual Literacy Box 6.1 ● ● ● ● ● ● ● ● ● ● ● ● ● ● ●

VISUALIZING DESCRIPTIONS

We can "see" that it is very hot because the two characters have "beads of sweat" on their faces.

The Arrangement of Details

When authors paint a picture with words, they must also present the details in an order that the reader can easily follow. In other words, the author thinks about the picture he wants to paint and then chooses a perspective from which to describe it. He tries to present the details in an order that helps the reader "see" what he "sees." The following are some ways in which the author can arrange the details as he visualizes or "looks at" the picture he is trying to describe:

1. From top to bottom

2. From bottom to top

3. From left to right

4. From right to left

5. From near to far

6. From far to near

7. From most to least noticeable

8. From least to most noticeable

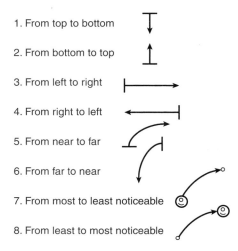

From Top to Bottom In the description below, the character is standing on the ledge of a building looking down at the street. The words "He stood where he was" indicate the author is starting his description at the top of his visualization. As we read further, the words "what lay below" and "down at the street" bring us to the bottom of the picture. So, the author begins his description at the top of the building and works his way toward the bottom. (The following examples are from Jack Finney, "Contents of a Dead Man's Pocket.")

> He stood where he was, breathing deeply, trying to hold back the terror of the glimpse of what lay below him; and he knew he had made a mistake in not making himself stare down at the street, getting used to it and accepting it, when he had first stepped out.

From Bottom to Top In the description below, the character is holding onto the bottom of a window and pushing up. The words "He heaved on the window" indicate the author is ordering the details from *bottom to top*. As we read further the author refers to the window shooting "open with a bang." This leads us to picture his arms first, at the bottom of the window, and then at the top as the window shoots upward.

> He heaved on the window with all his strength and it shot open with a bang, the window weight rattling in the casing.

From Left to Right In the description below, the character is watching a piece of paper move along the ledge of a building. In this case, the author is vague and does not specify the direction in which the paper is moving. But in order for us to visualize the paper moving "slowly along the ledge," *we* need to choose a direction for the paper to move with respect to the character's position.

> Even as he watched, it was moving, scraping slowly along the ledge, pushed by the breeze that pressed steadily against the building wall.

From Right to Left   Again, in the description below, the author does not specify the direction in which the paper is moving. We only know that it "scud steadily along the ledge to the south." Let's say we know from previous sentences that the character is standing by the window. We now need to decide whether "south" is to the right or left of the window. Let's say that we imagine "south" to be on the left. Now we can "draw the picture" as it unfolds because we are able to "see" in our mind's eye where the paper is going in relation to the window and the character.

> But the paper was past his reach and, leaning out into the night, he watched it scud steadily along the ledge to the south, half plastered against the building wall.

From Near to Far   We know in the description below that the paper, at first, had to be very near to the character because it was filled with his writing—"his own improvised shorthand."

The author describes the details of this sentence in a *near-to-far* pattern by directing our attention to where the paper had moved—"out there on the ledge."

> And there they all lay, in his own improvised shorthand—countless hours of work—out there on the ledge. . . . And he knew he was going out there in the darkness, after the yellow sheet.

From Far to Near   In the description below, the character is standing on the ledge of a building looking down at the street. The words "blocks ahead," "miles of traffic signals," and "moving dots of people" describe the farthest points of the scene. The author then brings us closer by describing a vision the character has of himself on the ledge and then even closer yet by describing the character's state of mind and physical condition.

> He saw, in that instant, the Lowe's theatre sign, blocks ahead; the miles of traffic signals; the lights of cars and street lamps; countless neon signs; and the moving dots of people. And a violent, instantaneous explosion of absolute terror roared through him. For an instant he saw himself externally—bent practically double, balanced on this narrow ledge, nearly half his body projecting out above the street far below—and he began to tremble violently, panic flaring through mind and muscles.

From the Least to the Most Noticeable Object or Characteristic   In the sentence below, the author starts his description with the least noticeable object, "a dangling shoestring," and moves to more obvious objects such as "the sole of his other shoe" and "his foot." He finishes by making reference to the most noticeable object, his whole body—"and felt his balance leaving him." In this way he moves the reader's attention from the least noticeable object to the most noticeable.

> He saw a dangling shoestring caught between the ledge and the sole of his other shoe, saw a foot start to move, to be stopped with a jerk, and felt his balance leaving him.

From Most to Least Noticeable Object   In the description below, the author calls attention to the most noticeable objects—the people in supermarkets—and moves our attention to the least noticeable object—the yellow piece of paper. He uses these objects to direct our attention from the most noticeable items to the least noticeable.

> On four long Saturday afternoons he had stood in supermarkets counting the people who passed certain displays, and the results were scribbled on that yellow sheet.

Reading Between the Lines Box 6.1

SIGNALS IN DESCRIPTIVE WRITING

Authors list details in the order they want us to notice them. They use the first detail to place our focus on a certain object or place and then connect it to the other details. Signal words and phrases help us recognize the order in which the details are being described. Below is a list of such signal words.

Signal Patterns	Signal Words	Signal Words	Signal Words
top to bottom	below that	down from there	toward the bottom
bottom to top	above that	up from that point	at the top
left to right	to the right of	next to	beside
right to left	to the left of	next to	beside
near to far	nearest to	not far from	farther away from
far to near	farthest from	nearer to	from a distance
most to least noticeable object	the most prominent	the most striking	the most obvious
least to most noticeable object	least prominent	least obvious	least striking

1. Study the signal words in the chart above.

(continued on next page)

2. Read the paragraph below and decide which signal pattern is used.

3. Underline the signal words or phrases in the paragraph that helped you decide which pattern was used.

> On stage, the New York City Ballet was getting ready to perform *Swan Lake*. The dancers were posed waiting for the music to begin. The orchestra was seated nearest to the stage. Not far from the orchestra pit were the front-row seats. They were completely full. Farther away from the stage were the back sections; they were also full. Farthest from the stage were the lawn seats. Blankets and lawn chairs covered the grass from the edge of the amphitheater to the top of the hill, almost reaching the area where the vendors sold their snacks. The orchestra started to play as the curtains opened and the ballet began.

4. Explain the reasons for your answer to question 2.

A Reading in Literature

The following selection is part of a story called "Contents of a Dead Man's Pocket." Read the paragraphs below and identify the order in which the author arranged the details: (a) top to bottom, (b) bottom to top, (c) left to right, (d) right to left, (e) near to far, (f) far to near, (g) most to least noticeable object or characteristic, (h) least to most noticeable object or characteristic. The first one has been done for you. (There are no questions to answer for the paragraphs in italics; they are included because they are part of the story and the story would not make sense without them.)

Contents of a Dead Man's Pocket

_e_ **1.** He got up, shoving his hands into the back pockets of his gray wash slacks, stepped to the living-room window beside the desk and stood breathing on the glass, watching the expanding circle of mist, staring down through the autumn night at Lexington Avenue, eleven stories below. He was a tall, lean, dark-haired young man in a pullover sweater, who looked as though he might have played basketball in college. Now he placed the heels of his hands against the top edge of the lower window frame and shoved upward. But as usual the window didn't budge, and he had to lower his hands and then shoot them hard upward to jolt the window open a few inches. He dusted his hands, muttering.

____ **2.** But still he didn't begin his work. He crossed the room to the hallway entrance and, leaning against the door-jamb, he called, "Clare?" When his wife answered, he said, "Sure you don't mind going alone?"

"No." Her voice was muffled, and he knew her head and shoulders were in the bedroom closet. Then the tap of her high heels sounded on the wood floor and she appeared at the end of the little hallway, both hands raised to one ear, clipping on an earring. She smiled at him—slender, very pretty girl with light brown, almost blond hair—her prettiness emphasized by the pleasant nature that showed in her face. "It's just that I hate you to miss this movie; you wanted to see it, too."

"Yeah, I know." He ran his fingers through his hair. "Got to get this done though."

She nodded, accepting this. Then, glancing at the desk across the living room, she said, "You work too much, though, Tom—and too hard."

____ 3.   Turning, he saw a sheet of white paper drifting to the floor in a series of arcs, and another sheet, yellow, moving toward the window, caught in the dying current flowing through the narrow opening. As he watched, the paper struck the bottom edge of the window and hung there for an instant, plastered against the glass and wood. Then, as the moving air stilled completely the curtains swinging back from the wall to hang free again, he saw the yellow sheet drop to the window ledge and slide over out of sight.

He ran across the room, grasped the bottom edge of the window and tugged, staring through the glass. He saw the yellow sheet, dimly now in the darkness outside, lying on the ornamental ledge a yard below the window. Even as he watched, it was moving, scraping slowly along the ledge, pushed by the breeze that pressed steadily against the building wall. He heaved on the window with all his strength and it shot open with a bang, the window weight rattling in the casing. But the paper was past his reach and, leaning out into the night, he watched it scud steadily along the ledge to the south, half plastered against the building wall. Above the muffled sound of the street traffic far below, he could hear the dry scrape of its movement, like a leaf on the pavement.

The living room of the next apartment to the south projected a yard or more farther out toward the street than this one. And now the yellow sheet, sliding along the stone ledge, nearly invisible in the night, was stopped by the projecting blank wall of the next apartment. It lay motionless, then, in the corner formed by the two walls—a good five yards away, pressed firmly against the ornate corner ornament of the ledge by the breeze.

____ 4.   He knelt at the window and stared at the yellow paper for a full minute or more, waiting for it to move, to slide off the ledge and fall, hoping he could follow its course to the street, and then hurry down in the elevator and retrieve it. But it didn't move . . .

*It was hard for him to understand that he actually had to aban-
don it—it was ridiculous—and he began to curse. Of all the papers
on his desk, why did it have to be this one in particular! On four long
Saturday afternoons he had stood in supermarkets counting the people who passed certain displays, and the results were scribbled on
that yellow sheet. From stacks of trade publications, gone over page
by page in snatched half hours at work and during evenings at home,
he had copied facts, quotations and figures onto that sheet. And he
had carried it with him to the Public Library, where he'd spent a
dozen lunch hours and early evenings adding more. All were needed
to support and lend authority to his idea for a new grocery-store display method; without them his idea was a mere opinion. And there
they all lay, in his own improvised shorthand—countless hours of
work—out there on the ledge. . . . And he knew he was going out there
in the darkness, after the yellow sheet.*

____ **5.** He swung a leg over the sill, then felt for the ledge a yard below
the window with his foot. Gripping the bottom of the window frame
very tightly and carefully, he slowly ducked his head under it, feeling on his face the sudden change from the warm air of the room to
the chill outside. With infinite care he brought out his other leg, his
mind concentrating on what he was doing. Then he slowly stood
erect. Most of the putty, dried out and brittle, had dropped off the
bottom edging of the window frame, and the flat wooden edging provided a good gripping surface, a half inch or more deep, for the tips
of his fingers.

Now, balanced easily and firmly, he stood on the ledge outside
in the slight, chill breeze, eleven stories above the street, staring into
his own lighted apartment, odd and different-seeming now.

____ **6.** First his right hand, then his left, he carefully shifted his finger-
tip grip from the puttyless window ledging to an indented row of
bricks directly to his right. It was hard to take the first shuffling
sideways step then—to make himself move—and the fear stirred in
his stomach, but he did it, again by not allowing himself time to
think. And now—with his chest, stomach, and the left side of his
face pressed against the rough cold brick—his lighted apartment
was suddenly gone, and it was much darker out here than he had
thought.

Without pause he continued—right foot, left foot, right foot, left—
his shoe soles shuffling and scraping along the rough stone, never
lifting from it, fingers sliding along the exposed edging of the bricks.
He moved on the balls of his feet, heels lifted slightly; the ledge was
not quite as wide as he had expected. But leaning slightly inward
toward the face of the building and pressed against it, he could feel
his balance firm and secure, and moving along the ledge was quite

as easy as he had thought it would be. He could hear the buttons of his jacket scraping steadily along the rough bricks and feel them catch momentarily, tugging a little, at each mortared crack. He simply did not permit himself to look down, though the compulsion to do so never left him; nor did he allow himself actually to think. Mechanically—right foot, left foot, over and over again—he shuffled along crabwise, watching the projecting wall ahead loom steadily closer. . . .

_____ 7.   Then he reached it and, at the corner—he'd decided how he was going to pick up the paper—he lifted his right foot and placed it carefully on the ledge that ran along the projecting wall at the right angle to the ledge on which his other foot rested. And now, facing the building, he stood in the corner formed by the two walls, one foot on the ledge of each, a hand on the shoulder-high indention of each wall. His forehead was pressed directly into the corner against the cold bricks, and now he carefully lowered first one hand, then the other, perhaps a foot farther down, to the next indentation in the row of bricks.

Very slowly, sliding his forehead down the trough of the brick corner and bending his knees, he lowered his fingerholds another foot and bent his knees still more, thigh muscles taut, his forehead sliding and bumping down the brick V. Half squatting, he dropped his left hand to the next indentation and then slowly reached with his right hand toward the paper.

He couldn't touch it, and his knees now were pressed against the wall; he could bend them no farther. But by ducking his head another inch lower, the top of his head now pressed against the bricks, he lowered his right shoulder and his finger had the paper by a corner, pulling it loose. At the same instant he saw between his legs and far below, Lexington Avenue stretched out for miles ahead.

He saw, in that instant, the Loew's theatre sign, blocks ahead; the miles of traffic signal; the lights of cars and street lamps; countless neon signs; and the moving dots of people. And a violent, instantaneous explosion of absolute terror roared through him. For an instant he saw himself externally—bent practically double, balanced on this narrow ledge, nearly half his body projecting out above the street far below—and he began to tremble violently, panic flaring through mind and muscles.

_____ 8.   In the fractional moment before horror paralyzed him, as he stared between his legs at that terrible length of street far beneath him, a fragment of his mind raised his body in a spasmodic jerk to an upright position again, but so violently that his head scraped hard against the wall, bouncing off it, and his body swayed outward to the knife edge of balance, and he very nearly plunged backward and fell. Then he was leaning far into the corner again, pushing into it, not only his face but his chest and stomach, his back arching; and his finger tips clung with all the pressure of his pulling arms to the shoulder-high half-inch indentation in the bricks.

____ 9.   He was more than trembling now; his whole body was racked with violent shuddering beyond control, his eyes squeezed so tightly shut it was painful, though he was past awareness of that. His teeth were exposed in a frozen grimace, the strength draining like water from his knees.

____10.   It was extremely likely that he would faint, to slump down along the wall, and then drop backward, a limp weight, out into nothing. And to save his life he concentrated on holding onto consciousness, drawing deep breaths of cold air into his lungs, fighting to keep his senses aware.

Then he knew he would not faint, but he could not stop shaking nor open his eyes. He stood where he was, breathing deeply, trying to hold back the terror of the glimpse of what lay below him; and he knew he had made a mistake in not making himself stare down at the street, getting used to it and accepting it, when he had first stepped out.

It was impossible to walk back. He couldn't bring himself to make the slightest movement. The strength was gone from his legs; his shivering hands—numb, cold and desperately rigid—had lost all deftness; his ability to move and balance was gone. Within a step or two, if he tried to move, he knew he would stumble clumsily and fall.

____11.   Seconds passed, with the chill faint wind pressing the side of his face, and he could hear the toned-down volume of the street traffic far beneath him. Again and again it slowed and then stopped, almost to silence; then presently, even this high, he would hear the click of the traffic signals and the subdued roar of the cars. During a lull in the sounds, he called out. Then he was shouting "help!" so loudly it rasped his throat. But the pressure of the wind, moving between his face and the blank wall, snatched up his cries as he uttered them, and he knew they must sound directionless and distant. And he remembered how habitually, here in New York, he himself heard and ignored shouts in the night. If anyone heard him, there was no sign of it, and presently Tom Benecke knew he had to try moving; there was nothing else he could do.

Eyes squeezed shut, he watched scenes in his mind like scraps of motion-picture film. He saw himself stumbling suddenly sideways as he crept along the ledge and saw his body arc outward, arms flailing. He saw a dangling shoestring caught between the ledge and the sole of his other shoe, saw a foot start to move, to be stopped with a jerk, and felt his balance leaving him. He saw himself falling with terrible speed as his body revolved into the air, knees clutched tight to his chest, eyes squeezed shut, moaning softly.

____**12.** Out of utter necessity, knowing that any of these thoughts might be reality in the very next seconds, he was slowly able to shut his mind against every thought but what he now began to do. With fear-soaked slowness, he slid his left foot an inch or two toward his own impossibly distant window. Then he slid the fingers of his shivering left hand a corresponding distance. For a moment he could not bring himself to lift his right foot from one ledge to the other; then he did it, and became aware of the harsh exhalation of air from his throat and realized that he was panting. As his right hand then began to slide along the brick edging, he was astonished to feel the yellow paper pressed to the bricks underneath his stiff fingers, and he uttered a terrible, abrupt bark that might have been a laugh or a moan. He opened his mouth and took the paper in his teeth, pulling it out from under his fingers.

____**13.** By a kind of trick—by concentrating his entire mind on first his left foot, then his left hand, then the other foot, then the other hand—he was able to move, almost imperceptibly, trembling steadily, very nearly without thought. But he could feel the terrible strength of the pent-up horror on just the other side of the flimsy barrier he had erected in his mind; and he knew that if it broke through he would lose this thin artificial control of his body.

____**14.** Dropping his palms to the sill, he stared into his living room—at the brown davenport, and a magazine he had left there; at the pictures on the walls and the gray rug; at his papers, typewriter and desk, not two feet from his nose. A movement from his desk caught his eye and he saw a thin curl of blue smoke; his cigarette, the ash long, was still burning in the ash tray where he'd left it—this was past all belief—only a few minutes before.

____**15.** He couldn't open the window. It had been pulled completely closed, and its lower edge was below the level of the outside sill; there was no room to get his fingers underneath it. Between the upper sash and the lower was a gap not wide enough to get his fingers into; he couldn't push it open. The upper window panel, he knew from long experience, was frozen tight with dried paint.

COMPARISON-CONTRAST

The comparison-contrast pattern is used in almost every type of writing. When we compare two or more people, places, or things, we look for their similarities,

VENN DIAGRAMS FOR COMPARISON AND CONTRAST

We can draw a Venn diagram to illustrate the information below concerning high and low achievers. Our diagram will compare and contrast successful students with unsuccessful students. We do this by first drawing two circles to represent the groups—successful and unsuccessful. We make the circles overlap so there is an area common to both. In the overlapping space, we list the shared characteristics of the groups, or their similarities. In the darker circle where there is no common area, we list only the characteristics of the successful students. In the lighter circle where there is no shared area, we list only the characteristics of the unsuccessful students. The separate areas represent their differences.

High and Low Achievers

Both the high- and low-achieving students described themselves as being "slackers" in high school. The two groups had similar scores on the SAT exam. Their high school grade averages were the same, and both groups were equal in their high school ranking. However, the high-achieving students revealed a change in their sense of self as students when they entered college: They saw themselves as low achievers in high school but viewed themselves as high-achievers in college. In contrast, most low-achieving students described no change in their academic self-concept from high school to college. They retained the same study habits, attitudes, and behavior. Also, no increase in motivation, interest, self-discipline, or desire to be in school was found in their reports.

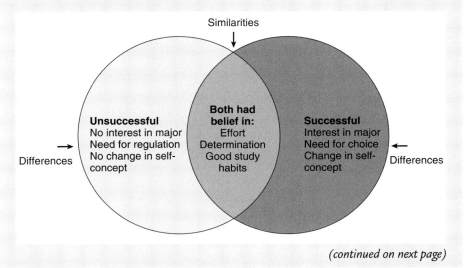

(continued on next page)

(continued from previous page)

Activity: (1) Read the paragraph below and identify the experiences that successful young career women have in common. (2) Using the numbers in the key, locate and label four spaces in the diagram that could illustrate each of these experiences. (3) Identify and label as #5 a space in the diagram that could represent all four of the experiences that help women to become successful.

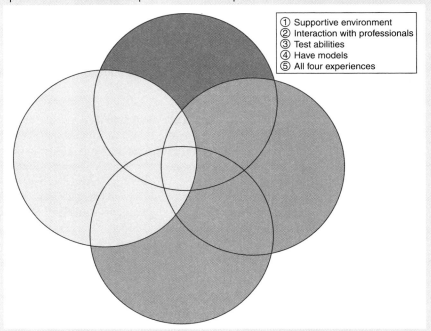

① Supportive environment
② Interaction with professionals
③ Test abilities
④ Have models
⑤ All four experiences

Research shows that the aspirations of young women rise in response to career guidance that encourages them to set goals that match their abilities, interests, and values. Those who continue to achieve usually have four experiences in common:

■ A college environment that values and supports the accomplishments of women and that attends to women's experiences in its curriculum.

■ Frequent interaction with faculty and professionals in their chosen fields.

■ The opportunity to test their abilities in a nurturing environment.

■ Models of accomplished women who have successfully dealt with family—career role conflict.

(Berk 447)

or what is common among them. When we contrast two or more items, we look for their differences. There are three ways an author can use this pattern. He may show (1) similarities between items, (2) differences between items, or (3) both similarities and differences between items.

Example 1: Similarities

There were three similarities in the way that both high- and low-achieving students defined success. Both groups indicated that effort was needed to achieve success in school. The high achievers were similar to the low achievers in their belief that determination was an important factor in achieving success. Like the high achievers, the low achievers also felt that good study habits were necessary for success in college. Both groups agreed that persistence, good study habits, and effort were needed to attain their goals.

Example 2: Differences

Several elements included in the high achievers' definition of success were not found in the low achievers' definition. The high achievers felt it was necessary to be interested in the subjects they were studying, whereas the low achievers showed little interest in their majors. The high achievers felt the choices in scheduling and freedoms of college life contributed to their success, whereas the low achievers felt lost without parents and teachers regulating their time.

Example 3: Similarities and Differences

Both the high- and low-achieving students described themselves as being "slackers" in high school. The two groups had similar scores on the SAT exam. Their high school grades averages were the same, and both groups were equal in their high school ranking. However, the high-achieving students revealed a change in their sense of self as students when they entered college: They saw themselves as low achievers in high school but viewed themselves as high achievers in college. In contrast, most low-achieving students described no change in their academic self-concept from high school to college. They retained the same study habits, attitudes, and behavior. Also, no increase in motivation, interest, self-discipline, or desire to be in school was found in their reports.

| EXERCISE 6-2 | **Identifying Comparison and Contrast I** |

Read the following paragraphs. Indicate if the paragraph shows (a) comparison, (b) contrast, or (c) comparison-contrast. The first one has been done for you.

    a   **1.** Another common feeling among both high- and low-achieving students concerning college was that success could be achieved by being organized, attending and paying attention in classes, completing all assigned work, and developing good study habits.

_____ **2.** Unlike the high achievers, the low achievers often mistook the less structured atmosphere of the college campus as a gift of free time that they could use for more social activity and recreation. Individual time management was confused with the notion that the college workday consisted of "all free time."

_____ **3.** In contrast with the high achievers, the low achievers admitted that they lacked the self-discipline to manage their time effectively. Many spoke of a need to have either parents or teachers prodding them to keep up with their academic work.

_____ **4.** Unlike the high achievers, the low achievers believed that students who studied were "nerdy" and that people who were smart did not have to study. Again, opposite from the high achievers, the low achievers thought that people who had good grades were just born to be smart and that intelligence was a fixed characteristic.

_____ **5.** Like the high achievers, the low achievers hoped for a fresh start in college. They also had the same academic backgrounds as the high achievers. However, unlike the high achievers, the low achievers battled against a fear of failure. They often did not try their best. They were afraid that if they tried and failed it would be an indication that they were not intelligent. However, if they put no effort into an assignment and failed, they could say that they failed because they did not try rather than saying they failed because they did not have the intelligence to succeed.

EXERCISE
6-3

Identifying Comparison and Contrast II

Read the following paragraphs. Indicate whether the paragraph shows (a) comparison, (b) contrast, or (c) comparison-contrast. The first one has been done for you.

___b___ **1.** Minority groups, in particular, face the problem of not having health coverage. In 1995, 85 percent of the children from the mainstream culture had health insurance that would pay for them to go to the hospital or to see a doctor if they became ill. In contrast, only 71 percent of Hispanic children had access to health care during that same year. (Bryjak and Soroka 350)

Reading Between the Lines Box 6.2

SIGNALS FOR COMPARISON AND CONTRAST

Authors may show how two or more items are alike (compare) or they may show how two or more items are different (contrast). They may also show both likenesses and differences. Signal words and phrases help us recognize these patterns or combinations of patterns. Below is a list of words and phrases that commonly signal when these patterns are being used.

Comparison Words		**Contrast Words**	
like	just like	unlike	however
as	just as	but	although
both	alike	instead	while
similarly	in a similar way	in contrast	on the other hand
comparable to	related to this	opposite from	different than

Activity

1. Read the excerpt below and identify the two items being compared: _____

A common example of mass behavior is rumor, unsubstantiated information people spread informally, often by word of mouth. Although people still pass along rumors through face-to-face communication, modern technology—including telephones, the mass media, and now the Internet—spreads rumors more rapidly and to a greater number of people than ever before.

Closely related to rumor is gossip, rumor about the personal affairs of others. Charles Horton Cooley (1962) explained that, while rumor involves issues or events of interest to a large segment of the public, gossip concerns a small circle of people who know a particular person. While rumors spread widely, then, gossip is more localized. (Macionis 618)

2. Underline the signal words, that helped you to identify the text pattern above.

3. What is the difference between rumor and gossip? _____

_____

4. How are rumor and gossip alike? _____

_____

_____ **2.** A primary group is characterized by intimacy, close association, and cooperation, whereas a secondary group is characterized by casual superficial relationships. Families and friends are generally a part of our primary groups, in contrast with classmates and co-workers, who make up our secondary groups. (Bryjak and Soroka 58–59)

_____ **3.** Black Africans make up 75% of the population of South Africa, while White Africans make up only 13% of the population. The Black Africans are the original people of South Africa, whereas the White Africans are of European descent, composed of English and Dutch heritages. The Blacks are from many different tribal and ethnic groups who have their own languages. In contrast, the White Africans are of only two ethnic cultures and, therefore, speak one of two languages, either English or Afrikaan. (Farr and Hammers 80)

_____ **4.** Scientists have discovered that perceptions of time provide important nonverbal cues, cues that vary from culture to culture. Western industrialized cultures, for example, think of time in linear-spatial terms related to past, present, and future. Thus, North Americans think of moving "through" time, with the present as the intermediate point between past and future. In contrast, other cultures stress "felt time," the "now" of living for each day and not for the past or future. Greeks, for instance, see themselves as stationary. Time comes up behind them, overtakes, them, and then becomes the past. Many Native Americans have the same concept. Indeed, the Sioux in the United States have no words for "time," "late," or "waiting." (Barker and Gaut 76–77)

_____ **5.** There are many types of teams. Teams can be formed for athletic purposes, such as football teams, soccer teams, baseball teams, etc. Teams can also be formed at work for the purpose of solving a problem or accomplishing a specific task. Whatever type of group, all teams have several elements in common. These elements include: commitment, trust, purpose, communication, involvement, and activities. (Barker and Gaut 147)

CAUSE-EFFECT

Cause-effect paragraph patterns are common in many textbooks, especially history, business, ecology, psychology, and sociology. Since scientists and scholars look for reasons why something has happened the way it did, cause-effect relationships also make up the backbone of research reports.

In our daily lives, we often look at cause-effect patterns. We may wonder, "What caused me to get a C on the exam?" or "What would be the effect of sending out this resume?" and "Will this aspirin cause my headache to go away?"

Although the idea that a certain action produces an effect does not seem difficult to grasp, cause-effect relationships can oftentimes be very tricky, causing seemingly simple sentences to become sources of confusion.

One reason this happens is because there are many different ways cause-effect relationships can be stated and many different combinations of causes and effects:

■ One cause leading to one effect

cause ⟶ effect

■ Two or more causes leading to one effect

cause
cause ⟶ effect
cause

■ One cause leading to two or more effects

effect
cause ⟵ effect
effect

■ Two or more causes leading to two or more effects

cause ⟶ effect
cause ⟶ effect
cause ⟶ effect

Another reason why cause-effect can be tricky is that sometimes the effect becomes a new cause that, in turn, creates a new effect. We call this "chains of reasoning."

cause ⟶ effect (cause) ⟶ effect

A third reason why cause-effect relationships are tricky is that the cause may be mentioned first, followed by the effect. Or, the effect may be mentioned first, followed by the cause. We must be careful not to assume that the first part of a cause-effect statement is always the "cause."

■ I woke up late; therefore, I missed my first class.

(cause) ⟶ (effect)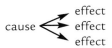

■ I missed my first class because I woke up late.

(effect) ⟶ (cause)

Reading Between the Lines Box 6.3

SIGNALS TO CAUSE AND EFFECT RELATIONSHIPS

If we are familiar with the words that signal the cause and those that signal the effect, we will not be stumped by the various arrangements of cause and effect statements.

Words that signal cause		Words that signal effect	
cause	reason	therefore	thus
since	many factors	resulting in	as a result
due to	if . . . then	so	consequently
because		effect	then
this prompted		affect	in conclusion

Activity

1. Read the excerpt below and underline the signal words related to cause and effect.

2. What is the overall cause? _____

3. List the effect and give examples

   a. effect: _____

   b. examples: _____

Self-Fulfilling Prophecy

A self-fulfilling prophecy occurs when you make a prediction or formulate a belief that comes true because you made the prediction and acted as if it were true (Merton, 1956; Insel & Jacobson, 1975). There are four basic steps in the self-fulfilling prophecy. First, you make a prediction or formulate a belief about someone (often, ourselves) or a situation. For example, you predict that Pat is awkward in interpersonal situations. Then, you act toward that person or situation as if the prediction or belief is true. For example, you act toward Pat as if she were, in fact, awkward. Then, because you act as if the belief were true, it becomes true. Because of the way you act toward Pat, she becomes tense and manifests awkwardness. Finally, your effect on the person or the resulting situation strengthens your beliefs. Seeing Pat's awkwardness reinforces your belief that Pat is, in fact, awkward.

If you expect people to act in a certain way, the self-fulfilling prophecy will frequently make your predictions come true. Consider, for instance, people who enter a group situation convinced that other members will dislike them. Almost invariably they're proved right, perhaps because they act in a way that

(continued on next page)

encourages people to respond negatively. Such people fulfill their own prophecies. The tendency to fulfill your own prophecies can lead you to:

- Influence another's behavior to conform to your prophecy.
- See what you predicted rather than what really is. For example, it can lead
  you to perceive yourself as a failure because you made this prediction
  rather than because of any actual failures.

(Devito, 56–57)

A way to make this easier is to look at the cause as being an action and the
effect as being a result of that action.

I woke up late (action); therefore, I missed my first class (result).
I missed my first class (result) because I woke up late (action).

EXERCISE 6-4	**Identifying Cause and Effect**

Identify the cause and the effect for each of the following sentences. The first one
has been done for you.

1. Neal wanted to become a lawyer, so he studied business law.

cause: Neal wanted to become a lawyer.

effect: He studied business law.

2. Neal studied business law because he wanted to become a lawyer.

cause: _____

effect: _____

3. Kendra worked in the bookstore because she needed money for tuition.

cause: _____

effect: _____

4. Kendra needed money for tuition, so she worked in the bookstore.

cause: _____

effect: _____

5. Vladimir wrote interesting papers; therefore, his professors enjoyed reading them.

cause: _____

effect: _____

More Complicated Cause-Effect Relationships

Some cause-effect relationships are more complicated. A cause can create an effect that becomes the cause of another effect. The pattern looks like this:

$\underline{A}$ caused $\underline{B}$ and $\underline{B}$ caused $\underline{C}$.

This pattern sometimes continues on and on because each cause creates a new effect:

$\underline{A}$ caused $\underline{B}$ and $\underline{B}$ caused $\underline{C}$. $\underline{C}$ caused $\underline{D}$ and $\underline{D}$ caused $\underline{E}$.

Example:

John worked hard to prepare his speech, which made him quite knowledgeable, so he went to class feeling confident.

$\underline{A}$ caused $\underline{B}$:

cause: John worked hard.

effect: John became knowledgeable.

$\underline{B}$ caused $\underline{C}$:

cause: John became knowledgeable.

effect: John felt confident.

EXERCISE	**Identifying One Cause and One Effect**
6-5	

#2, 3, 6, 8, 9, 10

Identify the causes and the effects in each of the following sentences. The first one has been done for you.

1. Mohammed missed lunch, which made him hungry, so he went to the dining hall for an early dinner.

$\underline{A}$ caused $\underline{B}$: **cause:** Mohammed missed lunch.

effect: Mohammed felt hungry.

Visual Literacy Box 6.3 ● ■ ■ ■ ■ ■ ■ ■ ■ ■ ■ ■ ■ ■ ■ ■ ■ ■ ■

DIAGRAMMING COMPLEX
CAUSE AND EFFECT CHAINS

When we look at complex cause-effect relationships, we see a chain type pattern in which a cause creates an effect that becomes the cause of another effect. Reread the passage in the Reading Between the Lines Box 6.3 on page 212 and identify a chain of causes and effects. Then write out each step in the pattern and fill in the diagram below.

Chain = A caused <u>B</u> *and* <u>B</u> caused <u>C</u> *and* <u>C</u> caused <u>D</u>.

Self-Fulfilling Prophecy

A self-fulfilling prophecy occurs when you make a prediction or formulate a belief that comes true because you made the prediction and acted as if it were true (Merton, 1956; Insel & Jacobson, 1975).

1. A caused <u>B</u>: _____

2. B caused <u>C</u>: _____

3. C caused <u>D</u>: _____

There are four basic steps in the self-fulfulling prophecy:

1. Formulate a belief.

2. Act toward that belief as if it is true.

3. Belief becomes true.

4. Effect strengthens your beliefs.

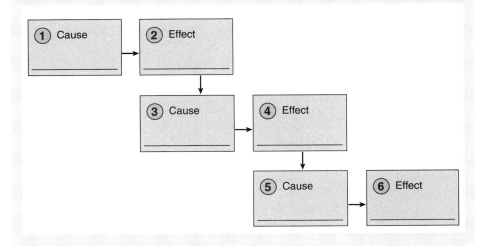

B caused **C**: cause: _____

effect: _____

2. Michaela caught a cold, which made him feel chilled, so he put another log in the fireplace.

A caused **B**: cause: _Michaela_____

effect: _____

B caused **C**: cause: _____

effect: _____

3. Cindy is was offered a spot in *Disney on Ice* because she skated beautifully due to daily practices.

A caused **B**: cause: _____

effect: _____

B caused **C**: cause: _____

effect: _____

4. Due to daily practices, Cindy skated beautifully, and so she was offered a spot in *Disney on Ice*.

A caused **B**: cause: _____

effect: _____

B caused **C**: cause: _____

effect: _____

5. Cindy became an excellent skater by practicing every day and, therefore, was offered a spot in *Disney on Ice*.

A caused **B**: cause: _____

effect: _____

B caused **C**: cause: _____

effect: _____

6. Tired from the ten-mile ride on his mountain bike, Glenn took a nap.

A caused **B**: **cause:** _____

                 effect: _____

B caused **C**: **cause:** _____

                 effect: _____

7. Because he was tired from the ten-mile ride on his mountain bike, Glenn took a nap.

A caused **B**: **cause:** _____

                 effect: _____

B caused **C**: **cause:** _____

                 effect: _____

8. After listening to the interesting lecture, the students were inspired to start working on their projects immediately.

A caused **B**: **cause:** _____

                 effect: _____

B caused **C**: **cause:** _____

                 effect: _____

9. The groundwater table was low from many years of irrigation; therefore, water restrictions were placed on farmers.

A caused **B**: **cause:** _____

                 effect: _____

B caused **C**: **cause:** _____

                 effect: _____

10. The shift in population from urban to suburban areas led to a tremendous increase in traffic, and this resulted in an increase in air pollution.

A caused **B**: **cause:** _____

effect: _____

B caused **C**:   cause: _____

effect: _____

Sometimes, relationships have two or more causes that create one effect. Look at the example below.

The weather was very hot and the pool was empty, so Shawna went swimming.

Cause 1:   The weather was very hot.

Cause 2:   The pool was empty.

Effect: Shawna went swimming.

It makes sense that Shawna went swimming because of the information that we have been given. People generally go swimming when the weather is warm. The fact that the pool is empty is also encouraging because we know there is room for her to swim. Therefore, the conclusion that Shawna went swimming makes sense according to the facts that are given.

EXERCISE
6-6

Identifying Two Causes and One Effect

Identify the causes and the effect in each of the following sentences. The first one has been done for you.

1. Marian liked working with computers and she was accepted into the computer science program, so she changed her major to computer science.

   Cause 1: _Marian liked working with computers._

   Cause 2: _She was accepted into the computer science program._

   Effect: _She changed her major to computer science._

2. Leo loved children and he enjoyed teaching, so he became a first-grade teacher.

   Cause 1: _____

   Cause 2: _____

   Effect: _____

3. Mei wrote her paper quickly because she was behind in her academic work and didn't want to miss the deadline.

Cause 1: _____

Cause 2: _____

Effect: _____

4. Rose Marie studied the project intently because she wanted to help stop the destruction of the rain forest, and she knew she had to understand the situation before she could be of any help.

Cause 1: _____

Cause 2: _____

Effect: _____

5. Upon finding the air pressure to be down, and because the weather map indicated that a warm front was moving in, the meteorologist predicted rain in the forecast.

Cause 1: _____

Cause 2: _____

Effect: _____

Sometimes when there are two causes and one effect, one cause is stated and the other cause is implied. In that case, we have to read between the lines to connect the gap between the stated cause and the effect. Look at the example below.

The soccer team was holding tryouts, so Maria went to the soccer field to participate in the competition.

Stated cause: Tryouts were being held on the soccer field.

Implied cause: Maria wanted to be on the soccer team.

Effect: Maria went to the soccer field to participate in the competition.

The sentence does not tell us why Maria decided to participate in the competition. We as readers have to read between the lines to fill in that information. We are given the information that tryouts were being held on the soccer field and that Maria went to join in the competition. Therefore, we would be safe in assuming she did so because she wanted to be on the soccer team.

Identifying Stated Cause, Implied Cause, and Effect

2–5

In each of the following sentences, identify the stated cause, the implied cause and the effect. The first one has been done for you.

1. Unrest in the Middle East led to peace talks between the United States and other countries that belong to the United Nations.

   Stated cause: There is unrest in the Middle East.

   Implied cause: Members of the United Nations would like to see peace.

   Effect: Peace talks were held between the U.S. and other members of the U.N.

2. Mexico City is the largest city in the world and therefore has tremendous problems with air pollution. Mexico City is now estimated to have a population of over 20 million people, making it the largest city in the world. (Farr and Hammers 19)

   Stated cause: _____

   Implied cause: _____

   Effect: _____

3. In Brazil, women are no longer considered to be the property of men because of the changes that took place under the constitution in 1988.

   Stated cause: _____

   Implied cause: _____

   Effect: _____

4. Since the Chinese Communist Party established new laws, commercial Web sites are only allowed to put state-published news on the Internet.

   Stated cause: _____

   Implied cause: _____

   Effect: _____

5. Over the next ten years, people in South Africa are not expected to live very long because many have the AIDS virus.

   Stated cause: _____

Implied cause: _____

Effect: _____

DRAWING CONCLUSIONS

Drawing a conclusion is similar to cause-effect relationships. In this case, facts are presented, and from these facts, the reader draws a logical conclusion. The conclusion must make sense based on the given facts.

> *Example*: It snowed today in Toronto. Patrice lives in Toronto. We can conclude that Patrice's house is covered in snow.

Fact 1: It snowed today in Toronto.
Fact 2: Patrice lives in Toronto.
Conclusion: Patrice's house is covered in snow.

EXERCISE
6-8

Drawing Conclusions

Identify the conclusion drawn from the facts provided. The first one has been done for you.

1. Students do not have to go to school during the summer. I am a student. Therefore, I do not have to go to school during the summer.

   Fact 1: Students do not have to go to school during the summer.

   Fact 2: I am a student.

   Conclusion: I do not have to go to school during the summer.

2. Everyone in the United States who is age 18 or over has the right to vote. Jackie is 21 years old, so Jackie is qualified to vote.

   Fact 1: _____

   Fact 2: _____

   Conclusion: _____

3. Trucks are not allowed on Route 7. Therefore, tractor-trailers are not allowed on Route 7 because tractor-trailers are trucks.

Fact 1: _____

Fact 2: _____

Conclusion: _____

4. We can conclude that tractor-trailers are not allowed on Route 7 because tractor-trailers are trucks and trucks are not allowed on Route 7.

Fact 1: _____

Fact 2: _____

Conclusion: _____

5. Connie must have gone to the beach today because she said she would either go to the beach or stay home, and we know she is not at home.

Fact 1: _____

Fact 2: _____

Conclusion: _____

6. Giovanni was going to major in either accounting or earth science. Since he didn't major in earth science, we can conclude that he majored in accounting.

Fact 1: _____

Fact 2: _____

Conclusion: _____

7. The coaches will probably ask Ryan to join the football team since they were looking for people to join either the football team or the baseball team. Ryan isn't very good at baseball.

Fact 1: _____

Fact 2: _____

Conclusion: _____

8. We can conclude that 20 to 40 wolves have radio ear tags since the researchers took 40 tags with them yesterday. The director said he wanted to tag 20 to 40 wolves.

   Fact 1: _____

   Fact 2: _____

   Conclusion: _____

9. In the election of 2000, Al Gore won the popular vote, so the popular vote must not carry much weight since George Bush became the president.

   Fact 1: _____

   Fact 2: _____

   Conclusion: _____

10. If the water table in Dallas fell more than 400 feet in the last 30 years, it is reasonable to predict that it will fall 800 feet during the next 30 years, since the rate of public water use has doubled since 1950.

    Fact 1: _____

    Fact 2: _____

    Conclusion: _____

EXERCISE
6-9

Identifying Multiple Causes and Effects

Identify the cause-effect relationships in each of the following paragraphs and/or passages. The first one has been done for you.

1. Another way to gauge the importance of listening is to look at the purposes that listening serves and the many benefits that you can derive from listening more effectively. Listening serves the same purposes already noted for interpersonal communication: to learn, to relate, to influence, to play, and to help. (DeVito 132)

   cause: listening _____

   effect 1: learning _____

effect 2: relating _____

effect 3: influencing _____

effect 4: playing _____

effect 5: helping _____

2. There are many factors that are causing the earth's fresh water supply to be used up. One reason for this is the rapid growth of the world's population. Also, much water is being used by industry and agriculture. Large-scale farming uses 65 percent of the world's water supply for irrigation and agricultural purposes. [Large-scale industry uses 22 percent of the world's water supply.] In the entire world, only 7 percent of all the fresh water is used for drinking and household purposes. (Bryjak and Soroka 300)

cause 1: _____

cause 2: _____

cause 3: _____

effect: _____

3. The results of a study show divorce has a negative effect on many children. The majority of children in the study felt that at least one parent had rejected them. When almost half of these children became adults, they had many difficulties to overcome. They spent more time worrying and had lower self-esteem than their peers from intact families. They were also underachieving and sometimes "angry individuals." From this research we know that the effects of divorce are more devastating and long-lasting for children than for their parents. (Davidson and Moore 688)

cause: _____

effect 1: _____

effect 2: _____

effect 3: _____

effect 4: _____

4. Nixon's announcement to bomb neutral Cambodia and expand the Vietnam War triggered many campus demonstrations. One college where feelings ran high was Kent State University in Ohio. For several days students there

clashed with local police. They broke windows and caused other damage to property. After students burned down the ROTC building, the governor of Ohio ordered the National Guard to the campus. When the governor of Ohio called out the National Guard, angry students showered the soldiers with stones. During a noontime protest on May 4 the guardsmen, who were poorly trained in crowd control, suddenly opened fire. Four students were killed, two of them women who were merely passing by on their way to class. (Garraty and Carnes 849)

cause: _____

effect 1: _____

effect 2: _____

effect 3: _____

effect 4: _____

effect 5: _____

effect 6: _____

5. Because of ever-increasing air pollution, some Chinese cities are no longer visible when photographed from satellites. A recent study concluded that the air quality in Beijing was at a "level 4," with "level 5" being the worst ("Heavy Breathing in China," 1998). Some school children in Mexico City and Taipei wear surgical masks to protect them from a variety of pollutants, as do many residents of Beijing. The U.S. State Department advises women assigned to Mexico City not to become pregnant lest their children suffer brain damage while still in the womb as a result of high rates of airborne toxins. A World Health Organization study in the Mexican capital found blood toxicity in 70 percent of the fetuses examined (Gardels and Snell, 1989). Another study discovered levels of lead in 41 percent of newborn babies (Walker, 1993). Lead levels of this magnitude could reduce the intelligence quotient (IQ) of an individual by as much as 10 percent. A Mexican lung specialist stated, "If we continue this way, Mexico will have very few intellectuals" (Sanchez, in Rodriguez, 1992, p. D7). (Bryjak and Soroka 324)

cause 1: _____

effect 1: _____

effect 2: _____

effect 3: _____

effect 4: _____

effect 5: _____

cause: _____

effect: _____

cause: _____

effect: _____

CLASSIFICATION

The classification pattern, also called *categorization*, is found in textbooks of all fields because it is rooted in the basic way that human beings think.

There is nothing more basic than categorization to our thought, perception, action, and speech. Every time we see something as a kind of thing, for example, a tree, we are categorizing. Whenever we reason about kinds of things—chairs, nations, illnesses, emotions, any kind of thing at all—we are employing categories. (Lakoff 5–6)

Whenever we identify divisions, groups, and classes, we are categorizing and classifying them. Read the paragraph below. What divisions have been created to represent the different types of people living in Mexico?

Modern Mexicans trace their heritage to two distinct *groups of* people, the Spanish conquistadores, and the indigenous Amerindians who lived in this area before the Spanish arrived. The people of this mixed ancestry, called Mestizos, *make up* 60 percent of the Mexican population. In addition, 30 percent of the population are Amerindian, and about 9 percent are listed as White, or European. (Farr and Hammers 16)

From reading the paragraph, we know that we could classify the conquistadores and the Amerindians as "modern Mexicans." We also know that we could classify the Mestizos, the Amerindians, and the Europeans as inhabitants of Mexico.

One clue to the classification pattern is the phrase "groups of." It helps us recognize that we are reading about categories, types, or classes of people. Another clue to the classification pattern is the phrase "make up 60 percent." It helps us recognize that the Mestizos are one part of one group that makes up the whole of the Mexican population. (See the Reading Between the Lines Box 6.4 on page 227 for more clue words and phrases common to the classification pattern.)

Reading Between the Lines Box 6.4

SIGNALS TO CLASSIFICATION PATTERNS

Authors use the classification pattern to define concepts that are interconnected. Our task is to make the connection between these groups and the major category that represents them. We are generally looking for "types" or "kinds" of things that belong together because they have something in common. Signal words can help us identify these relationships. Study the signal words below and complete the activity that follows.

Signals

categories	elements of	a form of
classify	characteristics of	part(s) of
include	characterized by	together make up
types of	categorized as	grouped by
kinds of	composed of	comprises

Activity

1. Read the paragraph below and underline the signal words that help you identify the classification pattern.

2. What is the major class or category discussed?_____

3. What are the items in this class?_____

> Astronomers classify galaxies into three major categories. **Spiral galaxies** look like flat white disks with yellowish bulges at their centers. The disks are filled with cool gas, as in the Milky Way, and usually display beautiful spiral arms. **Elliptical galaxies** are redder, more rounded, and often longer in one direction than in the other, like a football. Compared with spiral galaxies, elliptical galaxies contain very little cool gas and dust, though they often contain very hot, ionized gas. Galaxies that appear neither disk-like nor rounded are classified as **irregular galaxies**. The sizes of all three *types of* galaxies span a wide range, from dwarf galaxies containing as few as 100 million (10^8) stars to giant galaxies with more than 1 trillion (10^{12}) stars. The differing colors of galaxies arise from the different kinds of stars that populate them and reflect their star-formation histories. (Bennett, Donahue, Schneider, & Voit 591)

EXERCISE 6-10

Identifying Class and Category

All of the selections below are written in the classification pattern. For each selection, identify the category, or class, and indicate the parts that make up this class of items. Underline the signal words that helped you identify them. The first one has been done for you.

1. The Mexican middle <u>class</u> is <u>composed of</u> three groups; white-collar workers in the private and public sectors of the Mexican economy, the new urban professionals, and small businessmen. As in many developing countries, this class has little political or social cohesion, yet provides political and economic stability to the Mexican society. (Farr and Hammers 17)

   Class or category: <u>Mexican middle class society</u>

   Items within the class:

   1. <u>white-collar workers</u>

   2. <u>urban professionals</u>

   3. <u>small businessman</u>

2. Three types of teams that are found in organizations are work teams, task teams, and management teams. A **work team** is a collection of individuals who form natural work groups within an organization. A **task team** is a group that is formed for a specific period of time to work on a particular problem or issue. A **management team** is a collection of managers who meet on a regular basis to make decisions and determine the future direction of a unit or organization. These three types of teams have different purposes and needs. In order for any of them to work efficiently and effectively, it is best to continuously evaluate their performance. (Barker and Gaut 147–49)

   Class or category: _____

   Items within the class:

   1. _____

   2. _____

   3. _____

3. The American economy is characterized by (1) the private ownership of property and (2) a free market economy—two key tenets of capitalism, a form of economic system that favors private control of business and minimal governmental regulation of private industry. In capitalist systems the laws of supply and demand, interacting freely in the marketplace, set prices of goods and drive production. Under capitalism, sales occur for the profit of the individual. (O'Connor and Sabato 14)

   Class or category: _____

Items within the class:

1. _____

2. _____

3. _____

4. Capitalism is just one type of economic system. Others include socialism, communism, and totalitarianism. **Socialism** is a philosophy that advocates collective ownership and control of the means of economic production. Socialists call for governmental—rather than private—ownership of all land, property, and industry and, in turn, an equitable distribution of the income from those holdings. In addition, socialism seeks to replace the profit motive and competition with cooperation and social responsibility.

   Under **communism**, all class differences would be abolished and government would become unnecessary. A system of common ownership of the means of sustenance and production would lead to greater social justice.

   A **totalitarian system** is basically a modern form of extreme authoritarian rule. Totalitarian governments have total authority over their people and their economic system. The tools of totalitarianism are secret police, terror, propaganda, and an almost total prohibition on civil rights and liberties. (O'Connor and Sabato 15)

Class or category: _____

Items within the class:

1. _____

2. _____

3. _____

4. _____

5. **Types of Groups.** Throughout your life you will take part in many groups and teams. Let's take a look at some of the more distinctive ones.

   A **study group** is a gathering of people who get together to learn new information or skills. They may assemble as a group only one time or may come together periodically. Perhaps you are a member of several different study groups whose members help you review material to pass your exams.

A **support group** focuses on learning to cope with situations to meet the needs of its members. In the future, you may find that you need a support group to help you through a crisis in your life. Examples of organizations that sponsor support groups are Alcoholics Anonymous, American Cancer Society, Alzheimer's Family Association, and Students Against Drunk Drivers.

As part of your college career, you may be asked to participate as a member of **a focus group**. A focus group is comprised of members of a certain target audience that uses a particular product or service. For example, during an election year, you may see a group of people interviewed on C-SPAN about their view on presidential candidates. A professional facilitator usually leads focus group discussions. (Barker and Gaut 147)

Class or category: _____

Items within the class:

1. _____

2. _____

3. _____

PROBLEM-SOLUTION

The problem-solution pattern is common among most textbooks because every discipline seeks answers to problems. A problem is an undesirable condition that creates difficulties. The solution is the action or series of actions that will cure or solve the problem.

This pattern is often found in or near passages that describe cause-effect relationships. This is because some effects create problems that call for a solution. Once a problem is identified, there can be more than one solution. When this happens, people must decide which solution is best.

The problem-solution pattern is similar to the cause-effect pattern in that there can be many different combinations of problems and solutions:

■ One problem with one solution

     problem ⟶ solution

■ Two or more problems with the same solution

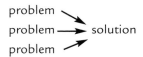

Visual Literacy Box 6.4

USING ORGANIZATION CHARTS TO SHOW CLASSIFICATION PATTERNS

Organization charts are useful for "seeing" the classification pattern. Read the paragraph below, taken from a biology textbook, study the organization chart below and answer the following questions.

Activity 1:

1. What is the major category? _____

2. What are the subcategories or classes?_____

3. What items come under the category of roots? grains? fruits of trees and vines? legumes? _____

Angiosperms have dominated the land for over 100 million years, and there are about 235,000 species of flowering plants living today. Most of our foods come from a few hundred domesticated species of flowering plants. Among these foods are roots, such as beets and carrots; the fruits of trees and vines, such as apples, nuts, berries, and squashes; the fruits and seeds of legumes, such as peas and beans; and grains, the fruits of grasses such as rice, wheat, and corn.

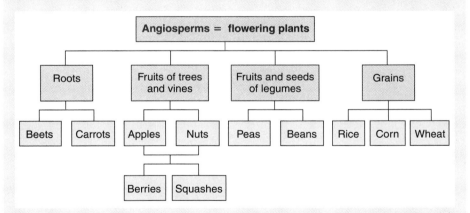

Activity 2:

1. Read the excerpt below and underline any words or phrases that signal the classification pattern.

2. Use the information provided in the excerpt to fill in the organization chart below.

Plant biologists classify angiosperms in two groups, called monocots and dicots, on the basis of several structural features, illustrated below. The names "monocot"

(continued on next page)

(continued from previous page)

and "dicot" refer to the first leaves that appear on the plant embryo. These embryonic leaves are called seed leaves, or cotyledons. A monocot embryo has one seed leaf while a dicot embryo has two seed leaves.

Monocots (about 85,000 species) include the orchids, bamboos, palms, and lilies, as well as the grains and other grasses. Most angiosperms (about 170,000 species) are **dicots**. This group includes most shrubs and trees (except for the conifers), as well as the majority of our ornamental plants and many of our food crops. (Campbell, Mitchell, and Reece 621)

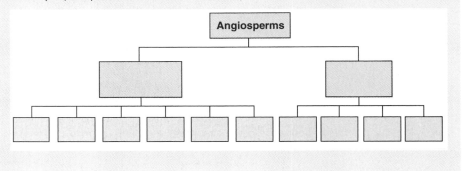

■ One problem with many solutions

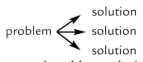

As we read problem-solution patterns, we should keep in mind the following questions:

1. What are the causes of the problem?
2. What are the effects?
3. What are the possible solutions?
4. Which solutions are the best?
5. Which solutions will cause more problems?

Read the following paragraph and identify the problem and the solution.

Lately we have been watching a lot of television, ordering out for pizza and ice cream, and sleeping quite a bit. My doctor said that I have to lose 40 pounds because the excess weight is putting a strain on my heart. He has suggested that I eat more fresh fruits and vegetables and whole grains. He has also suggested that I begin an exercise program, swimming for one hour three times a week. He believes this can be accomplished by simply turning off the television and taking the time to cook and go to the pool.

After reading the above paragraph, we learn that the narrator has a strained heart. This is the problem. The solution to this problem is diet and exercise. We can diagram this paragraph by looking at the causes, effects, problems, and solutions being described.

causes: watching television
eating pizza and ice cream
excessive sleep

effects: gained 40 pounds

problem: strained heart

solution: change diet
start exercise program

Reading Between the Lines Box 6.5

SIGNALS TO PROBLEM-SOLUTION PATTERNS

Problem-solution is a pattern common to sociology, ecology, science, and mathematics. Signal words such as "problem" and "solution" usually stand out quite well in mathematics textbooks. However, they are less obvious in other types of texts. Below is a list of signals that will help you recognize when the author is introducing a problem and/or a solution.

Signals

problem	the problem is	what can be done	the issue is
solution	one solution to this is	some strategies include	to solve this problem

Activity:

1. Read the except below and underline the signal words related to the problem-solution pattern.

2. What is the overall problem? _____

3. List the solutions:

_____

_____

_____

_____

What, if anything, can be done to alleviate chronic hunger/malnutrition-related diseases that affect 14 percent of humanity? The following is a list of solutions most often put forth by experts from a variety of backgrounds:

(continued on next page)

(continued from previous page)

1. Reduce fertility and slow population growth. While this strategy will not eliminate hunger in the short run, it will prevent the problem from getting substantially worse.

2. Take the necessary political and economic steps to bring about a more equitable distribution of the world's wealth.

3. Change our collective eating habits. Enough food is produced annually to feed a world of 10 billion vegetarians. However, a significant amount of grains, corn, and other crops goes to feed cattle, pigs, and chickens—animals later consumed by the planet's most affluent people.

4. Increase the food supply. According to one estimate, the current global food supply will have to double by 2025 to keep up with population growth. A report by the United Nations Food and Agricultural Organization concluded that to feed its citizens in the year 2050, Africa would have to increase food production by 300 percent, Latin America by 80 percent, and Asia by 70 percent. (Bryjak and Soroka 295–96)

EXERCISE
6-11

Identifying the Cause and Effect, Problem and Solution

Read the following paragraphs and identify the cause(s), effect(s), problem(s), and solution(s). The first one has been done for you.

1. When I was seven years old, my parents separated and later divorced. My parents are the most influential and persuasive people in my life, so their divorce had an incredible effect on my childhood. It caused me great grief and unhappiness. Over the years, I have managed to deal with these problems. My parents' divorce caused me to use my academics as a tool to get their attention. There are many ways to get through to my parents. Unfortunately, I used negative tools to gain their attention. For example, I used a "poor" general attitude to convey a message that I was unhappy. My parents' divorce was also a learning experience. I have learned that I am my own individual and that I must achieve my goals for myself. I gained this knowledge through maturity and the fact that I have felt alone for so many years.

   cause(s): _parent's divorce_

   effect(s): _great grief and unhappiness_

   problem(s): _poor general attitude_

   solution(s): _used academics to gain parent's attention_

2. Attempts to limit fertility in the poorer nations of the world have met with some success. These strategies include China's policy of one child per family and forced sterilization. Many nations have used media campaigns aimed at convincing people that having fewer children is to everyone's advantage. Governments have made various contraceptive devices available at low enough costs (or for free) so that even poor people can afford them. Educating women via formal schooling appears to be one of the most effective ways of lowering fertility. (Bryjak and Soroka 308)

   cause(s): _____

   effect(s): _____

   problem(s): _____

   solution(s): _____

3. In the developing world, slums are increasing at twice the rate of rapidly growing cities as a whole. Whereas the number of dwellings constructed annually in Third World nations is between 2 and 4 per 1,000 individuals, the urban population in these nations is increasing at between 25 and 60 persons per 1,000 (Hardoy and Satterthwaite, 1997). The housing shortage is so acute in many poor countries that in all likelihood it will never be resolved. For example, in Kenya, three million new units would have to be built each year to accommodate that country's urban growth. In Cairo, between 200,000 and 500,000 people live in cemeteries; and some residents of the infamous "City of the Dead" even have running water and electricity. Approximately 500 million urban dwellers (or one of every 12 people) worldwide (mostly in developing nations) are homeless or lack adequate housing (Harper, 1998). According to a United Nations report, an estimated 10 million people die each year in densely populated urban areas as a result of health problems brought about by sub-standard housing and poor sanitation (Wright, 1994).

   A partial solution to the housing shortage is for people to construct dwellings "illegally or informally." Hardoy and Satterthwaite (1997) note that it is not uncommon for 30 percent of a city's population to be housed in such a manner, with dwellings constructed by people who have "demonstrated remarkable ingenuity in developing their own homes and new residential area" (p. 267). (Bryjak and Soroka 324–28)

   cause(s): _____

   effect(s): _____

   problem(s): _____

   solution(s): _____

4. Lawns create more problems than they solve. First, lawns require a lot of water. Watering lawns accounts for up to 60 percent of the water used in cities in the Western states and 30 percent of the water used in the East. Second, lawns require herbicides to keep weeds from overtaking them. We use 33 million pounds of herbicide each year. Not only is this expensive, but these herbicides leave residues that contaminate our drinking water. In addition to these problems, our lawns require 580 million gallons of gasoline to power our mowers. We also need pesticides to ward off insects and fungus that are attracted to grass. The problem with this is that the pesticides do not stay in the soil for long; they have been found in 10 percent of our communities' wells. Landscapers have been working hard to present solutions to the public. They suggest incorporating more native species of grasses and vegetation that require less maintenance because they are adapted to the local environment. They have also suggested creating meadows and mixed-plant gardens that will attract wildlife in place of lawn. (Smith and Smith V-C)

cause(s): _____

effect(s): _____

problem(s): _____

solution(s): _____

5. Fossil fuels power most of our industries, agricultural equipment, and automobiles, and they heat most of our homes. One of the major side effects of the combustion of fossil fuels is an increase in atmospheric CO_2. Carbon dioxide is one of several so-called greenhouse gases—molecules that can trap heat and cause atmospheric warming, known as the greenhouse effect. Our current cause for alarm arises from the potential for too much warming. Studies of climatic changes through geological time and mathematical models lead some climatologists to predict that in the next 50–100 years, at the present rate greenhouse gases are increasing, atmospheric temperatures could rise by about 2C degrees. On a global scale, an increase of less than 2C degrees would be enough to melt polar ice and raise sea levels significantly. Unless massive dikes were built, the projected rise in sea level would, by the end of the twenty-first century, flood coastal areas, many of which are environmentally sensitive and heavily populated. In addition to flooding, a warming trend might alter patterns of global precipitation. For instance, the grain belts of the central United States and central Asia might become much drier and unable to support the crops currently grown there. Furthermore, forested areas in semiarid zones could lose their trees and become deserts.

What can be done to lessen the chances of a greenhouse disaster? International cooperation and national and individual action are needed to decrease fossil-fuel consumption and to reduce the destruction of forests and replant many areas throughout the world. Several nations have instituted tree-planting programs, and the leaders of many nations have called for efforts to stabilize CO_2 output by the end of the century. Because fossil-fuel combustion currently powers much of our industry and economic growth, meeting the terms of the treaty will require strong individual efforts and acceptance of some major lifestyle changes. There is much to gain by conserving energy at home, recycling, and reducing our use of cars by walking, bicycling, or taking mass transit. Other strategies include developing solar, wind, and geothermal energy sources to reduce our reliance on fossil fuels. Although such measures are expensive, so are building massive dikes to prevent coastal cities from flooding, or changing a food-producing nation such as the United States to a food-dependent one. (Campbell, Mitchell, and Reece 768–69)

cause(s): _____

effect(s): _____

problem(s): _____

solution(s): _____

Visual Literacy Box 6.5 ● ● ● ● ● ● ● ● ● ● ● ● ● ● ● ●

DIAGRAMMING COMPLEX PROBLEM-SOLUTION PATTERNS

Problem-solution patterns are closely linked to cause-effect relationships because a problem can be either a cause or an effect. For example, the fact that "lawns require a lot of water" is a problem, but it is also a cause. However, the effect "a huge water loss" is also a problem. Study the passage below and identify which **problems** are **causes** and which are **effects**, and fill in the chart below. After that, identify the **solutions** and add them to the chart. Finally, fill in the diagram at the bottom of the page with the appropriate problems and solutions. The first two have been done for you.

Chain = A caused B *and* B caused C *and* C caused D.

1. Problem (cause)— _____
2. Problem (effect)— _____
3. Problem (cause)— _____
4. Problem (effect)— _____
5. Problem (effect)— _____

6. Problem (cause)— _____
7. Problem (cause)— _____
8. Problem (effect)— _____
9. Solution— _____
10. Solution— _____

(continued on next page)

(continued from previous page)

Lawns create more problems than they solve. First, lawns require a lot of water. Watering lawns accounts for up to 60 percent of the water used in cities in the Western states and 30 percent of the water used in the East. Second, lawns require herbicides to keep weeds from overtaking them. We use 33 million pounds of herbicide each year. Not only is this expensive, but these herbicides leave residues that contaminate our drinking water. In addition to these problems, our lawns require 580 million gallons of gasoline to power our mowers. We also need pesticides to ward off insects and fungus that are attracted to grass. The problem with this is that the pesticides do not stay in the soil for long; they have been found in 10% of our communities' wells. Landscapers have been working hard to present solutions to the public. They suggest incorporating more native species of grasses and vegetation that require less maintenance because they are adapted to the local environment. They have also suggested creating meadows and mixed-plant gardens that will attract wildlife in place of lawn. (Campbell, Mitchell, and Reece 168–69)

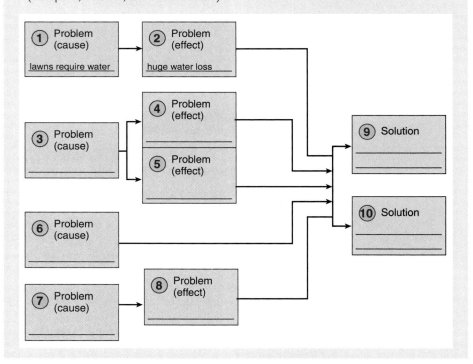

A Reading in Sociology

Have you ever wondered why some people have a lot of money and others have very little money? Read the following selection to find out why this happens. Complete the vocabulary exercise before reading the selection to learn the new terms. Then complete the comprehension exercises that follow the reading.

Vocabulary in Context

a. **converge**—come together

b. **tenfold**—ten times

c. **financial speculation**—investing money

d. **inequity**—unfairness; injustice; discrimination

e. **staples**—goods; supplies

Use the words above to complete the following statements. The first one has been done for you.

_____a_____ **1.** The directions were confusing because MLK Boulevard and Washington Street _____ at the intersection, becoming one road called Broad Street.

_____ **2.** Since 1970, the number of women who are unmarried and supporting children increased _____.

_____ **3.** The rich became wealthier since the 1980s because they were able to participate in investment opportunities and _____.

_____ **4.** Much_____ exists between the rich and poor; the rich do not need to work while the poor cannot find jobs.

_____ **5.** The homeless lack the necessary _____ that most Americans take for granted, such as food and shelter.

What Causes the Gap Between the Rich and the Poor?

[1]   Approximately 700,000 families fall into that lofty category of being in the top 1 percent of income earners in the United States. Even though it takes a family income of at least $250,000 to be part of the top 1 percent, the average for this group is considerably higher and is well over $500,000. The average family incomes for these people nearly doubled between 1980 and 1990.

[2]   Before 1973, incomes rose equally for poor, middle-class, and wealthy families. Since that time, the economy helped lift the incomes of the rich, but not of the poor. As the wealth of the rich doubled during the 1980s, the poor watched their already low incomes slide 5 percent to a 1990 average of $9,800. This helped to bring the gap between the rich and the poor to its widest in decades.

[3]   How did this happen? As with so many social issues, the answers are not all that easy, and they include a number of possible explanations.

[4]   Many people are inclined to say that the rich grew richer at the expense of the poor. This view is difficult to support. The poor had so little to begin

with that it is impossible for them to account for the dollar gains of the rich. Three trends **converged** to widen income inequality.

[5] 1. *Growth of the poorest poor.* The last decade saw a substantial growth in the number of people in extreme poverty, most of whom are minority and young. Unwed mothers, who head the poorest families of all, saw their numbers increase **tenfold** from 1970 to 1990 to 2.8 million. Politicians may argue over why this category of poverty is growing, but it appears that these people have fallen below the level where an upward turn in our economy can help them.

[6] 2. *Investment earnings.* Investment opportunities and financial **speculation** fueled during the 1980s helped increase the wealth of the rich. Census Bureau figures show that 99 percent of all families—even the well-off upper-middle class—depend on their paychecks for most of their income. Not so for the top 1 percent of families who make the majority of their income from interest, dividends, and other investment income.

[7] 3. *Need for educated workers.* Our society has become very dependent on an educated workforce, and in the middle class there has been a noticeable split between the earnings of the highly skilled and the unskilled. This is due to the decline in American manufacturing and blue-collar jobs. The median weekly wage of blue-collar workers, when adjusted for inflation, has dropped almost 10 percent in the last decade. At the same time, the earnings of college graduates have risen sharply in comparison with those of high-school graduates. Incomes of college-educated families have increased by nearly as much as those of the top 1 percent group. Families in the high-school education category have watched their incomes fall (U.S. Bureau of Census). Unless there are dramatic changes, the trend points in the direction of a nation with drastically greater **inequities** between the well-to-do and those who are unable to obtain the **staples** of the American dream. (Tischler 241).

Comprehension

Write the letter of the correct answer on the line provided. The first one has been done for you.

_____c_____ 1. The topic of this selection is:
   a. incomes of college-educated families.
   b. the need for educated workers.
   c. the gap between the rich and the poor.

_____ 2. The main point of this selection is:
   a. For various reasons, already wealthy families and college-educated families are becoming wealthier while families of blue-collar workers and high school graduates are earning less.
   b. Approximately 700,000 families fall into that lofty category of being in the top 1 percent of income earners in the United States.

    c. Unwed mothers, who head the poorest families of all, saw their numbers increase **tenfold** from 1970 to 1990 to 2.8 million.

_____ **3.** The overall text pattern of this selection is:
    a. description.
    b. cause-effect.
    c. classification.

_____ **4.** The text pattern for paragraph 2 is:
    a. cause-effect.
    b. problem-solution.
    c. contrast.

_____ **5.** How many families in the United States earn more than $250,000 per year?
    a. 500,000
    b. 1,000,000
    c. 700,000

_____ **6.** What percentage of the American people earn over $250,000?
    a. 1 percent
    b. 25 percent
    c. 50 percent

_____ **7.** What is the text pattern for the following sentence?

Unwed mothers, who head the poorest families of all, saw their numbers increase **tenfold** from 1970 to 1990 to 2.8 million.
    a. comparison
    b. contrast
    c. comparison-contrast

_____ **8.** What is the text pattern for the following sentence?

Incomes of college-educated families have increased by nearly as much as those of the top 1 percent group.
    a. comparison
    b. contrast
    c. comparison-contrast

_____ **9.** The text pattern for paragraph 6 is:
    a. comparison.
    b. contrast.
    c. comparison-contrast.

_____ **10.** Another text pattern used in this selection is:
    a. topic and list.
    b. term, definition, and example.
    c. description.

A Reading in Human Anatomy and Physiology

Being overweight is a real problem for many people in the United States. Read the following article to find out why it is so difficult to lose weight and what is the safest way to go about doing so. Because this selection is from a college-level anatomy and physiology textbook, you will probably not understand every detail. Therefore, as you read, focus on the main points and the overall textbook patterns. Complete the vocabulary exercise before reading the selection to learn the new terms. Then complete the comprehension exercises that follow the reading.

Vocabulary in Context

   a. relative—in relation to; in comparison with

   b. obesity—the state of being overweight

   c. perplexing—puzzling

   d. adverse—harmful

   e. stigma—condition that makes one feel shame

   f. syndrome—condition or disease

   g. successive—following one after another

   h. deviation—move away from; variation

   i. correlation—association; connection; relationship

   j. predisposition—tendency

Use the words above to complete the following statements. The first one has been done for you.

_____e_____ **1.** Because there is a social _____ attached to being obese, a fat person pays higher insurance premiums, is discriminated against in the job market, has fewer clothing choices, and is frequently humiliated during both childhood and adulthood.

_____ **2.** When people lose weight, then gain weight, and lose weight again, they are called yo-yo dieters. Each _____ time they diet, the weight loss occurs more slowly, and regaining lost weight occurs three times as fast.

_____ **3.** People who exercise develop more compact bones and will weigh more than a person of _____ size who doesn't exercise.

_____ 4. Any _____ from a well-balanced diet will have an effect on a person's weight.

_____ 5. Most experts agree that _____ occurs when a person is 20 percent heavier than the ideal weight.

_____ 6. It is well known that obesity has _____ effects on health such as diabetes and heart disease.

_____ 7. A disease is sometimes referred to as a _____.

_____ 8. Because weight loss is a _____ concept to many dieters, they often fail to achieve their goals.

_____ 9. Harvard Medical School found a _____ between obesity and those whose diets were highest in fat.

_____ 10. Only 5 percent of the United States population has a genetic _____ for obesity.

Obesity: Magical Solution Wanted

[1]   How fat is too fat? What distinguishes an obese person from one who is merely overweight? The bathroom scale is an inaccurate guide because body weight tells nothing of body composition. A skilled dancer with dense bones and well-developed muscles may weigh several pounds more than an inactive person of the same **relative** size. Most experts agree that a person is obese when he or she is 20% heavier than the "ideal weight" published in insurance company tables (which, by the way, are artificially low). What is really needed is a measure of body fat, because the most common view of **obesity** is that it is a condition of excessive triglyceride storage. Although we bewail our inability to rid ourselves of fat, the real problem is that we keep refilling the storehouses by consuming too many calories. A body fat content of 18% to 22% of body weight (males and females, respectively) is considered normal for adults. Anything over that is defined as obesity.

[2]   However it's defined, obesity is a **perplexing** and poorly understood disease. The term "disease" is appropriate because all forms of obesity involve some imbalance in food intake control mechanisms. Despite its well-known **adverse** effects on health (the obese have a higher incidence of arteriosclerosis, hypertension, coronary artery disease, and diabetes mellitus), it is the most common health problem in the United States. About 50% of adults and 20% of teenagers are obese. U.S. kids are not only getting fatter but, because they are opting for home video games and nachos instead of touch football, their general cardiovascular fitness is declining as well. In addition to the health problems mentioned, the obese may store excessive levels of fat-soluble toxic chemicals, such

as marijuana, the insecticide DDT, and PCB (a cancer-causing chemical) in their bodies. Because DDT interferes with the liver's ability to rid the body of other toxins, these effects may be very far-reaching.

[3] As if this were not enough, the social **stigma** and economic disadvantages of obesity are legendary. A fat person pays higher insurance premiums, is discriminated against in the job market, has fewer clothing choices, and is frequently humiliated during both childhood and adulthood.

[4] With all its attendant problems, it's a pretty fair bet that few people choose to become obese. So what causes obesity? Let's look at three of the more recent theories.

[5] (1) Large numbers of fat cells deliver signals that tend to stimulate overeating. Some believe that overeating behaviors develop early in life (the "clean your plate" **syndrome**) and set the stage for adult obesity by increasing the number of fat cells formed during childhood. During early adulthood and thereafter, increases in adipose tissue mass occur by depositing more fat in the existing cells. Thus, the more cells there are, the more fat can be stored. Further, when there are armies of incompletely filled fat cells, basal plasma levels of fatty acids and glycerol are lower, leading to abnormal hunger.

[6] Besides the signals delivered by blood-borne nutrients or so-called satiety chemicals (hormones and others), researchers have found hints that the fat cells themselves may stimulate overeating. Supporting this idea is the observation that when yo-yo dieters lose weight, their metabolic rate falls sharply. But when they subsequently gain weight, their metabolic rate increases like a furnace being stoked. Each **successive** weight loss occurs more slowly, and regaining lost weight occurs three times as fast. Thus, it appears that people, like laboratory animals subjected to alternating "feasts and fasts," become increasingly food efficient, and their metabolic rates adjust to counteract any **deviation** from their weight "set point." The instrument used to solve the problem—dieting (again and again)—becomes self-defeating.

[7] (2) Obese people are more fuel efficient and more effective "fat storers." Although it is often assumed that obese people eat more than other people, this is not necessarily true—many actually eat less than people of normal weight.

[8] Fat, the nutrient, is the obese person's worst enemy. Fats pack more wallop per calorie (are more fattening) than proteins or carbohydrates because of the way they are processed in the body. For example, when someone ingests 100 excess carbohydrate calories, the body uses 23 of them in metabolic processing and stores 77. However, if the 100 excess calories come from fat, only 3 calories are "burned" and the rest (97) are stored. Furthermore, since carbohydrates are the preferred energy fuel for most body cells, fat stores aren't tapped until carbohydrate reserves are nearly depleted.

[9]   These facts apply to everyone, but when you are obese the picture is even bleaker. For example, fat cells of overweight people "sprout" more alpha receptors (the kind that favors fat accumulation). Furthermore, the enzyme lipoprotein lipase, which unloads fat from the blood (usually to fat cells), is exceptionally efficient, and more of it is formed in the obese. In fact, obesity research done at Harvard Medical School found no **correlation** between caloric intake and body weight, but did find that those whose diets were highest in fat (especially saturated fats) were most overweight regardless of the number of calories consumed.

[10]   (3) Morbid obesity is the destiny of those inheriting two obesity genes. However, a true genetic **predisposition** for "fatness"—distributed "without compassion or fairness" by recently discovered recessive obesity genes—appears to account for only about 5% of the U.S. obese. These people, given excess calories, will always deposit them as fat, as opposed to those who lay down more muscle with some of the excess calories.

[11]   Rumors and poor choices for dealing with obesity abound. Some of the most unfortunate strategies used for coping with obesity are listed here.

1. **"Water pills."** Diuretics, which prompt the kidneys to excrete more water, are sought as a means of losing weight. At best, these may cause a few pounds of weight loss for a few hours; they can also cause serious electrolyte imbalance and dehydration.

2. **Diet pills.** Some obese [people] use amphetamines (best known are Dexedrine and Benzedrine) to reduce appetite. These work, but only temporarily (until tolerance develops) and can cause a dangerous dependency. Then the user has the problem of trying to dispense with the drug habit. Furthermore, none of the other "pill-type" diet aids cause fat to melt away either. Those that provide fiber to prevent absorption of nutrients can cause serious malnutrition.

3. **Fad diets.** Many magazines print at least one new diet regimen yearly, and diet products sell well. However, many of these diets are nutritionally unhealthy, particularly if they limit certain groups of nutrients. Some of the liquid high-protein diets popular now contain such poor-quality (incomplete) protein that they are actually dangerous. (The worst are those that contain collagen protein instead of a milk or soybean protein source).

4. **Surgery.** Sometimes sheer desperation prompts surgical solutions, all of which must be carefully considered. Surgical options include having the jaws wired shut, stomach stapling, intestinal bypass surgery, biliopancreatic diversion (BPD), and lipectomy (removal of fat by suction). BPD "rearranges" the digestive tract: Two-thirds of the stomach is removed; the small intestine is cut in half, and one 8-foot-long portion is sutured into the stomach opening. Since pancreatic juice and bile are diverted away from this "new intestine," far fewer nutrients (and no fats) are digested and absorbed. Although the

patients can eat anything they want without gaining weight, BPD is major surgery and carries all of its risks.

[12]   Unfortunately, there is no magical solution for obesity. The only way to lose weight is to take in fewer fat calories and increase physical activity to increase muscle mass (muscle consumes more energy at rest than fat). This prescription stresses the often-forgotten fact that there are two sides to the energy balance equation—caloric intake and energy output—and recognized the unique nature of fat handling in the body. Furthermore, low activity levels actually stimulate eating, while physical exercise depresses food intake and increases metabolic rate not only during activity but also for some time after. The only way to keep the weight off is to make these dietary and exercise changes lifelong habits. (Marieb 882–83)

Comprehension

Write the letter of the correct answer on the line provided. The first one has been done for you.

_____c_____ **1.** The topic of this selection is:
　　　　　a. why people become obese.
　　　　　b. why fad diets are a good solution for obesity.
　　　　　c. why there are no quick fixes for obesity.

_____ **2.** The main point of this selection is:
　　　　　a. Researchers have found that the only way to lose weight is to take in fewer fat calories and increase physical activity.
　　　　　b. About 50% of adults and 20% of teenagers are obese.
　　　　　c. The obese may store excessive levels of fat-soluble toxic chemicals, such as marijuana, the insecticide DDT, and PCB.

_____ **3.** The overall text pattern of this selection is:
　　　　　a. cause-effect.
　　　　　b. description.
　　　　　c. classification.

_____ **4.** The text pattern for paragraph 3 is:
　　　　　a. cause-effect.
　　　　　b. problem-solution.
　　　　　c. contrast.

_____ **5.** The only effect of taking a diet pill is:
　　　　　a. permanent weight loss of many pounds.
　　　　　b. temporary weight loss of a few pounds.
　　　　　c. loss of a couple of pounds for a few hours.

_____ **6.** When fad diets limit certain groups of nutrients such as proteins, they
   a. become dangerous.
   b. are relatively safe.
   c. are healthy.

_____ **7.** What is the text pattern of the following sentence?

Surgical options include having the jaws wired shut, stomach stapling, intestinal bypass surgery, biliopancreatic diversion (BPD), and lipectomy (removal of fat by suction).

   a. comparison-contrast
   b. cause-effect
   c. topic and list

_____ **8.** What is the effect in the following sentence?

The only way to lose weight is to take in fewer fat calories and increase physical activity to increase muscle mass.

   a. losing weight
   b. taking in fewer fat calories
   c. increasing physical activity

_____ **9.** What is the text pattern of the following sentence?

Furthermore, low activity levels actually stimulates eating, while physical exercise depresses food intake and increases metabolic rate.

   a. cause-effect
   b. comparison-contrast
   c. both cause-effect and comparison-contrast

_____ **10.** Another text pattern used in this selection is:
   a. topic and list.
   b. classification.
   c. description.

PART II
Critical Reading Strategies

CHAPTER

7

Inference

• •

In this chapter, we practice:

- making inferences;
- drawing conclusions;
- using logical reasoning.

On Halloween night, October 31, 1938, Orson G. Welles directed and narrated a play called the *War of the Worlds* over a nationwide radio network. In the play, Martians landed in Grovers Mills, New Jersey, defeated every army on earth, and took control of entire regions of the country. Of the six million people who listened to this broadcast, an estimated one million people believed it was a live newscast instead of a play. George Rodham, in *Making Sense of Media*, writes, "Soon, real-life residents there were running for cover with wet towels wrapped around their heads to protect their brains from Martian heat rays. Across the nation, police switchboards were jammed with calls from people who believed the invasion was real, and young men reported for military duty to fight the invaders"(179).

This example illustrates how important critical thinking skills are to listening. They are equally important to reading. The first step in developing good critical thinking skills is learning how to make accurate *inferences* from given *facts* (the information we learn when we read a text literally).

In chapter 1, you learned that while reading, you generally use your background knowledge to make predictions. In general, you connect what you know to the new information provided by the author. From these connections you make educated guesses, usually about what will happen next in the reading or about the point the author is trying to make. Making educated guesses allows you to become involved with the text. If you discover that your initial guess is incorrect, you review and reevaluate the information you have and make another guess. These guesses are called **inferences**.

Since chapter 1, you have been practicing your inference skills with the "Reading Between the Lines" boxes, so making inferences should not be new for you. So far, you have learned how to make inferences from

1. clues to action,
2. clues to word meaning,
3. experience clues,
4. clue words that signal patterns,
5. examples that illustrate the main point, and
6. descriptions that provide clues to character development.

You are now ready to make inferences based on facts. Go to Reading Between the Lines Box 7.1 on page 252 and test your skills.

From our knowledge of the world and the clues the author gives us, we infer what has happened or what will happen. The following diagram illustrates the process of making and evaluating an inference.

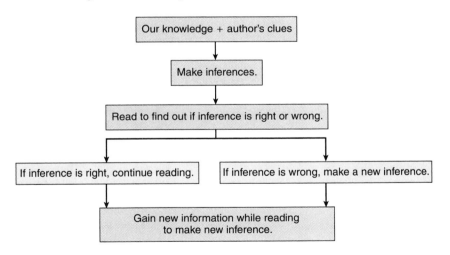

MAKING INFERENCES

Your success at making guesses or inferences depends on your background knowledge and the facts that you're given. In general, your background knowledge includes everything that you know about the world. **Logical reasoning** is the use of logic, analysis, and reasoning to make sense of our experiences as well

Reading Between the Lines Box 7.1

INFERENCE
The War of the Worlds

Before we can make a correct inference or draw a logical conclusion, we must know if our facts are true or false. In our *War of the Worlds* situation, people were given "facts" that were not true, such as the ones below:

- Martians landed in Grovers Mills, New Jersey.
- The Martians defeated every army on earth.
- The Martians took control of entire regions of the country.
- Martian heat rays could destroy human brains.

How were five million people able to recognize these facts to be false while one million people believed them to be true? Read the following excerpt about "The Invasion from Mars" study and learn how researchers from Princeton University answered this question.

> Listeners were frightened by the *War of the Worlds* broadcast because dramatic techniques such as simulated "on the spot" reporting and interviews with "experts" had fooled them. The researchers found that many of these listeners had accepted radio as their primary and most credible source of breaking news. This effect was heightened by the effect of "dial-twisting." While viewers were sampling other networks, deciding which program they liked best, many had missed the introductory disclaimer that the play was not a news report. Of equal importance, however, were the sociological conditions of the times. Americans had endured years of economic insecurity during the Great Depression and were facing the threat of World War II. This was an audience that felt on the edge of disaster, and they believed anything could happen at any time.
>
> In terms of why some people were frightened but others were not, the researchers found that those who were not good at critical thinking (the use of logic, analysis, and reasoning to make sense of their experiences) were most likely to be alarmed by the broadcast. Also, those with strong religious beliefs, those who were emotionally insecure to begin with, and those who listened with others who believed the broadcast, were more likely to be fooled. (Rodman 370–71).

List 5 reasons why one million people believed the facts given on the *War of the Worlds* broadcast were true.

1. _____

2. _____

3. _____

4. _____

(continued on next page)

5. _____

Are the following facts true or false?

_____ **1.** People who listened with others who believed the *War of the Worlds* broadcast was true were more likely to be fooled.

_____ **2.** A fact can be either true or false.

_____ **3.** Six million people believed the *War of the Worlds* broadcast was a real newscast.

_____ **4.** On Halloween night, October 31, 1938, Orson G. Welles directed and narrated a play called the *War of the Worlds* over a nationwide radio network.

_____ **5.** On October 31, 1938, young men reported for military duty to fight the Martians.

as to make inferences about ideas or concepts that the author has not directly stated. Thus, while we read we look at the important details and think of them as clues or evidence that will support our inferences or conclusions. Review the example below to see how we find clues within the facts and how we use these facts to make inferences.

> **Situation**: During the second quarter of the football game, the referee blew his whistle. The tackled quarterback lay motionless on the field. Two men with a stretcher rushed from the sidelines and carried him away.

What clues will help us infer what is happening in this scene?

■ The quarterback was tackled.

■ The quarterback was lying motionless.

■ The quarterback was carried away on a stretcher.

Based on these clues, what conclusion can we draw?

> **Inference:** The quarterback was hurt.

Visual Literacy Box 7.1 ● ● ■ ■ ■ ■ ■ ■ ■ ■ ■ ■ ■ ■ ■ ●

MAPPING INFERENCES

Based on what you've learned in previous Visual Literacy boxes, finish the maps that show how you would arrive at each inference about the scene described below:

It is a crisp autumn day, and fans have filled the bleachers to watch the game. Team Red has the ball. Members from Team Blue chase after player number 31,

(continued on next page)

(continued from previous page)

who is running toward the goalpost. In the bleachers Team Red fans are cheering him on, yelling "Go 31. Player 31 crosses the goal line while the coaches shoot their arms straight up, palms inward. Team Red fans jump up and down, waving banners and shouting for joy. The Team Red band starts playing a victory song.

The clues or facts provided are:

- Two teams are playing a game that involves a ball.
- Team Red has the ball.
- Team Red fans cheer for the person who has the ball.
- The coaches make the "goal" symbol with their arms.
- Team Red fans shout, jump up and down, and wave banners.
- Team Red band plays a victory song.

What can you guess or infer about this scene? Create a map that shows how you would reach an inference about the scene.

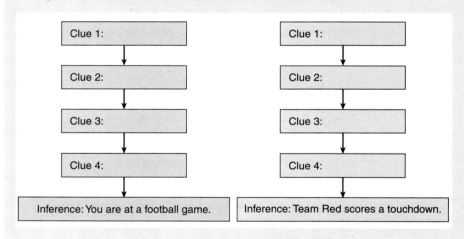

EXERCISE
7-1

Locating Clues to Inference

Study each situation. Locate the clues to help you make a logical inference or draw a reasonable conclusion. The first item is done for you.

1. **Situation**. It was the last lap around the Pocono Raceway. In the lead, Mario was only 500 yards from the finish line when the left front tire of his race car blew out.

Clues: There are race cars.

The race cars are doing laps around a raceway.

There is a finish line.

Mario's tire blew out.

Inference: Mario did not win the race.

2. **Situation:** In the dining room, customers were waiting for the roast beef to be served. Smoke filled the kitchen as the head chef ran to the oven where the roast had burned.

Clues: _____

_____

_____

_____

Inference: _____

3. **Situation:** Deep in conversation, the seven archaeologists compared the bones found on the site with those of prehistoric animals. As they argued, the neighbor's dog came out from the house with a bone in his mouth and buried it in the dirt behind them.

Clues: _____

_____

_____

_____

Inference: _____

4. **Situation:** Not wanting to be late for their 50-minute class on the third floor of the library, ten students hurried into the elevator. Before they could reach the third floor, the elevator jammed and they were stuck for 55 minutes.

Clues: _____

_____

_____

Inference: _____

5. **Situation:** Wanting to keep her jeans clean, the girl complained that her side of the canoe was dirty. The boy suggested they change seats as he pushed the canoe away from the shore. When they stood up to switch places, the canoe wavered and then tipped over.

Clues: _____

_____

_____

_____

Inference: _____

TYPES OF INFERENCE

Many different situations in reading require the reader to make inferences. Sometimes a sentence or paragraph does not give the reader all of the information he needs to know to be able to determine the _implied meaning_. (Remember, _implied_ means that hints or clues are given, but the idea is not directly stated.) In this case, the reader needs to read ahead to gain more information before he can identify and understand the inference or make the intended connections.

Instrumental Inferences

Sometimes we read a sentence and it is unclear as to what the author is "getting at," or implying. And so, we read the sentence over and over again and become frustrated because we still do not understand. In this case we need to read further; we need more information to "get" the author's point. Consider the example below:

Last year Sarita drove her sportscar everywhere. This year she has been in a lot of accidents again.

In this example, when we read the first sentence all we know is that Sarita has a sportscar and that she drives it a lot. It's not until we read the second sentence that we begin to understand what type of driver Sarita is. We know from the word "again" that Sarita was in a lot of accidents last year. However, had we stopped reading after the first sentence, we would have been unable to make this connection.

Other times we can read a sentence and pretty much determine the inference right away; when we read further, that inference is confirmed, as in this example:

The boy took pictures of all of his friends. His camera was very expensive.

In this case, we can pretty much infer that the boy used a camera to take pictures. The second sentence confirms that a camera was, in fact, the type of instrument he used to take the pictures. In both cases, a word or phrase in a following sentence helps us or is *instrumental* to our making the correct inference.

EXERCISE
7-2

Explaining Inferences

Read the sentences below and choose the letter that best explains the inference. The first one has been done for you.

_____b_____ **1.** Steve sold seven houses this month. His business is really booming.
   a. Steve works in the business industry.
   b. Steve is a realtor.
   c. Steve inherited a lot of properties.

_____ **2.** Glenn has been in graduate school for two years. He has one more year to go before he becomes a psychologist.
   a. It took Glenn two years to finish graduate school.
   b. Glenn will graduate three years from now.
   c. Glenn is enrolled in a three-year program.

_____ **3.** Brian learned a new song last night. He has really taken a liking to rap music.
   a. Brian learned a new rap song.
   b. Brian learned a new classical guitar song.
   c. Brian spent the evening playing heavy metal music.

_____ **4.** We watched television for two hours last Sunday. Although the movie was interesting, the commercial time in between segments took away 30 minutes.
   a. The movie lasted for two hours.
   b. The movie lasted about an hour.
   c. The movie lasted about one and a half hours.

_____ **5.** Tamika was asked to join the track team this year. She was also on the Olympic team two years ago.

   a. Tamika joined the Olympic track team again.
   b. Tamika joined a local track team.
   c. Tamika joined an Olympic soccer team.

Elaborative

Another situation that requires inference is when a general term is followed by a more specific term, or vice versa. This is called an **elaborative** inference because it adds information or *elaborates* on the subject.

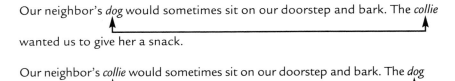

Our neighbor's *dog* would sometimes sit on our doorstep and bark. The *collie* wanted us to give her a snack.

Our neighbor's *collie* would sometimes sit on our doorstep and bark. The *dog* wanted us to give her a snack.

In the first case, the general term, "dog," is related to the specific term, "collie." In the second case, the specific term, "collie," is related to the general term, "dog." In both cases, the second sentence confirms that a collie is a type of dog. Let's look at another scenario.

Only one student in our sophomore class could afford a *car*. The rest of us depended on public transportation or walked if our destination was close enough. After the game on Friday night the temperature really dropped. None of us wanted to walk, so we all piled into Carmen's *car*. Twenty-one altogether. Boy, I don't know how that *Volkswagen Bug* ever got off the ground!

In this case, the general term, "car," is presented first. From this, we can infer that "Volkswagen Bug" is a type of car.

| EXERCISE 7-3 | **Explaining Elaborative Inferences** |

Read the sentences below and choose the letter that best explains the elaborative inference. The first one has been done for you.

___b___ **1.** The People's Express has the most competitive prices around. Jack booked a flight from Los Angeles to New York for under $99.00.
   a. People's Express is a train.
   b. People's Express is an airline.
   c. People's Express is a credit card.

_____ **2.** Francis counted the codlins and biffins before placing them in the baskets. In September, his farm stand always sold more apples than other types of produce.
   a. Codlins and biffins are types of baskets.

b. Codlins and Biffins is the name of the farm stand.

c. Codlins and biffins are apples.

_____ **3.** David packed to leave for Miramar. He was excited about his opportunity to go to a new Airforce base.

    a. Miramar is an Airforce base.

    b. Miramar is a city.

    c. Miramar is an airport.

_____ **4.** Although they were twice as expensive as other models, Anna Marie bought a new pair of Vokels. After trying several demo models of skis, she knew she would like them best.

    a. Vokels are demo models.

    b. Vokels are cars.

    c. Vokels are skis.

_____ **5.** Since the beginning of the year, Nabil met many new friends at Quinsigamond, including his girlfriend. He truly enjoyed going to college.

    a. Quinsigamond is a college.

    b. Quinsigamond is a dating service.

    c. Quinsigamond is a corporation.

Causal

Cause-effect relationships, or instances in which one event is the cause of another event, also require us to make inferences as we read. Review the sentences below. In order to explain how Rita's face went into the cake, what inference do we need to make?

> The passenger standing next to Rita on the subway was holding a box from the downtown bakery. Rita leaned forward as the passenger opened the lid to show her the beautifully decorated birthday cake. Just then the subway car came to a sudden stop. Rita's face went right into the cake.

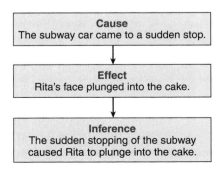

Explaining Causal Inferences

Read the sentences below and choose the letter that best explains the causal inference. The first one has been done for you.

_____b_____ 1. Although he was very intelligent, Josh had mixed results on his midterm scores: a D in math, an F in English, an A in psychology, and a B in sociology. He bought his psychology and sociology textbooks at the campus bookstore. However, he did not buy the math and English texts because he figured that he had taken English and math in high school and would not need to read those types of textbooks again.
     a. Josh is failing English because he is not very intelligent.
     b. Josh is failing English because he did not buy the textbook.
     c. Josh is failing English because he was only interested in psychology and sociology.

_____ 2. Every summer, countless numbers of vacationers drive to the coast to enjoy the ocean. Some even drive up to the water, as some resorts permit cars on the beach. However, major cities and small beach towns along the coast dump raw sewage into the ocean. Tides bring the contaminated water back to the shore, forcing some beaches to close.
     a. The water is contaminated from cities and towns dumping raw sewage into the ocean.
     b. The water is contaminated from vacationers swimming in the ocean.
     c. The water is contaminated from people driving cars along the beach.

_____ 3. Janet, an American student in Seattle, uses the Internet twice as many hours as her Japanese friend, Shuko. Although Shuko would like to go online more to promote her business, telecommunication charges are extremely high in Japan.
     a. Shuko doesn't use the Internet as much as Janet because telecommunication is expensive in Japan.
     b. Shuko doesn't use the Internet as much as Janet because she lives in Seattle.
     c. Shuko doesn't use the Internet as much as Janet because she wants to promote her business.

_____ 4. Mexico refused offers from the U.S. president to buy Texas and by 1830, Mexico closed the Texas borders to Americans. At that time, there were only a few thousand Mexicans living in Texas,

compared with the 20,000 white Americans who had already settled there. (Garraty and Carnes 329).

  a. In 1830, Mexico closed the Texas borders to Americans
     because the United States bought Texas.
  b. In 1830, Mexico closed the Texas borders to Americans
     because the United States refused to buy Texas.
  c. In 1830, Mexico closed the Texas borders to Americans
     because there were already more Americans than Mexicans.

_____ **5.** The Mexican-American War ended when the Americans took
     Mexico City. In the Treaty of Guadalupe Hidalgo (1848), Mexico
     agreed to sell much of its territory to the United States for 15 mil-
     lion dollars. This territory included areas that we know of today
     as Arizona, California, Colorado, Nevada, New Mexico, and
     parts of Utah and Wyoming. (Farr and Hammers 16)

  a. As a result of the Treaty of Guadalupe Hidalgo, Mexico gave
     up Arizona, California, Colorado, Nevada, New Mexico, and
     parts of Utah and Wyoming to the United States.
  b. As a result of the Treaty of Guadalupe Hidalgo, the United
     States lost Arizona, California, Colorado, Nevada, New Mex-
     ico, and parts of Utah and Wyoming to Mexico.
  c. As a result of the Treaty of Guadalupe Hidalgo, parts of Utah
     and Wyoming were sold to Mexico.

Metonymy—Inferences About People

Oftentimes we make inferences without realizing it. We use what linguists call
metonymy, or the use of symbols to simplify communication. We take a part of
something we know very well and use it to symbolize something else with
which it is associated. For example,

> A parking attendant tells his assistant, "The *Oldsmobile* has paid for the
> week, but you still need to collect $40.00 from the *Ford*."

The inference here is that the driver of the Oldsmobile has paid while the driver of the Ford has not. However, to the parking attendant, the words "Oldsmobile" and "Ford" are more familiar than the names of the people who own the cars,
and so he uses the names of the cars because they come most easily to the mind.

EXERCISE
7-5

Identifying Inferences About People

Read the sentences below and explain what the italicized term stands for. The
first one has been done for you.

1. Jan and Mike headed for the window as the cook called out "*Number 32, your pizza is ready.*"

   Number 32 stands for <u>Jan and Mike.</u>

2. As the bartender handed the waitress a glass of wine, he said "Send this over to the *redhead.*"

   Redhead refers to _____ .

3. One newspaper boy told another, "The *gray house* gets both the *Tribune* and the *Daily Local.*"

   The *gray house* stands for _____ .

4. As he collected the papers from students in the large auditorium, the graduate assistant told the professor. "*The green shirt* snored through the entire class."

   The *green shirt* refers to _____ .

5. One flight attendant said to another, "The *turkey club* wants another soda."

   The *turkey club* stands for _____ .

Metonymy—Inferences About Places

We also use inferences to let a place stand for events that occurred there. Look at the example below:

This is becoming another *Watergate.*

This sentence implies that people are secretly engaging in illegal information-gathering practices just as former President Nixon did at the Hotel Watergate.

A place can also stand for an organization that is located at that place. Read the example below and note the inference.

Wall Street is getting ready for a comeback.

Here, "Wall Street" refers to the entire U.S. investing network that is located in Manhattan, New York. The meaning implied is that the financial institutions in the United States will soon start making a profit again.

Identifying Inferences About Places

Read the sentences below and explain what the italicized term stands for. The first one has been done for you.

1. Don't cause any trouble at the demonstration; we don't want this to become another *Kent State*.

   Kent State stands for   the events that occurred at Kent State University in the

   1960s when the National Guard shot and killed two students who were

   protesting the Vietnam War and two who were on their way to class.

2. *India* said today that Pakistan would have to remove all of its missiles before talks can continue.

   India refers to _____

   _____

3. *Hollywood* lost millions when the latest film flopped.

   Hollywood stands for   _____

   _____

4. *Florida* said it will continue to recount the votes to settle the dispute from the 2000 presidential election.

   Florida refers to   _____

   _____

5. *Ocean City* called to say that the hotel is booked for the months of July and August.

   Ocean City stands for   _____

   _____

SITUATIONS THAT REQUIRE INFERENCE

Much of our daily communication depends heavily on inferences. Very few forms of writing, such as legal contracts and technical information, are written in a straightforward, precise manner. In most situations it is assumed that people have a certain amount of world knowledge and that every detail does not need to be spelled out. Take, for example, the statement "I'm late for work because I missed the bus." Even though the phrase "missed the bus" does not make much sense literally, everyone would understand what you meant. It is not necessary to explain that the bus had departed without you because your arrival time at the station was later than the departure time of the bus.

Figurative Language

Because we think in terms of images instead of words, much of our language depicts our imagination in a colorful way. For instance, it is more popular to say that we were "surfing the Net" instead of "searching for information through the use of the Internet system." Three common types of figurative language are *metaphors, imagery*, and *idioms*.

Metaphor   Authors require us to make inferences when they use metaphors in their writing. A **metaphor** is a comparison of two unlike things without using the words *like* or *as*. The metaphor just states that one unlike thing *is* another unlike thing. We have to use our inference skills to figure out the implied comparison. For example, look at the two sentences below. The first uses "as" to make a comparison, while the second does not.

She was as light as a feather.

We know that a human being is much heavier than a feather, but the inference is that she weighs less than most people.

I picked her up, and she is an absolute feather!

We know, of course, that a human being is a human being and not a feather. However, by saying that a human being *is* a feather, it is implied that compared with other human beings, this person weighs less.

EXERCISE
7-7

Explaining Metaphors

Choose the letter for the answer that best explains the metaphor. The first one has been done for you.

    b   **1.** Nik is the featherweight champion of wrestling.
   - a. Nik looks like a bird when he wrestles.
   - b. Nik is in the lighter-weight class of competitors.
   - c. Nik is not only a wrestler but also a bird watcher.

_____ **2.** LaToya thought Math 250 was a killer course.
   - a. LaToya knew people who died from taking Math 250.
   - b. LaToya thought Math 250 was an easy course.
   - c. LaToya thought Math 250 was a difficult course that took a lot of work.

_____ **3.** Laughter is the best medicine.
   - a. People should laugh when they take medicine.
   - b. It is healthy to laugh.
   - c. People become ill when they laugh and need medicine.

_____ **4.** A thin ribbon of smoke floated from the chimney.
   - a. Ribbons came out of the chimney.
   - b. The ribbon smelled like smoke because it was too close to the chimney.
   - c. The smoke has the appearance of a ribbon.

_____ **5.** The moon is a large round cookie.
   - a. The moon is large and full and resembles the shape of a cookie.
   - b. The cookies are cut into moon shapes.
   - c. The Moon Bakery has cookies for sale.

Imagery   Imagery is the process by which an author's description helps the reader create mental images—we try to create a picture of the author's experiences in our mind. When authors use imagery, we, as readers, interpret the mood or the meaning by making inferences based on the images or descriptions the author presents. Let's look at some images that Jack Finney provides in his short story "Contents of a Dead Man's Pocket." How can we tell that the character in this story is high up on the ledge of a building and that he is very frightened?

> He saw, in that instant, the Loew's theatre sign, blocks ahead; the miles of traffic signals; the lights of cars and street lamps; countless neon signs; and the moving dots of people. And a violent, instantaneous explosion of absolute terror roared through him. For an instant he saw himself externally—bent practically double, balanced on this narrow ledge, nearly half his body projecting out above the street far below—and he began to tremble violently, panic flaring through mind and muscles.

Reading Between the Lines Box 7.2

COMMUNICATION THROUGH METAPHOR

Throughout history, great speakers have used metaphor to communicate their thoughts and to reach out to massive audiences. Their speeches were overwhelmingly successful because the images helped people relate to and comprehend their messages. For example, one of the greatest speeches ever delivered is Dr. Martin Luther King Jr.'s "Address on the March on Washington for Jobs and Freedom." It is commonly called the "I Have a Dream Speech" because it is easier to picture the word "dream" than it is to picture the words "address on freedom." His speech contains many other vivid metaphors.

1. Read the following excerpts and explain what King meant by the metaphors in italics.

2. What is King's dream?

3. What does King suggest the Negro community to do when they come up against physical force?

4. King said the Negro community cannot walk alone; with whom did he suggest they walk?

1. "In a sense we have *come to our nation's capital to cash a check.* When the architects of our republic wrote the magnificent words of the Constitution and the Declaration of Independence, *they were signing a promissory note to which every American was to fall heir.*"

_____

2. "It is obvious today that *America has defaulted on this promissory note* insofar as her citizens of color are concerned. Instead of honoring this sacred obligation, *America has given the Negro people a bad check, a check which has come back marked "insufficient funds."*

_____

3. "But we refuse to believe that the *bank of justice is bankrupt.* We refuse to believe that there are insufficient funds in the great vaults of opportunity of this nation. *So we have come to cash this check, a check that will give us upon demand the riches of freedom and the security of justice.*"

_____

4. Let us not seek to *satisfy our thirst for freedom by drinking from the cup of bitterness and hatred.* We must ever conduct our struggle on the *high plane of dignity and discipline.* We must not allow our creative protest to degenerate into physical violence. Again and again we must rise to the majestic heights of *meeting physical force with soul force.*

_____

(continued on next page)

5. The marvelous new militancy which has engulfed the Negro community must not lead us to distrust of all white people, for many of our white brothers, as evidenced by their presence here today, have come to realize that *their destiny is tied up with our destiny.* They have come to realize that their freedom is inextricably bound to our freedom. *We cannot walk alone.*

_____

6. I have a dream that this *nation will rise up and live out the true meaning of its creed* (beliefs)—we hold these truths to be self-evident that all men are created equal.

_____

7. This is our hope . . . With this faith we will be able to work together, to pray together, to struggle together, to go to jail together, to stand up for freedom together, knowing that *we will be free one day.*

_____

8. . . . we will be able to *speed up that day* when all of God's children, black men and white men, Jews and Gentiles, Protestants and Catholics, will be able to join hands and sing in the words of the old Negro spiritual, "Free at last. Thank God Almighty, we are free at last."

_____

Through the use of imagery, the writer shows us that the character is very high above ground. The clues that help us to experience this perspective lie in the descriptive details in the passage. The character is so high above ground that he can see:

- blocks ahead to the Loew's theater sign
- miles of traffic signals
- countless neon signs
- the moving dots of people

We can also infer from the passage that the character is frightened because the author describes him as being in a dangerous position. It is logical that anyone "balanced on a narrow ledge" high above the ground would feel fright. We can also "see" the character's fear in the following details:

- absolute terror roared through him,
- he began to tremble violently,
- panic flaring through mind and muscles.

A Reading in Literature

Read the following excerpts from Jack Finney, "Contents of a Dead Man's Pocket," and decide what inference we should make based on the images the author projects. The first one has been done for you.

_____b_____ **1.** Very carefully observing his balance, the finger tips of his left hand again hooked to the narrow stripping of the window casing. Tom drew back his right hand, palm facing the glass, and then struck the glass with the heel of his hand. His arm rebounded from the pane, his body tottering, and he knew he didn't dare strike a harder blow.
   a. Tom broke the window with the palm of his hand.
   b. Tom tried to break the window, but his hand bounced off the glass when he hit it.
   c. Tom knew if he hit the window a little bit harder he could break the glass.

_____ **2.** But in the security and relief of his new position, he simply smiled; with only a sheet of glass between him and the room just before him, it was not possible that there wasn't a way past it. Eyes narrowing, he thought for a few moments. But nothing occurred to him. Still, he felt calm: the trembling, he realized, had stopped. At the back of his mind there still lay the thought that once he was again in his home, he could give release to his feelings. He actually would lie on the floor rolling, clenching tufts of the rug in his hands. He would literally run across the room, free to move as he liked, testing and reveling in his absolute security, letting the relief flood through him, draining the fear from his mind and body. His yearning for this was astonishingly intense, and he knew he had better keep this feeling at bay.
   a. Tom let out all of his pent-up feelings when he got into his home.
   b. Tom thought of a way to get into his home.
   c. Tom could not get into his home, but he thought about how he would act once he got in.

_____ **3.** He took a half dollar from his pocket and struck it against the pane, but without any hope that the glass would break and with very little disappointment when it did not. After a few moments he drew his leg up onto the ledge and picked loose his shoelace. He slipped off the shoe and, holding it across the instep, drew back his arm as far as he dared and struck the leather heel against the glass. The pane rattled, but he knew he'd been a long way from breaking it. His foot was cold and he slipped the shoe back on. He shouted again, experimentally, but there was no answer.

    a. Tom felt discouraged and did not try to get back into his home.

    b. Tom tried to break the window by rattling it.

    c. Tom first tried to break the window with a half dollar, then with his shoe, and finally he tried shouting for help.

_____ 4. The realization suddenly struck him that he might have to wait here till Clare came home, and for a moment the thought was funny. He could see Clare opening the front door, withdrawing her key from the lock, closing the door behind her and then glancing up to see him crouched on the other side of the window. He could see her rush across the room, face astounded and frightened, and hear himself shouting instructions: "Never mind how I got here! Just open the wind—" She couldn't open it, he remembered; she'd always had to call him. She'd have to get the building superintendent or a neighbor, and he pictured himself smiling and answering their questions as he climbed in. "I just wanted to get a breath of fresh air, so—"

    a. Tom knew that once Clare got home, she would be able to let him into the house.

    b. Tom was afraid that his wife would be angry with him when she found him on the ledge.

    c. Tom pictured himself being witty and humorous when people finally arrived to help him.

_____ 5. He couldn't possibly wait here till Clare came home. It was the second feature she'd wanted to see, and she'd left in time to see the first. She'd be three hours or—. He glanced at his watch; Clare had been gone eight minutes. Only eight minutes ago he had kissed his wife good-by.

    a. Tom felt as though hours had passed since his wife had left for the movies.

    b. Tom felt as though he had only been on the ledge for a few minutes.

    c. Tom felt as though he had only been on the ledge for eight minutes.

_____ 6. It would be four hours before she could possibly be home, while all the time he hung out here. He might possibly get to his feet, but he was afraid to try. Already his legs were cramped, his thigh muscles tired; his knees hurt, his feet felt numb and his hands were stiff. He couldn't possibly stay here for four hours, or anywhere near it. Long before that his legs and arms would give out; he would be forced to try changing his position often—stiffly, clumsily, his coordination and strength gone—and he would fall.

   a. Tom felt discouraged.

   b. Tom felt energized.

   c. Tom felt hopeful.

_____ 7. A dozen windows in the apartment building across the street were lighted. Looking over his shoulder, he could see the top of a man's head behind a newspaper. In another window he saw the blue-gray flicker of a television screen. No more than twenty-odd yards from his back were scores of people, and if just one of them would walk idly to his window and glance out. . . . For some moments he stared over his shoulder at the lighted rectangles, waiting. But no one appeared. The man reading his paper turned a page. A figure passed another of the windows and was immediately gone.

   a. Several of Tom's neighbors noticed him on the ledge.

   b. None of Tom's neighbors noticed him on the ledge.

   c. The man reading the newspaper glanced out of his window and saw Tom.

_____ 8. In the inside pocket of his jacket he found a little sheaf of papers, and he pulled one out and looked at it in the light from the living room. It was an old letter, an advertisement of some sort; his name and address, in purple ink, were on a label pasted to the envelope. Gripping one end of the envelope in his teeth he twisted it into a tight curl. From his shirt pocket he took a book of matches. He didn't dare let go the casing with both hands, but with the twist of paper in his teeth, he opened the matchbook with his free hand; then he bent one of the matches in two without tearing it from the folder, its red-tipped end now touching the striking surface. With his thumb, he rubbed the red tip across the striking area.

   a. Tom wanted to set fire to the papers that he pulled out of his pocket.

   b. Tom wanted to write a message on one of the papers.

   c. Tom wanted to light a match to warm his hands.

_____ 9. He did it again, then again, and still again, pressing harder each time, and the match suddenly flared, burning his thumb. But he kept it alight, shielding it with his body. He held the flame to the paper in his mouth till it caught. Then he snubbed out the match with his thumb and forefinger, careless of the burn, and replaced the book in his pocket. Taking the paper in his hand, he held it flame down, watching the flame crawl up the paper, till it flared bright. Then he held it behind him over

the street, moving it from side to side, the flame flickering and
fluttering in the wind.

    a. Tom set the paper on fire to keep from becoming bored.

    b. Tom set the paper on fire to warm his hands.

    c. Tom set the paper on fire to call attention to himself.

_____ **10.** There were three more letters in his pocket and he lit each of
them, holding each until the flame touched his hand and then
dropping it to the street below. At one point, watching over his
shoulder while the last of the letters burned, he saw the man
across the street put down his paper and stand—even seeming,
to Tom, to glance toward his window. But when he moved, it
was only to walk across the room.

    a. The man reading the paper finally noticed Tom.

    b. The man reading the paper noticed Tom and left to get help.

    c. The man reading the paper did not notice Tom.

*There was a dozen coins in Tom Benecke's pocket and he dropped
them, three or four at a time. But if they struck anyone, or if anyone
noticed their falling, no one connected them with their source.*

_____ **11.** His arms had begun to tremble from the steady strain of clinging
to this narrow perch, and he did not know what to do now and
was terribly frightened. Clinging to the window stripping with
one hand, he again searched his pockets. But no—he had left his
wallet on the dresser when he'd changed clothes—there was
nothing but the yellow sheet. It occurred to him irrelevantly that
his death on the sidewalk would be an eternal mystery; the window closed—why, how, and from where could he have fallen?
No one would be able to identify his body for a time, either—the
thought was somehow unbearable and increased his fear. All
they'd find in his pockets would be the yellow sheet—*contents of
the dead man's pockets, one sheet of paper bearing penciled notations—
incomprehensible.*

    a. The thought that nobody would be able to identify Tom's
dead body if he fell increased his fear.

    b. The yellow sheet of paper contained all the information that
people would need to know to identify his body if Tom fell.

    c. If Tom fell, people would know who he was because he
could be identified from the information in his wallet.

_____ **12.** It occurred to him with all the force of a revelation that, if he fell,
all he was ever going to have out of life he would then, abruptly,
have had. Nothing, then, could ever be changed; and nothing
more—no least experience or pleasure—could ever be added to
his life. He wished, then, that he had not allowed his wife to go
off by herself tonight—and on similar nights. He thought of all

the evenings he had spent away from her, working; and he regretted them. He thought wonderingly of his fierce ambition and of the direction his life had taken; he thought of the hours he'd spent by himself, filling the yellow sheet that had brought him out here. *Contents of the dead man's pockets*, he thought with sudden fierce anger, a wasted life.

    a. Tom was pleased with the accomplishments that he has made so far in his life.

    b. Tom wished that he had spent more time enjoying himself with his wife and less time working.

    c. Tom had enjoyed all of the time he spent working after hours and was glad that he had been so ambitious.

_____ 13. He was simply not going to cling here until he slipped and fell; he told himself that now. There was one last thing he could try; he had been aware of it for some moments, refusing to think about it, but now he faced it. Kneeling here on the ledge, the fingertips of one hand pressed to the narrow strip of wood, he could draw his other hand back a yard perhaps, fist clenched tight, very slowly until he sensed the outer limit of balance, then, as hard as he was able, he could drive his fist forward against the glass. If it broke, his fist smashing through, he was safe; he might cut himself badly, and probably would, but with his arm inside the room, he would be secure. But if the glass did not break, the rebound, flinging his arm back, would topple him off the ledge.

    a. Although he cut himself badly, Tom broke the glass with his fist and was safe inside the room.

    b. Tom tried to break the glass with his fist but when he hit the glass it threw him off the ledge.

    c. Tom imagined what would happen if he was able to break the glass with his fist *and* if he was unable to break the glass with his fist.

_____ 14. He tested his plan. The fingers of his left hand claw-like on the little stripping, he drew back his other fist until his body began teetering backward. But he had no leverage now—he could feel there would be no force to his swing—and he moved his fist slowly forward till he rocked forward on his knees again and could sense his swing would carry its greatest force. Glancing down, measuring the distance from his fist to the glass, he saw it was less than two feet.

    a. Tom held onto the frame of the window with the fingers of his left hand.

    b. Tom practiced striking the window with his left hand.

    c. Tom needed to swing his right arm backward more than two feet to acquire the force he needed to break the window.

_____ 15. It occurred to him he could raise his arm over his head, to bring it down against the glass. But experimenting in slow motion, he knew it would be an awkward girl-like blow without the force of a driving punch, and not nearly enough to break the glass.
   a. The phrase "awkward girl-like blow" projects an image of confidence and competence.
   b. The phrase "awkward girl-like blow" projects an image of a punch lacking effectiveness.
   c. The phrase "awkward girl-like blow" projects an image of tremendous strength and power.

_____ 16. Facing the window, he had to drive a blow from the shoulder at a distance of less than two feet; and he did not know whether it would break through the heavy glass. It might; he could picture it happening; he could feel it in the nerves of his arm. And it might not; he could feel that too—feel his fist striking this glass and being instantaneously flung back by the unbreaking pane, feel the fingers of his other hand breaking loose.
   a. The phrase "feel the fingers of his other hand breaking loose" creates an image of Tom falling off the ledge.
   b. The phrase "feel the fingers of his other hand breaking loose" creates an image of Tom breaking the window.
   c. The phrase "feel the fingers of his other hand breaking loose" creates an image of Tom using both hands to break the glass.

_____ 17. He waited, arm drawn back, fist balled, but in no hurry to strike; this pause, he knew, might be an extension of his life. And to live even a few seconds longer, he felt, even out here on this ledge in the night, was infinitely better than to die a moment earlier than he had to. His arm grew tired, and he brought it down and rested it.
   a. Tom was anxious to see if he could break the glass.
   b. Tom was less worried about breaking the glass because he knew his wife would be home in four hours.
   c. Tom wanted to stay alive as long as possible.

_____ 18. Then he knew it was time to make the attempt. He could not kneel here hesitating indefinitely till he lost all courage to act, waiting till he slipped off the ledge. Again he drew back his arm, knowing this time that he would not bring it down till he struck. [His elbow protruding over Lexington Avenue far below, the fingers of his other hand pressed down bloodlessly tight against the narrow stripping, he waited, feeling the sick tenseness and terrible excitement building.] It grew and swelled toward the moment of action, his nerves tautening. He thought of Clare— just a wordless, yearning thought—and then drew his arm back just a bit more, fist so tight his fingers pained him, and knowing he was going to do it. Then with full power, with every last scrap of strength he could bring to bear, he shot his arm forward toward the glass, and he shouted, "Clare!"

a. Tom finally acted on his plan to break the glass because he missed his wife.

b. Tom finally acted on his plan to break the glass because he knew if he waited any longer he would have no more strength to hold onto the ledge.

c. Tom finally acted on his plan to break the glass because he was anxious to get back to work.

_____ **19.** He heard the sound, felt the blow, felt himself falling forward, and his hand closed on the living-room curtains, the shards and fragments of glass showering onto the floor. And then, kneeling there on the ledge, an arm thrust into the room up to the shoulder, he began picking away the protruding slivers and great wedges of glass from the window frame, tossing them in onto the rug. And, as he grasped the edges of the empty window frame and climbed into his home, he was grinning in triumph.

a. When the glass broke, Tom fell head-first through the window and onto the rug.

b. When the glass broke, Tom fell feet-first through the window and landed on the rug.

c. When the glass broke, only Tom's arm and shoulder went through the window.

He did not lie down on the floor or run through the apartment, as he had promised himself; even in the first moments it seemed to him natural and normal that he should be where he was. He simply turned to his desk, pulled the crumpled yellow sheet from his pocket and laid it down where it had been, smoothing it out; then he absently laid a pencil across it to weight it down. He shook his head wonderingly, and turned to walk toward the closet.

_____ **20.** There he got out his topcoat and hat and, without waiting to put them on, opened the front door and stepped out, to go find his wife. He turned to pull the door closed and the warm air from the hall rushed through the narrow opening again. He saw the yellow paper, the pencil flying, scooped off the desk and, unimpeded by the glassless window, sailed out into the night and out of his life. Tom Benecke burst into laughter and closed the door.

a. Tom no longer cared if he had the yellow paper.

b. Tom was upset that he lost the yellow paper after all the trouble he went through to get it back.

c. Tom was going down to the street to get the yellow paper back.

Idioms   Sometimes authors use idioms to emphasize a point. **Idioms** are colorful expressions that project an image of a common situation. Idioms require inference skills, especially if we are unfamiliar with the expression. Let's look at some common expressions:

It's pouring buckets of water.

This expression creates an image of something larger than life dumping buckets of water upon our surroundings. In actuality, it simply means that it is raining very hard. Look at the idiom below and decide which of the following best explains the inference.

The crooks *flooded* the market with counterfeit bills.

a. The crooks poured water onto the supermarket floor.
b. The criminals took the counterfeit money to the supermarket.
c. The criminals used fake money to buy a lot of goods.

The idiom is not literal. In other words, it does not mean exactly what it says but projects a picture that emphasizes a point. In this case, "c" is the correct answer. The word *flooded* is meant to emphasize the point that there was not just *some* counterfeit money but *a lot* of counterfeit money being used as real money.

EXERCISE 7-8	**Explaining Idioms**

Read each idiom and explain its implied meaning. The word or words that make each statement an idiom are italicized. The first one has been done for you.

1. Everyone was making a ton of money until the stock market took a *nosedive*.

The stocks decreased in value.
_____

2. You cannot go to the picnic until your room is cleaned and that is the *bottom line*!

_____

_____

3. You *hit the nail on the head* when you said this place was fancy—just look at those chandeliers!

_____

_____

4. That guy is a real *number-cruncher*; he is always calculating everyone's GPAs.

_____

_____

5. We think our new computer product *will sell like hotcakes* because everybody will need it to get onto the Internet more quickly.

_____

_____

DRAWING CONCLUSIONS

When we make an inference, we start with a guess and then we read or gather more information that confirms or verifies our guess. If the information checks out, our inference is correct. If later information or clues conflict with our initial guess, we must rethink the situation and make a new guess. Drawing a conclusion is very similar to making an inference. However, when we draw a conclusion, we look at the information first, and then we create a logical explanation based on the facts. Look at the example below. How do we know the hurricane destroyed Mike and Jennifer's house?

> Yesterday, the hurricane destroyed all of the houses on Fourth Avenue. Mike and Jennifer owned a beach house on Fourth Avenue. Therefore, we can conclude that the hurricane destroyed Mike and Jennifer's house.

First we look at the information provided:

Fact 1: The hurricane destroyed all of the houses on Fourth Avenue.

Fact 2: Mike and Jennifer owned a house on Fourth Avenue.

And then, we make an inference based on that information.

Inference: Since we know that Jennifer and Mike lived on Fourth Avenue and that all of the houses on Fourth Avenue were destroyed, we have no reason to believe that their house was an exception.

From this, we draw the logical conclusion that Mike and Jennifer's house was also destroyed.

Conclusion: Mike and Jennifer's house was destroyed by the hurricane.

EXERCISE
7-9

Drawing Reasonable Conclusions

Draw a reasonable conclusion from the facts provided. Follow the steps as described above. The first one has been done for you.

1. In Crawford County, Little League football players must be between the ages of six years old and eight years old. Harry is nine years old.

   Fact 1: In Crawford County, Little League football players must be ages six years old to eight years old.

Fact 2: Harry is nine years old.

Inference: Harry is older than the Little League football players.

Conclusion: Harry is not allowed to play Little League football.

2. At age 16, people in Pennsylvania can get a learner's permit to drive a car. Paul is 15 years old.

   Fact 1: People in Pennsylvania can get a learner's permit to drive a car at age 16.

   Fact 2: Paul is 15 years old and wants a learner's permit.

   Inference: Paul is under the minimal age to get a learner's permit.

   Conclusion: _____

3. The M & D company requires two years of mechanical experience to run a machine in their shop. Rick wants to work in M & D's machine shop, but only has one year of experience working on machinery.

   Fact 1: M & D requires two years of experience to work in its machine shop.

   Fact 2: Rick has only one year of experience working on machinery.

   Inference: Rick does not have enough experience to work at the M & D Company.

   Conclusion: _____

4. Americo Airlines hires only pilots with 20/20 vision. Karina has been flying for Jetko Airlines for 17 years and has 20/20 vision.

   Fact 1: Americo Airlines hires only pilots with 20/20 vision.

   Fact 2: Karina has 20/20 vision.

   Inference: Karina has been flying for Jetko Airlines with 20/20 vision.

   Conclusion: _____

5. Psychologists are required to have a four-year college degree in any subject plus a Master's degree in counseling psychology. Antoine would like to look for a job as a psychologist. He has a Bachelor's degree in broadcasting and a Master's degree in counseling psychology.

   Fact 1: Psychologists are required to have a four-year college degree plus a Master's degree in counseling psychology.

   Fact 2: Antoine has a four-year degree and a Master's degree in counseling psychology.

   Inference: Antoine satisfies all the requirements.

   Conclusion: _____

6. Teachers cannot receive their permanent certification until they have completed three years of successful teaching and acquired 30 graduate credits (credits beyond the Bachelor's degree) in the field of education. Boris has a temporary certificate, but would like to get the permanent certificate. He has a Bachelor's degree, three years of teaching experience, and 18 graduate credits in Education.

   Fact 1: A permanent teacher's certificate requires three years of teaching, a Bachelor's degree, and 30 graduate credits.

   Fact 2: Boris has three years of teaching, a Bachelor's degree, and 18 graduate credits.

   Inference: Boris is missing some of the requirements he needs to qualify.

   Conclusion: _____

7. Olympic figure skaters generally practice on the ice for six hours each day, six days of the week, all year round. Miranda practices for two hours every Monday and Wednesday.

   Fact 1: Olympic figure skaters generally practice on the ice for six hours each day, six days of the week, all year round.

   Fact 2: Miranda practices for two hours every Monday and Wednesday.

   Inference: Miranda does not practice as much as Olympic figure skaters do.

   Conclusion: _____

8. Coal miners risk their lives every day and the work is dirty. Daniel does not like the idea of going down in the deep mines and getting dirty.

   Fact 1: A coal miner's job is risky and dirty.

   Fact 2: Daniel does not like to get dirty.

   Inference: Daniel is not the ideal candidate for a coal-mining job.

   Conclusion: _____

9. The food in the dining hall at White Mountain College is usually good on Parents' Day. Today is Parents' Day.

   Fact 1: The food in the dining hall at White Mountain College is usually good on Parents' Day.

   Fact 2: Today is Parents' Day.

   Inference: The food is not usually good on other days.

   Conclusion: _____

10. All of the students at Center University who studied 30 hours or more per week had a grade point average of over 3.0. All of the students at this same

institution who studied less than five hours per week were on academic probation. Between practices and traveling to games, Margie spent 30 hours a week with the soccer team and approximately two to three hours studying.

Fact 1: All of the students who studied less than five hours per week were on academic probation.

Fact 2: Margie studied two to three hours per week.

Inference: Margie studied less than the average five hours per week.

Conclusion: _____

Using Logical Reasoning

Logical reasoning is the ability to both make inferences (verify or disprove a hypothesis, or an educated guess) and to draw conclusions that make sense based on given information. Read the following description of a scene from John Steinbeck's novel *The Grapes of Wrath*. Pay close attention to the actions of the character Mae.

A man and two little boys come into a modest little restaurant somewhere on the highway leading to California, the highway traveled by so many of the dispossessed, trying desperately to make it to the land of sun and fruit trees, where they dream of making big salaries. He asks Mae, the waitress, to sell him ten cents worth of bread. He cannot afford to buy restaurant food for his family. Then he notices the little boys hungrily eyeing two peppermint sticks.

"Is them penny candy, ma'am?"

Mae moved down and looked in. "Which ones?"

"There, them stripy ones."

The little boys raised their eyes to her face and they stopped breathing; their mouths were partly opened, their half-naked bodies were rigid.

"Oh—them. Well, no—them's two for a penny."

Eagerly, the man gives her a penny, then hands each excited boy a stick of the candy. After they have gone, one of the two truck drivers who were having coffee at the counter and witnessed the incident reminds her on his way out: "Them was nickel apiece candy." She asks him curtly what that was to him, whereupon each man drops a half-dollar next to his empty cup of five-cent coffee and walks out. (Janaro and Altshuler 56)

What could you tell about Mae from her speech and her actions? Although the text does not tell us that Mae is a sensitive and kind-hearted person, we can come to this conclusion through logical reasoning. Let us review the passage for some clues to Mae's nature. First, we know from the text that the man cannot afford to buy candy for his two children.

He cannot afford to buy restaurant food for his family.

We also know from the description of the children that they would really like to have the candy.

Then he notices the little boys hungrily eyeing two peppermint sticks.

In addition to this, we know Mae did not hurt the man's pride by giving the candy away for free.

"Oh—them. Well, no—them's two for a penny."

Finally, we know from the truck driver's statement that she sold the man two pieces of candy worth 10 cents for what he could afford (one penny).

One of the two truck drivers who were having coffee at the counter and witnessed the incident reminds her on his way out: "Them was nickel apiece candy."

From this information it would be reasonable to say that Mae is a sensitive and kind-hearted person because she sold the candy to the man for less than its value, knowing that one penny was all that he could afford to spend.

What would be logical to assume about the truck drivers?

    a. The truck drivers could not afford to eat in the restaurant.

    b. The truck drivers were selfish people.

    c. The truck drivers believed Mae was wrong for not charging full price for the candy.

    d. The truck drivers believed Mae was a kind-hearted person and approved of her actions.

It would be reasonable to say that the truck drivers believed Mae was a kind-hearted person and approved of her actions. How do we know this? If we review the story, we recall that although a cup of coffee cost only five cents, each man left 50 cents ("half-dollar") as a tip. Had the men not approved of Mae's actions, they probably would not have given her the large tip.

A Reading in Sociology

Technology is spreading to even Third World countries. Read the following selection to find out how it is being used in a society that is very different from our own. Complete the vocabulary exercise before reading the selection to learn the new terms. Comprehension questions follow each paragraph and are meant to be completed as you read through the selection.

scents; and even the gifts you give would be considered artifacts. Let's look at each of these briefly.

[2]   Color Communication. When you're in debt, you speak of being "in the red"; when you make a profit, you're "in the black." When you're sad, you're "blue"; when you're healthy, you're "in the pink"; and when you're jealous, you're "green with envy." To be a coward is to be "yellow" and to be inexperienced is to be "green." When you talk a great deal, you talk "a blue streak," and when you are angry, you "see red." As revealed through these time-worn clichés, language abounds in color symbolism.

[3]   There is some evidence that colors affect us physiologically. For example, respiratory movements increase in the presence of red light and decrease in the presence of blue light. Similarly, eye blinks increase in frequency when eyes are exposed to red light and decrease when exposed to blue. This seems consistent with our intuitive feelings that blue is more soothing and red more **provocative**. After changing a school's walls from orange to white to blue, the students' blood pressure decreased and their academic performance improved.

[4]   Colors surely influence our perceptions and behaviors (Kanner, 1989). People's acceptance of a product, for example, is largely determined by its package. For example, among consumers in the United States the very same coffee taken from a yellow can was described as weak, from a dark brown can it was described as too strong, from a red can it was described as rich, and from a blue can it was described as mild. Even our acceptance of a person may depend on the colors worn. Consider, for example, the comments of one color expert (Kanner, 1989). "If you have to pick the wardrobe for your defense lawyer heading into court and choose anything but blue, you deserve to lose the case. . . . " Black is so powerful that it can work against the lawyer with the jury. Brown lacks sufficient authority. Green will probably **elicit** a negative response.

[5]   Clothing, Body Adornment, and Odor. People make inferences about who you are—in part by the way you dress. Whether these inferences are accurate or not, they will influence what people think of you and how they react to you. Your social class, your seriousness, your attitudes (for example, whether you are conservative or liberal), your concern for **convention**, your sense of style and, perhaps, even your creativity will all be judged—in part at least—by the way you dress.

[6]   College students will perceive an instructor dressed informally as friendly, fair, enthusiastic, and flexible; the same instructor dressed formally is perceived as prepared, knowledgeable, and organized (Melandro, Barker, & Barker, 1989).

[7]   Your jewelry also communicates messages about you. Wedding and engagement rings are obvious examples that communicate specific messages. College rings and political buttons likewise communicate specific messages. If you wear a Rolex watch or large precious stones, for example, others are likely to infer that you're rich. Men who wear earrings will be

judged differently from men who don't. Body piercing and tattoos likewise communicate something about the individual.

[8]   The way you wear your hair communicates about who you are—from caring about being up-to-date to a desire to shock, to perhaps a lack of concern for appearances. Men with long hair, to take just one example, will generally be judged as less conservative than those with shorter hair.

[9]   <u>Space Decoration.</u> The way you decorate your private spaces also tells a lot about you. The office with the mahogany desk and bookcase set and oriental rugs communicates your importance and status within the organization, just as the metal desk and bare floors indicate an entry-level employee worker much further down in the company **hierarchy**.

[10]   Similarly, people will make inferences about you based on the way you decorate your home. The expensiveness of the furnishings may communicate your status and wealth, their coordination, and your sense of style. The magazines may reflect your interests while the arrangement of chairs around a television set may reveal how important watching television is to you. Bookcases lining the walls reveal the importance of reading. In fact, there is probably little in your home that would not send messages that others could use in making inferences about you. Computers, widescreen televisions, well-equipped kitchens, and oil paintings of great-grandparents, for example, all say something about the people who live in the home.

[11]   Similarly, the lack of certain items will communicate something about you. Consider what messages you would get from a home where there is no television, telephone, or books.

[12]   <u>Gifts.</u> Gift giving is a little discussed aspect of nonverbal communication but actually communicates a great deal. A gift can signify the level of intimacy you attribute to the relationship. If you perceive your relationship to be a very close one then you might give personal items like pajamas and underwear, which would be highly inappropriate if given between, say, two persons who just started dating. A gift can also signify the level of commitment; an expensive gift of jewelry would signify a level of commitment much greater than would a scarf or an umbrella.

[13]   Consider, for example, the "Pygmalion gift." This type of gift is designed to change the person into what you want that person to become. The parent who gives a child books or science equipment may be asking the child to be a scholar. The romantic partner who gives a gift of stylish clothing may be asking the person to dress differently.

[14]   Not surprisingly, gift giving is a practice in which rules and customs vary according to each culture. Even with good intentions, gift giving without sensitivity to cultural norms can backfire. Here are a few situations where gift giving created barriers rather than bonds. What might

have gone wrong in each of these situations? These few examples should serve to illustrate the wide variations that exist among cultures in the meaning given to artifacts and in the seemingly simple process of giving gifts (Axtell 1990; Dresser 1996).

1. You bring chrysanthemums to a Belgian colleague and a clock to a Chinese colleague. Both react negatively.
2. Upon meeting an Arab businessman for the first time—someone with whom you wish to develop business relationships—you present him with a gift. He seems to become disturbed. To smooth things over, when you go to visit him and his family in Oman, you bring a bottle of your favorite brandy for after dinner. Your host seems even more disturbed now.
3. Arriving for dinner at the home of a Kenyan colleague, you present flowers as a dinner gift. Your host accepts them politely but looks puzzled. The next evening you visit your Swiss colleague and bring 14 red roses. Your host accepts them politely but looks strangely at you. Figuring that the red got you in trouble, on your third evening out you bring yellow roses to your Iranian friend. Again, there was a similar reaction.
4. You give your Chinese friend a set of dinner knives as a gift but she does not open it in front of you; you get offended. After she opens it, she gets offended.
5. You bring your Mexican friend a statue of an elephant drinking water from a lake. Your friend says he cannot accept it; his expressions tell you he really doesn't want it.

Possible reasons:

1. Chrysanthemums in Belgium and clocks in China are both reminders of death and that time is running out.
2. Gifts given at the first meeting with Arabs (or in the Middle East generally) may be interpreted as bribes. Further, since alcohol is prohibited by Islamic law, it should be avoided when selecting gifts for most Arabs or religious Muslims.
3. In Kenya, flowers are only brought to express condolence. In Switzerland red roses are a sign of romantic interest. In addition, an even number of flowers (or 13) is generally considered bad luck, so should be avoided. Yellow flowers to Iranians signify the enemy and send a message that you dislike them.
4. The Chinese custom is simply not to open gifts in front of the giver. Knives (and scissors) symbolize the severing of a relationship.

5. Among many Latin Americans the elephant's upward trunk symbolizes a holding of good luck; an elephant's downward trunk symbolizes luck slipping away. (DeVito 131–36)

Comprehension

Draw a reasonable conclusion from the facts provided. The first one has been done for you.

1. You bring chrysanthemums to a Belgian colleague and a clock to a Chinese colleague. Both react negatively.

    Fact 1: Chrysanthemums in Belgium are a reminder of death.

    Fact 2: Clocks in China are reminders of death and that time is running out.

    Inference: Your gifts were reminders of death to your colleagues.

    Conclusion: If you are trying to please your Belgian or Chinese colleagues, you should not give these types of gifts.

2. Upon meeting an Arab businessman for the first time—someone with whom you wish to develop business relationships—you present him with a gift. He seems to become disturbed.

    Fact 1: Gifts given at the first meeting with Arabs (or in the Middle East generally) may be interpreted as bribes.

    Fact 2: You gave an Arab a gift at a first meeting.

    Inference: _____

    Conclusion: _____

3. You bring yellow roses as a gift to your Iranian friend, and your friend looks puzzled.

    Fact 1: Yellow flowers to Iranians signify the enemy.

    Fact 2: Yellow flowers send the message that you dislike the person you are sending them to.

    Inference: _____

    Conclusion: _____

4. You give your Chinese friend a set of dinner knives, and she becomes offended.

Fact 1: Knives symbolize the severing of a relationship.

Fact 2: You gave your friend a set of knives.

Inference: _____

Conclusion: _____

5. You bring your Mexican friend a statue of an elephant drinking water from a lake, and he does not want to accept it.

Fact 1: Among many Latin Americans, an elephant's downward trunk symbolizes luck slipping away.

Fact 2: The elephant statue that you gave your Latin American friend had a downward trunk (the trunk would be pointing downward if the elephant lowered his head to drink from a lake.)

Inference: _____

Conclusion: _____

6. There is some evidence that colors affect us physiologically. For example, respiratory movements increase in the presence of red light and decrease in the presence of blue light. Similarly, eye blinks increase in frequency when eyes are exposed to red light and decrease when exposed to blue. This seems consistent with our intuitive feelings that blue is more soothing and red more **provocative**. After changing a school's walls from orange to white to blue, the students' blood pressure decreased and their academic performance improved.

Fact 1: Respiratory movements increase in the presence of red light and decrease in the presence of blue light.

Fact 2: Eye blinks increase in frequency when eyes are exposed to red light and decrease when exposed to blue.

Fact 3: After changing a school's walls from orange to white to blue, the students' blood pressure decreased and their academic performance improved.

Inference: _____

Conclusion: _____

7. Colors surely influence our perceptions and behaviors (Kanner, 1989). People's acceptance of a product, for example, is largely determined by its package. For example, among consumers in the United States the very same coffee taken from a yellow can was described as weak, from a dark brown can it was described as too strong, from a red can it was described as rich, and from a blue

can it was described as mild. Even our acceptance of a person may depend on the colors worn. Consider, for example, the comments of one color expert (Kanner, 1989). "If you have to pick the wardrobe for your defense lawyer heading into court and choose anything but blue, you deserve to lose the case...." Black is so powerful that it can work against the lawyer with the jury. Brown lacks sufficient authority. Green will probably **elicit** a negative response.

Fact 1: In the United States the very same coffee taken from a yellow can was described as weak.

Fact 2: Coffee taken from a dark brown can was described as too strong.

Fact 3: Coffee taken from a red can was described as rich.

Fact 4: Coffee taken from a blue can was described as mild.

Inference: _____

Conclusion: _____

8. College students will perceive an instructor dressed informally as friendly, fair, enthusiastic, and flexible; the same instructor dressed formally is perceived as prepared, knowledgeable, and organized.

Fact 1: College students will perceive an instructor dressed informally as friendly, fair, enthusiastic, and flexible.

Fact 2: College students will perceive an instructor dressed formally as prepared, knowledgeable, and organized.

Inference: _____

Conclusion: _____

9. The way you decorate your private spaces also tells a lot about you. The office with the mahogany desk and bookcase set and oriental rugs communicates your importance and status within the organization, just as the metal desk and bare floors indicate an entry-level employee worker much further down in the company hierarchy.

Fact 1: The office with the mahogany desk and bookcase set and oriental rugs communicates your importance and status within the organization

Fact 2: The office with a metal desk and bare floors indicates an entry-level employee worker who has very little status within the organization.

Inference: _____

Conclusion: _____

10. Similarly, people will make inferences about you based on the way you decorate your home. The expensiveness of the furnishings may communicate

your status and wealth, their coordination, and your sense of style. The magazines may reflect your interests while the arrangement of chairs around a television set may reveal how important watching television is to you. Bookcases lining the walls reveal the importance of reading. In fact, there is probably little in your home that would not send messages that others could use in making inferences about you. Computers, wide-screen televisions, well-equipped kitchens, and oil paintings of great-grandparents, for example, all say something about the people who live in the home.

Fact 1: There are no magazines in your house.

Fact 2: There are no books in your house.

Fact 3: There are two televisions and three computers in your house.

Inference: _____

Conclusion: _____

Visual Literacy Box 7.2 ● ● ● ● ● ● ● ● ● ● ● ● ● ● ● ●

USING TABLES TO ORGANIZE INFORMATION

Some Cultural Meanings of Color

Read the excerpt below concerning the cultural meanings of color. Then use the following chart to organize this information.

In China, the color red signifies prosperity and rebirth and is used for festive and joyous occasions. However, in France and the United Kingdom, red is identified with masculinity. In many African countries, blasphemy or death is signaled by the color red while in Japan it signifies anger and danger. Red ink, especially among Korean Buddhists, is used only to write a person's name at the time of death or on the anniversary of the person's death. This creates lots of problems when American teachers use red ink to mark homework.

In Thailand as well as many Muslin and Hindu countries white signifies purity while in Japan and other Asian countries, it represents death and mourning. However, black symbolizes old age and death in Thailand, and in much of Europe and North America.

The color green also has many symbolic meanings. In the United States green signifies capitalism, go ahead, and envy whereas in Ireland, it stands for patriotism. Among some Native Americans, however, green symbolizes femininity. And to the Egyptians, it represents fertility and strength. Similar to this, the Japanese are reminded of youth and energy when they look at green.

In Iran blue signifies something negative. Similar to this blue signifies defeat among the Cherokee. However, it reflects positive aspects in many

(continued on next page)

(continued from previous page)

other countries. For example, in Egypt blue symbolizes virtue and truth and in Ghana it represents joy.

Purple has many different symbolic meanings. In Latin America purple signifies death while in Europe it represents royalty. In Egypt purple is a symbol of virtue and faith and to the Japanese it means grace and nobility. Purple, however, signifies barbarism in China.

Yellow, too, has a host of different meanings around the world. In China yellow signifies wealth and authority while in the United States it symbolizes caution and cowardice. The Egyptians, however, look at yellow as a sign of happiness and prosperity. (DeVito 132)

Color	Country	Cultural Meanings and Comments
Red		
Green		
Black		
White		
Blue		
Yellow		
Purple		

8

Purpose and Tone

● ●

*Authors write to express themselves, and, usually, they have something to say to a particular audience. In other words, they have a **purpose** for their writing. This purpose generally directs the author's **tone** of voice or the way he expresses himself about a chosen subject.*

In this chapter we:

▪ learn how to determine the author's purposes;

▪ learn how to recognize how the author uses tone of voice to communicate specific messages to his audience.

AUTHOR'S PURPOSE

The three common purposes for writing are:

■ to inform,

■ to entertain, and

■ to persuade.

As a reader, it is important for you to be able to distinguish between facts that are presented in an informative way and those that are presented in a persuasive way. You need to be able to recognize when the author is being serious and when he is being humorous. Understanding the author's purpose will also help you identify the **main idea** of the writing. Let's look more closely at these three types of purpose.

To Inform

If the author's purpose is to **inform**, you can expect to find factual information on a given subject. College textbooks, for example, provide information on specific topics. These facts may be used to explain an idea; compare or contrast two things; show cause-and-effect relationships; define a term; illustrate a process; demonstrate solutions to problems; and so forth. The paragraph below, for example, is informative. What information does it provide? Is the author's purpose to explain an idea or to compare or contrast two things? Does he define a term or provide solutions to problems?

> A final pattern that crime data have uncovered is that of the **career criminal,** or chronic offender. The idea of the chronic offender was established by the pioneering research of Marvin Wolfgang, Robert Figlio, and Thorsten Sellin. The trio used official records to follow a cohort of 9,945 males born in Philadelphia in 1945 until they turned eighteen years of age in 1963. Released in 1972, the resulting study showed that 6 percent of the cohort had committed five or more offenses. Furthermore, this "chronic 6 percent" were responsible for 72 percent of the murders attributed to the cohort, 82 percent of the robberies, 69 percent of the aggravated assaults, and 73 percent of the rapes. The existence of chronic offenders has been corroborated by further research, such as that done by Lawrence Sherman in Kansas City. Sherman found that although only 2.7 percent of the city's roughly 500,000 inhabitants were arrested twice or more in 1990, these offenders accounted for over 60 percent of all arrests that year. (Gaines, Kaune, and Miller 44)

This excerpt is informative because it provides information or facts about career criminals. First, the term *career criminal* is defined, and then the research concerning career criminals is explained. If we did not know what a career criminal was, the fact that most of the crimes were committed by only 6 percent of the population studied would help us understand the idea that career criminals commit crimes repeatedly (See Visual Literacy Box 8.1 on page 295).

To Entertain

If the author's purpose is to **entertain,** you may read humorous, dramatic, or historical accounts. They may be either fictional (such as a mystery novel) or nonfictional (such as an autobiography). The paragraph below is an excerpt from a dramatic short story by Gloria Naylor.

> The judge set bail the next day, and Basil was given an early trial date. Cecil Garvin tried to appeal the bail, but the court denied his plea.
> "I'm sorry, Mrs. Michael, it's the best I could do. There's no need, really, to try and raise so much money. The case goes to trial in only two weeks, and it won't be a complicated proceeding. I've talked to the district attorney, and they won't push too heavily on the assault charge if we drop the implications of the undue force in the arrest. So it's going to work out well for all the parties involved. And your son will be free in less than fifteen days."

Visual Literacy Box 8.1

READING CHARTS IN SOCIOLOGY: CAREER CRIMINALS

It is often easier to understand what we read if we can see a picture of the information. The chart below is a visual picture of information concerning career criminals. The horizontal axis (across) shows a box for each crime. If you look at the top of each box and follow across to the left side, you will see the vertical axis (up and down) scale. The number on the vertical axis at that point *represents the percentage of crimes committed by 6 percent of those studied*. For example, we can tell that this group committed 72 percent of all murders. Without looking back at the text, decide which percentages of the following crimes were committed by 6 percent of those studied.

Robberies: _____

Assaults: _____

Rapes: _____

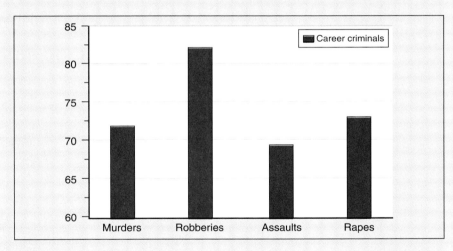

Of the 9,945 males studied, most of the crimes were committed by only 6 percent.

"I still want to put up the bail," Mattie said.

Garvin looked worried.

"It's a great deal of money, Mrs. Michael, and you don't have the ready assets for something like that."

"I've got my house; it's mine and paid for. Can't I put that up for bail?"

"Well, yes, but you do understand that bail is only posted to insure that the defendant appears for trial. If they don't appear, the court issues a bench warrant for the truant party and you forfeit your bond. You do understand that?"

"I understand." (Naylor).

As we begin reading the account, we sense that a serious situation is about to be resolved. However, Mattie's insistence on putting up the bail at extreme risk to herself leads us to believe that there is more to the story, and, as in all dramas, the tension builds. We are hooked. Will Mattie's son be safe in jail if she doesn't put up the bail? Will she lose her house if she decides to do so? We begin to imagine ourselves in this situation and read on to find out what happens in the end (See Visual Literacy Box 8.2 on page below). Drama, humor, mystery, biography, autobiography, and current news stories are among the many types of writing that authors may use to entertain.

Visual Literacy Box 8.2   ● ■ ● ● ● ● ● ● ● ● ● ● ● ● ● ● ●

READING FLOW CHARTS

The Women of Brewster Place

A s you read the excerpt below, think of the judicial process within the story line. Use the boxes below to arrange the following information in the correct sequence.

The judge set bail the next day, and Basil was given an early trial date. Cecil Garvin tried to appeal the bail, but the court denied his plea.

"I'm sorry, Mrs. Michael, it's the best I could do. There's no need, really, to try and raise so much money. The case goes to trial in only two weeks, and it won't be a complicated proceeding. I've talked to the district attorney, and they won't push too heavily on the assault charge if we drop the implications of the undue force in the arrest. So it's going to work out well for all the parties involved. And your son will be free in less than fifteen days."

"I still want to put up the bail," Mattie said.

Garvin looked worried. "It's a great deal of money, Mrs. Michael, and you don't have the ready assets for something like that."

"I've got my house: it's mine and paid for. Can't I put that up for bail?"

"Well, yes, but you do understand that bail is only posted to insure that the defendant appears for trial. If they don't appear, the court issues a bench warrant for the truant party and you forfeit your bond. You do understand that?"

"I understand." (Naylor)

■ Cecil tells Mattie that bail is not necessary because the trial is in two weeks.

■ Cecil warns Mattie that she would lose her house if her son did not appear in court.

■ Court denies plea.

■ Mattie wants to put up bail.

(continued on next page)

(continued from previous page)
- Cecil tries to appeal.
- Mattie decides to use her house as bail.
- Judge sets bail.

To Persuade

If the author's purpose is to **persuade**, he will offer information in his writing that supports a particular position. When an author writes to persuade, he intends to convince his audience to share his views, adopt his position, or take a particular course of action. Occasionally an author may have plenty of factual support for an issue but for only one side of it. Ideally, though an author may clearly and strongly favor one side of a case over another; if he is conscientious, he will present both. In either case, in order to convince his audience to see his **point of view** (position from which something is considered), he will use persuasive techniques and strategies. The paragraph below, for example, is persuasive. What is the author's point of view? What position does he want his readers to adopt?

> Forget Osama bin Laden, the real terrorists plaguing the American public this summer have been the meat executives at Corporation X. After allowing more than 19 million pounds of potentially e.coli-contaminated meat to be distributed throughout the nation, Corporation X wants to sterilize unclean beef through the irradiation process. It doesn't take much more than common sense to question the wisdom of consuming irradiated products when merely handling irradiated mail causes health problems such as cancer. Scientists have known for decades that exposing red meat to high doses of radiation creates a host of known carcinogens, including the very potent benzene. The public needs to let Corporation X know that irradiated fecal matter is not OK for dinner. (Colby 14)

Although this passage is informative, we can tell the author's purpose is to persuade. First of all, by comparing Corporation X with terrorists, we can tell the author would like us to take a stand against irradiation. The author also tries

DIAGRAMMING PROBLEM-SOLUTION AND
CAUSE-EFFECT PATTERNS: OSAMA CONAGRA

The problem-solution text pattern is often combined with the cause-effect pattern because problems have both causes and effects. Read the passage below and label each part of the diagram as one of the following: (1) cause, (2) effect, (3) problem, (4) solution. Note that some boxes will have more than one label.

> Forget Osama bin Laden, the real terrorists plaguing the American public this summer have been the meat executives at Corporation X. After allowing more than 19 million pounds of potentially e.coli-contaminated meat to be distributed throughout the nation, Corporation X wants to sterilize unclean beef through the irradiation process. It doesn't take much more than common sense to question the wisdom of consuming irradiated products when merely handling irradiated mail causes health problems such as cancer. Scientists have known for decades that exposing red meat to high doses of radiation creates a host of known carcinogens, including the very potent benzene. The public needs to let Corporation X know that irradiated fecal matter is not OK for dinner. (Colby 14)

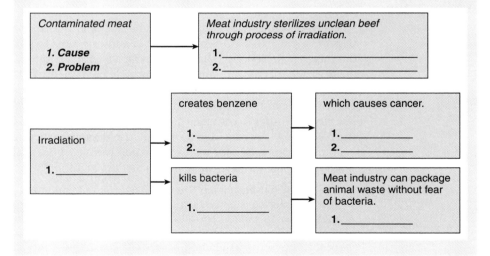

to persuade us to adopt his stand by providing facts about the carcinogens that are created by this process. The author's final point of persuasion comes in the form of a warning that we will end up eating animal waste products if it is allowed to be sterilized through the process of irradiation and sold as part of the meat (See Visual Literacy Box 8.3 on page above).

EXERCISE	**Using Titles to Identify the Author's Purpose**
8-1	

Read each of the following articles and book titles and decide whether the author's purpose is to inform, to entertain, or to persuade. Explain your answers below. The first one has been done for you.

_____b_____ 1. *Gaining Weight on the "See Food" Diet*
          a. to inform
          b. to entertain
          c. to persuade

        Explanation: <u>The author jokingly states that he would rather gain</u>

        <u>weight by eating everything he sees, rather then stick to the limits of</u>

        <u>a "seafood" diet.</u>

_____ 2. *How to Invest in the Stock Market*
          a. to inform
          b. to entertain
          c. to persuade

        Explanation: _____

_____ 3. *The Ten Best Investments and Why Every Person Should Choose Them*
          a. to inform
          b. to entertain
          c. to persuade

        Explanation: _____

_____ 4. *How to Build a Web Site Using Netscape Navigator*
          a. to inform
          b. to entertain
          c. to persuade

        Explanation: _____

_____ 5. *The Smart People's Guide to Avoiding Technology*
          a. to inform
          b. to entertain
          c. to persuade

        Explanation: _____

_____ 6. *Slacker's Tips for Perfecting Academic Procrastination*
          a. to inform
          b. to entertain
          c. to persuade

        Explanation: _____

_____ **7.** *Life on the Nile River*
     a. to inform
     b. to entertain
     c. to persuade

Explanation: _____

_____ **8.** *Catalysts of the Russian Revolution*
     a. to inform
     b. to entertain
     c. to persuade

Explanation: _____

_____ **9.** *The Japanese Economy Since 1945*
     a. to inform
     b. to entertain
     c. to persuade

Explanation: _____

_____ **10.** *Why Everyone Should Own a Duel-Powered Automobile*
     a. to inform
     b. to entertain
     c. to persuade

Explanation: _____

EXERCISE
8-2

Using Topic Sentences to Identify the Author's Purpose

Read each of the following topic sentences and decide on the author's purpose. Explain your answers below. The first one has been done for you.

___a___ **1.** One of the most serious problems facing the survivors of an airplane crash is the lack of food, water, and shelter.
     a. to inform
     b. to entertain
     c. to persuade

Explanation: The purpose is to inform the reader about what is
needed for survival in the event of an airplane crash.

_____ **2.** Bony fishes, the largest class of vertebrates (about 29,000), are common in the seas and freshwater habitats.
     a. to inform
     b. to entertain
     c. to persuade

Explanation: _____

_____ **3.** Cigarette smoking should be banned from all public places.
　　a. to inform
　　b. to entertain
　　c. to persuade

Explanation: _____

_____ **4.** Working as a volunteer is fun and rewarding.
　　a. to inform
　　b. to entertain
　　c. to persuade

Explanation: _____

_____ **5.** A three-sided war among Serbs, Croats, and Muslims was fought in Bosnia from 1991 to 1995.
　　a. to inform
　　b. to entertain
　　c. to persuade

Explanation: _____

_____ **6.** As he stepped from the mansion into the shadows, Adam thought about the many reasons he did not want to be seen.
　　a. to inform
　　b. to entertain
　　c. to persuade

Explanation: _____

_____ **7.** Children have many funny misunderstandings about songs that they hear.
　　a. to inform
　　b. to entertain
　　c. to persuade

Explanation: _____

_____ **8.** All Americans should vote in presidential elections.
　　a. to inform
　　b. to entertain
　　c. to persuade

Explanation: _____

_____ **9.** There are many different branches of psychology.
　　a. to inform
　　b. to entertain
　　c. to persuade

Explanation: _____

_____ **10.** Frustrated, the child sat down on a bench after running several blocks in an unsuccessful attempt to escape his shadow.
   a. to inform
   b. to entertain
   c. to persuade

   Explanation: _____

EXERCISE 8-3	**Reading Paragraphs to Identify the Author's Purpose**

Read each of the following paragraphs and decide on the author's purpose. Explain your answers below. The first one has been done for you.

____a____ **1.** In the child's first several years, skill in spoken language develops naturally and easily. Children discover what language does for them. They learn that language is a tool that they can use and understand in interactions with others in their environment. They also learn that language is intentional; it has many purposes. Among the most obvious is communication. The more children use language to communicate, the more they learn the many special functions it serves. (Vacca, Vacca, and Grove 26)
   a. to inform
   b. to entertain
   c. to persuade

   Explanation: The purpose is to inform the reader of what children learn about language in their first several years of life.

_____ **2.** Did you know that 80 percent of the firefighters in the United States work on a volunteer basis? In other words, if you were trapped in your car after a collision with a truck or if your house were on fire, chances are the people helping you would not be getting paid for their efforts. However, when volunteer firefighters go to the grocery store, their food is not free. When they buy a house or rent an apartment, their mortgage/rent is not free. When they visit a doctor or dentist, their bills are not automatically paid. It is not fair to expect firefighters to risk their own lives to save us or to save our property without providing them some compensation. All firefighters should be paid for their work, just as workers in other professions are paid.
   a. to inform
   b. to entertain
   c. to persuade

   Explanation: _____

_____ **3.** Around the beginning of the twentieth century, American newspapers began to concentrate into chains. Chains, defined as one company owning the same type of medium in more than one market area, were not a new idea. Benjamin Franklin started the first chain in the U.S. when he owned both the *Pennsylvania Gazette* and the *New England Courant* in 1729. Many other publishers followed Franklin's lead in the early years, but the first one to make it work on a large scale, and therefore the one who today is considered the founder of the first modern chain, was Edward Wylis Scripps. (Rodman 79)

    a. to inform

    b. to entertain

    c. to persuade

Explanation: _____

_____ **4.** It was 4:30 p.m. and the December daylight was beginning to fade. My father gave one more tug at the broken chain saw and then pronounced it useless. We still had 500 more trees to cut before the truck arrived in the morning. If we didn't sell them this year, the trees would grow too tall for the next Christmas season. Aside from that, my father needed the money to pay this year's taxes. My mom and I walked back to the house in silence as the darkness set in. Then, suddenly, from the depths of the pine grove came the wail of the chain saw. As we grabbed flashlights and gloves, I noticed a bright moon rising. We worked all through the night. With the help of the strong moonlight and my mom's flashlight, my father cut each tree as I caught and dragged them through the snow to the end of the drive where the truck would pick them up in the morning.

    a. to inform

    b. to entertain

    c. to persuade

Explanation: _____

_____ **5.** Many merchants advertise their products in newspapers claiming their products are better and cost less. They give some information, but *not all of the information* consumers need to know. For example, automobile dealers will advertise cars by offering savings of $3,000. However, they will not indicate the price from which the customer is saving. They just advertise "Save $3,000."

    a. to inform

    b. to entertain

    c. to persuade

Explanation: _____

> ### Reading Between the Lines Box 8.1
>
> ### AUTHOR'S PURPOSE
> *Common Misconceptions: The Greenhouse Effect Is Bad*
>
> Read the passage below and determine the author's purpose:
>
> The greenhouse effect is often in the news, usually in discussions about environmental problems. But the greenhouse effect itself is not a bad thing. In fact, we could not exist without it. Remember that the "no greenhouse" temperature of the Earth is well below freezing. Thus, the greenhouse effect is the only reason why our planet is not frozen over. Why, then, is the greenhouse effect discussed as an environmental problem? It is because human activity is adding more greenhouse gases to the atmosphere—which might change the Earth's climate. After all, while the greenhouse effect makes the Earth livable, it is also responsible for the searing 740 K temperature of Venus—proving that it's possible to have too much of a good thing. (Bennett, Donahue, Schneider, and Voit 270)
>
> Circle the author's purpose from the choices below:
>
>   **1.** to inform
>
>   **2.** to persuade
>
>   **3.** to entertain
>
> The text pattern of this paragraph is both cause-effect and problem-solution.
>
> **1.** When can the greenhouse effect be a problem? <u>When human activity</u>
>
> <u>changes to the Earth's climate by adding more greenhouse gases to the atmosphere.</u>
>
> **2.** In what sense can we look at the greenhouse effect as a solution? _____
>
> _____
>
> **3.** In what ways is the greenhouse effect a cause? _____
>
> _____
>
> **4.** What is the effect of the greenhouse gases on Venus? _____
>
> _____

AUTHOR'S TONE

When authors write, they voice their thoughts on paper. These thoughts express how the author feels about a particular subject and, thus, can be as varied as our human emotions. As we read his thoughts, it is important for us to recognize the author's feelings or *attitude* toward the subject so that we can understand his intended meaning. We call this the author's **tone of voice**, or simply **tone**. The author gives us clues to interpret his mood through the words in the text—namely, the supporting details.

In addition to describing the author's feelings on a subject, tone can also depict the overall *atmosphere* or *mood* of a passage or the mood created by a character's emotions. In order to identify the author's tone, imagine that the author is speaking directly to you. Ask yourself the following questions:

- How does he sound?
- Is the author's tone of voice or the voices of his characters cheerful, depressed, fearful, or worried?
- Is the author being **objective** (sticking to the facts) or **subjective** (giving his opinion of the facts)?
- Is his manner of expressing himself **formal** (following the rules for precise language) or **informal** (using everyday language)?
- Does the author show excitement toward the subject, or does he display anger?
- Is the author's mood **optimistic** (hopeful) or **pessimistic** (doubtful)?
- Does her mood appear to be **nonchalant** (unconcerned) or **nostalgic** (homesick for past circumstances)?

Below is a list of words commonly associated with the author's tone. These words clue us in to the author's tone in general. For example, if the author's tone is joyous, lighthearted, or hopeful, the reader senses an overall positive feeling as he reads. On the other hand, if the author's tone is angry, hostile, or fearful, the overall tone becomes negative. Sometimes, the author's tone is neutral, meaning it is neither positive nor negative. Other times, tone depends on the situation presented. For example, a serious tone can be positive, as in a description of a graduation ceremony. However, it can be negative if the description is of a terrorist attack. A serious tone could be just plain neutral as in a description of writing an essay.

amused *(positive)*	curious *(neutral)*	formal *(neutral)*	joyous *(positive)*
angry *(negative)*	depressed *(negative)*	helpless *(negative)*	loving *(positive)*
anxious *(negative)*	disappointed *(negative)*	hopeful *(positive)*	nonchalant *(neutral)*
authoritative *(neutral)*	doubtful *(negative)*	hostile *(negative)*	nostalgic *(neutral)*
cheerful *(positive)*	encouraging *(positive)*	humorous *(positive)*	objective *(neutral)*
concerned *(positive)*	enthusiastic *(positive)*	informal *(neutral)*	optimistic *(positive)*

pessimistic *(negative)* respectful *(positive)*	sympathetic *(positive)*	sad *(negative)*
critical *(negative)* fearful *(negative)*	ironic *(contextual)*	serious *(contextual)*
sarcastic *(contextual)* lighthearted *(positive)*	subjective *(contextual)*	

Now read the sentences below and note the author's tone in each.

objective   The student body comprises youth of ages 18 to 21 from 37 states and 17 foreign countries.

subjective   Our outstanding student body is made up of energetic, enthusiastic young people who come from the most interesting parts of the world.

formal   The preceding discussion focused on technically correct information.

informal   What I told you yesterday was right.

optimistic   College students who are well trained in the area of computer programming can always find jobs when they graduate.

pessimistic   With the economy the way that it is, even students who graduate with degrees in the Allied Health Option will have a tough time finding places to work.

EXERCISE
8-4

Recognizing the Author's Mood

Practice recognizing the author's mood by reading each sentence or paragraph below and identifying the overall tone. Determine whether each statement or paragraph is *positive, negative,* or *neutral.* The first one has been done for you.

___b___   **1.** Our state educational system is flawed. Many teachers are not qualified to teach. Some school districts are even hiring people with only a two-year degree.
    a. positive
    b. negative
    c. neutral

_____   **2.** High-speed railroad systems have been long in the planning but never undertaken because many industries would suffer from their success. For twenty-five years, people have been talking

Reading Between the Lines Box 8.2

AUTHOR'S TONE

The Economy

Read the passage below and place an X next to the following adjectives that describe the author's tone.

❑ lighthearted *(positive)*	❑ optimistic *(positive)*	❑ authoritative *(neutral)*
❑ helpless *(negative)*	❑ fearful *(negative)*	❑ angry *(negative)*
❑ hopeful *(positive)*	❑ serious *(contextual)*	❑ cheerful *(positive)*
❑ hostile *(negative)*	❑ critical *(negative)*	❑ concerned *(positive)*
❑ joyous *(positive)*	❑ sarcastic *(contextual)*	❑ enthusiastic *(positive)*
❑ pessimistic *(negative)*	❑ anxious *(negative)*	❑ doubtful *(negative)*
❑ sympathetic *(positive)*	❑ encouraging *(positive)*	

The past decade has seen a dramatic worsening of the economic climate. For college students, this means increased pressure to get a good job, which in turn promotes an atmosphere of competitiveness rather than cooperation. There is tremendous anxiety, in both college and graduate school, about being able to make a "good living."

In college, as in society, pressures abound, competition is fierce, and the ethos is "do it for yourself," for your own development. But how can these be reconciled with commitment? Most college students want to be committed not only to a person, but to a relationship—and yet they are truly afraid of making the commitment.

Women in particular have been struggling long and hard for "self-hood," which often is based on the male model of success. In an eastern women's college, women are expected to put their own careers first: "If you are going with somebody, and you both get into grad school in different parts of the country, there are no more of the old rules, which said that women were supposed to follow the men's careers. But there's no new model of relationship. It's everyone for herself." This leaves students with a terrible fear and doubt about whether to get involved and committed. Women and men want relationships badly, but they are told to put their own careers first. (Manis 73)

about upgrading our transportation systems, but industry will simply not allow progress.

    a. positive

    b. negative

    c. neutral

_____ **3.** Hiking is an extremely pleasurable and healthy activity. It's wonderful to hike in the mountains during the fall when the leaves display brilliant color. Even more fabulous is the wonderful feeling that comes from exercising in the cool, crisp air.
a. positive
b. negative
c. neutral

_____ **4.** The New York City Ballet will perform _A Midsummer Night's Dream_ at the amphitheater in Saratoga Springs during the second week in August.
a. positive
b. negative
c. neutral

_____ **5.** Unfortunately, there are many signs of a recession. Thousands of workers are being laid off from their jobs each week. Consumer confidence is down. Our economy will definitely not flourish for a long, long time.
a. positive
b. negative
c. neutral

_____ **6.** The career center is a wonderful place for freshmen to visit. Students with undeclared majors can find much information on countless numbers of exciting careers.
a. positive
b. negative
c. neutral

_____ **7.** Our products are not competitive with those of other nations. Everything is made in China. And, if it's not made in China, then it's made in Japan. We can hardly compete with the quantity of goods these nations are producing.
a. positive
b. negative
c. neutral

_____ **8.** The architecture of our library, with its Doric columns and marble stairs, is beautiful. Many students enjoy going there just for the thrill of walking through its stately doors.
a. positive
b. negative
c. neutral

_____ **9.** The football game started at 6:00 in the evening. The band played the usual "fight" songs. The bleachers on both sides of the field were filled. Neither football team was playing on its own turf, so neither had the advantage.
   a. positive
   b. negative
   c. neutral

_____ **10.** There have been no incidents since all of the schools in the districts installed metal detectors. They seemed out-of-place at first, but no one seems to notice them now. Students and faculty alike have reported feeling safer since their installation, and we feel optimistic that this has solved the problem.
   a. positive
   b. negative
   c. neutral

Irony

Whether his work is fiction or nonfiction, an author may attempt to amuse the audience through the use of humor or **irony**. Irony is when the opposite of what we normally expect to happen happens. Usually, background experience and world knowledge guide our expectations for how a situation or an event will unfold. When the opposite of what we expect to happen occurs instead, we refer to the situation as *ironic*.

When an author purposely writes one thing while actually meaning another, he is writing with an *ironic* tone. He does this to get the reader's attention. Study the examples of irony below and then complete Exercise 8.5.

Example 1: The warmth and brightness danced off the clear blue water as it reflected a glittery combination of sunlight, multicolored leaves, and crystal blue sky. Tom looked across the lake at the sleepy village in the distance. The mountains surrounding the lake seemed to create a natural barrier from the world. "Another peaceful Indian summer morning," thought Tom as his canoe reached the cove. Suddenly cries, as if from whooping Indians, pierced the silence as 30 small children climbed out of a school bus and dashed toward the water's edge.

Example 2: The canine did not process any command correctly. When the boy gave the command to sit, the dog ran and brought back a rubber ball. When asked to retrieve, man's best friend simply sat. The boy finally nicknamed the dog "Einstein."

EXERCISE
8-5

Identifying Irony

Read the sentences and/or paragraphs below and check those that describe an ironic situation or make an ironic statement.

_____ **1.** "He has made more home runs than any other player in the history of baseball. He's not _too_ good, is he?"

_____ **2.** He made more home runs than any other player in the history of baseball, and ceremonies were arranged in his honor.

_____ **3.** The editorial board of the Modern Library drew up a list of the 100 best English-language novels of the 20th century. I, of course, read every book on the list, despite that fact that, like most others who were getting ready to graduate, I had senioritis, prom fever, and social priorities.

_____ **4.** The editorial board of the Modern Library drew up a list of the 100 best English-language novels of the 20th century. These included novels such as John Steinbeck's _The Grapes of Wrath_ and William Faulkner's _The Sound and the Fury_.

_____ **5.** Daggers of lightning split the black blanket of clouds while thunder shook the valley. As buckets of water soaked through their waterproof jackets, Bob said, "What a wonderful idea it was to go camping this weekend."

EXERCISE
8-6

Using Adjectives to Identify Tone and Mood

Often the author's tone or the mood of a story can be described by more than one adjective. Read the following story and check the adjectives that apply.

A Lesson for Living

"Everything happens for the best," my mother said whenever I faced disappointment. "If you carry on, one day something good will happen. And you'll realize that it _wouldn't_ have happened if not for that previous disappointment."

Mother was right, as I discovered after graduating from college in 1932. I had decided to try for a job in radio, then work my way up to sports announcer. I hitchhiked to Chicago and knocked on the door of every station and got turned down every time.

In one studio, a kind lady told me that big stations couldn't risk hiring an inexperienced person. "Go out in the sticks and find a small station that'll give you a chance," she said.

I thumbed home to Dixon, Ill. While there were no radio-stations announcing jobs in Dixon, my father said Montgomery Ward had opened a store and wanted a local athlete to manage its sports department. Since Dixon was where I had played high-school football, I applied. The job sounded just right for me. But I wasn't hired.

My disappointment must have shown. "Everything happens for the best," Mom reminded me. Dad offered me the car to drive 70 miles to the Tri-Cities. I tried WOC Radio in Davenport, Iowa. The program director, a wonderful Scotsman named Peter MacArthur, told me they had already hired an announcer.

As I left his office, my frustration boiled over. I asked aloud, "How can a fellow get to be a sports announcer if he can't get a job in a radio station?"

I was waiting for the elevator when I heard MacArthur calling, "What was that you said about sports? Do you know anything about football?" Then he stood me before a microphone and asked me to broadcast an imaginary game.

The preceding autumn, my team had won a game in the last 20 seconds with a 65-yard run. I did a 15-minute buildup to that play, and Peter told me I would be broadcasting Saturday's game!

On my way home, as I have many times since, I thought of my mother's words: "If you carry on, one day something good will happen—something that *wouldn't* have happened if not for that previous disappointment."

I often wonder what direction my life might have taken if I'd gotten the job at Montgomery Ward. (Reagan)

Check all of the adjectives that describe Ronald Reagan's mood or tone in the above narrative. One has been done for you.

_____X_____ **1.** ironic

_____ **2.** angry

_____ **3.** encouraging

_____ **4.** critical

_____ **5.** formal

_____ **6.** informal

_____ **7.** loving

_____ **8.** sarcastic

_____ **9.** hopeful

_____ **10.** optimistic

EXERCISE 8-7

Distinguishing Tone

Read each sentence or paragraph and determine which word below best describes the author's tone. The first one has been done for you.

_____c_____ 1. Many women went to college to find husbands—and dropped out if they succeeded. Almost two-thirds of the women in college, but less than half the men, left before completing a degree. Women were expected to marry young, have children early, and support their husbands' careers. An article in *Esquire* magazine in 1954 called working wives a "menace." Adlai Stevenson, Democratic presidential candidate in 1952 and 1956, defined the female role in politics, telling a group of women "the assignment for you, as wives and mothers, you can do in the living room with a baby in your lap or in the kitchen with a can opener in your hand." As in much of the nineteenth century, a woman was "to influence man and boy" in her "humble role of housewife" and mother. (Nash et al. 700)
   a. anxious
   b. optimistic
   c. straightforward
   d. cheerful
   e. concerned

_____ 2. Of all the knowledge and skills you have, those concerning communication are among your most important and useful. Whether in your personal, social, or work life, your communication ability is your most vital (important) asset. Through intrapersonal communication, you talk with, learn about, and judge yourself. You persuade yourself of this or that, reason about possible decisions to make, and rehearse messages that you plan to send to others. (DeVito 4)
   a. amused
   b. enthusiastic
   c. lighthearted
   d. respectful
   e. doubtful

_____ 3. Another problem with lawns is that they need watering. Since 1950, the rate of public water use . . . grew at more than twice the rate of our population increase. Water tables are falling, and stream flow is decreasing in many river basins. For instance, water tables in the Dallas–Fort Worth area have fallen more than 400 feet in the last 30 years. Some states in the West are now battling over water rights among themselves and with Mexico, and water shortages are now also frequent on the typically much wetter East Coast. With lawn watering accounting for up to 60 percent of urban water use in the West and 30 percent in the East, it's not surprising that an increasing number of communities are restricting the use of water for lawns. (Smith and Smith V-C)

a. angry
b. serious
c. lighthearted
d. amused
e. nostalgic

_____ **4.** Conservationists are increasingly concerned about the toxic con-
tamination of our water supply and the depletion of our underground water sources. Extensive irrigation projects in the western
states use more than 150 billion gallons of water a day—seven
times as much water as all the nation's city water systems combined. The Ogallala aquifer (a 20-million-acre lake beneath the
beef-and-breadbasket states of Colorado, Kansas, Nebraska, New
Mexico, Oklahoma, and Texas) has been dropping by three feet per
year because 150,000 wells are pumping water out faster than
nature can replenish it. (Miller, Benjamin, and North 39)
a. hostile
b. concerned
c. joyous
d. curious
e. subjective

_____ **5.** Let's begin with the passenger pigeon, which provides the most
famous example of the role of human beings in the extinction of
a species. At one time these birds were the most numerous
species of birds in North America and perhaps in the world.
They nested and migrated together in huge flocks and probably
numbered in the billions. When flocks passed overhead, the sky
would be dark with pigeons for days at a time.

The famous naturalist John James Audubon measured one
roost at forty miles long and three miles wide, with birds stacked
from treetop down to nearly ground level. Although the Native
Americans had long hunted these birds, the demise of the passenger pigeon is usually tied to the arrival of the white man,
which increased the demand for pigeons as a source of food and
sport. The birds were shot and netted in vast numbers; by the
end of the nineteenth century, an animal species that had been
looked on as almost indestructible because of its enormous numbers had almost completely disappeared. The last known passenger pigeon died in the Cincinnati Zoo in 1924. (Miller, Benjamin,
and North 157–58)
a. encouraging
b. sad
c. sarcastic
d. nonchalant
e. ironic

Thinking About the Author's Purpose and Tone

Read the article below and think about the author's purpose and the tone of voice. Answer the multiple-choice questions by choosing the correct letter. The first one has been done for you.

If you touch a hot stove, thermal energy enters your hand because the stove is warmer than your hand. When you touch a piece of ice, on the other hand, thermal energy passes out of your hand and into the colder ice. The direction of thermal energy flow is always from a warmer thing to a neighboring cooler thing. A physicist defines heat as the thermal energy transferred from one thing to another due to a temperature difference between the two things.

According to this definition, matter does not contain heat. Matter contains thermal energy, not heat. Heat is thermal energy in transit. Once heat has been transferred to an object or substance, it ceases to be heat. It becomes thermal energy.

For substances in thermal contact, thermal energy flows from the higher-temperature substance to the lower-temperature one but not necessarily from a substance that has more thermal energy to one that has less thermal energy. For instance, there is more thermal energy in a large bowl of warm water than in a red-hot thumbtack; if the tack is immersed in the water, thermal energy doesn't flow from the warm water to the tack. Instead, it flows from the hot tack to the cooler water. Thermal energy never flows of itself from a low-temperature substance to a higher-temperature substance. (Hewitt, Suchocki, and Hewitt 138)

_____a_____ **1.** The author's purpose is:
a. to inform.
b. to entertain.
c. to persuade.

_____ **2.** The tone of this article is:
a. formal.
b. informal.
c. nostalgic.

_____ **3.** Thermal energy enters your hand if you touch a hot stove because:
a. The direction of thermal energy flow is always from a cooler thing to a neighboring warmer thing.
b. Your hand is warmer than the stove.
c. The stove is warmer than your hand.

_____ **4.** According to the author, matter contains:
a. heat.
b. thermal energy.
c. heated substances.

_____ **5.** Thermal energy always flows from:
a. the higher-temperature to the lower-temperature substance.
b. the lower-temperature to the higher-temperature substance.
c. a substance that has more thermal energy to one that has less thermal energy.

A Reading in Memoir

Is it better to study alone or with a study group? Read the passage below, taken from former congresswoman Barbara Jordan's autobiography, to see how she found a way to succeed in law school. Complete the vocabulary exercise before reading the selection to learn the new terms. After reading the selection, complete the comprehension exercises that follow it.

Vocabulary in Context

a. colleagues—classmates; coworkers; equals

b. compensate—pay damages; make up for

c. tolerated—put up with; endured; allowed

d. unmitigated—total; complete; utter

e. orator—public speaker

Use the above terms to complete the following statements. The first one has been done for you.

____a____ **1.** Barbara Jordan felt that she had to try harder than her _____ because she had attended inferior high schools and colleges.

_____ **2.** She tried to _____ for her inadequate training by studying by herself for long hours every night.

_____ **3.** Jordan said she would not make it through law school on public speaking skills alone. She had to learn to think, read, and reason because there was a huge difference between being a lawyer and a(n) _____.

_____ **4.** During that time, according to Jordan, the female students at Boston University were not considered "top drawer;" they were just _____.

_____ **5.** Jordan felt that failing law school would be a(n) _____
disaster.

Becoming a Student

[1]   So I was at Boston University in this new and strange and different
world, and it occurred to me that if I was going to succeed at this strange
new adventure, I would have to read longer and more thoroughly than
my **colleagues** at law school had to read. I felt that in order to
compensate for what I had missed in earlier years, I would have to work
harder, and study longer, than anybody else. I still had this feeling that
I did not want my colleagues to know what a tough time I was having
understanding the concepts, the words, the ideas, the process. I didn't
want them to know that. So I did my reading not in the law library, but
in a library at the graduate dorm, upstairs where it was very quiet,
because apparently nobody else studied there. So I would go there at
night after dinner. I would load my books under my arm and go to the
library, and I would read until the wee hours of the morning and then go
to bed. I didn't get much sleep during those years. I was lucky if I got
three or four hours a night, because I had to stay up. I had to. The professors would assign cases for the next day, and these cases had to be
read and understood or I would be behind, further behind than I was.

[2]   I was always delighted when I would get called upon to recite in class.
But the professors did not call on the "ladies" very much. There were certain favored people who always got called on, and then on some rare
occasions a professor would come in and would announce: "We're going
to have Ladies Day today." And he would call on the ladies. We were just
tolerated. We weren't really considered top drawer when it came to the
study of the law.

[3]   At some time in the spring, Bill Gibson, who was dating my new roommate, Norma Walker, organized a black study group, as we blacks had to
form our own. This was because we were not invited into any of the other
study groups. There were six or seven in our group—Bill, and Issie, and
I think Maynard Jackson—and we would just gather and talk it out and
hear ourselves do that. One thing I learned was that you had to talk out
the issues, the facts, the cases, the decisions, the process. You couldn't
just read the cases and study alone in your library as I had been doing;
and you couldn't get it all in the classroom. But once you had talked it
out in the study group, it flowed more easily and made a lot more sense.

[4]   And from time to time I would go up to the fourth floor at 2 Rawley
Street to check on how Louise was doing. She was always reading
Redbook. Every time I was in there and wanted to discuss one of the

cases with her, she was reading a short story in *Redbook*. I don't know how she could do that. She was not prepared in class when the professors would call on her to discuss cases, but that did not bother her. Whereas it was a matter of life and death with me. I had to make law school. I just didn't have any alternatives. I could not afford to flunk out. That would have been an **unmitigated** disaster. So I read all the time I was not in class.

[5] Finally I felt I was really learning things, really going to school. I felt that I was getting educated, whatever that was. I became familiar with the process of thinking. I learned to think things out and reach conclusions and defend what I had said.

[6] In the past I had got along by spouting off. Whether you talked about debates or oratory, you dealt with speechifying. Even in debate it was pretty much canned because you had, in your little three-by-five box, a response for whatever issue might be raised by the opposition. The format was structured so that there was no opportunity for independent thinking. (I really had not had my ideas challenged ever.) But I could no longer orate and let that pass for reasoning. Because there was not any demand for an **orator** in Boston University Law School. You had to think and read and understand and reason. I had learned at twenty-one that you couldn't just say a thing is so because it might not be so, and somebody brighter, smarter, and more thoughtful would come out and tell you it wasn't so. Then, if you still thought it was, you had to prove it. Well, that was a new thing for me. I cannot, I really cannot describe what that did to my insides and to my head. I thought: I'm being educated finally. (Jordan and Hearon)

Comprehension Questions

_____b_____ **1.** The author's purpose is to:
   a. to inform.
   b. to entertain.
   c. to persuade.

_____ **2.** The tone of this article is:
   a. sad.
   b. determined.
   c. humorous.

_____ **3.** In paragraph 2, Jordan wrote, "We were just tolerated." She was referring to the fact that
   a. African Americans were not welcome in study groups.
   b. Louise was never prepared for class.
   c. Women were not fully welcome in law school at that time.

_____ **4.** At first, law school was very difficult for Barbara Jordan because:
   a. She read short stories in *Redbook* instead of studying.
   b. She was trying to study alone.
   c. She was not really making an effort to succeed.

_____ **5.** The author suggests that:
   a. Discussion is extremely important for understanding what we read.
   b. Women should not go to law school.
   c. Structured responses are more important than independent thinking in law school.

A Reading in Human Interest

Have you ever felt that life would not be complete if you did not have a particular experience? Read the article below to see how one man was determined to have an unforgettable experience. As you read, think about the author's purpose and his tone of voice. Complete the vocabulary exercise before reading the selection to learn the new terms. After reading the selection, complete the comprehension exercises that follow it.

Vocabulary in Context

a. memento—souvenir; keepsake; reminder

b. propelled—moved by some type of force

c. unceremoniously—quickly and abruptly

d. descend—go down

e. generated—created, as in generated heat or generated work

Use the above terms to complete the following statements. The first one has been done for you.

___a___ **1.** Larry Walters wanted a _____ as a reminder of his flight in a most unusual aircraft.

_____ **2.** Unlike regular aircraft, Larry's vehicle was not _____ by jet fuel.

_____ **3.** With regard to landing, Larry used a BB gun to make his aircraft _____.

_____ **4.** When he ran into severe flying conditions, Larry's flight ended _____.

_____ **5.** Larry's flight _____ much publicity because his experience was so unusual.

Lawn Chair Pilot Says One Flight Is Enough

[1]   Los Angeles (AP)—All Larry Walters has is a **memento** of his 3-mile-high flight in a balloon-**propelled** lawn chair is an empty plastic soda bottle.

[2]   "I'm going to hold onto it. I'm going to have it bronzed," said the 33-year old truck driver.

[3]   But it will be a long time before he forgets taking off Friday morning from the back yard of his fiancée's home in San Pedro, lashed to an aluminum lawn chair buoyed by 45 weather balloons and weighted with jugs of spring water for ballast.

[4]   During the 45-minute flight, he soared to 16,000 feet, was spotted by pilots of two jetliners, got so cold he became numb and had to shoot out some of the balloons with a BB gun to make his flying chair **descend**.

[5]   His Journey Ended **unceremoniously** with his contraption wrapped around a power line in Long Beach, about 20 miles from where he started.

[6]   "My mother thought I should be institutionalized and probably still does, but she's proud of me," Walters said Saturday, adding that he'd dreamed of soaring into the skies on a weather balloon since he was 13 years old.

[7]   He was surprised at the widespread publicity his antics **generated**.

[8]   "I knew it would bring a little attention, but I thought they would have the space shuttle on the front page," he said. "The phone wouldn't stop ringing. We finally had to unplug it."

[9]   He added with a grin, "My sister wants me to get an agent."

[10]   As for the trusty lawn chair, Walters gave it away to some youngster who helped pull his contraption off the power lines—police had turned off the electricity when they saw where he was heading. He also gave the kids autographed pieces of the 6-foot balloons.

[11]   "I would have junked it, to be honest," he said of the chair. "It served its purpose."

[12]   He took along the soda for refreshment.

[13]   The Federal Aviation Administration said Walters had been spotted at 16,000 feet by pilots for Delta Air Lines and Trans World Airlines. Land FAA regional safety inspector Neal Savoy said Friday, "We know he broke some part of the Federal Aviation Act, and as soon as we decide which part it is, some type of charge will be filed."

[14]   On Saturday, FAA officials were still scratching their heads. It's all new to everybody around here. We're just trying to get the facts together," said an FAA duty officer who refused to give his name. The officer said some set of charges probably would be filed this week.

[15]   But Walters said he has no second thoughts about the adventure.

[16]   "God, no," he said. "The more I look at it, the more I'm glad I did it. It's something for when I'm an old man. So many people have dreams and they never follow through on them."

[17]   Still, Walters said, "One flight is enough."

[18]   "It was a one-shot deal," he said. "You couldn't pay me a million dollars to do it again."

[19]   But he added, "I will endorse Sears lawn chairs."

Questions for Discussion

1. Why do you think Larry Walters wants to have the soda bottle bronzed?

_____

_____

_____

2. Why hasn't the FAA regional safety inspector pressed charges against the balloonist?

_____

_____

_____

3. Why do Larry Walters and his family feel good about his adventure?

_____

_____

_____

4. How do you think the airline pilots reacted when they saw Larry Walters flying around in a lawn chair?

_____

_____

_____

5. Do you think the FAA will eventually press charges? Find the words in the article that lead you to believe this and record them below.

_____

_____

_____

Comprehension Questions

_____ b _____ **1.** The author's purpose is:
   a. to inform.
   b. to entertain.
   c. to persuade.

_____ **2.** The tone of this article is:
   a. humorous.
   b. serious.
   c. disapproving.

_____ **3.** The height that Larry Walters went up to in his lawn chair was:
   a. 1 mile.
   b. 21,000 feet.
   c. 16,000 feet.

_____ **4.** Larry Walters was a:
   a. 35-year-old doctor.
   b. 33-year-old truck driver.
   c. 31-year-old pilot.

_____ **5.** The plastic soda bottle will be:
   a. bronzed and kept as a souvenir.
   b. thrown away.
   c. given to the youngster who pulled the balloons from the power lines.

_____ **6.** Larry said he would endorse the Sears lawn chair because:
   a. His fiancée liked to sit in the chair.
   b. He used it for years until it finally fell apart.
   c. It didn't fall apart after going 16,000 miles in the air.

_____ **7.** Walters said he had no second thoughts about the adventure because:
   a. It was not that dangerous.

   b. He felt he had lived out his dream.
   c. He was not breaking any laws.

_____ **8.** Walter's journey ended:
   a. 20 miles from where he started.
   b. 13 miles from where he started.
   c. 16,000 miles from where he started.

_____ **9.** To carry him on his 45-minute flight, Larry used:
   a. a BB gun.
   b. a hot air balloon.
   c. 45 weather balloons.

_____ **10.** The FAA is having a hard time filing charges because
   a. Larry Walters has not broken any laws with his flying lawn chair.
   b. No one has ever been charged with flying an unauthorized lawn chair before.
   c. Complaints were already filed against the lawn chair by the pilots.

Reading Between the Lines Box 8.3

PURPOSE AND TONE
The Lawn Chair Pilot

The tone of an article helps us determine the author's overall purpose. For example, at the end of the lawn chair pilot article, the author was quoted in saying that he would endorse Sears lawn chairs. Does this mean the author's purpose is to persuade us to buy at Sears? The answer is "no" because, although the author is impressed with the quality of the lawn chair, the tone of the article lets us know that he is making a joke instead of trying to sell a product.

Reread the article on the lawn chair pilot and check the adjectives that describe the author's tone.

❏ lighthearted *(positive)*   ❏ informal *(neutral)*   ❏ encouraging *(positive)*
❏ helpless *(negative)*   ❏ optimistic *(positive)*   ❏ authoritative *(neutral)*
❏ hopeful *(positive)*   ❏ fearful *(negative)*   ❏ angry *(negative)*
❏ hostile *(negative)*   ❏ serious *(contextual)*   ❏ cheerful *(positive)*
❏ joyous *(positive)*   ❏ critical *(negative)*   ❏ humorous *(positive)*
❏ pessimistic *(negative)*   ❏ sarcastic *(contextual)*   ❏ enthusiastic *(positive)*
❏ formal *(contextual)*   ❏ objective *(contextual)*   ❏ subjective *(contextual)*

After assessing the adjectives that describe the author's tone, determine the author's overall purpose for writing this article.
_____ **1.** inform
_____ **2.** persuade
_____ **3.** entertain

CHAPTER
9

Critical Thinking

- -

PREPARING TO THINK CRITICALLY

All of us are bombarded with persuasive messages every day. Advertisers study our lifestyles and try to persuade us to buy products whether we actually need them or not. Politicians try to convince us to support issues that affect the quality of our lives. The food industry tries to lure us into eating products that may or may not be healthy.

In this chapter, we prepare to think critically by:

- understanding and describing events;
- identifying the issues;
- identifying the argument;
- finding evidence to support the argument;
- understanding propaganda.

Most adult decisions require skill in weighing the pros and cons involved with each choice we make. *We* are the ones who need to be informed and able to make good decisions about what is safe to eat and drink and what is safe to feed our children. It takes careful thought to distinguish between what we actually need and what advertisers and politicians tell us we need. And, it takes skill to make good decisions on ordinary business agreements such as insurance policies, car loans, work contracts, apartment leases, and mortgage loans.

How can we develop the skill to make good decisions in our everyday lives? We know we are making good decisions when we are able to explain why we choose one item or opportunity over another and when our reasons make sense. In other words, decisions are sound when they are logical and relevant. **Relevant** means that our reasons are directly connected to our choice, while **logical** means that our reasons for a particular action make sense under given circumstances. When we make good decisions based on sound reasons, we are **thinking critically**.

When we are influenced or even pressured to make choices that sound good but may not, in the end, be to our benefit, critical thinking can become challenging. For example, salespeople may try to persuade us to buy things we don't need. Politicians may try to try to talk us into voting for things that we don't believe in. The news media may try to influence the way we feel about situations in our neighborhoods, our nation, and the world. Sometimes their tactics are questionable or even involve trickery. For these types of situations, an understanding of logic and propaganda (discussed later in this chapter) is needed. In this chapter we practice strategies that *prepare* us to think critically.

Understanding Events

The first step in preparing to think critically is to understand a situation or event. This is necessary because misunderstandings or errors in comprehension can prevent us from drawing logical conclusions. The ability to describe a situation or an event is also important because it allows us the opportunity to "play back" what we have heard or read and, thus, enables us to recognize whether or not we have actually understood the event. "Playing back" or "describing" checks our comprehension.

Describing Events

Have you ever read a newspaper or magazine article and wanted to talk about it with a friend but could not remember the details? Your retelling might have sounded like this:

> "I read this really great article. I can't remember where I read it, but it was really awesome; you should read it. It was about some students—can't remember where they were from—going on a spring break vacation. I can't remember where they went, some island somewhere. But, you would really like the article; you should read it."

Remembering details makes our conversations more interesting. For example, your friends would probably become more interested in reading the spring break article and talking about it if they knew some of the details. A more effective "playing back" of the article might be:

> There's an article in our campus newspaper today about seven seniors from our school who went to Greece during spring break. It tells how they cut expenses by camping and backpacking and taking advantage of Super Express's low airfares.

What details are provided in this retelling that were not included in the previous description? Why are they important to generating interest in the article?

Reading Between the Lines Box 9.1

RETELLING AND TIME ORDER

The Life of Frederick Douglass

When events are introduced in the order in which they occurred, this textbook pattern is known as chronological order, or time order. Read the excerpt from "The Life of Frederick Douglass" on page 326. Then, arrange the following events in the order in which they occurred in his autobiography. Place numbers 1 through 10 on the blanks provided. One has been done for you.

　__3__ The slaves conclude their plan by deciding to take the water route.

　_____ The slaves who were planning the escape were seized.

　_____ The slaves, although anxious, felt determined to escape rather than live their lives in slavery.

　_____ Henry was beaten when he refused to be tied.

　_____ Frederick Douglass thinks about the protections keeping them safe through the bay area.

　_____ One slave, Sandy, changed his mind about Frederick Douglass's escape plan.

　_____ Without knowing why, both Sandy and Frederick Douglass felt they had been betrayed.

　_____ Frederick Douglass managed to put the false travel papers in the fire before being tied.

　_____ Frederick Douglass and five other slaves decided to escape.

　_____ Frederick Douglass wrote several false protections for the slaves to travel.

A Reading in Autobiography

Complete the vocabulary exercise before reading this selection to learn the new terms. Then, as you read the excerpt from Frederick Douglass's account of how he attempted to escape from slavery, take notice of the details. Think of what and how much you would need to remember in order to play back this event to someone else, then complete the exercises that follow the reading.

Vocabulary in Context

a. **resolved**—firmly decided

b. **agitated**—restless, troubled, disturbed

c. **hazardous**—having obstacles; dangerous

d. **indescribable**—beyond description, beyond words, inability to express

e. **betokening**—indicating

Use the above terms to complete the following statements. The first one has been done for you.

_____e_____ 1. Mr. Hamilton, Mr. Freeland, and three constables came to the house in haste, _____ great troubles.

_____ 2. Frederick Douglass and his friends _____ upon freedom and were determined to run away.

_____ 3. Escape was extremely _____ because slaves had to have official documents that gave them permission to travel.

_____ 4. Right before they were betrayed, both Frederick Douglass and Sandy had feelings that were _____.

_____ 5. While waiting for the day of escape, Frederick Douglass felt _____ by thoughts of what would happen if they were caught.

From *The Life of Frederick Douglass*

[1]   In coming to a fixed determination to run away, we did more than Patrick Henry, when he **resolved** upon liberty or death. With us it was a doubtful liberty at most, and almost certain death if we failed. For my part, I should prefer death to hopeless bondage.

[2]   Sandy, one of our number, gave up the notion, but still encouraged us. Our company then consisted of Henry Harris, John Harris, Henry Bailey, Charles Roberts, and myself. Henry Bailey was my uncle, and belonged to my master. Charles married my aunt: he belonged to my master's father-in-law, Mr. William Hamilton.

[3]   The plan we finally concluded upon was, to get a large canoe belonging to Mr. Hamilton, and upon the Saturday night previous to Easter holidays, paddle directly up the Chesapeake Bay. On our arrival at the head of the bay, a distance of seventy or eighty miles from where we lived, it was our purpose to turn our canoe adrift, and follow the guidance of the

north star till we got beyond the limits of Maryland. Our reason for taking the water route was, that we were less liable to be suspected as runaways; we hoped to be regarded as fishermen; whereas, if we should take the land route, we should be subjected to interruptions of almost every kind. Any one having a white face, and being so disposed, could stop us, and subject us to examination.

[4]   The week before our intended start, I wrote several protections, one for each of us. As well as I can remember, they were in the following words, to wit:

> "This is to certify that I, the undersigned, have given the bearer, my servant, full liberty to go to Baltimore, and spend the Easter holidays. Written with mine own hand, &c., 1835.
>   "William Hamilton, Near St. Michael's, in Talbot county, Maryland."

[5]   We were not going to Baltimore; but, in going up the bay, we went toward Baltimore, and these protections were only intended to protect us while on the bay.

[6]   As the time drew near for our departure, our anxiety became more and more intense. It was truly a matter of life and death with us. The strength of our determination was about to be fully tested. At this time, I was very active in explaining every difficulty, removing every doubt, dispelling every fear, and inspiring all with the firmness indispensable to success in our undertaking; assuring them that half was gained the instant we made the move; we had talked long enough; we were now ready to move; if not now, we never should be; and if we did not intend to move now, we had as well fold our arms, sit down, and acknowledge ourselves fit only to be slaves. This, none of us were prepared to acknowledge. Every man stood firm; and at our last meeting, we pledged ourselves afresh, in the most solemn manner, that, at the time appointed, we would certainly start in pursuit of freedom. This was in the middle of the week, at the end of which we were to be off. We went, as usual, to our several fields of labor, but with bosoms highly **agitated** with thoughts of our truly **hazardous** undertaking. We tried to conceal our feelings as much as possible; and I think we succeeded very well.

[7]   After a painful waiting, the Saturday morning, whose night was to witness our departure, came. I hailed it with joy, bring what sadness it might. Friday night was a sleepless one for me. I probably felt more anxious than the rest, because I was, by common consent, at the head of the whole affair. The responsibility of success or failure lay heavily upon me. The glory of the one, and the confusion of the other, were alike mine. The first two hours of that morning were such as I never experienced before, and hope never to again. Early in the morning, we went, as usual, to the field. We were spreading manure; and all at once while thus engaged, I was overwhelmed with an **indescribable** feeling, in the fullness of which I turned to Sandy, who was near by, and said, "We are betrayed!"

[8]   "Well," said he, "that thought has this moment stuck me." We said no more. I was never more certain of any thing.

[9]   The horn was blown as usual, and we went up from the field to the house for breakfast. I went for the form, more than for want of any thing to eat that morning. Just as I got to the house, in looking out at the lane gate, I saw four white men, with two colored men. The white men were on horseback, and the colored ones were walking behind, as if tied. I watched them a few moments till they got up to our lane gate. Here they halted, and tied the colored men to the gatepost. I was not yet certain as to what the matter was. In a few moments, in rode Mr. Hamilton, with a speed **betokening** great excitement. He came to the door, and inquired if Master William was in. He was told he was at the barn. Mr. Hamilton, without dismounting, rode up to the barn with extraordinary speed. In a few moments, he and Mr. Freeland returned to the house. By this time, the three constables rode up, and in great haste dismounted, tied their horses, and met Master William and Mr. Hamilton returning from the barn; and after talking awhile, they all walked up to the kitchen door. There was no one in the kitchen but myself and John. Henry and Sandy were up at the barn. Mr. Freeland put his head in at the door, and called me by name, saying, there were some gentlemen at the door who wished to see me. I stepped to the door, and inquired what they wanted. They at once, seized me, and, without giving me any satisfaction, tied me—lashing my hands closely together. I insisted upon knowing what the matter was. They at length said, that they had learned I had been in a "Scrape," and that I was to be examined before my master; and if their information proved false, I should not be hurt.

[10]   In a few moments, they succeeded in tying John. They then turned to Henry, who had by this time returned, and commanded him to cross his hands. "I won't!" said Henry, in a firm tone, indicating his readiness to meet the consequences of his refusal. "Won't you?" said Tom Graham, the constable. "No, I won't!" said Henry, in a still stronger tone. With this, two of the constables pulled out their shining pistols, and swore, by their Creator, that they would make him cross his hands or kill him. Each cocked his pistol, and, with fingers on the trigger, walked up to Henry, saying, at the same time, if he did not cross his hands, they would blow his damned heart out. "Shoot me, shoot me!" said Henry; "you can't kill me but once, Shoot, shoot,—and be damned! I won't be tied!" This he said in a tone of loud defiance; and at the same time, with a motion as quick as lightning, he with one single stroke dashed the pistols from the hand of each constable. As he did this, all hands fell upon him, and, after beating him some time, they finally overpowered him, and got him tied.

[11]   During the scuffle, I managed, I know not how, to get my pass out, and, without being discovered, put it into the fire. We were all now tied. . . .

Retelling

In your own words and *without looking back at the excerpt*, retell Frederick Douglass's plan to escape and the events that followed his attempt. Pretend that you are explaining this event to a friend who has not read the excerpt.

_____

_____

_____

_____

Next, review the excerpt and make sure you have included the following details for both the escape plan and the following events. Check your retelling for accuracy and add any details that you may have forgotten.

Who? _____

What? _____

When? _____

Where? _____

How? _____

Why? _____

Finally, compare your retelling with those of other students' in the class. What details did you include that were different from others? Which details did you include that were similar to others?

Similar: _____

_____

Different: _____

_____

Multiple-Choice Questions

Check your understanding of events surrounding Frederick Douglass's failed escape plan. The first one has been done for you.

_____d_____ **1.** While contemplating the escape plan, Frederick Douglass thought about what would happen to him if it failed. If his plan failed, he was sure he:
   a. would go to jail.
   b. would be sent back to their master.
   c. would be beaten severely.
   d. would be killed.

_____ **2.** The escape plan involved going up the Chesapeake Bay in a canoe for 70 to 80 miles and then following the North Star until they crossed the Maryland border. Their reason for going by canoe instead of walking on land was:
   a. They would look like fishermen and have less chance of being questioned.
   b. It was faster to go by water than by land.
   c. It was easier to ride in a canoe than it would be to walk.
   d. They had no identification or written permissions to leave the plantation.

_____ **3.** The group of slaves that was planning to escape consisted of:
   a. Henry Harris, John Harris, Henry Bailey, Charles Roberts, and Frederick Douglass.
   b. Sandy, Henry Harris, Henry Bailey, Charles Roberts, and Frederick Douglass.
   c. John Harris, Henry Bailey, Charles Roberts, and Frederick Douglass.
   d. Henry Harris, John Harris, Henry Bailey, Charles Roberts, and Sandy.

_____ **4.** Frederick Douglass was trying to escape from:
   a. Baltimore.
   b. the bay area of Boston.
   c. Talbot County, Maryland.
   d. Atlanta, Georgia.

_____ **5.** During the week before the date they had set for the escape, Frederick Douglass felt:
   a. anxious and fearful.
   b. hopeless.
   c. doubtful and depressed.
   d. joyful and lighthearted.

_____ **6.** On the Saturday morning of the planned escape, Frederick Douglass knew their plan had been discovered because:
   a. Sandy told him they had been betrayed.
   b. Henry Harris had never been trustworthy.
   c. Mr. Freeland questioned them suspiciously the day before.
   d. He had an instinctive feeling that they had been betrayed.

_____ 7. Frederick Douglass's master learned of the escape plan through:
   a. the three constables.
   b. Master William.
   c. Mr. Hamilton.
   d. Mr. Freeland.

_____ 8. When Henry refused to be tied, the constables said they would shoot and kill him if he did not comply. Once again, Henry refused to be tied, and the constables:
   a. beat him to death.
   b. shot him to death.
   c. tied him.
   d. beat him and then tied him.

_____ 9. While they were tying Henry, Frederick Douglass managed to destroy his fake travel permission by:
   a. swallowing it.
   b. passing it to another slave.
   c. throwing it out the window.
   d. putting it into the fire.

_____ 10. At the end of the passage, Frederick Douglass wrote that "We were all now tied. . . . " "We" refers to:
   a. Henry and Frederick Douglass.
   b. Sandy, Henry, John, and Frederick Douglass.
   c. Sandy and Frederick Douglass.
   d. Henry, John, and Frederick Douglass.

IDENTIFYING THE ISSUE

Think of an occasion when you found yourself trying to persuade another person to see your point of view, and, in turn, that person tried just as hard to persuade you to see *her* point. In other words, the two of you **argued** in favor of your own opinions—that is, *made cases* for your individual points.

When authors write persuasively, their intention is to convince readers to adopt their opinion. **Persuasive writing** is, therefore, like an argument. The topic of a persuasive passage is called the **issue**. To find the issue, we must read the passage, locate the topic, and consider whether there are differing opinions about the topic. If so, the topic is then thought of as the *issue* and is often stated as a question. The topic sentence of a persuasive passage is called the **argument** because it states the author's opinion of the issue. Read the passage below and identify the issue and the argument.

Every building on campus should have a nonsmoking entrance in which smoking is prohibited within 100 feet. The need for this is very clear. First of all, some people are allergic to cigarette smoke and need to enter and exit buildings without exposure to it. Also, researchers have found that secondary cigarette smoke is even more deadly than the original smoke, and the right to fresh air could become a legal issue. Finally, nonsmokers may simply want to enter and exit buildings without smelling as though they just came from a smoky bar.

> The issue is *Should all buildings on campus have nonsmoking entrances?*
>
> The argument is *Every building on campus should have a nonsmoking entrance.*
>
> We know this is the *argument* because it states the author's opinion about the *issue* of whether all campus buildings should have nonsmoking entrances.

EXERCISE
9-1

Identifying the Argument

Read the following paragraphs and write the issue in the form of a question. Then identify the statement that contains the argument by choosing a, b, c, or d. The first one has been done for you.

1. (a) Since psychologists have found that sounds are linked to our emotions, advertisers have become very sneaky about including certain sounds we associate with good times in their ads, a process called *psychoacoustic persuasion*. (b) Advertisers also use a questionable practice called *subliminal seduction*— disguised scenes in television and magazine ads—to trick us into associating a product or service with a desirable emotion. (c) *Psychographics* is another deception that advertisers use to calculate what type of products we are most likely to buy based on our income, social status, and locale. (d) Advertisers use unfair methods to trap consumers into buying their products.

   Issue: Do advertisers use unfair methods to trap consumers into buying their products?

   Argument: ___d___

2. (a) Virologists found that when plant cells having virus genes implanted in them come into contact with new viruses, the implanted virus can be transferred into the new virus. (b) This can create a new virus that is stronger. (c) Genetically altered soil bacteria can upset the natural soil balance necessary for the growth of crops, grasses, and trees. (d) Genetic engineering can cause more problems than it solves. (e) For example, fragments of DNA and genet-

ically engineered bacteria can remain in rivers, sewers, and soil much longer than scientists originally thought possible.

Issue: _____

Argument: _____

3. (a) Corporate farms are putting the family farm out of business. (b) The family farm cannot compete with the huge corporate farms in both resources and prices. (c) As are result, family farms, with their natural methods of food production, are disappearing. (d) Replacing them are huge corporate farms that use artificial means to meet their goal of mass production and large profits. (e) Therefore, corporate farms are responsible for the destruction of natural methods of food production.

Issue: _____

Argument: _____

4. (a) Hypnosis should be used for treating some psychological ills. (b) It has been used successfully to treat anxiety, insomnia, and other minor psychological symptoms. (c) It has no side effects, unlike many drugs. (d) Under hypnosis, subjects will not do anything that goes against their basic morals and ethical codes.

Issue: _____

Argument: _____

5. (a) Overdoses of vitamin D may cause calcification of organs and arteries. (b) It is not easy to control the amount of vitamin D obtained through vitamin supplements. (c) Vitamin D supplements should be taken only under the supervision of a doctor or nutritionist.

Issue: _____

Argument: _____

FINDING EVIDENCE TO SUPPORT OPINIONS

As we read or listen to others' ideas, we form opinions. **Opinions** are the judgments we make based on our impressions and perceptions of an event or situation. The quality of our arguments may be good or poor depending on the evidence we use to "back up" or support our opinions.

If we have "done our homework" and are knowledgeable about a topic, we will have an **informed opinion**. If, however, we know very little about a subject, we hold an **uninformed opinion**. Arguments based on informed opinions are more convincing than arguments based on uninformed opinions.

In other words, to convince someone to adopt our opinion, we need to build an argument that is supported by a series of logical reasons offering a valid conclusion. Look again at the passage that argues for nonsmoking entrances to buildings on campus. What are the author's reasons for wanting nonsmoking entrances?

> Every building on campus should have a nonsmoking entrance in which smoking is prohibited within 100 feet. The need for this is very clear. First of all, some people are allergic to cigarette smoke and need to enter and exit buildings without exposure to it. Also, researchers have found that secondary cigarette smoke is even more deadly than the original smoke and the right to fresh air could become a legal issue. Finally, nonsmokers may simply want to enter and exit buildings without smelling as though they just came from a smoky bar.

The author provides three reasons:

1. Some people are allergic and cannot be exposed to cigarette smoke.
2. Researchers found that secondary cigarette smoke is even more deadly than the original smoke.
3. Nonsmokers may not want to smell smoky.

All three reasons are related to the issue, and they make sense in this situation. Therefore, we can say that this argument is well supported. In other words, the author has a good argument or case for the creation of nonsmoking entrances based on the reasons that he provides.

In persuasive writing, the argument can also be called the **point**. The reasons we give to defend our point are called the **support**. If our reasons are grounded with facts that can be verified, then we can say that we are giving evidence to support our point. For example, if we argued that the Food-O-Rama Supermarket is not a safe place to shop, our point would simply be:

> The Food-O-Rama Supermarket is not a safe place to shop.

If we provided facts that verified how dangerous the Food-O-Rama has become for shoppers, our support would be as follows:

1. There was a shootout in the Food-O-Rama last Saturday night between a robber and the police.
2. Gangs congregate in front of the store in the afternoons.
3. Seven people were held hostage while they were buying their groceries last fall.

Visual Literacy Box 9.1

DIAGRAMS: ARGUMENT

The argument pattern is similar to the "topic with a list" pattern. The argument is like the topic and the support for the argument is like a list of reasons.

Topic: Types of Parking Facilities	**Argument**: The Food-O-Rama is not safe.
1. Item: parking garages	**1. Reason:** There was a shoot out.
2. Item: parking lots	**2. Reason:** Gangs congregate in front.
3. Item: metered spaces along streets	**3. Reason:** Seven people were held hostage.

Identify the argument from the list below.

Argument: _____

City college can afford to build a parking garage.

Many students cannot find a place to park because the lots are full by 8:00 A.M.

City college should build a parking garage.

There are not enough metered parking spaces along the streets.

All of these reasons are related to the lack of safety at the Food-O-Rama, and based on these reasons, it makes sense that we would feel unsafe to go there. Therefore, we can say that our argument or point is well supported. Our opinion is backed up by sound evidence.

Sometimes the point is stated first and the support is listed afterward. Other times the support is listed first and the point is stated last. In the second case, the point is considered to be the author's conclusion. In the case of the Food-O-Rama example, the evidence (support) concerning shootouts, gangs, and hostages led us to draw the conclusion (or make the point) that the Food-O-Rama is not a safe place to shop.

Let's practice identifying point and support. Remember, the *point* is a general statement or a conclusion that can be drawn from more specific information. The *support* is evidence that leads you to believe the point or conclusion is accurate or correct.

A Reading in Education

The professor said, "Since the university library was closed due to the snow storm, I am extending the deadline for the research papers. You do not need to turn them in until Friday." I told my colleagues the professor said, to his students, "You do not need to turn in the research papers until Friday." By telling only part of the story, I led my colleagues to believe that the professor had no legitimate reason for extending the deadline. One question that could be raised after reading the following segment of the book One Child by Torey L. Hayden is: Can the public schools serve Sheila's needs or should she be placed in a psychiatric hospital? This issue has two arguments:

1. Sheila should stay in the special education classroom at the public school.
2. Sheila should be moved to a psychiatric hospital.

After you complete the reading, decide which argument you agree with and write down five facts that support your argument.

Argument: _____

Support: _____

1. _____

2. _____

3. _____

4. _____

5. _____

Vocabulary in Context

a. perplexing—confusing, puzzling, mystifying

b. verbose—wordy, longwinded

c. erudite—well educated; well read; knowledgeable; learned

d. discourse—dialogue, conversation, discussion

e. lurid—awful, disgusting, appalling, graphic

Use the above terms to complete the following statements. The first one has been done for you.

_____c_____ **1.** Many _____ teachers and psychologists wrote lengthy reports describing Sheila's problems.

Reading Between the Lines Box 9.2

RESPONSE JOURNALS

One Child

A response journal permits the reader to discuss especially thought-provoking parts of a text and express his/her feelings in an honest way.

1. Use the following questions to write a response or reaction to the excerpt from *One Child*.

   a. What were your reactions to Sheila's family and upbringing?
   b. What were your reactions to the chain of events that took place in the classroom?
   c. How do you feel about the lunch aides and their responsibilities to the school?
   d. What would you do if you were the teacher?

2. Find reasons or support from the passage to back up each of your points or responses. Put quotation marks around sentences that you take word for word from the passage. Use the "Sample Response Journal Entry" below as a model.

Sample Response Journal Entry:

If I were the teacher, I don't think that I would want Sheila in my classroom. The reports that Torey read indicated that Sheila had a terrible childhood. I realize that it is not Sheila's fault that all of the adults in her life refused to take care of her. **"Sheila had been shifted around among relatives and friends of the family, mostly on the mother's side, before finally being abandoned on a roadside, where she was found clinging to a chain-link fence that separated the freeway lanes."**

However, her actions are not appropriate for a public school. They are even disturbing to the children with severe disabilities. **"Freddie had joined Max in circling the room. Tyler was wailing; Guillermo hid under that table; William stood in one corner and cried, Whitney was off trying to capture Max and Freddie as they reeled around the perimeter of the room screaming."**

It seems that Sheila is a danger to the children, the aides, and the teachers. For example, Sheila stabbed Torey with a pencil, she kicked Whitney in the shins, and she killed all of the children's goldfish. **"She had apparently caught the goldfish one by one and poked their eyes out with a pencil."** Even Torey described her as being wild and beyond control when Sheila was threatening to stab anybody that came near her with a pencil. **"I had no doubt she would attack if at all provoked. Her eyes had the glazed wildness of a threatened animal."**

_____ 2. Throughout the year, much of the _____ among Anton, Torey, and Whitney concerned Sheila.

_____ 3. The _____ details of child abuse were included in the social worker's report to the school.

_____ 4. Because the children she taught had so many special needs, Torey spent many hours reading _____ and detailed reports from psychologists.

_____ 5. Torey had never worked with such a troubled child before. Therefore, Sheila's actions were _____ to her.

One Child

[1]   After escorting Sheila to the lunchroom I retired to the office to have a look at her file. I wanted to know what others had done with this **perplexing** child. From watching her, it was apparent that she did not suffer from the crippling, unexplainable disturbances such as Max and Susannah displayed. Instead, she was in surprisingly good control of her behavior, more so than most of the children coming into my class. Behind those hate-filled eyes I saw a perceptive and most likely intelligent little girl. She had to be in order to manipulate her world with such conscious effort. But I wanted to know what had been tried before.

[2]   The file was surprisingly thin for one that had worked its way to me. Most of my children had thick, paper-bloated folders, glutted with **verbose** opinions of dozens of doctors and therapists and judges and social workers. It was plain to me every time I read one of those files that the people filling them never had to work with the child day in and day out for hours at a time. The words on the papers were **erudite discourses**, but they did not tell a desperate teacher or frightened parent how to help. I doubt anyone could write such words. In reality, each of the children was so different and grew in such unpredictable ways that one day's experience was the only framework for planning the next. There were no textbooks or university courses specializing in Max or William or Peter.

[3]   But Sheila's file was thin, only a few bits of paper: a family history, test results, and a standard data form from Special Services. I paged through the social worker's report of the family. Like so many others in my room, it was filled with **lurid** details that, despite my experience, my middle-class mind could not fully comprehend. Sheila lived alone with her father in a one-room shack in the migrant camp. The house had no heat, no plumbing, and no electricity. Her mother had abandoned Sheila two years earlier but had taken a younger son. She now lived in California, the form stated, although no one actually knew her whereabouts. The mother had been only fourteen when Sheila was born, two months after a forced wedding, while her father was thirty. I shook my head in grim amazement. The mother would only be twenty years old now, barely more than a child herself.

[4]   The father had spent most of Sheila's early years in prison on assault-and-battery charges. Since his release two-and-a-half years before, he had also had stays at the state hospital for alcoholism and drug dependency. Sheila had been shifted around among relatives and friends of the family, mostly on the mother's side, before finally being abandoned on a roadside, where she was found clinging to a chain-link fence that separated the freeway lanes. Taken to the juvenile center, Sheila, then four, was discovered to have numerous abrasions and healed multiple fractures, all the results of abuse. She was released to her father's custody and a child-protection worker was assigned to the case. A court statement appended to the file said that the judge felt it was best to leave the child in her natural home. A county-appointed physician had scrawled across the bottom that her small size probably resulted from malnutrition, but otherwise she was a healthy Caucasian female with well-healed scars and fractures. Loose behind these two assessments was a memo from the county's consulting psychiatrist with the single statement: Chronic Maladjustment to Childhood. I smiled at it in spite of myself; what an astute conclusion this man had drawn. How helpful to us all. The only normal reaction to a childhood like Sheila's would be chronic maladjustment. If one did adjust to such pornography of life, it would surely be a testimony to one's insanity.

[5]   The test results were even more obscure. Beside each title on the battery, written in tight, frustrated printing: Refused. The bottom summary simply stated she was untestable and underlined the fact twice.

[6]   The Special Services questionnaire contained only demographics. The father had filled out the form and he had been in prison all those crucial years. She had been born with no apparent complications in a local hospital. Nothing was known of her early developmental history. She had attended three schools in her short educational history, not including the one she was in now. All the moves had resulted from her uncontrollable behavior. At home she was reported to eat and sleep within the normal limits. But she wet the bed every night and she sucked her thumb. She had no friends among the migrant workers' children at the camp; nor did she appear to have any solid relationships with adults. The father wrote that she was a loner, hostile, and unfriendly even to him. She spoke erratically at home, usually only when she was angry. She never cried. I stopped and reread that statement. She never cried? I could not conceive of a six-year-old who did not cry. He must have meant she seldom cried. That must have been a mistake.

[7]   I continued reading. Her father saw her as a wayward child and disciplined her frequently, mostly by spanking or taking away privileges. I wondered what sort of privileges there were in her life to be taken away. In addition to the burning incident, she had been reprimanded for setting fires in the migrant camp and for smearing feces in the restroom of a bus station. By six-and-a-half, Sheila had encountered the police three times.

[8]   I stared at the file and its bits of random information. She was not going to be an easy child to love because she worked at being unlovable. Nor was she going to be an easy child to teach. But she was not unreachable. Despite her exterior, Sheila was indeed probably more reachable than Susannah Joy or Freddie, because there was no indication that her functioning was garbled with retardation, or neurological impairments or other mysteries of the brain. From what I could glean, Sheila was a normally functioning child in that respect. Which made the battle ahead for me even harder because I knew it rested solely with us on the outside. We had no cute phrases, no curtains like autism or brain damage to hide behind when we failed with the Sheilas. We had only ourselves. Deep down behind those hostile eyes was a very little girl who had already learned that life really isn't much fun for anybody; and the best way to avoid further rejection was to make herself as objectionable as possible. Then it would never come as a surprise to find herself unloved. Only a simple fact.

[9]   Anton came in while I was paging through the file. He pulled up a chair beside me and took the forms as I finished them. Despite our clumsy beginning, Anton and I had become a fully functioning team. He was an adroit worker with these children. Having spent all his life prior to this year in the fields, and still living in the migrant camp in a small hut with his wife and two sons, Anton knew much more intimately than I the world my kids came from. I had the training and the experience and the knowledge, but Anton had the instinct and the wisdom. Certain aspects of their lives I never would understand because in my existence warm houses and freedom from violence and hunger and cockroaches was my due. I had never had reason to expect otherwise. Now as an adult, I had learned that others lived differently and that this different way of life, to them, was also normal. I could accept that fact, but I could not understand it. I do not believe that anyone for whom it is not a living reality can; anyone claiming that extra measure of understanding either lies to himself or is a deluded braggart. But Anton compensated for my lack and together we had managed to build a supportive relationship. He had come to know without being told when and how and whom to help. An additional benefit was that Anton spoke Spanish, which I did not. Thus, he saved me innumerable times when Guillermo went beyond his limit of English. Now Anton sat beside me, quietly reading Sheila's folder.

[10]   "How did she do at lunch?"

[11]   He nodded without looking up from the papers. "Okay. She eats like she never sees food. But she probably doesn't. And, oh, so bad on the manners. But she sat with the children and did not fuss."

[12]   "Do you know her father out at the camp?"

[13]   "No. That's the other side of the camp, where the whites live. The junkies are all over there. We never go over."

[14]   Whitney came in and leaned over the counter. She was a pretty girl in a nondescript way: tall, slender, with hazel eyes and long, straight,

dishwater-blond hair. Although Whitney was an honors student at her junior high and came from one of the community's most prominent families, she was a painfully shy girl. When she had come in the fall she had carried out all her tasks in great silence, never looking me in the eye, always smiling nervously, even when things were going wrong. The only time she did talk was to criticize her work, to put herself down or to apologize for doing everything wrong. Unfortunately, in the beginning that seemed all too true. Whitney made every mistake in the book. She dropped half a gallon of freshly mixed green tempera paint on the gym floor. She forgot Freddie in the men's room at the fairgrounds. She left the door to our room ajar one afternoon after school and Benny, the class boa constrictor, escaped and went to visit Mrs. Anderson, the first grade teacher. For me, Whitney was like having another child. If I had not been so desperate in those early months for a third set of hands to help, I might not have had the patience for her. Those first weeks I was always re-explaining, always cleaning something up, always saying, "Don't worry about it," when I did not mean it. Whitney was always crying.

[15]   But like Anton, Whitney had been worth the trouble, because she cared so much about the kids. Whitney was hopelessly devoted to us. I knew she skipped classes occasionally to stay longer with us, and she often came over on her lunch hour or after school to help me. From home she brought her own outgrown toys to give the children. She came with ideas for me that she had found in teaching magazines she read in her spare time. And always that hungry, pleading look to be appreciated. Whitney very seldom talked about the rest of her life outside my classroom. Yet, despite her affluence and the prominent name of her family, Whitney, I suspected, was no better off in some ways than the kids in the class. So I remained tolerant of her clumsiness and ineptitude and tried to make her feel a valued part of our team because she was.

[16]   "Did you get your new girl?" Whitney asked, stretching over the counter and causing her hair to tumble onto the papers I was reading.

[17]   "Yes, we did," I said and mentioned briefly what had transpired during the morning. That was when I heard the screaming.

[18]   I knew it was one of my children. None of the regular kids seemed to have that high vibrant note of desperation in their voices when they yelled. I looked at Anton, asking him wordlessly what was going on. Whitney went to look out the door of the office.

[19]   Tyler came careening in, wailing. She motioned out the door, but her explanation was strangled in her sobs. Then she turned and ran.

[20]   All three of us sprinted after her toward the door that led to the annex. Normally over the lunch hour, lunch aides were in charge of the children. In the cold months the kids all played inside in their rooms and the aides patrolled up and down the halls keeping order. I kept telling them that my children could not be left unattended at any time, but the aides hated supervising my room and avoided it by congregating outside the annex

door and keeping an ear cocked for disaster. My children had the latest lunch hour, which meant the aides only had about twenty minutes of actual supervision. But they still protested and still refused to stay in the room with the kids. I usually ignored the aides, because I had worked hard to instill in my kids the independence to function without my physical presence. Lunch hour was a daily test of this skill. Moreover, both Anton and I desperately needed that half-hour break. Still things occasionally got out of hand.

[21]   Tyler was sobbing something out to us as we ran, something about eyes and the new girl. I came storming into a room in chaos.

[22]   Sheila stood defiantly on a chair by the aquarium. She had apparently caught the goldfish one by one and poked their eyes out with a pencil. Seven or eight of the fish lay flopping desperately on the floor around the chair, their eyes destroyed. Sheila clutched one tightly in her right fist and stood poised threateningly with the pencil in the other. A lunch aide was near her, dancing nervously about, but too frightened to attempt disarming Sheila. Sarah was wailing. Max was flying about the room flapping his arms wildly and screeching.

[23]   "Drop that!" I shouted in my most authoritative voice. Sheila glared at me and shook the pencil meaningfully. I had no doubt she would attack if at all provoked. Her eyes had the glazed wildness of a threatened animal. The fish flopped hopelessly about, leaving little bloody spots on the floor where their empty eye sockets hit. Max crunched through one on his flight around the room.

[24]   Suddenly a high-pierced shriek knifed the air. Behind us Susannah had entered the room. She has a psychotic fear of blood, of any red liquid, and would go into a frenzy of crazed screaming while darting senselessly about when she thought she saw blood or even hallucinated it. Now, seeing the fish, she bolted off across the room. Anton moved after her and I took that moment of surprise to disarm Sheila who was not so off-guard as I had suspected. She slammed the pencil into my arm with such vehemence that for a moment it stuck, waving uncertainly before falling to the ground. My mind was filled with too much confusion to feel any real pain. Freddie had joined Max in circling the room. Tyler was wailing; Guillermo hid under that table; William stood in one corner and cried, Whitney was off trying to capture Max and Freddie as they reeled around the perimeter of the room screaming. The decibel level was unbearable.

[25]   "Torey!" came William's cry. "Peter's having a seizure!" I turned to see Peter collapse to the floor. Passing Sheila to Whitney, I ran for Peter to remove the chairs among which he had fallen.

[26]   Sheila gave Whitney an audible crack in the shins and won her freedom. Within seconds she was out the door. I fell onto the floor beside Peter, still writhing in his seizure, and felt the pressure of what was happening lie upon me. It had all happened within minutes. (Hayden 26–32)

True/False

Place a *T* next to the statements that are true and an *F* next to the statements that are false. The first one has been done for you.

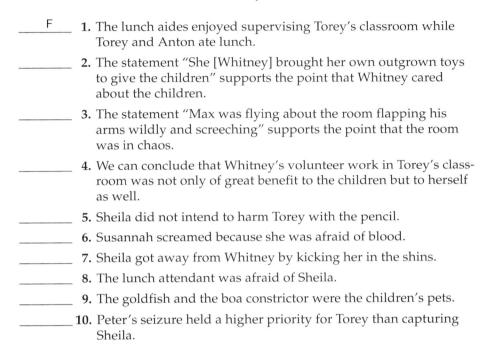

_____F_____ **1.** The lunch aides enjoyed supervising Torey's classroom while Torey and Anton ate lunch.

_____ **2.** The statement "She [Whitney] brought her own outgrown toys to give the children" supports the point that Whitney cared about the children.

_____ **3.** The statement "Max was flying about the room flapping his arms wildly and screeching" supports the point that the room was in chaos.

_____ **4.** We can conclude that Whitney's volunteer work in Torey's classroom was not only of great benefit to the children but to herself as well.

_____ **5.** Sheila did not intend to harm Torey with the pencil.

_____ **6.** Susannah screamed because she was afraid of blood.

_____ **7.** Sheila got away from Whitney by kicking her in the shins.

_____ **8.** The lunch attendant was afraid of Sheila.

_____ **9.** The goldfish and the boa constrictor were the children's pets.

_____ **10.** Peter's seizure held a higher priority for Torey than capturing Sheila.

Identifying Points and Support

Place a *P* in front of the statement that is the point and an *S* in front of the statements that provide support for the point. The first one has been done for you.

1. __S__ Two of the children in Tory's class, Max and Susannah, suffered from crippling, unexplainable disturbances.

__S__ Most of Torey's students had thick, paper-bloated folders, glutted with verbose opinions of dozens of doctors and therapists and judges and social workers.

__P__ Torey was a special education teacher who worked with severely disturbed children.

2. ____ Torey wanted to know how to help Sheila.

____ Torey read Sheila's file because she wanted to know what other teachers had tried with Sheila.

____ Torey asked Anton what he knew about Sheila's neighborhood and circumstances.

3. ____ Sheila was an abused child.
   ____ Sheila had been abandoned on a roadside.
   ____ Sheila had numerous abrasions and healed multiple fractures.
   ____ Sheila's father disciplined her by spanking her or taking away privileges.

4. ____ "The words on the papers . . . did not tell a desperate teacher . . . how to help."
   ____ Torey was not sure she could help Sheila.
   ____ Torey realized that Sheila tried very hard to be unteachable.

5. ____ The house had no heat, no plumbing, and no electricity.
   ____ Sheila lived alone with her father in a one-room shack in the migrant camp.
   ____ Sheila survived under extremely difficult conditions.
   ____ Sheila's small size probably resulted from malnutrition.

6. ____ Sheila's father had been in the state hospital for alcoholism and drug dependency.
   ____ Sheila's father had spent most of Sheila's early years in prison on assault-and-battery charges.
   ____ Sheila's father was not capable of caring for his daughter.

7. ____ Torey described Sheila as being filled with hate.
   ____ A frustrated psychiatrist had written in her folder that Sheila was untestable.
   ____ Sheila had been removed from three schools because of her uncontrollable behavior.
   ____ Sheila had many emotional problems.
   ____ Sheila had no friends among the other children at the migrant camp.
   ____ Sheila had no warm and caring relationships with any adults.
   ____ Her father wrote that Sheila was hostile and unfriendly.
   ____ Sheila spoke only when she was angry and never cried.
   ____ Sheila set fires in the migrant camp.
   ____ Sheila had a police record at the age of six and one-half.

8. ____ Anton spoke Spanish and could communicate with the Hispanic child.
   ____ Anton was a good worker with the children.
   ____ Anton understood the conditions under which the children grew up.

9. ____ Whitney did not speak much as she completed her duties.
   ____ Whitney was a shy girl.
   ____ Whitney never looked Torey in the eyes.
   ____ Whitney smiled nervously and spoke only to criticize herself.

10. ____ At first, Whitney made a lot of mistakes.
    ____ Whitney dropped half a gallon of paint on the gymnasium floor.
    ____ Whitney left one of the children at the fairgrounds.
    ____ Whitney accidentally left the class snake out of its cage.

Reading Between the Lines Box 9.3

ARGUMENT

Should Metal Detectors Be Installed in Schools?

It is difficult to find solutions to many problems that we face every day because most issues do not have right and wrong answers. However, through debate and argument we can make our thoughts clear and understand those of others. We do this by considering all sides of an issue. We build a case for each side by first stating the reasons for supporting it. Only when we can see the issue from all sides can we make an informed decision concerning which side to support.

Read the selection about metal detectors in the schools on page 346. As you read, list the reasons given in favor of metal detectors in schools and then list the reasons given opposing the use of metal detectors in schools.

For Metal Detectors:

_____

_____

_____

Against Metal Detectors:

_____

_____

_____

What Do You Think?

Answer the following questions. Then discuss these issues with a group of three people from your class. Compare your responses. On which issues did you agree? On which issues did you disagree?

1. How do schools and airports compare in their need for metal detectors?

2. What are zero-tolerance policies? Should they be used?

3. How can teachers and students help prevent violence in schools?

4. With which position do you agree? Why?

5. What compromise position can you suggest?

A Reading in Current Controversy

Have you ever felt unsafe in school? What do you think is the solution? Some people believe that installing metal detectors in schools is the solution. Read the article below to gain an understanding of both sides of this issue. Complete the vocabulary exercise before reading the selection to learn the new terms. After reading the selection, complete the comprehension exercises that follow it.

Vocabulary in Context

a. decline—decrease

b. juvenile—adolescent, minor

c. lethality—ability to cause death

d. abhorrent—disgusting, horrible, sickening

e. ludicrous—absurd, foolish, ridiculous

Use the above terms to complete the following sentences. The first one has been done for you.

___d___ **1.** It is awful, if not _____, to think that our children are legally forced to become sitting ducks in a shooting gallery simply because some would feel offended by a metal detector.

_____ **2.** To think that anyone can learn history, English, and mathematics while in a state of constant fear is unreasonable, if not completely _____.

_____ **3.** The overall _____ in our youth's violence rate does not include deaths due to guns.

_____ **4.** We should not allow guns to fall into the hands of children or _____ (s).

_____ **5.** The increase in _____ is due mainly to the increase in the number of young people who have access to guns and to the school's inability to regulate these weapons within its own walls.

Should Metal Detectors Be Installed in Schools?

[1]   Ten days after the Columbine High School shooting spree in 1999 that took the lives of fourteen students and a teacher and wounded over twenty others, the U.S. Secretary of Education, Richard Riley, sought to make sense of the tragedy. Speaking at Walt Whitman High School in

Bethesda, Maryland, he told his audience, "We have always had school-yard fights, but now there is a new level of fear because of these weapons of deadly violence." Crime statistics at the time indicated an actual **decline** in the **juvenile** violence rate, but **lethality** had increased, mainly due to guns.

[2]   "Guns and youth are a particularly deadly combination," observed a report by the Center for the Study and Prevention of Violence at the University of Colorado at Boulder. "Guns give youth the feeling of power, and during adolescence, abstract reasoning about the consequences of gun use and the capacity to read social cues are incomplete." The need to separate the two is obvious. But the way to do that is a challenge. Should metal detectors be installed in schools? Are there less ominous ways to handle the problem? Can schools be kept safe without becoming fortresses?

Metal Detectors Should Be Installed in Schools

[3]   A shooting in a school is like an earthquake in a city: It shakes the very foundation of what was thought to be solid, secure, and safe. Children and youth need to feel confident that their school is a safe and secure place. The thought of requiring students to spend their days in environments that make them vulnerable to violence is **abhorrent**. Expecting students to tackle their studies and find learning engaging when they are fearful for their lives is **ludicrous**. And yet that is exactly what we are doing if we fail to install metal detectors in schools.

[4]   After bombings occurred in air travel, metal detectors were installed in airports in order to protect passengers. Few complained, realizing that the personal inconvenience assured them of greater protection and peace of mind. They accepted the need to lose a liberty for the good of all. If adults are granted such protection from the violence in our society, should we not provide the same for our children and youth?

[5]   Metal detectors and similar devices are technological advances that help reduce crime in a variety of settings. In addition to the security they provide in airports, they prevent people from taking library books they haven't checked out and protect stores from shoplifters. Just as we have learned to accept metal detectors in libraries, airports, and stores, so their presence in schools would soon be hardly noticed.

[6]   Model programs that have decreased student weapon violations by 70 to 86 percent include weapon scanning with metal detectors along with random searches conducted by police. Other features of such model programs include eliminating building areas that cannot be viewed by surveillance cameras and training school security officers by local police forces. These model programs also call for teachers and students to be trained in how to handle dangerous situations and ways to avoid them. The installation of metal detectors is clearly where protection from school violence must begin.

Metal Detectors Should Not Be Installed in Schools

[7]   Using metal detectors to prevent school violence is like putting an adhesive bandage on an infected wound. Not only will it not remedy the problem, but it could also make it even worse. Students who have not considered bringing a weapon to school might decide to do so simply to challenge the system. Like gang members who write graffiti on dangerous highway overpasses, similar minds will be motivated to find ways to bypass the metal detector. Metal detectors also present a foreboding welcome to a school campus and convey to students the messages "We have problems here" and "We don't trust you."

[8]   Instead, the way to prevent school violence is to get to the heart of students' problems. What causes the anger and alienation that eventually explodes in destructive, and sometimes deadly, acts? Teaching students how to solve their problems, handle disappointments, and seek help when it's needed are ways in which some schools have tried to reduce violence. Conflict management, peace building, using literature to teach empathy, forbidding teasing, and anti-bullying programs are other approaches.

[9]   In his speech at Walt Whitman High, Secretary Riley urged community members, parents, and students themselves to play active roles in reversing the trend toward greater violence. "I ask all Americans to believe as I do in this generation of young people . . . We must send . . . a powerful message of hope and security. We will do everything we can to protect you, to listen to you, and to reach out to you so that you feel connected. . . . This is why I ask parents again and again to slow down your lives." He told students to speak to adults when they believe something violent is about to happen. He never mentioned metal detectors, and rightly so. Finding ways to reduce alienation and create community in our schools is a better approach to promoting school safety. (Parkay and Stanford 150–51)

Multiple-Choice Questions

Complete the following multiple-choice questions to test your understanding of the issues and arguments presented concerning metal detectors in schools. The first one has been done for you.

_____d_____ **1.** The issue of this article is:
    a. Should Zero-tolerance policies be used in schools?
    b. Do airports really need metal detectors?
    c. Teachers and students should work together to prevent violence in schools.
    d. Should schools install metal detectors?

_____ **2.** The two basic arguments or points are:
   a. Parents should slow down their lives and spend more time with their children versus school security officers should be trained by local police forces.
   b. Metal detectors should be placed in schools versus metal detectors should not be placed in schools.
   c. Airports should not infringe on people's rights versus metal detectors installed in airports should provide greater protection and peace of mind.
   d. All Americans should be taught conflict management and peace-building strategies versus Americans should be taught to accept the loss of some liberties when it involves the good of all.

_____ **3.** All of the following were given as reasons for installing metal detectors in schools EXCEPT:
   a. Metal detectors make students feel they have problems and cannot be trusted.
   b. Without metal detectors in schools, we are requiring students to spend their days in environments that are vulnerable to violence.
   c. Adults are granted protection from violence in public places and so should children.
   d. In a short period of time, metal detectors would become an acceptable feature of life, with their presence in schools hardly noticed.

_____ **4.** All of the following were given as reasons for leaving schools free of metal detectors EXCEPT:
   a. Students who have not considered bringing a weapon to school might decide to do so simply to challenge the system.
   b. Violence can be better prevented by getting to the heart of students' problems by teaching them how to solve problems, handle disappointments, and seek help when it's needed.
   c. Model programs using metal detectors have decreased student weapon violations by 70 to 86 percent.
   d. Students will bring weapons to school anyway because they will become motivated to find ways to bypass the metal detector.

_____ **5.** According to U.S. Secretary of Education Richard Riley:
   a. Schoolyard fights have become deadly because children have access to guns.
   b. Young people's access to guns is not a problem.

c. The Columbine High School shooting is an isolated incident, and we should not expect to see that type of behavior played out in other schools.

d. Crime statistics indicate a decline in the juvenile violence rate and a decrease in lethality.

Reading Between the Lines Box 9.4

DEBATE

Television

When authors take a stand on an issue, they may mention some favorable aspects of the opposing argument, but they mostly concentrate on presenting evidence to support their case. Read the excerpt about television (page 351) and identify the following:

The issue:

_____

_____

The favorable aspects of television:

_____

_____

The unfavorable aspects of television:

_____

_____

The solutions proposed by the author:

_____

_____

The author's position or stand on this issue:

_____

_____

A Reading in Debate

Television is often a topic for debate. People can find good reasons for watching television, and they can find reasons why television viewing is harmful. Read the following excerpt to see if you agree with the author's argument. Complete the vocabulary exercise before reading the selection to learn the new terms. After reading the selection, complete the comprehension exercises that follow it.

Vocabulary in Context

a. dictum—rule, decree

b. redeeming—making up for bad qualities or behavior

c. obesity—state of being considerably overweight

d. indiscriminately—by chance; at random; without rhyme or reason

e. initiative—will or desire to do things of one's own accord or without being told

Use the above terms to complete the following sentences. The first one has been done for you.

___b___ 1. Some people believe television is a poisonous pastime. Others feel we can learn from television and that it has some _____ qualities.

_____ 2. Children gain weight when they watch television because they lose their _____ to participate in more active pastimes.

_____ 3. Rather than planning special times for watching favorite programs, some children watch television _____.

_____ 4. Karl Marx's famous _____ " Religion is the opiate of the masses" meant that people become dependent on religion just as the drug opium becomes addictive to those who take it. The author feels that television has the same power of addiction.

_____ 5. Watching television requires no physical effort and thus has been linked to _____.

Television

[1]   If Karl Marx were to wander among the homes of America, he would probably change his famous **dictum** to "Television is the opiate of the masses." Children between the ages of six and eleven watch, on the

average, twenty-seven hours of television a week, the equivalent of two months a year.

[2]   Television is not inherently bad. It has some **redeeming** value. We can see history in the making, science and medicine as they are practiced, and join in the varied splendor of the human arts. However, television is severely polluted. Like contaminated water, it can appear seemingly harmless and inviting. It is only much later that the illness is evident. TV viewing is the most significant predictor of **obesity** in children, with excess weight increasing 1 percent for each hour of TV watched per week. By the time the average child graduates from high school, he or she will have watched 18,000 murders, been exposed to an hourly average of more than 13 examples of explicitly sexual behavior, and have viewed 24,000 beer and wine commercials.

[3]   The mind processes information. That is a fact. Television is information. That is a fact. Much of the information on television is rubbish. That's a value. Children who **indiscriminately** watch television continuously process rubbish. That's an opinion. Studies do show a relationship between adverse effects on the imaginative and creative abilities of children and heavy exposure to standard commercial television programming. However, from a scientific perspective, it has not been demonstrated that watching vast amounts of television is a direct cause of poor school performance.

[4]   It is not the corrosive potential of television upon the mind that alone bothers us; its destructive force upon the soul also deeply disturbs us. Motivation is more spirit than thought. It is the stuff of will, determination, and endurance. Television viewing erodes such qualities because it literally replaces them. It deposes activity with passivity. It eliminates **initiative** with docility and displaces thoughtfulness with stupor. Children do not want to do their homework because they would rather watch television. They sloppily rush through their homework in order to watch television, which offers the opportunity for a continuous dismal pleasure without any requirement of responsibility, effort, or courage. That is why watching it will never build a child's confidence, character, or sense of justifiable pride. Television is a terrible seduction. It can turn a young person into a "couch potato" in the worst sense that this image can convey. We genuinely believe television sets should come, as cigarettes do, emblazoned with a warning about their hazards to a person's well-being. We suggest:

1. Limiting your children's television viewing to no more than ten hours weekly.
2. Planning television viewing with your children and helping them select quality programs. (Teachers can be helpful by alerting families to programs that are supportive of academic learning and relevant to current lessons.)

3. Deliberately not offering television viewing as a reward or incentive for homework completion because such action would make television only more desirable and contradict other measures being taken to lessen the influence of TV.

4. Replacing television viewing with an involving and productive set of activities; for example, reading, sports, exercise, games, puzzles, and, best of all, doing things together, such as making something, cooking, reading, and having conversations.

5. Practicing what you preach by applying standards to your own television viewing that are similar to the ones you advocate for your children.

[5]   One of the most important conclusions drawn from motivation research is that the amount of time people spend on particular tasks often reflects the strength of their motivation for the task. With this reasoning, a case can be made that young Americans are more motivated to watch television than they are motivated to learn. It is estimated that of the average of six hours that students spend in school [each day], approximately three and a half of them are spent actually engaged in learning. That is a total of seventeen and a half hours per week. In the 1981 High School and Beyond Study of more than 55,000 students, the students themselves reported that they were averaging four to five hours of homework and about twenty-eight hours of television per week. That makes a total of about twenty-two hours of learning versus twenty-eight hours of watching television, not including summers and holidays. Because many students do other things while watching television, including homework, we cannot pin down the exact ratio. However, these estimates are enough to make us very concerned.

[6]   Without a doubt, too many children are more motivated to watch television than they are motivated to learn. When you think of the content of a good book compared to the superficial entertainment of the average television program, the exponential folly of this predicament is frightening—a waste of the minds and the motivation of our youth. Parents can change this. (Wlodkowski and Jaynes 49–51)

Multiple-Choice Questions

Write the letter of the correct answer in the blank provided. The first one has been done for you.

_____d_____ **1.** All of the following support the argument that television has become polluted EXCEPT:

a. By the time the average child graduates from high school, he or she will have watched 18,000 murders.

    b. By the time the average child graduates from high school, he or she will have been exposed to an hourly average of more than 13 examples of explicitly sexual behavior.

    c. By the time the average child graduates from high school, he or she will have viewed 24,000 beer and wine commercials.

    d. We can see history in the making, science and medicine as they are practiced, and join in the varied splendor of the human arts.

_____ 2. Children between the ages of six and eleven watch, on the average, twenty-seven hours of television a week, the equivalent of two months a year. The author:

    a. sees nothing wrong with this trend.

    b. feels that too much of children's lives are wasted in front of the television.

    c. believes that television has no assets.

    d. believes that television should be done away with completely.

_____ 3. Which of the following are solutions that the author would agree with?

    a. Children's television viewing should be limited to 10 or fewer hours per week.

    b. Parents do not need to plan television viewing with their children because children are quite capable of selecting quality programs by themselves.

    c. Television viewing should be offered as a reward or incentive for homework completion.

    d. It is not necessary for parents get their children involved in activities such as reading, sports, exercise, games, puzzles, or cooking because television is a wonderful resource to use for entertaining children.

_____ 4. The authors pointed out that young Americans spend a total of seventeen and a half hours per week engaged in learning at school in order to:

    a. Show that young Americans spend a lot of time engaged in learning.

    b. Show that education is highly valued in America.

    c. Show that American children do not spend very much time engaged in learning activities at school.

    d. Show that education is the top priority in American schools.

_____ 5. Studies show a relationship between:

    a. adverse effects on the imaginative and creative abilities of children and heavy exposure to standard commercial television programming.

    b. watching vast amounts of television and poor school performance.

    c. television watching and building children's confidence, character, and pride.

    d. television watching and children's happiness.

Questions for Discussion

Answer the following questions. Then discuss your responses with a group of three people from your class. Compare your responses. In what ways were your responses similar? In what ways were they different?

1. Why does the author believe that parents should regulate their children's exposure to television?

_____

2. Do you agree with the author's five suggestions for monitoring children's use of the television?

_____

3. Why do you think young Americans are more motivated to watch television than they are motivated to learn?

_____

4. What suggestions would you offer parents with respect to television watching and child development?

_____

5. How many hours per week do you spend watching television? If you were unable to watch television, how would you spend this time?

_____

UNDERSTANDING PROPAGANDA

Propaganda refers to the spread of information. Propaganda can be good or bad depending on its purpose and on the writer's intention in employing it. According to *Merriam-Webster's Collegiate Dictionary*, "Propaganda is the spreading of ideas,

Visual Literacy Box 9.2   ● ● ● ● ● ● ● ● ● ● ● ● ● ● ● ● ●

MAKING CHARTS: TELEVISION

Sometimes it takes mathematical calculations to truly understand a sentence. Look at the following statement:

TV viewing is the most significant predictor of **obesity** in children, with excess weight increasing 1 percent for each hour of TV watched per week during the course of the year.

Let's say a 120-pound girl begins to watch 25 hours per week. We would multiply 120 by 1 percent to get the weight increase for 1 hour per week and then multiply by 25 to predict how much she would gain by watching television for 25 hours per week.

Step 1: 120 pounds × .01 = 1.2 pounds
Step 2: 1.2 pounds × 25 hours per week = 30 pounds
Step 3: 30 pounds × 1 year = 30 pounds per year

We can predict she would gain 30 pounds by watching television for 25 hours each week. Finish the chart by using the formula above.

Weight	Hours spent watching television per week	Weight gain
120 pounds	1	1.2 pounds
120	5	
120	10	
120	25	30 pounds
130	25	

information, or rumor for the purpose of helping or injuring an institution, a cause, or a person. [These] ideas, facts, or allegations are deliberately spread to further one's cause or to damage an opposing cause." (996)

Good Versus Bad Propaganda

Propaganda is good when:

1. The author clearly states his purpose for writing.
2. The information is based on facts.
3. The message is used to inform or to teach.
4. The purpose is to help the reader.

For example, a message may be sent out to warn people of an approaching hurricane or to inform the public about a direct link between cigarette smoking and cancer. This type of propaganda enables cultures to pass their world knowledge down from generation to generation.

Visual Literacy Box 9.3

VISUAL PROPAGANDA

Look at the picture below. Is this an example of good or bad propaganda?

Give!
It's the American way!

Send your contributions to:
P.O. Box 10009
Philadelphia, PA 10002

Propaganda is bad when it serves only to benefit the writer. Typically he employs strategies that trick the reader into accepting an idea or buying a product. Every day, individuals who try to influence our behavior—politicians, advertisers, journalists, and others—hit us with bad propaganda. Rather than present us with sound, logical arguments, they use tactics that manipulate our thoughts and emotions. They gamble on the chance that we will not analyze the messages they send us. For this reason, it is essential that we take the time to think critically about the propaganda we face in our daily lives. This will then assure us that we are making good decisions based on facts and logic.

A Reading in Propaganda

Read the article on page 358 to determine if it is good propaganda or bad propaganda. As you read, check any of the following statements that describe the article or the author's purpose for writing it. Then compare your responses to those that follow the article.

_____ **1.** The author clearly states his purpose for writing.

_____ **2.** The author's purpose is to make a profit for himself.

_____ **3.** The information is based on facts.

_____ **4.** Strategies are used to trick the reader into accepting an idea.

_____ **5.** The purpose is to inform or to teach the reader.

_____ **6.** Strategies are used to trick the reader into buying a product.

_____ **7.** The purpose is to help the reader.

Researcher Says Teacher Shortage Is "Misdiagnosed"

The nation's teacher shortage is not due to an inadequate supply of teachers, as is widely believed, but because of widespread job dissatisfaction that makes new recruits leave the profession, according to a study by a University of Pennsylvania researcher.

The study, which examined national data from the U.S. Department of Education from 1987 to 2000, found that the high rates of teacher turnover have less to do with an aging work force or a shortage of applicants and more to do with new teachers quitting.

"There are lots of recruitment programs but when almost 40 percent leave within five years, what do we end up with? It's like pouring water into a bucket with holes in the bottom," said Penn education professor Richard M. Ingersoll, the study's author.

The study appears in the current issue of *American Educational Research Journal* and includes data on teachers from kindergarten through grade 12 in public and private schools nationwide. Of the 39 percent of teachers who leave the profession within five years, nearly 29 percent give the reason as job dissatisfaction. Only about 13 percent left because of retirement.

Ingersoll said the term "teacher shortage" implies that the problem is a short supply of teachers, when the real problem is too many new teachers leaving the profession.

"Blaming teacher shortages on supply or on large demographic trends is kind of assuming that the problem's out there somewhere," he said. "The data is telling us that the problem is not out there—it's in here, in the way our schools are set up."

According to teachers surveyed by the Education Department, their main reasons for leaving—even above low salaries—are student disciplinary problems, too little a say in decision-making, and lack of support for new teachers, Ingersoll said.

"The data doesn't say that changing these things will be easy, but the data does tell us if we fix these things we will significantly fix our turnover problems and do a lot to alleviate these so-called shortages," Ingersoll said.

Education officials have long recognized that job dissatisfaction is a major problem, said Jamie Horwitz, spokesman for the American Federation of Teachers. (B–9)

Now that you have selected your own statements that describe the article or the author's purpose for writing it, compare your choices with those below:

_____√_____ **1.** The author clearly states his purpose for writing.

_____ **2.** The author's purpose is to make a profit for himself.

_____√_____ **3.** The information is based on facts.

_____ **4.** Strategies are used to trick the reader into accepting an idea.

_____√_____ **5.** The purpose is to inform or to teach the reader.

_____ **6.** Strategies are used to trick the reader into buying a product.

_____√_____ **7.** The purpose is to help the reader.

- Number 1 is checked because the author states his purpose in the first sentence. There he explains that we do not have a shortage of people who are trained as teachers but rather a shortage of people who are willing to work in our public schools.
- Number 2 is not checked because there is no indication in the article that the author will profit from informing the public that the educational system needs to be changed.
- Number 3 is checked because there are many facts to support the author's statements. One example is the fact that almost 40 percent of new teachers quit within the first five years.
- Number 4 is not checked because there are no appeals to our emotions or tricks to influence our thoughts. The researcher is simply trying to explain the results of a research study.
- Number 5 is checked because the researcher is trying to inform the public about the results of his study and explain why there is a need for more teachers when we have more than enough qualified people.
- Number 6 is not checked because the author does not offer any products for sale.
- Number 7 is checked because the author is trying to help educators understand what they need to do to solve the problem of high teacher turnover.

From our analysis of the article, we can conclude that (1) the article contains propaganda because it educates the public about the causes of the teacher shortage, and (2) it is good propaganda because the researcher is presenting facts and advice that can be used to solve the problem.

EXERCISE
9-2

Identifying Types of Propaganda

Analyze the following information to determine if it is good propaganda or bad propaganda. As you read, check any of the following statements that describe the article or the author's purpose for writing it. Then check the type of propaganda you believe the article to be. One response has already been checked for you.

Wherever you go. Wherever you are. The Big Buddy Corporation is behind you 100 percent. At our nationally respected research center, we have been setting the standards in the pharmaceutical industry for years. Our involvement with new advancements in medical research is on the cutting edge. When you invest in our company, you can feel assured that you are with the best. And at all times, the power is behind you!

_____ **1.** The author clearly states his purpose for writing.

___√___ **2.** The author's purpose is to make a profit for himself.

_____ **3.** The information is based on facts.

_____ **4.** Strategies are used to trick the reader into accepting an idea.

_____ **5.** The purpose is to inform or to teach the reader.

_____ **6.** Strategies are used to trick the reader into buying a product.

_____ **7.** The purpose is to help the reader.

_____ **8.** Good propaganda

_____ **9.** Bad propaganda

_____ **10.** Not propaganda

Denotative and Connotative Meaning

Bad propaganda contains carefully selected words that are intended to rouse a particular response. According to the famous novelist Jean-Paul Sartre, words are "loaded pistols." The writer's choice of words affects how readers will respond to them. For example, what does it mean to you when an instructor uses any of the following adjectives to describe a mathematics exam?

■ complex

■ tricky

■ terribly hard

■ impossible

■ challenging

The word *complex* brings to mind a multistep problem; the word *tricky* may suggest a sense of unfairness. *Terribly hard* may mean that the exam is very long and requires tremendous concentration. The word *impossible* suggests that the exam is too long and overwhelming to pass. On the other hand, the word *challenging* is less threatening. It suggests, instead, that the exam will stimulate the student to think.

   In general, in order for a writer to provoke a specific reaction in his readers, he will have to think carefully about his choice of words—that is, he will need to consider both the denotative and connotative qualities of his language. The

denotative meaning of a word refers to the strict dictionary definition, while the **connotative** meaning refers to the feelings or emotions attached to that word.

Let's look at an example. The *Meriam Webster Dictionary*, 11th Edition says the word *assertive* describes something stated or declared positively and often forcefully or aggressively. If you are known to exhibit assertive behavior, what does that mean? Review the list of synonyms for *assertive* below and think about which words you would use to describe yourself. Keep in mind that certain attitudes and emotions are attached to each adjective and will therefore influence your selections.

insistent	opinionated	self-assured
militant	sure	self-confident
pushy	cocksure	certain

In general, because of the **positive** connotations associated with words like "self-confident" and "self-assured," most of us would rather describe ourselves as such rather than "pushy" or "opinionated," which have more **negative** connotations.

EXERCISE 9-3

Identifying Positive versus Negative Connotations

Read the following sentences and determine whether the underlined words hold positive or negative connotations. Place a P in front of the sentence if the underlined word carries a positive connotation and an N if it carries a negative connotation. The first one has been done for you.

If you made the Dean's List, which of the following comments would you like to hear?

_____P_____ **1.** He made the Dean's List; he's a real <u>brain</u>.

_____ **2.** He made the Dean's List; he's a real <u>nerd</u>.

_____ **3.** He made the Dean's List; he's really <u>smart</u>.

_____ **4.** He made the Dean's List; he's really <u>intelligent</u>.

_____ **5.** He made the Dean's List; he's a real <u>brown noser</u>.

Our word choices can make any person, place, or situation sound good or bad. Let's look at other techniques that propagandists use to sway our opinions.

Propaganda Techniques

Some propaganda techniques rely on connotation to persuade. The writer carefully chooses words with connotative meanings that evoke strong emotions either in favor or against a person or idea. Let's look at some propaganda techniques that turn words into "loaded pistols."

Reading Between the Lines Box 9.5

CONNOTATION

Shades of Meaning

Words have shades of meaning—slight differences due to the attitudes and emotions attached to them. For example, most of us would rather be described as "self-confident" or "self-assured" than "pushy" or "opinionated." What connotations do the words in italics carry? What would you rather have said about you?

❏ She is having a *bad* day.

❏ She is in an *unpleasant* mood today.

❏ She is in a *disagreeable* mood today.

❏ She is in a *rotten* mood today.

❏ She is in a *sour* mood today.

If you had a lot of money, how would you rather be described?

❏ He is extremely *wealthy*.

❏ He is *very* rich.

❏ He is *filthy rich*.

❏ He is a *money-monger*.

❏ He was born with a *silver spoon* in his mouth.

❏ He is *greedy* for money.

If you went to a cooking class and burned everything you made, what would you rather have your instructor say about you?

❏ She's a real *terror* in the kitchen.

❏ She's just *trying out* some *new* recipes.

❏ She's a walking *disaster* when it comes to cooking.

❏ She's *experimenting* with some new dishes.

---

1. **Name-calling**: A writer or speaker may use offensive names to win an argument or to encourage rejection of a person or an idea instead of analyzing the evidence or reviewing the facts.

   <u>*Example:*</u> As marketers try to find out everything they can about their consumers, they have become *professional spies and nosy pests*.
   <u>*Analyzing the propaganda:*</u> Is the name flattering or insulting? Does the name try to undermine the credibility of the person or organization?

2. **Glittering generalities**: By identifying a person, idea, or product with a "good" name, a writer or speaker tries to lead the reader to accept his thoughts as "good" without evaluating the evidence.

Example: If *Abraham Lincoln* were here today, he would tell us, in all honesty, that Tylarex is the best medicine for headaches.
Analyzing the propaganda: Does the "good name" have any logical connection with the person, idea, or product? In reality, would that "good name" want or choose to be associated with the person, idea, or product mentioned?

3. **Euphemism**: The speaker or writer substitutes a more pleasant-sounding word to represent an unpleasant reality.

   Example: Former President Clinton's plan for cutting government jobs was called the *Reinventing Government Streamlining Project*.
   Analyzing the propaganda: What is the actual or precise meaning of the substitution word or phrase?

4. **Plain folks**: A writer or speaker attempts to convince his audience that they, and their ideas, are the same as those of the average ordinary person's.

   Example: Former President Carter tried to convince the American public that he was just an average guy by referring to himself as *Jimmy* Carter instead of *James* Carter. On many occasions, he wore *blue jeans* instead of a suit and had *fireside chats* with the public instead of formal press conferences.
   Analyzing the propaganda: Can you separate the speaker or writer's image from what he is actually saying? Would you still like his ideas if they were presented in a different style or manner?

5. **Repetition**: In general, people don't like change. They feel more comfortable with things they are used to than they do with new things. Persuaders, such as advertisers and political campaign managers, use repetition to make a product seem familiar and comfortable.

   Example: A restaurant merchant plays an ad on the radio between every song. After a while, everyone knows this advertisement by heart and eventually, the ad and the product become a part of everyday life. Soon people choose that restaurant over others because it is so familiar.
   Analyzing the propaganda: Do I really like this product or idea, or am I just buying or accepting it because it is familiar?

6. **Quotation out of context**: A statement or several statements are taken from an article, speech, or interview and used to persuade without the audience or reader knowing the details or the meaning of the entire work.

   Example: The professor said, "Since the university library was closed due to the snow storm, I am extending the deadline for the research papers. You do not need to turn them in until Friday." I told my colleagues the professor said, to his students, "You do not need to turn in the research papers until Friday." By telling only part of the story, I led my colleagues to believe that the professor had no legitimate reason for extending the deadline.

Analyzing the propaganda: Do I have the whole story, or do I only have a part of it? What information is missing? Does the missing information change the meaning?

7. **Appeal to fear**: A fearful event or circumstances are emphasized followed by a suggestion or solution that removes the threat. This type of appeal is meant to scare people into acting on their feelings of fear instead of using logic to guide their choices.

   Example: X-rays are the leading cause of brain cancer. If you buy an ultrasound machine instead of an x-ray machine, your patients will not have to worry about getting brain cancer.
   Analyzing the propaganda: Is the fear real or exaggerated? Will the suggestion actually stop the problem? In the example above, the ultrasound machine cannot produce the same results as an x-ray machine. Therefore, if purchased, the buyer will still have to get an x-ray machine.

8. **Appeal to loyalty**: One of our basic needs is to belong. Persuaders know this and often try to get people to do things for the good of the group without thinking whether or not it is in the individual's best interest.

   Example: You should help out with the fraternity's fund-raiser. So what if you fail your first biology exam? You can make up for it on the next one. But the fraternity needs your help this week.
   Analyzing the propaganda: Aside from the members of the group, do you personally feel that this is a good decision, argument, purpose, or cause?

9. **Appeal to pity**: Bad propaganda may appeal to our sense of pity at the expense of rational thought. You can tell if it is a fake attempt to get you to feel sympathy instead of a sincere request for help if the problem is exaggerated, if the request is unreasonable, if the request is inappropriate for the problem, or if the appeal is illogical.

   Example: *Please give Sunitra an A on her research paper*. The reason it has a lot of mistakes is that she was sick all week.
   Analyzing the propaganda: Has the problem been exaggerated? Is the request reasonable, logical, and appropriate for the problem?

10. **Appeal to sentiment**: This type of persuasion makes us feel sentimental, that we want to return to a certain place or time in our lives. It brings out a nostalgic feeling or a homesickness for the past.

    Example: Television ads that target people in a particular age bracket play top musical hits from the decade that they were teenagers behind the pitch for the product. The music is meant to make the target group feel sentimental about their teen years and buy the product associated with it.
    Analyzing the propaganda: What is suggested? What evidence supports the claim or appeal?

11. **Appeal to vanity**: This type of emotional appeal encourages agreement by complimenting the target audience or reader while relating the compliment to the argument, persuasion, or issue.

Example: You people are *so smart*, I know you will not go home without buying the Celamar II phone.
Analyzing the propaganda: Is any flattery connected with the proposed outcome?

12. **Bandwagon appeal:** The writer or speaker uses the argument that because everyone is doing something or believes in something, it must be right or true.

Example: Everyone is buying jeans at the "Blue Jean Factory." You will look out of style if you don't buy your jeans there too.
Analyzing the propaganda: How does the writer try to appeal to the masses?

EXERCISE
9-4

Identifying Propaganda Techniques

Read each of the statements below. Which propaganda technique makes it a poor argument? The first one has been done for you.

_____d_____ 1. Toasty Oat Bran Cereal contains 75 percent more fiber than other brands of cereal. According to the National Health Organization, studies have shown that people who eat oat bran as a regular part of their diet have a lower risk of cancer.
    a. plain folks
    b. quotation out of context
    c. name-calling
    d. appeal to fear

_____ 2. A television advertisement shows a jeans-clad, middle-aged gentleman hiking in the Rockies. The announcer asks the audience, "Who should you trust with your tax dollars?" A subtitle displays the words "Roy Hobson for Senate."
    a. plain folks
    b. quotation out of context
    c. repetition
    d. appeal to loyalty

_____ 3. During the first presidential debate of 2000, George Bush said of Al Gore, "This man has been disparaging [discrediting] my plan with all his Washington fuzzy math."
    a. name-calling
    b. glittering generalities
    c. euphemism
    d. appeal to pity

_____ **4.** An ad for a presidential candidate appears on television every day at half-hour intervals until viewers can mimic the content word for word and almost feel as though they know the candidate personally.
   a. glittering generalities
   b. plain folks
   c. repetition
   d. name-calling

_____ **5.** Old age is referred to as the *golden years*.
   a. euphemism
   b. glittering generalities
   c. quotation out of context
   d. appeal to sentiment

_____ **6.** The good citizen is smart enough not to be fooled by a tax plan that excludes 30 million Americans.
   a. plain folks
   b. name-calling
   c. quotation out of context
   d. appeal to vanity

_____ **7.** This is an American tax cut plan, based on the principles of democracy and designed for a new generation of prosperity.
   a. repetition
   b. appeal to fear
   c. glittering generalities
   d. name-calling

_____ **8.** This is not the best solution—but, after all, we are members of the union, and we should support this proposal for the good of the union.
   a. quotation out of context
   b. euphemism
   c. appeal to loyalty
   d. plain folks

_____ **9.** "I failed the midterm because I had the flu. Then I missed the final exam because I had pneumonia and my doctor's appointment was scheduled at the same time. I should get an A on the exam because I have been sick a lot."
   a. inference as fact
   b. repetition
   c. plain folks
   d. appeal to pity

Visual Literacy Box 9.4

FLOW CHARTS: PROPAGANDA TECHNIQUES

When making decisions based on propaganda, you must ask yourself a series of questions to determine if it is good or bad propaganda. Read the "Factual News Report" in Exercise 9.5 and then ask yourself the series of questions in the diagram below. Your answer to each question will take you to the words "good propaganda" or "bad propaganda." Then follow the same procedure to determine if the "News Report Slanted in Favor of Irradiation" and the "News Report Slanted Against Irradiation" are good or bad propaganda.

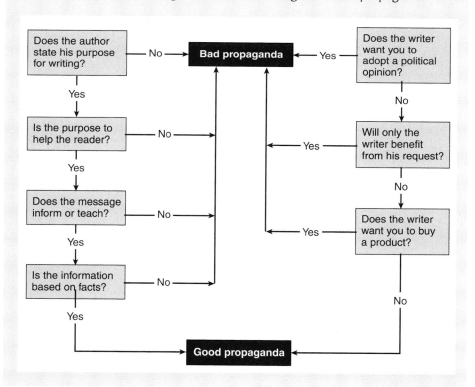

_____ **10.** A television commercial for insurance shows a mother baking cookies while three children are sitting in the kitchen drinking milk and eating cookies. The message is that this type of insurance is as comforting as your mother's kitchen.
   a. repetition
   b. name-calling
   c. glittering generalites
   d. appeal to sentiment

EXERCISE	**Factual Reports versus Slanted Reports**
9-5	

Read the following imaginary news reports and compare the slanted reports in favor of and against irradiation with the factual account.

Factual News Report

Members from Consumers for Clean Food demonstrated in front of Irradiate-Tech, Inc., protesting the company's plans to build a food irradiation factory in town. The facility would irradiate fruits before distribution and exportation. Although the Food and Drug Administration has approved the irradiation of fresh fruits, vegetables, nuts, pork, poultry, and other foods, the group claims the process poses serious health risks. Irradiate-Tech CEO Tom Doe believes the process is 100 percent safe and has called on the federal government to provide more support to inform the public of the benefits of food irradiation.

News Report Slanted in Favor of Irradiation

In response to the protests of radical grassroots organizers, Irradiate-Tech's fair-minded CEO, Tom Doe, reaffirmed the Food and Drug Administration's sound judgment that irradiation is a miraculously effective method for destroying insects and bacteria and is undoubtedly a safe means for controlling food-borne illnesses. "It is 100 percent safe; we are denying people the benefits," stated Doe. In response to the lack of national education effort, and in the interest of fair play, Doe called on the federal government to begin an education program to inform the public of the health benefits of food irradiation. If given good information, smart people will support the process of irradiation. Aside from solving the nation's problem with food poisoning, the construction of irradiation plants will boost the economy. And who can argue against a strong economy with more money in the hardworking citizen's pocket?

News Report Slanted Against Irradiation

A scientific and political noose appears to be tightening around Irradiate-Tech's controversial method of food processing. Instead of supporting the cleanup of filthy conditions in meat packaging and food processing plants, Irradiate-Tech has been aggressively marketing food bombarded with gamma rays. This deadly process alters the chemical composition of food by exposing it to as much as 300,000 rads of radiation—the equivalent of 30 million chest x-rays—just to extend shelf life *and profit*. Although irradiation was approved by the Food and Drug Administration as a safe method for killing bacteria, political troubles for Irradiate-Tech are mounting as new scientific studies suggest health risks such as cancer. Volunteers from Consumers for Clean Food tried to reason with CEO Tom Doe of Irradiate-Tech, Inc., by patiently explaining the risks associated with the creation of nuclear food in our "Brave New World."

1. Analyze the paragraph slanted in favor of irradiation and list the propaganda techniques it employs.

_____

_____

2. Analyze the paragraph slanted against the use of irradiation and list the propaganda techniques it employs.

_____

_____

A Reading in Propaganda

Do you drink milk? If so, how can you tell whether or not the milk you are drinking causes cancer? Read the following news report to find out more about new health issues related to milk. As you read, identify the type of support and propaganda techniques that are used. Complete the vocabulary exercise before reading the selection to learn the new terms.

Vocabulary in Context

a. traditional—usual, long-established, habitual, accepted

b. posilac bovine somatotropin—rBGH; recombinant bovine growth hormone; hormone given to cows to make them produce more milk

c. synthetic—man-made, artificial

d. prolong—make longer; extend; lengthen

e. incremental—increasing

Use the above terms to complete the following sentences. The first one has been done for you.

_____a_____ **1.** Those who live on _____ family farms feel they must inject their cows with rBGH in order to compete with the huge corporate-like farms.

_____ **2.** The hormone given to cows to make them produce milk is called

_____ .

_____ **3.** The use of rBGH has caused an _____ increase in the production of milk.

_____ **4.** When farmers inject rBGH into their cows, they know it will cause them to produce more milk because this hormone _____ (s) the length of a cow's lactation time.

_____ **5.** rBGH is considered to be a _____ drug because it does not occur naturally.

Got rBGH?

The McElmurray Farm, which was recently renamed Two Sisters' Dairy when Julia and Marie McElmurray purchased the farm from their father, is what many consider a dying breed. The traditional family farms are having to compete in a huge dairy industry, and many are losing the battle. But in order to help their farm remain competitive, the McElmurrays use a product called Posilac bovine somatotropin (BST), also known as rBGH, recombinant bovine growth hormone.

Basically, rBGH is a synthetic hormone which is intended to prolong the period of a cow's lactation in order for dairy farmers to boost milk production. Every two weeks the farmer injects rBGH into a cow, which can raise the cow's milk production from 10 to 15 percent.

And the benefits for the farmers also appear profitable. According to the manufacturer's figures, Posilac (rBGH) users report a productivity increase of cows giving 5 to 15 pounds [of milk] per day. Gary Barton, [director of environmental communications for rBGH manufacturer Monsanto corporation] said, since commercial sales began in 1994, he estimates that the use of Posilac has resulted in an incremental profit to dairy farmers of over $300 million.

_____d_____ **1.** Which propaganda technique is the author using when she includes the name of the McElmurray Farm, Two Sisters' Dairy?
   a. appeal to pity
   b. quotation out of context
   c. name-calling
   d. plain folks

_____ **2.** Which propaganda technique is the author using by describing small farms as "traditional family farms"?
   a. appeal to fear
   b. quotation out of text
   c. appeal to vanity
   d. appeal to loyalty

_____ **3.** Which propaganda technique can be related to this statement? "Traditional family farms are having to compete in a huge dairy industry, and many are losing the battle."
   a. appeal to pity
   b. name-calling
   c. appeal to vanity
   d. repetition

_____ **4.** Which propaganda technique can be related to this phrase? "help their farm remain competitive."
   a. glittering generalities
   b. name-calling
   c. euphemism
   d. appeal to vanity

Even though the Federal Drug Administration (FDA) approved rBGH in November 1993 there are still some nagging concerns over milk from rBGH-treated cows. The use of rBGH increases the level of an insulin-like growth factor (IGF-1) in a human's digestive tract. According to Dr. Samuel Epstein, a professor of occupational and environmental medicine at the University of Illinois Medical Center, "high levels of IGF-1 are associated with risk factors for breast, colon and childhood cancers." In March, 1998 Epstein announced "men with high blood levels of naturally occurring IGF-1 are over four times more likely to develop full-blown prostate cancer than are men with lower levels." rBGH milk has high levels of abnormally potent IGF-1, with "up to 10 times the level in natural milk."

The manufacturer's public position since 1994 has been that IGF-1 levels are not elevated in milk from rBGH-treated cows.

However, the British researcher T.N. Mepham recently reminded Monsanto [the manufacturer of rBGH] that in its 1993 application to the British government for permission to sell rBGH, Monsanto reported that "the IGF-1 level went up substantially."

[The FDA along with some industries] have consistently refused to make available their raw data," Epstein said in a statement sent to The Metropolitan Spirit. He thinks the FDA and other industry sources should publish detailed studies on the oral toxicity of IGF-1.

_____ **5.** Which propaganda technique can be related to this statement? "[The FDA along with some industries] have consistently refused to make available their raw data."
   a. incomplete facts
   b. overgeneralization
   c. testimonials
   d. circular reasoning

Gary Barton, director of environmental communications for Monsanto's corporate office in St. Louis, said "The FDA, the World Health Organization, the American Medical Association, the American Dietetic Association and regulatory agencies in 30 different countries agree that Posilac is safe."

But Posilac does not have unanimous approval. A 14-nation European Union voted 34 to 31 not to allow the product's use in Europe. But Barton said ever since November 1996, when the results of a post-approval monitoring program (PAMP) were announced and Monsanto received unanimous support from the FDA's Veterinary Medicine Advisory Committee, Posilac has been more widely accepted.

_____ **6.** Which propaganda technique can be related to this statement? "The FDA, the World Health Organization, the American Medical Association, the American Dietetic Association and regulatory agencies in 30 different countries agree that Posilac is safe."
   a. glittering generalities
   b. name-calling

        c. bandwagon appeal

        d. appeal to vanity

PAMP was designed to collect information about the use of Posilac and determine whether the product affects the quality or safety of milk. The study, representing 1,213 cows, focused on the general herd health in commercial operations ranging from 40 to more than 1,500 head per herd. The results of PAMP, which were endorsed by the FDA, confirmed the safety of Posilac for cows and the safety of the milk supply.

Many critics dismissed the study as biased since PAMP was conducted and developed by Monsanto.

Dr. Von Meyer, an opponent of rBGH, claims that Monsanto failed to collect chronic safety data on the whole milk prior to its approval. "By chronic safety data we are speaking of a year or more feeding trial on sufficient animals," Dr. Von Meyer said. "I have found that Monsanto only tested IGF-1 for 14 days. Fourteen days isn't going to tell you anything." Dr. Von Meyer also points out that Michael Taylor and two other FDA officials who approved Posilac had all previously been paid by Monsanto to do either legal or scientific research on the product.

_____ **7.** Which propaganda technique can be related to this statement? "Fourteen days isn't going to tell you anything."

        a. bandwagon appeal

        b. glittering generalities

        c. euphemism

        d. incomplete facts

Former U.S. Surgeon General C. Everett Koop said since BST is the exact copy of the hormone naturally produced in cows, the rBGH-treated milk is safe. He declared the allegation against Posilac incorrect, saying, "Unfortunately, a few fringe groups are using misleading statements and blatant falsehoods as part of a long-running campaign to scare consumers about a perfectly safe food."

_____ **8.** Which propaganda technique can be related to this phrase? "fringe groups"

        a. repetition

        b. name-calling

        c. plain folks

        d. appeal to vanity

_____ **9.** Which propaganda technique can be related to this phrase? "perfectly safe food"

        a. repetition

        b. name calling

        c. plain folks

        d. glittering generalities

In 1996, a survey was conducted by researchers at the University of Wisconsin to better understand what factors influence consumers' perception of rBGH. Approximately 1,900 people were surveyed and some of the results are as follows: 85 percent of all respondents acknowledge some level of concern over rBGH, with over 70 percent indicating their level of concern as moderate to very concerned; approximately 66 percent were aware of rBGH; 69 percent said they prefer milk from non-rBGH treated herds; 70 percent of those surveyed said that the long-run health implications of rBGH are not known; and 94 percent said there should be a way that you could distinguish between milk from treated and untreated cows. (Eidson 15–17)

_____ **10.** What type of support is used to indicate that the general public is against the use of rBGH to increase milk production?
    a. analogies
    b. personal experience
    c. statistics
    d. authority

EXERCISE 9-6

Identifying Support, Fallacy, and Propaganda

Read the following items and identify the type of propaganda technique used in each. The first one has been done for you.

___a___ **1.** Come to Quality Furniture at our downtown location for the greatest sales ever! You will find the best prices around! Everything at Quality Furniture is half off! At Quality Furniture you will find only the best craftsmanship and friendly service. So, if you want a good deal, remember, come to Quality Furniture!
    a. repetition
    b. quotation out of context
    c. name-calling
    d. appeal to loyalty

_____ **2.** The sophisticated, worldly woman travels on Pan-World Airlines because she is smart enough to know that her work is too important to jeopardize for cheaper and perhaps unreliable fares.
    a. appeal to vanity
    b. quoting out of context
    c. repetition
    d. appeal to loyalty

_____ **3.** We have to free ourselves from the greedy oil companies who purposely destroy our environment, through their intentional dumping of oil in pristine waters, to force consumers to pay top dollar.
   a. name-calling
   b. glittering generalities
   c. euphemism
   d. plain folks

_____ **4.** If you vote for that unscrupulous Tim Miller, he will put conservative, small-minded people into office who will give away our nation's best farmland to the corrupt developers for next to nothing.
   a. glittering generalities
   b. plain folks
   c. repetition
   d. name-calling

_____ **5.** Our state comes together to do what's right. We come together, both Republicans and Democrats.
   a. quotation out of context
   b. euphemism
   c. appeal to loyalty
   d. plain folks

_____ **6.** The Roll-Um Tire Company said they would close their doors today because of economic recession. Their spokesman said their departure from the industry had nothing to do with the thousands of lawsuits pending concerning allegations of placing defective retreads on new cars.
   a. plain folks
   b. name-calling
   c. euphemism
   d. appeal to vanity

_____ **7.** Teachers, I know you feel a sense of accomplishment from your dedicated service in this time-honored and noble profession. Your rich rewards come from the opportunity to work with young people and to see them grow. I know the salary freeze will not affect your motivation because we all know we are not here for capital gains but for the knowledge that sets us all free!
   a. euphemism
   b. appeal to fear
   c. glittering generalities
   d. name-calling

_____ **8.** Global warming is upon us. We knew about it yesterday and we did nothing. We know about it today and we are still doing nothing. As a result we are seeing more and more usual and unseason-

able weather patterns. If we don't plan for the future, will we be too late? Will severe weather patterns become irreversible? Will we have uncontrollable droughts and floods? Starting today, everyone must buy a hybrid automobile or who knows what will happen.
    a. euphemism
    b. appeal to fear
    c. glittering generalities
    d. name-calling

_____ **9.** Congress has been in session for thirty grueling days. They have been away from their families, friends, and neighbors for the good of the country. They suffer through long and hard debates on tough issues. They deserve the pay increases the new bill they passed will bring.
    a. appeal to vanity
    b. name-calling
    c. plain folks
    d. appeal to pity

_____ **10.** President Jimmy Carter always appeared in blue jeans and a jeans jacket in his televised addresses to the nation. He sat in an easy chair next to a fireplace and, thus, referred to his presidential speeches as "fireside chats."
    a. repetition
    b. name-calling
    c. glittering generalities
    d. plain folks

10

Argument

● ●

In this chapter, we learn how to:
- identify an issue;
- identify an argument;
- recognize good support for an argument;
- identify fallacies in reasoning;
- recognize when an argument is undermined by faulty reasoning.

SUPPORT FOR GOOD ARGUMENTS

We read in the newspaper that a new research study proves secondary cigarette smoke (the smoke from other people's cigarettes) is more dangerous than smoke inhaled directly from a filtered cigarette. We also read that secondary smoke causes more than 5,000 people to die of lung cancer each year and that some people are working very hard to have cigarette smoking banned in all public places, including bars and restaurants.

Let's say that we believe that the ban on smoking in public places is a good idea. We explain this to our friends, believing that they will heartily agree.

However, our friends, being smokers themselves, panic at the thought of having to go without a cigarette for any length of time. After reading the article, our friends become upset at the thought of someone telling them where, when, and if they can smoke. To our surprise, they strongly disagree with our view that smoking should be banned in all public places.

What we have here is called an **issue**. A topic of discussion becomes an issue when two or more knowledgeable parties disagree on the ways to solve a problem. Issues are generally expressed in the form of a question. Key words that help us to recognize the issue include *is, does*, and *should*. In this case, the issue is:

Should cigarette smoking, because of its dangers, be banned from all public places?

The statements that people make to explain how they feel about an issue are called **arguments**. For example, our smoking issue involves two arguments:

Argument 1: Smoking should be banned in public places.

Argument 2: Smoking should *not* be banned in public places.

An argument can be *good* or *poor*, depending on how well it is supported. Support for good arguments includes one or more of the following:

facts	accurate statistics
examples	inductive reasoning
analogies	common knowledge
deductive reasoning	authority

Visual Literacy Box 10.1 ● ▬ ● ● ● ● ● ● ● ● ● ● ● ● ● ● ●

USING GRAPHS TO SUPPORT AN ARGUMENT: SMOKING

Let's say that you would like to argue the following point:

Smoking should be banned in public places because most of the population does not smoke.

The following statistic would surely support your argument.

The dissemination (spread) of information on the harmful effects of cigarette smoking has helped reduce its prevalence from 40 percent of American adults in 1965 to 25 percent in 1997. . . . Most of the drop is among college graduates. (Berk 432)

However, your statistics will probably be easier for others to understand if you make a graph.

1. How can we tell from the graph that in 1965, the majority of people did not smoke?

_____

_____

_____

2. How can we tell from the graph that in 1997 and the year 2000, the overwhelming majority of people did not smoke?

_____

_____

(continued on next page)

(continued from previous page)

3. Does the graph provide good support for the argument that people should not smoke in public because "most people do not smoke?"

_____

_____

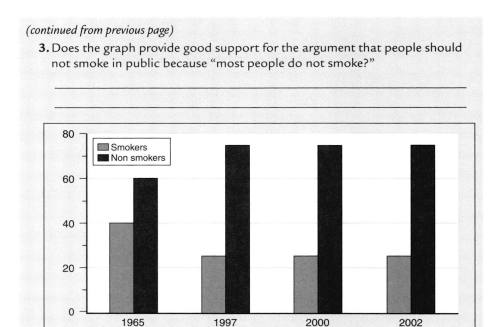

Source: From *Development through the Lifespan*, 432.

1. **Accurate statistics** are numerical data that have been prepared by experts who have a good reputation for analyzing statistics.

   Example: According to researchers from the University of Minnesota, 25 percent of all Americans and 33 percent of all British smoke cigarettes.
   Ask yourself: Are the statistics accurate, and were they prepared by a knowledgeable professional?

2. **Facts** provide verifiable, observable, or reliable proof.

   Example: Thirty thousand nonsmokers die each year from breathing in secondary smoke.
   Evaluate the evidence: Can I prove the statement true or false? Did I see it for myself? Did other people see it happen?

3. **Examples** illustrate the facts.

   Example: Many people with asthma cannot dine out. For example, so far this year, a total of forty asthmatics have been rushed to Spencer Hospital's Emergency Room with attacks triggered by inhaling the secondary smoke in restaurants.
   Evaluate the evidence: Is the evidence given in the example adequate to justify the argument?

4. **Analogies** make comparisons that allow the reader/listener to transfer the qualities of one item to another extremely different category.

   Example: Allowing people to smoke in public places is like giving your car keys to a drunk driver. (Chances are that both will hurt others through their enjoyable but harmful habits.)
   Ask yourself: What is similar about the two items being compared?

5. **Deductive reasoning** starts with the argument and provides support in the form of reasons, examples, or data.

   Example: Secondary smoke is harmful to nonsmokers. Over 30,000 nonsmokers die each year from passive smoke. Being exposed to secondary smoke for one hour per week does 20 percent as much damage to a person's arteries as smoking does.
   Ask yourself: Do the reasons support the conclusion?

6. **Inductive reasoning** starts with the support in the form of reasons, examples, or data and then draws a conclusion based on the evidence.

   Example Over 30,000 nonsmokers die each year from passive smoke. Being exposed to secondary smoke for one hour per week does 20 percent as much damage to a person's arteries as smoking does. Therefore, researchers have concluded that secondary smoke is harmful to nonsmokers.
   Ask yourself: Do the reasons, examples, or data add up to support for the conclusion? Based on the evidence, would you draw a different conclusion?

7. **Common knowledge** refers to what is generally known and accepted.

   Example: Smoking causes lung cancer.
   Ask yourself: Do most people know or believe this?

8. **Personal experience** involves information accumulated within the realm of your own knowledge of the world.

   Example: My Aunt Marge, a nonsmoker, died of lung cancer from working in an office where her coworkers smoked.
   Ask yourself: What do I know about this subject based on my experience?

9. **Authority** refers to the author's credentials, background knowledge, experience, position, or power.

   Example: According to Neil A. Campbell, Lawrence G. Mitchell, and Jane B. Reece, authors of *Biology*, the most widely used textbook for biology majors, lung cancer from cigarette smoke nearly always kills its victims.
   Ask yourself: What makes these authors experts?

Reading Between the Lines Box 10.1

INTERPRETING STATISTICS

Smoking I

Read the following passage. From the Information provided, can you calculate the exact number of young people expected to die prematurely from a smoking-related disease?

> The ingredients of cigarette smoke—nicotine, tar, carbon monoxide, and other chemicals—leave their damaging mark throughout the body. As the person inhales, delivery of oxygen to tissues is reduced, and heart rate and blood pressure rise. Over time, insufficient oxygen results in limited night vision, more rapid wrinkling of the skin, and a lower sperm count and higher rate of male sexual impotence. More deadly outcomes include increased risk of heart attack, stroke, and cancer of the mouth, throat, larynx, esophagus, lungs pancreas, kidneys, and bladder. *One of every three young people who become regular smokers will die from a smoking-related disease.*
>
> The link between smoking and mortality is dose related. The more cigarettes consumed, the greater the chance of premature death. At the same time, the benefits of quitting are great, including return of disease risks to nonsmoker levels within 3 to 8 years. (Berk 432–33)

EXERCISE 10-1

Identifying the Type of Support I

Below are examples of strong cases for both arguments concerning our smoking issue. Read the arguments below and identify the type of support used to defend each. The first one has been done for you.

Argument 1: Smoking should be banned in public places.

Support: According to the Centers for Disease Control and Prevention, each year 30,000 to 60,000 deaths are caused by secondary smoke.

Type(s) of Support: Statistics; facts; authority

Support: Passive cigarette smoke does about 40 percent as much damage to a person's arteries as smoking does, according to a January 14th report in the *Journal of the American Medical Association*.

Type(s) of Support: _____

Support: People who reported being in close contact with a smoker for at least 1 hour per week experienced 20 percent more thickening of the main blood vessel that goes from the neck to the brain than nonsmokers who didn't breathe any cigarette smoke.

Type(s) of Support: _____

Argument 2: Smoking should *not* be banned in public places.
Support: Smokers are addicted to cigarettes and cannot go for long periods of time without them.

Type(s) of Support: _____

Support: Twenty-five percent of all Americans and 33 percent of the British population smoke.

Type(s) of Support: _____

Support: In a survey of 2,500 smokers, the majority felt they could not enjoy restaurant dining and other activities without smoking. Most also felt they had the right to pursue enjoyment.

Type(s) of Support: _____

Reading Between the Lines Box 10.2

INTERPRETING STATISTICS

Smoking II

Percentages represent one type of statistic. (A percent sign (%) may be used to indicate when numbers represent a percentage.) We interpret percentages by comparing a number with the entire amount possible and expressing it AS IF the entire amount possible were 100. In the passage below, for example, 25 percent means that for every 100 people in the United States, 25 of them smoked in the year 2000.

> The dissemination (spread) of information on the harmful effects of cigarette smoking has helped reduce its prevalence from 40 percent of American adults in 1965 to 25 percent in 1997. Most of the drop is among college graduates.

1. If 25 percent of the population smokes, what percentage of the population does not smoke?

   Hint: Subtract the number of smokers from 100 percent of the population.

   _____

   To calculate the exact number of smokers in the year 2000, we need to know the exact number of people living in the United States at that time. Once we know that number, we would simply multiply it by 25 percent (0.25 × exact number of people = the number of people who smoke).

2. In the year 2000, there were 275,000,000 people living in the United States. How many people smoked?

   Hint: Multiply the number of people in the United States by the number of smokers (25 percent or 0.25).

   _____

(continued on next page)

(continued from previous page)

3. How many people do not smoke?

Hint: Multiply the number of people in the United States by the number of nonsmokers (75 percent or 0.75).

Identifying the Issue, Argument, and Support

Read the situation below. Then identify the issue, the arguments, and the reasons/support for both arguments. The first part of the exercise has been started for you.

> **Situation**: Some parents believe their children should be involved in as many activities as they can afford to provide for them. They want to give their children a head start on the competition they will face in school and career. Their children may be expected to keep up with a strict after-school, evening, and weekend schedule that includes team sports such as soccer, football, swimming, and gymnastics. Other events scheduled on the children's calendar may include artistic and cultural lessons such as piano, ballet, water color painting, and French. In addition to these activities, they may also be expected to keep up with clubs and church activities such as Boy Scouts, 4-H Club, and bible studies.
>
> The positive outcomes of these activities are that the children acquire good time management skills, learn how to interact well with others their age, and are kept out of negative situations that spring up from boredom.
>
> On the other hand, keeping up with the constant activity causes unwanted stress in the children. It cuts down on quality family time. In addition, the situation causes much stress for the parents; they lose all of their leisure time driving the children from one activity to another.

Issue: Aside from school, should children be engaged in as many activities as they can fit into the week?

Argument 1: Outside of school, children should be engaged in as many different activities as possible throughout the day.

Reason/support: _____

Reason/support: _____

Reason/support: _____

Argument 2: _____

Reason/support: _____

Reason/support: _____

Reason/support: _____

| EXERCISE 10-3 | **Identifying the Type of Support II** |

Read each of the statements below and identify the type of support it represents. The first one has been done for you.

___a___ **1.** According to Mike Rose in his award-winning book, *Lives on the Boundary*, many college students have difficulty in (1) framing an argument, (2) dismantling someone else's argument, (3) systematically inspecting an issue, event, or document, (4) synthesizing different points of view, and (5) applying theories.
 a. authority
 b. statistics
 c. personal experience
 d. analogy

_____ **2.** In 1983, the national Commission on the Excellence in Education identified the lack of preparation of entering college freshmen as a major concern in higher education.
 a. deductive reasoning
 b. inductive reasoning
 c. analogy
 d. facts

_____ **3.** The types of questions that were most frequently asked, for example, were comparison, analysis, discussion, and definition.
 a. analogy
 b. example
 c. deductive reasoning
 d. inductive reasoning

_____ **4.** Going to class without having read the assignment beforehand is like watching a foreign-language film without subtitles.
 a. personal experience
 b. common knowledge
 c. facts
 d. analogy

_____ **5.** Encouragement from mentors is important for student success. I couldn't draw in high school. I almost changed my major because of my drawing. I just couldn't do it. I went to my advisor and he talked me through it. He said that everybody could draw. He took extra time to help me. I struggled through that class and now I am really good at it. I'm one of the best figure drawers right now.
 a. accurate statistics
 b. analogy
 c. deductive reasoning
 d. personal experience

_____ **6.** More than half of the colleges surveyed during the 1930s and 1940s had reading/study skills programs.
 a. common knowledge
 b. accurate statistics
 c. authority
 d. example

_____ **7.** Understanding the organization of a text increases comprehension and recall. Evidence for this was found in a 1980 study showing that students who could focus on the main ideas and supporting details recalled more information than students who were not focused on this task. This study also found that students who could find the author's outline were able to identify the most important information.
 a. deductive reasoning
 b. inductive reasoning
 c. analogy
 d. accurate statistics

_____ **8.** A century ago, very few people graduated from high school (6.7 percent in 1890). By 1980, 75 percent of the population completed high school. Therefore, we can conclude that there is an increasing number of students attending American colleges and universities.
 a. common knowledge
 b. inductive reasoning
 c. deductive reasoning
 d. analogy

_____ **9.** Moore's (1915) program at Harvard University was the first reading program designed to give academic support to college students.
 a. personal experience
 b. inductive reasoning

     c. facts

     d. deductive reasoning

_____ **10.** The term *college freshman* refers to a first-year college student.

     a. examples

     b. analogy

     c. authority

     d. common knowledge

A Reading in Psychology

Read the following excerpts from an article (taken from *Understanding Human Behavior* by Clifford R. Mynatt and Michael E. Doherty) in which the author argues that television affects the way people behave. From each sentence below, identify which type of support the authors use as evidence for their arguments. Complete the vocabulary exercise before reading this selection to learn the new terms.

Vocabulary in Context

  a. aggression—violent behavior; hostility; anger

  b. interact—act together; relate to

  c. initially—at first

  d. comprehensive—complete, thorough, all-inclusive

  e. presumably—probably; most likely

Use the terms above to complete the following statements. The first one has been done for you.

____c____ **1.** Even though the children did not _____ exhibit violent behavior, after watching the model attack the doll, they did the same thing.

_____ **2.** The doll was rarely attacked by the children who watched the adult model _____ with the doll in a nonaggressive way.

_____ **3.** Most likely, or _____, the children rarely attacked the doll because they thought they would be punished if they did.

_____ **4.** When nursery school children were shown a film in which an adult attacked a doll, later these children modeled the adult's _____.

_____ **5.** George Gerbner has completed several thorough reports on children and aggression. These _____ studies that show the content of television have a great effect on children.

Television and Aggression

_____b_____ **1.** Watching television two to four hours per day translates into about 1,000 hours per year.
   a. examples
   b. facts
   c. cause-effect relationship
   d. common knowledge

_____ **2.** Behavior can be powerfully affected by observational learning, even when no classical or operant conditioning is involved. Here is an example: Perhaps *the* classic observational learning study was conducted many years ago by Albert Bandura and colleagues (Bandura, Ross & Ross, 1961). One group of nursery school children saw a film in which an adult modeled **aggression** by attacking a large inflated doll. Later these children were frustrated by being told that they couldn't play with several attractive toys. They were left alone in a room containing the same doll they had previously seen attacked by the adult. Most of them also attacked the doll and did so in ways that were very similar to the adult model's behavior. In contrast, children in a control group who had seen the adult model **interact** with the doll in a nonaggressive way rarely attacked it.
   a. examples
   b. analogy
   c. authority
   d. statistics

_____ **3.** The thing to note here is that the children in the condition in which the adult model was "punished" had learned to attack the doll, even though they did not **initially** exhibit this learning. **Presumably** this was because they believed that if they did, they too would be punished. When told that they wouldn't be punished, they acted just like the kids in the condition in which no punishment had taken place. This suggests that performance and learning are two different things.
   a. examples
   b. analogy
   c. deductive reasoning
   d. inductive reasoning

_____ **4. Comprehensive** studies of the content of television have been done by George Gerbner, who has been measuring the amount of violence on television for over twenty years.
   a. examples
   b. common knowledge
   c. personal experience
   d. authority

_____ **5.** Between 1940 and 1980 the percentage of U.S. households with at least one TV set rose from less than 1 percent to over 98 percent. Other industrial countries show a similar pattern; in 1985 the number of homes with television ranged from 90 percent in Ireland to 99 percent in Japan. In 1960 in an average American home, a television set was on about five hours per day. By 1984 it was on about seven hours per day. (Mynatt and Doherty 353–56)

    a. accurate statistics
    b. common knowledge
    c. personal experience
    d. authority

Visual Literacy Box 10.2 ● ● ● ● ● ● ● ● ● ● ● ● ● ● ●

LINE GRAPHS: WATCHING TELEVISION

Line graphs can be used to represent statistical relationships. Read the following statement:

    Watching TV _two to four_ hours per day translates into about 1,000 hours per year.

    From this sentence we understand that if we watch 2 hours of television per day, it will add up to 730 hours per year (2 hours × 365 days/year = 730). How many hours of television will we watch in one year if we watch 4 hours per day? 6 hours per day? 8 hours per day? Plot these points on the line graph below by first locating the hours/day on the horizontal axis (across) and then the number of hours of television watching per day on the vertical axis (up and down). The place where these two lines meet shows the number of hours watched for that year.

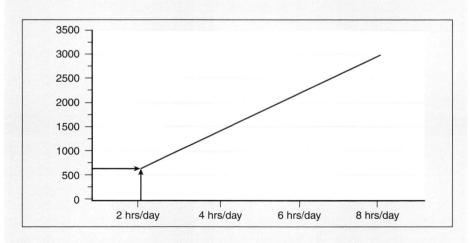

FALLACIES IN POOR ARGUMENTS

Poor arguments lack support; they do not have much evidence to prove or convince us to agree with or adopt the stated opinion. Poor arguments also contain errors in reasoning. These errors are called **fallacies**. Fallacies may trick us into agreeing with someone or into doing something we otherwise would not have done had we known all the facts. Other times, it is simply faulty logic that persuades us because we are not aware of the error in reasoning.

Types of Fallacies

Earlier in this chapter we analyzed the argument "Smoking should be banned in all public places." If we review this argument more closely and examine its points of support, we can see how this argument may actually be viewed as poor or weak.

Argument 1: Smoking should be banned in public places.

Support: Only really weird people smoke anyway.

Support: Smoking should be banned because it is not the type of thing that should be allowed in public places.

Support: Smoking should be banned because everyone wants to go to smoke-free places.

Our first point of support contains a fallacy called **ad hominem**. A writer uses this type of faulty reasoning to attack the person instead of the issue. The point that smoking should be banned in public places "because only really weird people smoke anyway" is attacking the smoker rather than the issue.

Our second point of support contains a fallacy called **circular reasoning**. The writer's error, in this case, is using a *restatement* of the point to *support* the point. When we take a closer look, we realize that the words "not allowed" mean the same as "banned." So, the statement "Smoking should be banned because it is not the type of thing that should be allowed in public places" means, "Smoking should be banned because smoking should be banned." Once we realize the statement contains no facts, examples, statistics, or other types of support for good arguments, we must question the value of the argument itself.

Our third point of support, "Smoking should be banned because everyone wants to go to smoke-free places," is also a fallacy. It is called the **bandwagon appeal**. In earlier times, a bandwagon was a horse-drawn wagon that contained musicians who played music as it traveled from town to town. People were encouraged to follow it through the streets. Eventually they would end up at an event or function such as a dance or a political campaign. Thus, the expression "jump on the bandwagon" means that since everyone else is going somewhere or doing something, you should go too; if you don't, then, as the expression implies, you will be left out.

In the banning public smoking argument, the final point of support implies that everyone is going to smoke-free places and therefore you should too. The idea alone that "everyone is doing this" is not a convincing enough reason for us to join in or accept a point of view.

Following is a complete list of fallacies that weaken arguments:

1. **Begging the Question/Circular Reasoning**—The writer makes a point that restates the point just made—for example, saying "A" is "B" so therefore "A" is "B."

   Example: There should be a ruling against professors giving most of the students A's because it should be against school policy for the majority of the students to receive A's.

Circular Reasoning
A is B. $\longrightarrow$ A is B.

2. **Straw Man**—The writer creates a false image or blows the argument out of proportion to make the opposition's ideas seem weak.

   Example: The postman tells a customer that the post office is closed on Saturday afternoons and Sundays. The customer replies, "This post office doesn't give good service; it is never open on weekends."

Straw Man
A is true. $\longrightarrow$ B is always the case.
B is not true.

3. **Ad Hominem**—In Latin, the full term *argumentum ad hominem* means "argument against the man." In this situation, rather than dealing logically with the issue itself, the person who presents the issue is attacked. The attack may be against another person's personality, affiliation, situation, or origin, and may involve inconsistent statements or beliefs.

   Example: Don't go by Lisa's opinions about child raising; she has never had any children.

Ad Hominem
A = issue
B = insult $\longrightarrow$ Argue B only

4. **Appeal to Loyalty**—An individual appeals for one to act in concert with the group's best interests, regardless of the merits of the particular case being argued.

   Example: All Democrats should vote for the Democratic candidate so the Republicans do not win the election.

Appeal to Loyalty
A = loyal feelings for B $\longrightarrow$ A should always make decisions for the good of B.

5. **Red Herring/Ignoring the Question**—An argument that dodges the real issue by drawing attention to an irrelevant issue.

Example: I don't know whether or not metal detectors should be installed in the public schools, but the cafeteria food in this school needs to serve better food.

Red Herring/Ignoring the Question
A = the issue
B = unrelated issue ⟶ Argue only about B.

6. **Bandwagon Appeal**—The writer or speaker uses the argument that because everyone is doing something or believes in something, it must be right or true.

Example: Everyone is buying their jeans at the Blue Jean Factory. You will look out of style if you don't buy your jeans there too.

Bandwagon Appeal
A = you
B = everyone else ⟶ A should do what B does.

7. **Oversimplification**—The issue of an argument is viewed as having only two alternatives when, in fact, it has more than two.

Example: All children should either attend the public schools or be schooled at home.

Oversimplification
A = one solution
B = one solution
C = one solution   ⟶ There are only two solutions to choose
D = one solution   from, A and B.
E = one solution
F = one solution

8. **Slippery Slope**—This is the assumption that allowing one thing will lead to a downward spiral.

Example: If you give my ninth-grade daughter an F for cheating, she will fail for this term. That will bring down her average for the year, and it will bring down her high school average. Then she will never be able to get into a good college. It will ruin her chances of getting a good job and ruin her entire life.

Slippery Slope
A = small consequence
B = more significant consequence ⟶   A will lead to B and
C = large consequence   B will lead to C.

9. **Overgeneralization**—An individual applies an example to all cases instead of to a few.

Example: I saw in today's paper that four teenagers were involved in a terrible car accident; all teenagers are terrible drivers.

Overgeneralization

Group 1 was involved in X.   Group 1 was involved in
Group 2 was *not* involved in X.   → X, therefore all groups
Group 3 was *not* involved in X.   were involved in X.

10. **Incomplete Facts or Card Stacking**—An individual attempts to mislead an audience by leaving out the facts.

Example: Advertisers encourage people to use a new prescription drug for colds and flu. They advertise that it stops sneezing and coughing. However, they leave out the fact that it may have serious side effects such as dizziness and vomiting.

Incomplete Facts or Card Stacking

Fact 1   You should believe this because of fact 1 *(facts 2*
Fact 2   → *and 3 are not mentioned because they do not*
Fact 3   *support the argument).*

11. **Testimonials/False Authority**—One falsely assumes that an expert in one field is also an expert in another.

Example: A famous football player endorses a cereal. (If he is a famous athlete and he is promoting a cereal, then you falsely conclude the cereal will make you energetic like him.)

Testimonials/False Authority

Joe Cool is an expert in field A. Joe Cool is speaking as an authority about field B.

12. **Guilt or Virtue by Association (also called Transfer)**—A situation in which one associates a positively or negatively regarded person or object with an issue and hopes that the association will lend the same credibility to the argument.

Example: The car salesman tried to convince the customers to buy a particular car by telling them that it was the same type featured in the James Bond movies.

Transfer/Guilt by Association

Everyone like sports hero X. Joe Cool argues that sports hero X would also agree with Joe Cool's argument.
Everyone hates politician Y. Joe Cool associates politician Y with his opponent.

Identifying Types of Fallacies

After studying the fallacies discussed on the previous page, write examples from your own experience in the spaces provided below. Then shut your book and try to recall the types of fallacies and their definitions. Quiz yourself on these items.

1. begging the question/circular reasoning

   _____

   _____

2. straw man

   _____

   _____

3. ad hominem

   _____

   _____

4. appeal to loyalty

   _____

   _____

5. red herring/ignoring the question

   _____

   _____

6. bandwagon appeal

   _____

   _____

7. oversimplification

   _____

   _____

8. slippery slope

_____

_____

9. overgeneralization

_____

_____

10. incomplete facts or card stacking

_____

_____

11. testimonials/false authority

_____

_____

12. guilt or virtue by association (transfer)

_____

_____

EXERCISE
10-5

Identifying the Fallacy

Read each of the statements below and identify the fallacy that makes it a poor argument. The first one has been done for you.

____a____ **1.** If Martin Luther King Jr., were alive today, I know he would have voted to have this bill passed.
    a. guilt or virtue by association/transfer
    b. incomplete facts or card stacking
    c. slippery slope
    d. bandwagon appeal

_____ **2.** Everyone is going to college, so you should too.
    a. circular reasoning
    b. testimonials

      c. slippery slope
      d. bandwagon appeal

_____ **3.** A student is told that he cannot have more than three absences before he is dropped from the course, and he replies, "That's not fair to say that I can never be absent."
      a. guilt or virtue by association
      b. straw man
      c. circular reasoning
      d. bandwagon appeal

_____ **4.** True Americans who clearly see the benefits of health care reform will support this initiative.
      a. guilt or virtue by association
      b. ad hominem
      c. slippery slope
      d. appeal to loyalty

_____ **5.** The American people must choose; they must either elect a Republican president or face an unstable economy with accelerating recession.
      a. false authority
      b. incomplete facts or card stacking
      c. straw man
      d. oversimplification

_____ **6.** Candidate X's argument concerning taxes is not convincing because he is too stiff and formal to win the vote of the average American.
      a. guilt or virtue by association
      b. ad hominem
      c. slippery slope
      d. bandwagon appeal

_____ **7.** College students spend too much time drinking beer and, therefore, do not have much time left over to study.
      a. guilt or virtue by association
      b. overgeneralization
      c. slippery slope
      d. ignoring the question

_____ **8.** You should sign a contract to buy this condominium because our company is the most successful agency in the area and we sell more condominiums than almost any agencies in the country.
      a. red herring
      b. transfer
      c. slippery slope
      d. bandwagon appeal

_____ **9.** If we don't fight communism in Asia, pretty soon it will spread to surrounding countries, and then to other continents, and eventually threaten our freedom here in the United States.
 a. overgeneralization
 b. begging the question
 c. slippery slope
 d. bandwagon appeal

_____ **10.** Nobody should be able to purchase a gun without a background check because background checks should be done whenever anyone purchases a gun.
 a. appeal to loyalty
 b. incomplete facts or card stacking
 c. slippery slope
 d. begging the question

A Reading in Education

Read the article that follows and identify the issue, the argument, the support, and any fallacies that would undermine the argument. Complete the vocabulary exercise before reading this selection to learn the new terms.

Vocabulary in Context

 a. emergence—coming out; surfacing; materializing

 b. inflation—price increase or expansion

 c. injunctions—restrictions, bans, rulings, orders, commands, embargoes

 d. curtail—limit, hold back, cut back, restrict

 e. dispose—get rid of

Use the above terms to complete the following sentences. The first one has been done for you.

____a____ **1.** According to the author, most students at Harvard University are starting to receive only grades of A or A–. The author especially feels that the _____ of this new way of grading has nothing to do with an increase in the quality of his students' work.

_____ **2.** The university may issue _____ telling the professors that they must cut out grade inflation.

_____ **3.** The college or university may not want to hurt its students' feelings by giving them low grades. It may go so far as to _____ of professors who give students low grades even if the students have not done anything to earn a high grade.

_____ **4.** Students who go on to get a degree beyond the Bachelor's degree often accept graduate assistant positions. They are usually provided free tuition and a minimum wage salary to assist professors with teaching and research. They often witness grade _____, in which professors calculate their students' grades on a curve.

_____ **5.** Grading papers is one job that a graduate assistant may be assigned. Professors sometimes tell their assistants to _____ grade inflation by making sure the average grade is a C. Other professors tell their assistants to curve the grade by raising the average to a B+.

How Should We Grade Our Students?

Issue:_____

Argument:_____

_____

_____

___d___ **1.** I had to laugh last month when administrators at Harvard University said that the **emergence** of an A or A– grading system reflects the increasing excellence of their students. Talk about spin.
   a. appeal to loyalty
   b. incomplete facts or card stacking
   c. slippery slope
   d. ad hominem

_____ **2.** I taught at Harvard as a teaching fellow and lecturer in the humanities for seven years, and the only time I felt safe giving a grade lower than an A– was when students didn't show up or turn in major assignments.
   a. analogy
   b. common knowledge
   c. statistics
   d. personal experience

_____ **3.** For PR purposes, the big administrators will hold a few well-publicized meetings. But the people who can most easily explain grade **inflation**—the underpaid and overworked teaching fellows and post-doc lecturers who do almost all of the grading—will not be invited. Or, if any are invited, they will act "professionally" and say there is no problem (just more excellence) rather than risk speaking the "unprofessional" truth.

    a. incomplete facts
    b. statistics
    c. slippery slope
    d. begging the question

_____ **4.** I found that . . . my primary duty was to insulate the supervising professor from undergraduates. If one of my students went to see the professor about something that occurred in my section—to contest a grade, say—then I would be sure to hear about it from the professor, and it would not be a pleasant encounter. I learned quickly that more than a few student complaints almost always meant the loss of future teaching fellowships with that professor.

    a. facts
    b. personal experience
    c. analogy
    d. example

_____ **5.** I have been told by professors—following regular administrative **injunctions** to **curtail** grade inflation—that the average grade in a section should be a B+.

    a. common knowledge
    b. personal experience
    c. authority
    d. statistics

_____ **6.** If I had followed this suggestion, I suspect that student complaints would have prevented me from ever teaching for that faculty member again. No one is fired, mind you. Teaching fellows are just not rehired. No one ever says why . . . it is worrisome to give any grade lower than an A–. . . . Even an A– is no guarantee against student complaints—all the way to the college president and into the legal system.

    a. appeal to loyalty
    b. incomplete facts or card stacking
    c. slippery slope
    d. begging the question

_____ **7.** The students know about the pressures faced by at-risk faculty, and they have entered into a silent agreement: Make this course an easy A, and we will give you a good evaluation. If not, we'll go to your superiors and complain about some species of unfairness—and the superior will get angry about having to spend time dealing with undergraduates—whether the complaints are justified or not.

    a. overgeneralization
    b. incomplete facts or card stacking

        c. slippery slope

        d. begging the question

_____ 8. When grades are inflated, everybody seems to win in the short term. Of course, the bottom has to fall out eventually. . . . What happens when employers learn that degrees, even with high grade-point averages, are not a good indication of ability? What happens when students realize, years later, they have been cheated out of an education?

        a. oversimplification

        b. incomplete facts or card stacking

        c. red herring

        d. begging the question

_____ 9. Of course, it's not Harvard's fault. No single institution can do anything about grade inflation. Paying student–customers are scarce, but teaching faculty members are a dime a dozen. At present the students have the power, and they are, in essence, buying not only their degrees but their high GPAs.

        a. transfer

        b. statistics

        c. slippery slope

        d. testimonials

_____ 10. The present system re-educates or **disposes** of anyone who might be overly inclined to maintain high standards. And grades will continue to inflate until everyone graduates summa cum laude. (The Chronicle: *Daily News,* December 13, 2001)

        a. transfer

        b. incomplete facts or card stacking

        c. slippery slope

        d. overgeneralization

A Reading in World Politics

The author of the article below argues that charities that give money to free the slaves in Sudan are actually causing more people to be enslaved. Complete the vocabulary exercise before reading this selection to learn the new terms.

Vocabulary in Context

  a. redemption—rescue, release, liberation

  b. suppressed—stopped by force

  c. humanitarian—caring; kind; civilized; charitable

d. inception—beginning; start; origin

e. incentive—reason; motivation; encouragement; enticement

Use the terms above to complete the following sentences. The first one has been done for you.

    _e_   **1.** Knowing that they can get a lot of money for selling human beings has been a(an) _____ for some members of the Muslim Baggara tribe to capture people from the Dinka tribe and sell them as slaves.

_____ **2.** Since the _____ of slave redemption, the number of people who have been captured for the purpose of slave trade has steadily increased.

_____ **3.** Although they meant well, the _____ groups who began buying slaves for the purpose of setting them free have actually created a larger economic market for slaves.

_____ **4.** Earlier in history, the British had _____ the slave raids. However, recently the Baggara have started these raids once more.

_____ **5.** The purpose of slave _____ is to free people from slavery.

From each sentence below, identify which type of support the author uses as evidence to back up his argument.

Slave Redemption in Sudan

    _b_   **1.** Slavery is a centuries-old practice in Sudan, one that colonial British rulers finally managed to halt during World War I. This changed in 1989, when the National Islamic Front (NIF) took control of the government. The NIF quickly began arming the Muslim Baggara tribe in the northern part of the country to fight against the rebellious Christian tribes of the south. The Baggara previously had made a regular practice of enslaving members of the southern Dinka tribe, and once armed by the NIF the Baggara resumed the slave raids the British had **suppressed**. Perhaps as many as 20,000 Dinkas, mostly women and children, were enslaved and taken north, selling for as little as $15 each.
    a. examples
    b. facts
    c. cause-effect relationship
    d. common knowledge

_____ **2.** Within a few years, word of the revived slave trade began filtering out of Sudan. In response, a variety of **humanitarian** groups from other nations began buying slaves in large batches and setting

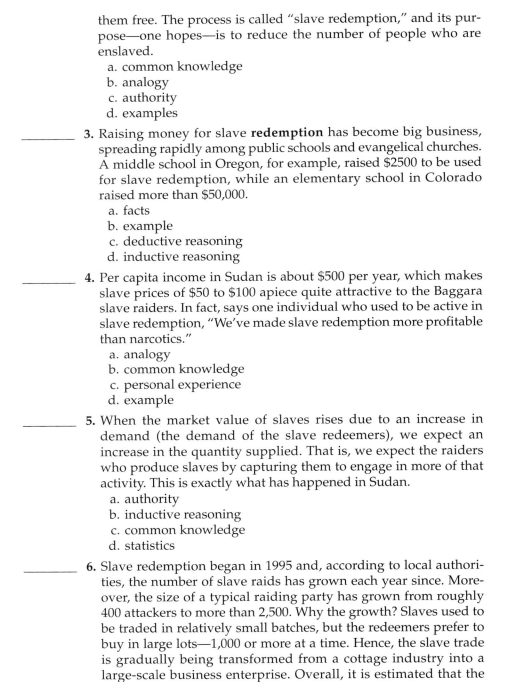

them free. The process is called "slave redemption," and its purpose—one hopes—is to reduce the number of people who are enslaved.
  a. common knowledge
  b. analogy
  c. authority
  d. examples

_____ **3.** Raising money for slave **redemption** has become big business, spreading rapidly among public schools and evangelical churches. A middle school in Oregon, for example, raised $2500 to be used for slave redemption, while an elementary school in Colorado raised more than $50,000.
  a. facts
  b. example
  c. deductive reasoning
  d. inductive reasoning

_____ **4.** Per capita income in Sudan is about $500 per year, which makes slave prices of $50 to $100 apiece quite attractive to the Baggara slave raiders. In fact, says one individual who used to be active in slave redemption, "We've made slave redemption more profitable than narcotics."
  a. analogy
  b. common knowledge
  c. personal experience
  d. example

_____ **5.** When the market value of slaves rises due to an increase in demand (the demand of the slave redeemers), we expect an increase in the quantity supplied. That is, we expect the raiders who produce slaves by capturing them to engage in more of that activity. This is exactly what has happened in Sudan.
  a. authority
  b. inductive reasoning
  c. common knowledge
  d. statistics

_____ **6.** Slave redemption began in 1995 and, according to local authorities, the number of slave raids has grown each year since. Moreover, the size of a typical raiding party has grown from roughly 400 attackers to more than 2,500. Why the growth? Slaves used to be traded in relatively small batches, but the redeemers prefer to buy in large lots—1,000 or more at a time. Hence, the slave trade is gradually being transformed from a cottage industry into a large-scale business enterprise. Overall, it is estimated that the

number of slaves captured in raids each year has risen steadily since the **inception** of slave redemption.
   a. inductive reasoning
   b. deductive reasoning
   c. authority
   d. facts

_____ **7.** All of the slaves subsequently "freed" by the redeemers are in fact individuals who never would have been enslaved had the redeemers not first made a market for them. In addition, because large numbers of new slaves now spend some time in captivity awaiting redemption, it is even possible that the total number of people in slavery at any point in time is actually higher because of the well-intentioned efforts of the slave redeemers.
   a. accurate statistics
   b. analogy
   c. inductive reasoning
   d. deductive reasoning

_____ **8.** In addition to encouraging the capture of new slaves, redemption also reduces any **incentive** for owners to set free their less productive slaves. Prior to 1995, about 10 percent of all slaves, chiefly older women and young children were allowed to escape or even told to go home, because the costs of feeding, clothing, and housing them exceeded their value to their owners. The final effect of redemption has been to create a trade in fictitious slaves—individuals who are paid to pose as slaves for the purposes of redemption, and who are then given a cut of the redemption price after they are "freed."
   a. personal experience
   b. analogy
   c. inductive reasoning
   d. statistics

_____ **9.** Is there another way to combat slavery in Sudan? On the demand side, the U.S. government has long refused to negotiate with terrorists or pay ransom to kidnappers, simply because it believes that such tactics encourage terrorism and kidnapping.
   a. authority
   b. examples
   c. common knowledge
   d. inductive reasoning

_____ **10.** The British were originally successful in ending the slave trade in Sudan and elsewhere in their empire by dispatching soldiers to kill or disarm slave raiders and by sending warships to close off maritime slave-trading routes. Sudan is an independent nation today,

---

Reading Between the Lines Box 10.3

UNDERSTANDING FALLACIES:

Slave Redemption in Sudan

The fallacy **oversimplification** occurs when an issue is viewed as having only two alternatives when it actually has more. In the article "Slave Redemption in Sudan," the author explains why slave redemption is not a good solution. At the end of his article, he proposes a second solution as an only alternative.

Solution 1: Humanitarian groups from other nations could buy slaves in large batches and set them free. The process is called *slave redemption*, and its purpose is to reduce the number of people who are enslaved.

Solution 2: The British were originally successful in ending the slave trade in Sudan and elsewhere in their empire by dispatching soldiers to kill or disarm slave raiders and by sending warships to close off maritime slave-trading routes. This could be done again.

Are there only two solutions to this problem of slave trading in Sudan? What other solutions can you think of? _____

---

and the British electorate would likely oppose military action by the British government against Sudanese slave traders. Yet even the people who used to be subject to British colonial rule have mixed feelings. When asked to compare the colonial British policies to the redeemers' policies of today, a schoolmaster in the affected area remarked, "If the colonial government were standing for election, I would vote for them." (Miller, Benjamin, and North 44–47)

   a. analogy
   b. example
   c. personal experience
   d. statistics

A Reading in American History

Alan Canfora was an eyewitness of the Kent State massacre. Read his account of the incident. Then identify the issue, the argument, and the facts that support the argument. Complete the vocabulary exercise before reading this selection to learn the new terms.

Vocabulary in Context

a. vandalized—damaged; wrecked; broke; smashed

b. ignite—catch fire; go up in to flames; burst into flames

c. reserve—emergency supply (e.g., reserve officers are troops used in an emergency)

d. arson—deliberate attempt to destroy by fire

e. eradicate—eliminate; wipe out; destroy; massacre

Use the terms above to complete the following sentences. The first one has been done for you.

_____a_____ **1.** The students of Kent State _____ downtown Kent, breaking windows as a way of protesting the Vietnam War.

_____ **2.** Two thousand angry students tried to set the ROTC building on fire. Their attempts to_____ the building and prevent firefighters from putting it out angered the governor of Ohio.

_____ **3.** The governor was so angry that he publicly denounced the students as being worse than communist enemies and threatened to _____ the problem.

_____ **4.** The governor called out the _____ forces to help local police get the situation under control.

_____ **5.** Although the ROTC building was burned to the ground, no student was ever convicted of _____.

The Kent State Massacre

May 1

[1]   Forty-three windows are broken in downtown Kent during a spontaneous, militant rampage by hundreds of angry anti-war students and some anti-war Vietnam veterans too. Mostly banks, loan companies, public utility offices and other "political" windows were **vandalized**. Only $5,000 worth of damage occurred but major anti-war momentum was created that continued until May 4.

May 2

[2]   Kent State University's **Reserve** Officers Training Corps (ROTC) building, a rickety, old wooden military science barracks, was attacked and

burned to the ground. It's true that 2,000 angry students surrounded the building, attempted to **ignite** the longstanding target and prevented firefighters from extinguishing the flames. However, the mysterious lack of police intervention for 90 minutes and the suspicious fire AFTER the ROTC building was finally under control by law enforcement officials leaves many unanswered questions.

[3]   Did the authorities stay away so the students would burn the building and create an excuse to bring the Ohio National Guard to Kent State? Did the inept arson attempts by the students fail? Why did the building burn AFTER the students were chased away? Why has no student ever been convicted of **arson** at Kent State in 1970? Who really burned the ROTC building at Kent State? Why?

[4]   All these questions aside, the National Guard arrived on the Kent State campus while the building was afire during that night of May 2. Two days of anti-property violence by Kent students on May 1 and 2 were followed by two days of anti-student violence by the Ohio National Guard on May 3 and 4.

May 3

[5]   The conservative Republican, pro-war Ohio Governor James Rhodes arrived at KSU for a tour of the damage and a news conference. Rhodes was facing a tough May 5 US Senate primary election and he was behind in the pre-election polls. This desperate politician exaggerated the situation to further his own political election and career. He condemned the Kent students as "the worst type of people we harbor in America . . . worse than the Communists. . . . We're going to **eradicate** the problem!"

[6]   The angry rhetoric of a desperate politician worsened the situation at Kent State. Hours later, Ohio National Guardsmen attacked peaceful students with tear gas and rifles. Several students were slashed and stabbed by the bayonets on the ends of National Guard rifles. The stage was set for May 4, 1970, a day of tragedy for Kent State, Ohio, and America.

May 4

[7]   My frightened girlfriend stayed in my apartment after I prepared two black protest flags. I purposefully chose black material to match my dark mood of despair and anger following the recent death of my friend Bill Caldwell in Vietnam. Four hundred Ohio national guardsmen (ONG) were in the city of Kent and 800 were on the campus. Leaving my apartment, I walked past many of these soldiers, went several blocks east to the Kent State campus, and joined my friends on the KSU Commons at noon. About 1,000 students had joined the protest rally, but classes were being held on campus as usual.

[8]   We assumed we still could exercise our Constitutional rights of freedom of speech, freedom of assembly, and freedom to dissent. Immedi-

ately as our peaceful anti-war rally began, approximately 75 members of the Ohio National Guard attacked our peaceful gathering. As these guardsmen wearing helmets and gas masks marched and fired tear gas, we ran away from the KSU Commons up over "Blanket Hill" and down into the Prentice Hall dormitory's parking lot.

[9]   The armed guardsmen followed us over the hill and then settled on a practice football field for perhaps 10 minutes. During this time, a stand-off occurred as a few rocks were thrown back and forth by both students and guardsmen. Because we stood hundreds of feet apart the rocks were ineffective and both sides ceased that activity.

[10]   As some of us walked closer to shout our anti-war and anti-National Guard anger, perhaps 250 feet away, about a dozen guardsmen kneeled and aimed toward us. I stood my ground and shouted towards the armed troops who had their fingers on their rifle triggers. Since there was no logical reason to aim or shoot, I assumed they would not fire and I was correct—at that moment. Soon, however, the troops regrouped and began to march away back up the hill. We assumed they were marching in a retreat back over the hill to the KSU Commons.

[11]   We were quite shocked when, at the hilltop, perhaps a dozen members of Troop G simultaneously stopped, turned and aimed their rifles. What followed was a 13-second barrage of gunfire, mostly from M-1 rifles, into our crowd of unarmed students. Some other guardsmen from Company A also fired non-lethal shots.

[12]   A total of 67 bullets were fired by the guardsmen from the hilltop. Most of the bullets were fired over 300 feet into the distant Prentice Hall parking lot. Two of the students killed, Allison Krause and Jeff Miller, were protesters. Two others, Sandy Scheuer and Bill Schroeder, were bystanders. Jeff was killed 275 feet away from his killer. Allison was 350 feet away. Sandy and Bill were approximately 390 feet away. Nine others, including myself, were wounded. Dean Kahler remains in a wheelchair after he was shot in the back.

Getting Shot

[13]   Years of pro-war/anti-war division among the American people culminated during those 13 seconds of bloody mayhem at Kent State. American citizens fired high-powered rifles into a crowd of unarmed American students. For a brief moment, I assumed they were firing blanks because there was no reason whatsoever to fire live ammunition, as they seemed to be retreating over the hilltop. At the moment the massacre occurred, as I stood and watched carefully, I saw several of my fellow-students run away and drop to the ground.

[14]   As the bullets began to fly, my survival instinct caused me to make a quick dash behind an oak tree a few feet away—the only tree in the direct line of fire. Because I had been taunting the guardsmen, I am convinced

they shot at me (and others) intentionally. As I ran behind the tree during the first seconds of gunfire I felt a sharp pain in my right wrist. An M-1 rifle bullet passed through my right wrist. My wound was quite painful and bloody. At that nightmarish moment, I realized that the triggermen were firing live ammunition. With shock and utter disbelief, I immediately thought to myself: "I've been shot! It seems like a nightmare but this is real. I've really been shot!" My pain was great during that unique moment of unprecedented anguish but I had another serious concern: the bullets were continuing to rain in my direction for another 11 or 12 seconds.

[15]   That narrow young tree absorbed several bullets intended for me. It was a chilling, unbelievable situation. The bullets continued to fly—some striking the tree, others zipping and cracking through the air and grass on both sides of the tree that saved my life—past me into the parking lot behind where other students were killed and wounded. Only a few feet away, my roommate, Tom Grace, was also wounded—shot through the foot. I heard him screaming in severe pain after a bullet passed through his left ankle.

[16]   While the bullets were still flying, I yelled over to him, "Stay down! Stay down! It's only buckshot!" I wrongly assumed we were wounded by shotguns because I knew that 30 students at nearby Ohio State University were slightly wounded a week earlier by police using such weapons on High Street in Columbus, Ohio. According to the FBI, eleven of the thirteen victims were either shot in the back or from the side. When the gunfire ceased, after a moment of eerie silence, we saw the killers begin to march away while students screamed in pain and shock and called out for ambulances.

[17]   I ran to Tom Grace and consoled him with assurances our wounds were only "caused by buckshot!" Soon, other students began to assist Tom Grace and I decided to run to somehow get a ride to the hospital. As I ran past Jeff Miller, I saw a crowd of students gathering and someone shouted: "Get an ambulance! This guy's been shot! AMBULANCE!" I ran up to Jeff Hartzler and showed him my bloody arm and said, "They shot me and Tom Grace too. He's over there. Go help him!" He ran away toward Tom Grace. My pain and blood distressed me as I ran through the chaotic bloody parking lot. I knew I had to get treatment for my injured wrist at a hospital soon.

[18]   When I ran into the home economics building and rinsed my wound a female student provided a clean, white towel and I ran back outside. I stopped the first car out front of the home economics building and convinced the driver to take me to the hospital. I was then driven by that KSU graduate student and his wife six miles east to the old Robinson Memorial Hospital in nearby Ravenna. As I rode along sitting, bleeding, in the back seat of that Ford, my pain and shock increased as the sound of ambulance and police sirens filled the air.

At the Hospital

[19]   When I got to the hospital I walked alone toward the emergency room door. Before entering I looked inside the open rear door of a parked ambulance. I saw my friend Jeff Miller lying dead and bloody on a stretcher. I assumed he was only unconscious from a facial flesh wound. I still wrongly assumed we were shot by non-lethal shotguns.

[20]   During those terrible seconds, as I stood alone gazing at my friend's bloody form, I vainly hoped that plastic surgery would repair Jeff's face that was clearly hit where a gaping 2-inch bloody hole destroyed his always-smiling face. I did not know that a powerful M-1 bullet had passed through his head. Once inside the hospital, I tried to calm Tom Grace (who had arrived in another vehicle) who was screaming a plea for morphine or "something to stop the pain!"

[21]   After I was hustled into a treatment room I was told that students were killed. My concern about my sister was alleviated by a doctor who checked the names of the slain students. Although I suffered extreme physical pain, the deaths of my fellow students overwhelmed me with feelings of great despair and anger. I immediately understood we were the victims of a great injustice. I feared immediate arrest in that police-state atmosphere.

[22]   After my wounds were treated, I convinced hospital authorities to permit my departure. Outside, I soon was reunited with my sister, my girlfriend, and other Kent friends who had just arrived at the hospital. We had to evade Main Street roadblocks and we sneaked back into Kent through Brady Lake on Lake Street. At my apartment, our many friends gathered and expressed horror and outrage about the murders.

[23]   We were also quite concerned about Tom Grace who was seriously injured and remained hospitalized because his ankle was blown open by a powerful bullet. He later developed a serious gangrene infection and nearly lost his maimed foot. Some expressed the need for revenge and others their grief and anger as we all discussed the historic massacre we had just survived. We were fortunate we were still alive.

[24]   We knew that we had witnessed a cold-blooded, calculated, planned massacre. Years later, we learned there were orders to fire those 67 bullets. Later, during testimony in Federal Court in Cleveland in 1975, we learned that there was an order to fire at Kent State on May 4, 1970. At least one of the Ohio National Guard officers admitted he gave an order to fire on the unarmed students at Kent State.

[25]   Were others involved in a conspiracy to terrorize the student movement at Kent State on May 4, 1970? We are still attempting to uncover the cover-up of murder at Kent State on May 4, 1970. Someday, hopefully, we'll learn the entire truth about Kent State.

The Victims of May 4, 1970

[26]   On May 4, 1970, four Kent State University students were killed and nine others wounded (including me) when numerous members of the Ohio National Guard—mostly from Troop G, the death squad—fired 67 bullets into a crowd of unarmed students during an anti-war demonstration under the noonday sun.

Those Killed On May 4, 1970

[27]   Jeffrey Miller was shot through the head 275 feet away. Allison Krause was shot through the arm and chest 350 feet away. Bill Schroeder was shot in the back nearly 400 feet away. Sandy Scheuer was shot through the throat nearly 400 feet away.

Full-Time Students

[28]   All 13 of the Kent State massacre victims were full-time students. This fact dispels the myth of "outside agitators" in the student demonstration. Kent State was where the most American students were killed in one incident (4) and the only incident where women were killed (2). Allison and Jeff were active protesters. Allison was an aspiring artist in the Honors College at Kent State. Jeff Miller had recently transferred to Kent from Michigan State University. Sandy and Bill were bystanders killed as they walked away toward their classrooms. Bill Schroeder was an "all-American boy" and an ROTC student of military science and business administration. Sandy Scheuer had been a member of Alpha Xi Delta sorority. (Canfora)

Multiple-Choice Questions

Read each of the statements below and identify the support that makes it a good argument or the fallacy that makes it a poor argument. The first one has been done for you.

____a____   **1.** He condemned the Kent students as "the worst type of people we harbor in America … worse than the Communists … "
a. guilt by association
b. incomplete facts or card stacking
c. slippery slope
d. bandwagon appeal

_____   **2.** Hours later, Ohio National Guardsmen attacked peaceful students with tear gas and rifles. Several students were slashed and stabbed by the bayonets on the ends of National Guard rifles.
a. personal experience
b. analogy

Visual Literacy Box 10.3

● ● ● ● ● ● ● ● ● ● ● ● ● ● ● ●

CAUSE-EFFECT TIME LINES: THE KENT STATE MASSACRE

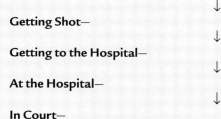

Sometimes it is easier to grasp a chain of events if we can see it in a time line. Study the time line below and then continue it on through the events of May 4.

May 1—Downtown Kent was vandalized by angry students protesting the Vietnam War.

↓

May 2—Kent State's ROTC Building is burned down.

↓

May 3—Ohio Governor James Rhodes threatens to "eradicate the problem."

↓

May 4—The student protest is interrupted by the National Guard and four students are killed.

↓

Getting Shot—

↓

Getting to the Hospital—

↓

At the Hospital—

↓

In Court—

　　　　　　c. inductive reasoning
　　　　　　d. facts

_____ **3.** As I ran behind the tree during the first seconds of gunfire I felt a sharp pain in my right wrist. An M-1 rifle bullet passed through my right wrist.
　　　　　　a. personal experience
　　　　　　b. analogy
　　　　　　c. inductive reasoning
　　　　　　d. statistics

_____ **4.** A total of 67 bullets were fired by the guardsmen from the hilltop. Most of the bullets were fired over 300 feet into the distant Prentice Hall parking lot. Two of the students killed, Allison Krause and Jeff Miller, were protesters. Two others, Sandy Scheuer and Bill Schroeder, were bystanders. Jeff was killed 275 feet away from his killer. Allison was 350 feet away. Sandy and Bill were approximately 390 feet away. Nine others, including myself, were

wounded. Dean Kahler remains in a wheelchair after he was shot in the back.
   a. personal experience
   b. analogy
   c. inductive reasoning
   d. statistics

_____ 5. It's true that 2,000 angry students surrounded the building, attempted to ignite the longstanding target, and prevented fire-fighters from extinguishing the flames. However, the mysterious lack of police intervention for 90 minutes and the suspicious fire AFTER the ROTC building was finally under control by law enforcement officials leaves many unanswered questions.
   a. authority
   b. common knowledge
   c. analogy
   d. inductive reasoning

_____ 6. All 13 of the Kent State massacre victims were full-time students. This fact dispels the myth of "outside agitators" in the student demonstration.
   a. deductive reasoning
   b. inductive reasoning
   c. analogy
   d. authority

_____ 7. On May 4, 1970, four Kent State University students were killed and nine others wounded (including me) when numerous members of the Ohio National Guard—mostly from Troop G, the death squad—fired 67 bullets into a crowd of unarmed students during an anti-war demonstration under the noonday sun.
   a. common knowledge
   b. facts
   c. inductive reasoning
   d. deductive reasoning

_____ 8. We knew that we had witnessed a cold-blooded, calculated, planned massacre. Years later, we learned there were orders to fire those 67 bullets. Later, during testimony in Federal Court in Cleveland in 1975, we learned that there was an order to fire at Kent State on May 4, 1970. At least one of the Ohio National Guard officers admitted he gave an order to fire on the unarmed students at Kent State.
   a. analogy
   b. example
   c. authority
   d. personal experience

_____ **9.** That narrow young tree absorbed several bullets intended for me. It was a chilling, unbelievable situation. The bullets continued to fly—some striking the tree, others zipping and cracking through the air and grass on both sides of the tree that saved my life—past me into the parking lot behind where other students were killed and wounded. Only a few feet away, my roommate, Tom Grace, was also wounded—shot through the foot. I heard him screaming in severe pain after a bullet passed through his left ankle.
   a. authority
   b. analogy
   c. personal experience
   d. statistics

_____ **10.** Allison and Jeff were active protesters. Allison was an aspiring artist in the Honors College at Kent State. Jeff Miller had recently transferred to Kent from Michigan State University. Sandy and Bill were bystanders killed as they walked away toward their classrooms. Bill Schroeder was an "all-American boy" and an ROTC student of military science and business administration. Sandy Scheuer had been a member of Alpha Xi Delta sorority.
   a. statistics
   b. inductive reasoning
   c. deductive reasoning
   d. facts

Reading Between the Lines Box 10.4

IDENTIFYING THE SUPPORT

The Kent State Massacre

Good arguments rely on the quality of their support. If, for example, an argument is supported only by opinions that cannot be backed up by facts, it is weak. Reread Alan Canfora's account of the Kent State Massacre. He argues that it was wrong for the National Guard to fire upon unarmed students. How much support does he provide for his argument?

Check the types of support that are provided in Alan Canfora's account of the Kent State massacre. One has been done for you.

__√__ **1.** facts   _____ **6.** common knowledge

_____ **2.** examples   _____ **7.** accurate statistics

_____ **3.** analogy   _____ **8.** personal experience

_____ **4.** deductive reasoning   _____ **9.** authority

_____ **5.** inductive reasoning

Short-Answer Questions

Identify the issue, the arguments, and the evidence that supports the arguments.

1. What is the issue?

   _____

2. What are the arguments?

   Argument 1: _____

   Argument 2: _____

3. List ten facts that could be used to support the argument that the killing of the Kent State students was planned. One fact has been listed for you.

   1. On May 4, 1970, four Kent State University students were killed and nine others wounded (including me) when numerous members of the Ohio National Guard fired 67 bullets into a crowd of unarmed students during an anti-war demonstration.

   2. _____

      _____

      _____

   3. _____

      _____

      _____

   4. _____

      _____

      _____

   5. _____

      _____

      _____

6. _____

_____

_____

7. _____

_____

_____

8. _____

_____

_____

9. _____

_____

_____

10. _____

_____

_____

EXERCISE
10-6

Comparing Accounts

Now read these accounts of the Kent State massacre from two history books. Which statements are the same as the ones Alan Canfora provided? Which statements are different? What did Canfora say that was not in the history books?

Account 1: Nixon's 1970 invasion of Cambodia brought renewed campus demonstrations two with tragic consequences. At Kent State University in Ohio, the antiwar response was fierce. After students burned down the ROTC building, the governor of Ohio ordered the National Guard to the campus, and without provocation the soldiers fired on a gathering crowd. Two demonstrators, who were more than 250 feet away were killed; so were two bystanders, almost 400 feet from the troops. (Nash, Jeffrey, Howe et al.)

Same as Canfora's account:

Four people were killed.

_____

_____

_____

_____

_____

_____

Different from Canfora's account:

Students burned down the ROTC building.

_____

_____

_____

Not mentioned in history book:

_____

_____

_____

_____

Account 2: Nixon's shocking announcement (that he was dispatching thousands of troops to destroy enemy bases in Cambodia) triggered many campus demonstrations. One college where feelings ran high was Kent State University in Ohio. For several days students there clashed with local police; they broke windows and caused other damage to property. When the governor of Ohio called out the National Guard, angry students showered the soldiers with stones. During a noontime protest on May 4 the guardsmen, who were poorly trained in crowd control suddenly opened fire. Four students were killed, two of them women who were merely passing by on their way to class. (Garraty and Carnes 849)

Same as Canfora's account:

It took place at Kent State in Ohio.

_____

_____

_____

_____

_____

_____

Different from Canfora's account:

The ROTC building was burned.

_____

_____

Not mentioned in history book:

_____

_____

_____

_____

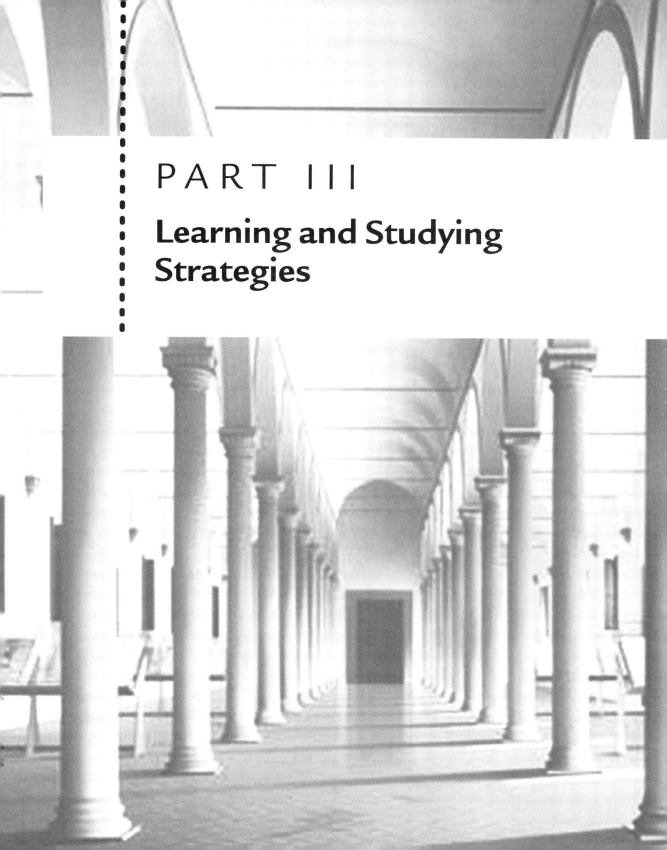

PART III
Learning and Studying Strategies

CHAPTER

11

Reading and Studying Textbooks

- -

This chapter shows you:

- strategies for reading college-level textbooks;
- strategies for studying from college-level textbooks.

JEN: If the teacher mentions a book, we think that, you know, oh, we just have to get it, but this one teacher, she never mentioned that we had to **READ** it. She told us to take out a piece of paper for a pop quiz and none of us had read the book because she had never **TOLD** us to.

Jen and the other students in her class are not the only ones who have ever had misunderstandings about the expectations of being a college student. Since the early 1900s, many students have gone to college unprepared to cope with the huge demands of college-level work. As far back as 1915, parents complained that their sons and daughters were failing classes at Harvard because they did not know how to study. It was then that Harvard created the first college reading course (Moore 1915). Other colleges and universities followed Harvard's example, and today almost every college or university has some type of program to help students cope with college reading and studying.

Sometimes, students don't need help with the actual reading of a textbook. In Jen's case, the students didn't understand that they were responsible for all of the readings listed on the syllabus whether or not the professor told them so directly.

Also, students frequently misunderstand that college-level courses cover three times the amount of information of high school–level classes. For example, in the first ten weeks of a college Spanish class you will learn as much information as you did after taking one full year of high school Spanish while spending just one-third the amount of time in class.

In other words, in high school you spent 40 hours per week in class learning from a classroom teacher. In college, you will spend 15 hours in class learning from a professor and 25 hours per week learning on your own from a textbook.

Therefore, it is extremely important to learn how to learn from a textbook. This chapter shows you strategies for reading and studying from college-level textbooks.

READING, DAYDREAMING, AND SLEEPING

TINA: My mind drifts, like I'm reading . . . a page and all of a sudden I think of something. I'm reading, but I'm not really reading. I'm totally thinking of something different and have to start that page again.

TONI: If I am not interested in a subject . . . I read the whole page, but don't learn learning the information that I just read.

Have you ever fallen asleep while reading a book? Have you ever been glad to reach the end of a chapter—and then realize that you don't remember a thing that you read? Like Tina and Toni, most us have experienced this at one time or another.

What happened? Why were we either snoring or not remembering what we read? This happens when we do not *think* about what we read. We may have read the words, but we let our minds wander to other things. Maybe we were thinking about our plans for next weekend or what we will eat for supper. As soon as we realize that we are *not* reading, we have to stop and go back to the place where we lost our concentration, *even if that was at the very beginning of the chapter*. This can be time-consuming and discouraging. We can apply many reading and study strategies to prevent this from happening. Before we discuss them, however, take the following survey to determine whether you need to develop new study and/or reading habits.

EXERCISE
11-1

Study Skills Survey

Below is a study skills survey. For each item on the list, check one of the following: frequently, sometimes, or rarely. Then, read the directions for scoring your answers.

Survey: Do You Fall Asleep When You Read?	Frequently	Sometimes	Rarely
1 I fall asleep shortly after I begin reading.			

(continued on next page)

Survey: Do You Fall Asleep When You Read?	Frequently	Sometimes	Rarely
2 I skip over introductions and conclusions.			
3 I daydream when I read.			
4 I read only the information that the author highlights, such as terms and their definitions.			
5 I close the book and put it away as soon as I am finished reading the chapter.			
6 I stay up all night cramming for exams.			
7 I mark, underline, or highlight main ideas as I read.			
8 I look through my reading assignments before I read them.			
9 I read the assigned chapter before I go to class.			
10 I take notes from the information that I mark in my textbooks.			
11 I prepare for exams by repeatedly reviewing all of the information covered so far.			
12 I have good grades when I take the time to read and study for exams.			

If you answer *frequently* to any of the first six statements and *rarely* to any of the second six statements, you may have some misunderstandings about learning from textbooks. The following study system is a great method for reading textbook chapters. It is the most widely used and researched study strategy around. In fact, more research has been done on this strategy than on any other reading and study strategy. And guess what? It has been proven over and over and over again to work. There exists so much evidence that this study strategy really does work that no future research needs to be done to prove its effectiveness.

THE PQ4R

PROFESSOR: When I was in school trying to earn my Bachelor's degree, I did not know of any study strategies. I just read and reread the information in my textbooks and my notes. I really struggled. By the end of college, however, my GPA was around a 3.0. Then, while I was working on my Master's degree, I learned about the PQ4R method (**P**review-**Q**uestion-**R**ead-**R**eflect-**R**ecite-**R**eview). I was told to apply this method when teaching people how to improve their reading skills. One day I decided to try it for myself to see if it would help with all the reading that I had to do for the graduate program. I began to incorporate the PQ4R method into my own reading and study routine. My GPA went up to a 3.5. I continued to use this method as a student in my doctoral program. The more I used this method, the easier it became for me to read and understand a large number of books and articles. As I became better at using the PQ4R, my GPA increased even more until I graduated with an almost 4.0 GPA. So, in short, I am very fond of the PQ4R method because it helped me a lot.

You, too, should learn to apply the PQ4R method regularly to your own reading and study routine. Depending on the material you need to learn, you can apply either the whole method or just parts of it. At first, the PQ4R may seem like a lot of work, but with persistent practice, it will become a habit—an automatic response to textbook reading. See Reading Between the Lines Box 11.1 below for an overview of the PQ4R.

Reading Between the Lines Box 11.1

PQ4R: A METHOD FOR READING AND STUDYING

In experiments, researchers have found over and over again that the PQ4R method is extremely effective. If you don't believe it, try this method for yourself. Take the textbook from your most difficult course and find the chapter that you will be tested on next. Read this chapter using the PQ4R method. Follow the guidelines below; do not skip any of the steps. It will take you approximately two hours to complete all of the steps. Be sure to review, or you will forget about 80 percent of what you read, even if you understood it completely. *Don't forget to do an additional review immediately before the exam!*

PQ4R

1. Preview

    a. Read title/introduction of chapter.

    b. Read conclusion or summary.

    c. Read major headings (main ideas)—this makes an outline of the chapter.

(continued on next page)

(continued from previous page)

d. Read subheadings (subtopics).

e. Read first and last sentences of each paragraph (topic sentences and transition sentences).

f. Figure out charts, graphs, diagrams.

g. Summary will tell you what information is important and what to concentrate and spend most time on.

2. Question

a. Convert each section heading and subheading into a question.

Sample Heading: Leadership Traits

Sample Question: What traits are needed for leadership in the business world?

b. If headings are missing, make topic sentences into questions.

c. Read to find the answers to your questions.

3. Read and Reflect

a. Think over each sentence to be sure the meaning is clear.

b. Mentally summarize each paragraph after reading it.

c. Ask yourself:

1. Can I give an example of this?

2. What is the basic meaning of this?

3. Can I sum this up into a generalization?

4. What evidence supports this?

5. How does this relate to the main topic?

4. Recite

a. Use an index card to cover paragraphs, look at subject headings, and try to remember what each section is about.

b. Choose 10–15 facts that you want to remember.

c. Write them down.

d. Memorize them.

5. Review

a. Repeat the Recite step several times as spaced reviews before the exam.

<u>Example</u>: If you read the chapter Sunday night and the exam is on Friday morning, you might repeat the Recite step on Monday night, Wednesday night, and Friday morning before your exam.

Steps in the PQ4R.

Previewing (P) Let's suppose we have two identical puzzles sitting on your dining room table. One is put together and the other one is piled up in pieces. In which puzzle would it be easier to see the whole picture? Although the puzzles are identical and have all of the same pieces, the image in the completed puzzle would be instantly detected. In order to figure out the image of the incomplete puzzle, however, we would have to examine each puzzle piece to see how the whole puzzle fits together.

Reading a textbook chapter is very much like putting together a puzzle. We try to imagine how each sentence fits together with the others, as we do with puzzle pieces.

Sometimes we may need to skim individual sentences or paragraphs in order to get a sense of what the whole chapter is about. This is known as **previewing**. Previewing is similar to looking at the border of a puzzle—that is, we try to identify the main pieces that help us to determine the basic outline of the image. We apply the same concept when previewing a chapter. Doing so allows us to see the main points and how they fit together. Previewing reveals the author's outline. Understanding the author's outline helps us to read much faster because we know what to expect as we read and understand how the details fit in.

So how do we preview? Following is a list of helpful hints:

a. <u>Read the title</u>. First, examine the title of the chapter to get a clue to its general content. A title provides lots of information; unfortunately, in our hurry to get through the chapter itself, it is often too easy for us to skip over it. Following is an example of how a title, had we known it, could have helped to set the stage for the reading.

> The procedure is actually quite simple. First you arrange things into different groups. Of course, one pile may be sufficient depending on how much there is to do. If you have to go somewhere else due to lack of facilities that is the next step, otherwise you are pretty well set. It is important not to overdo things. That is, it is better to do too few things at once than too many. In the short run this may not seem important but complications can easily arise. A mistake can be expensive as well. At first the whole procedure will seem complicated. Soon, however, it will become just another facet of life. It is difficult to foresee any end to the necessity for this task in the immediate future, but then one never can tell. After the procedure is completed one arranges the materials into different groups again. Then they can be put into their appropriate places. Eventually they will be used once more and the whole cycle will then have to be repeated. However, that is part of life. (Bransford and Johnson 722)

Until we find out the title of the passage above, it will be difficult, if not impossible, to make sense of it. Once we know that the title is "Doing Laundry," all of the details actually begin to make sense and the passage becomes understandable. We realize that "the procedure" refers to doing laundry. We can then infer that "arranging things into different groups" refers to separating clothing and that "one pile" means a pile of clothing or one load of laundry. We realize too that "going somewhere else due to lack of facilities" means going to a laundromat that has washers, dryers, detergent, and so forth. A mapping of this paragraph would look like this:

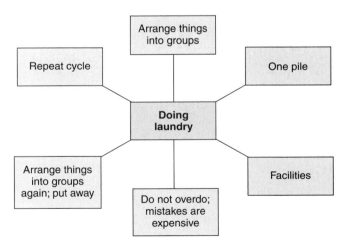

As we can see, a small effort such as paying attention to a title in our textbooks can make a difference in how quickly we understand what we read.

b. <u>Read the introduction</u>. After reading the title, the next step in previewing is to read the introduction of the chapter. In the introduction, the author announces the general content and tells us what information is included in the chapter.

c. <u>Read the summary</u>. After reading the introduction, read the conclusion or the summary. At this point, it is a good idea to compare the introduction with the summary. It should look pretty similar. Just as the opening section introduces the main ideas in the chapter, the conclusion sums up all of the main points that were explained in the chapter. The author wraps up the important content and reviews the major principles and concepts.

There are two reasons why you should be aware of a chapter's main points as you read. First, the knowledge will help you to focus on the important information. Second, reading the summary first will help you to recognize the information most likely to appear on an exam. If a point is made in both the introduction and in the summary, there is a good chance that you will be tested on it.

d. <u>Skim the body of the chapter</u>. After reading the title, the introduction, and the summary, you should read the chapter headings. These generally appear in dark boldface print and provide the general subject of each section. Herein lies the author's outline. The chapter division headings and subheadings set off the author's main thoughts and announce the subtopics. There are usually four to five major headings in a chapter and three to six subheadings under each of these. The subheadings may appear in smaller dark print or italics.

e. <u>Read the first and last sentences of each paragraph</u>. The first sentence of each paragraph is usually the topic sentence, and the last sentence is usually a transition (link) to the next paragraph. By reading the first and last sentences of each paragraph, you will find out what the main ideas are and how they are related to the topic. Oftentimes, it is possible to get a general understanding of an article simply by reading the first and last sentences. You will not know the details, but you will know what the article is about.

f. <u>Look at graphic aids: pictures, charts, graphs, and diagrams</u>. Sometimes complicated concepts are difficult to understand if they are explained in words alone. It may take pages for an author to explain, for example, a scientific process. However, the explanation may be simplified through the use of a picture, chart, diagram, or graph, which often takes only minutes to study and understand. Once we have grasped a concept through the diagram or chart, it becomes much easier for us to read the words that explain it. For example, read the passage below and try to interpret its meaning. It will probably not make much sense. Then look at the picture on the next page and reread the passage.

> If the balloons popped, the sound wouldn't be able to carry since everything would be too far away from the correct floor. A closed window would

also prevent the sound from carrying, since most buildings tend to be well insulated. Since the whole operation depends on a steady flow of electricity, a break in the middle of the wire would also cause problems. Of course, the fellow could shout, but the human voice is not loud enough to carry that far. An additional problem is that a string could break on the instrument. Then there could be no accompaniment to the message. It is clear that the best situation would involve less distance. Then there would be fewer potential problems. With face-to-face contact, the least number of things could go wrong. (Bransford and Johnson 718–19)

After looking at the picture, it is much easier to understand the meaning of the words. In fact, after seeing the picture, it takes almost no effort to read the passage, whereas before seeing the picture, it appeared to be a real brainteaser.

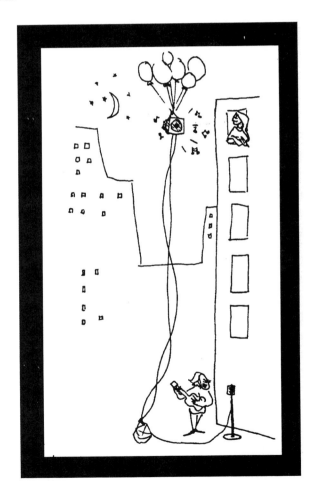

Visual Literacy Box 11.1   ● ● ● ● ● ● ● ● ● ● ● ● ● ●

CHARTS, MATH, AND READING:
THE ANATOMY OF A DRINK II

Read the following paragraph. A pie chart represents 100 percent (%) of a total number of items. Each piece of the pie represents a portion of the 100 percent. Read the paragraph and answer the following questions.

Of the 142 million Americans in the United States, 95 million drink something alcoholic at least once a year; that leaves about 47 million of the adult United States populace as absolute teatotalers. Of the 95 million drinkers, at least 10 million develop serious alcohol-related problems.

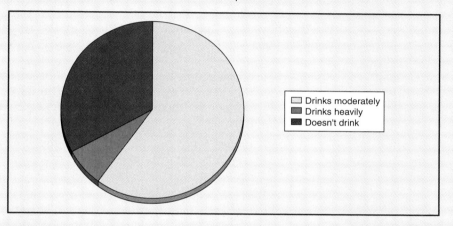

- **a.** What percentage of the population drinks?
- **b.** What percentage of the population drinks heavily?
- **c.** What percentage of the population does not drink at all?

(Hint: Divide 100 by the total number of Americans. Then multiply that answer by a. the number of people who drink, b. the number of people who drink heavily, c. the number of people who do not drink.)

A Reading in Health Science

Alcohol is commonly included in many social activities and in many ways is a part of the American lifestyle. But how can we tell if we or others drink too much? The following article can help us answer these questions. Preview the article and then complete the vocabulary exercise to learn the new terms. Finally, read the article and answer the comprehension questions as you read.

Vocabulary in Context

a. **premise**—idea, principle, basis of an argument

b. **diluted**—weakened, watered down, thinned

c. **retard**—slow down, delay, hinder

d. **unadulterated**—pure, untouched, unmodified

e. **contrary**—the opposite, different, unlike

Use the above terms to complete the following statements. The first one has been done for you.

_____a_____ 1. Many people believe that they cannot possibly have an alcohol problem if they only drink beer. This false _____ makes it difficult for them to believe doctors when diagnosed with alcoholism.

_____ 2. Liquor is not _____ and is therefore taken in smaller amounts. For example, one shot of liquor has the same alcohol content as an entire glass of beer.

_____ 3. Some people brag about how much they drink. But, _____ to their beliefs, hardly anyone can have two drinks that include several liquors each and still function normally.

_____ 4. Hard liquor consists of _____ alcohol; it contains no water or other buffering agents.

_____ 5. The drinker can slow down, or _____, the effects of hard liquor by diluting it with water, fruit juice, or mixes.

The Anatomy of a Drink II

[1]   Every year, doctors treat patients for alcoholism who swear that they can't be alcoholics. They base this belief on the **premise** that all they've ever drunk in their lives is beer. So they have one or two six-packs a day, so what? Beer, after all, has almost "no alcohol." On first glance, it seems a pretty logical argument. Beer does contain only four percent alcohol. But the alcohol is by volume, and therein lies the rub. An ounce of beer contains four percent alcohol. An ounce of 86 proof whiskey contains 43 percent alcohol. While many people stop drinking after one shot of whiskey, who has ever drunk just one ounce of beer? You drink 10

ounces, or 20 ounces, and you have increased your alcohol ingestion in direct proportion to the alcohol content by volume. Therefore, one average mug-and-a-half of beer equals, in alcohol content, about that of one drink. Likewise, a normal-sized glass of wine equals one beer, or approximately one drink.

_b_ **1.** The alcohol content in a normal-sized glass of wine is equal to the alcohol content of
     a. 86 ounces of proof whiskey.
     b. one drink of whiskey.
     c. 20 ounces of beer.
     d. 43 ounces of beer.

Visual Literacy Box 11.2 ● ▪ ● ● ● ● ● ● ● ● ● ● ● ● ● ● ▪ ●

GRAPHS, MATH, AND READING: THE ANATOMY OF DRINK II

The following graph shows how many ounces an average mug of beer, glass of wine, or shot of liquor contains. An ounce of beer contains 4 percent alcohol. An ounce of whiskey contains 43 percent alcohol.

1. Which drink contains the most fluid?

2. Which drink contains the most alcohol?

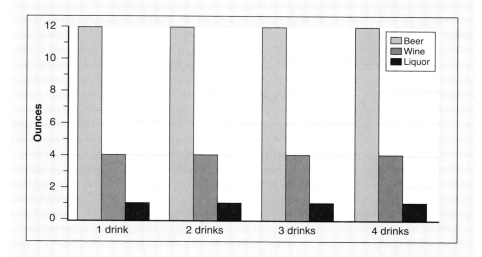

[2]   The effects of wine and beer are slightly less noticeable because the alcohol is more **diluted** by volume than in straight spirits. Similarly, one can **retard** the effects of hard liquor by mixing it with water or a commercial mixer. On the other hand, about the fastest-acting popular cocktail is the straight-up martini, either of the gin or vodka variety. The proof is high, and the drink **unadulterated**; consequently, robbed of any "buffering" agent such as water, the alcohol from such a drink enters the bloodstream very quickly. Few are the men, boasts to the **contrary**, who can imbibe two martinis at lunch and have their work for the rest of the day unimpaired. It would be impossible to calculate the number of man-hours lost every week in the United States as a direct result of the martini luncheon.

_____ **2.** The effects of wine and beer are
  a. much less noticeable than the effects of liquor.
  b. the same as the effects of liquor.
  c. slightly less noticeable than the effects of liquor.
  d. much more noticeable than the effects of liquor.

[3]   **Who drinks, and why?** Ninety-five million Americans drink something alcoholic at least once a year; that leaves about 32 percent of the adult United States populace as absolute teatotalers. Of the 95 million drinkers, at least 9 million develop serious alcohol-related problems. But, the most startling fact of all, the 9 million problem drinkers affect the lives of more than 36 million people! This is the awful legacy of the problem drinker. If his drinking harmed only himself, his problem would not fall too heavily upon the shoulders of society. But when 36 million people are involved as a result of his problem, the situation becomes an urgent one.

_____ **3.** What percentage of the American population does not drink alcohol?
  a. 32 percent
  b. 36 percent
  c. 95 percent
  d. 9 percent

[4]   The fact is that heavy drinking kills—and not just the drinker. Fully half of all highway fatalities are alcohol-related. This means that on the average more than 28,000 people lose their lives on the United States highway system a year as a partial contribution to alcohol misuse. This fact alone is enough to rivet us all into a position of taking a serious look at alcohol in the daily pattern of our social fabric.

[5]   But the statistics don't end on the highway. Fully one-third of all homicides in our country are also alcohol-related. And arrests where alcohol is a factor average close to 2 million a year.

[6]   In dollars, something we are fond of considering, alcohol costs industry, and the American worker and taxpayer, more than $15 billion annu-
ally in medical expenses, lost time, accidents, and impaired job efficiency.

_____ **4.** The author uses statistics to
a. inform us of the number of people who drink.
b. entertain us with trivia.
c. persuade us to believe that alcohol creates many problems.
d. provide information about the United States highway system.

[7]   On the other side of the coin, Americans spend more than $20 billion
each year on alcoholic beverages. The federal government spends less
than $4 million a year on alcohol research and alcohol facilities.

[8]   Grim as these statistics are, they do not mean that alcohol should once
again be prohibited. Clearly, the majority of United States drinkers drink
in a sane and safe way. What the figures do prove is that urgent work is
needed on the gigantic problem of alcoholism. Nine million lives are
directly at stake, plus millions of others who suffer, in one form or
another, from the consequences of the alcoholic's problem.

[9]   Virtually all medical groups, including the AMA, now recognize alcoholism as an illness. So do many insurance companies and health
groups.

[10]   We must first instruct the general public in ways of safe drinking, then
we must reach the alcoholic himself. Prevention of alcoholism is the first
and most important step. This prevention can come about only when all
are made aware of the problem. After this, treatment of the alcoholic
becomes a much simpler process.

_____ **5.** What is the most obvious text pattern in paragraphs 8–10?
a. comparison-contrast
b. term, definition, and example
c. topic with a list
d. problem-solution

[11]   **I drink. Am I an alcoholic?** One of the most insidious aspects of the
disease of alcoholism is its ability to completely mask itself. Few alcoholics, while in the grips of alcoholism, can admit to themselves that they
are diseased. Since no one opens their mouths and physically pours
drinks down them, they can always delude themselves that they are in
control; i.e., to drink they must make the conscious decision to put glass
or bottle in hand, and then to raise that hand to their lips. Since this
action is seemingly a voluntary one, alcoholics are provided with the comforting notion that they are operating under their own steam. They can
stop drinking any time by closing their fists and their mouths. Nothing
could be further from the truth. Alcoholism, regardless of what form it
may take, is a physical and/or psychological addiction, and the alcoholic

is no more capable of altering his disease than a heroin addict is capable of taking one fix for the day. The disease itself demands alcohol, and an alcoholic cannot be written off as a person with poor willpower. Willpower has nothing to do with the disease itself, although willpower has a lot to do with treatment. There is a very subtle, but very vital difference contained in the last statement. We do not tell cancer patients to cure their disease through willpower, and alcoholism cannot be cured by that approach. Cancer and alcoholism are diseases. Both are treatable, although alcoholism cannot be cured, only arrested.

_____ **6.** The author clearly defines alcoholism as
    a. a problem with willpower.
    b. a voluntary decision.
    c. a cancer.
    d. a disease.

[12]   So, who is the safe drinker? And the question can be a difficult one to answer. Simplistically speaking, the safe drinker is one within whom no rationalization, regardless of how subtle, is necessary for the taking of a drink. Whenever rationalization for drinking comes into play, the danger signal should go up.

[13]   If you have a drink because you are offered a drink, and think nothing more beyond that, it's probably quite all right for you to have that drink. If you attend a cocktail party and have one or two drinks, that's probably all right too. But if you habitually desire a drink before one is offered, or if you attend that cocktail party solely because you want to drink, then these are potential danger signals. Preoccupation with alcohol—planning when you will drink, what you will drink—are sure signs that alcohol may be playing too large a part in your life. Here again is where the rationalizations become so simple. It is so easy to say, "I'll just have these drinks to be sociable," or, "Of course I want a drink. I've had such a lousy day." The safe drinker is one who does not drink because an excuse is handy. He drinks. Or he doesn't drink. And he doesn't think of the why and wherefores. He takes it, or he leaves it—and one situation is as easy for him to do as the other. Alcohol makes absolutely no difference in his life.

_____ **7.** The main point of paragraph 13 is:
    a. Most people drink when offered a drink.
    b. Preoccupation with alcohol and a habitual desire to drink are signs of alcoholism.
    c. Most people drink when they have a bad day.
    d. Most people attend cocktail parties only to drink.

[14]   Alcoholism is difficult to define because there are so many types of the disease. It is impossible to give hard-and-fast rules that say this is alco-

holism, and this is not. Even the person who drinks daily will not necessarily become an alcoholic, although such a pattern would certainly predispose one to the disease.

_____ 8. According to the author,
   a. Alcoholism is defined as daily drinking.
   b. Alcoholism is difficult to define.
   c. There are ten hard-and-fast rules that define alcoholism.
   d. Alcoholism is easy to define because there are so many different types.

[15]   Most medical authorities now agree that it is not necessarily how much one drinks that may lead to alcoholism, but why one drinks. And this goes right back to the fact of rationalizing drinking behavior. If you must think about booze, then you should probably give it up. If you crave a drink, you should give it up. If drink is more important than food, stop now and seek help. If alcohol in any way alters your life or work, you're facing trouble. If a lunch without a drink sounds dull, booze has become too much a part of your life. All these things, and many more, are urgent red flags on the road to alcoholism; only the foolhardy—or the alcoholic—will fail to notice them.

_____ 9. All of the following are indicators of alcoholism except:
   a. craving a drink.
   b. buying alcohol before you would buy food.
   c. feeling that lunch would be boring without alcohol.
   d. feeling indifferent about accepting an alcoholic drink.

[16]   If you drink frequently to relieve problems, soothe tensions, forget cares, get happy, have a fight, go to bed, calm your stomach, increase your sex life, take a trip, meet people—you are drinking for wrong reasons. Drink for the wrong reasons long enough, and you will have a real reason to drink—alcoholism. Nine million Americans are all drinking for the wrong reasons.

[17]   Think all alcoholics are skid row bums? Not so. Less than 3 percent of all United States derelicts have drinking problems. Today's alcoholic individual is likely to be bright, well-educated, middle or top management, 35 to 50 years of age, a family man, and well-respected in his community and profession. He simply drinks too much, for all the wrong reasons, and his drinking has led to alcoholism. (Halegood)

_____ 10. According to the author, most alcoholics are
   a. skid row bums.
   b. well-educated family men.
   c. teenagers.
   d. bartenders.

Reading Between the Lines Box 11.2

OUTLINING

The Anatomy of a Drink II

Just as it is easier to see the picture of a puzzle once it is put together, it is easier to read an article when you visualize the author's organization. Reread the article. "The Anatomy of a Drink II" and find the author's outline. Use the list of scrambled topics and support to fill in the outline below.

Scrambled List of Topics

Beer and wine	Alcohol as a disease	Solving the problem
Who drinks, and why?	Hard liquor	Ninety-five million Americans
Heavy drinking kills	Costs of alcohol	I drink. Am I an alcoholic?
Alcohol profits	Alcoholism as an illness	Difficulties in defining alcoholism
Prevention of alcoholism	Safe drinkers	Excuses for drinking
Red flags	Drinking for wrong reasons	Alcohol content

Author's Outline

I. Alcohol content

    a. _____

    b. _____

II. _____

    a. _____

    b. _____

    c. _____

    d. _____

    e. _____

    f. _____

    g. _____

III. _____

    a. _____

    b. _____

    c. _____

(continued on next page)

d. _____

e. _____

f. _____

g. _____

Question (Q) The next step in the PQ4R method will keep you from falling asleep when you read. It is much like playing the television game show *Jeopardy*. You review a section heading and the information from that section to figure out what test question that section answers. While your mind actively ponders a question and searches for an answer, you will not fall asleep.

The questioning step is actually quite a simple process. Start by converting a section heading into a question. Next, read further to see whether the material that follows answers your question. As you continue to read, you may find that your question is too general or too specific. If this turns out to be the case, you need to change your question to reflect the information in the passage.

For example, imagine you are reading for your geology course and come across a section heading in your textbook that reads "Physical and Chemical Changes." You may ask yourself, "What are physical and chemical changes?" As you read, however, you realize that the author is making comparisons between physical and chemical changes. You would then revise your question accordingly so that it asks, "What is the difference between a physical and a chemical change?"

If the reading has no section headings or subheadings, you can turn each topic sentence (generally the first sentence in a paragraph) into a question. If there is no topic sentence, skim the content. Glance through the paragraph and ask yourself, "What question was the author trying to answer when he wrote this?"

If you create a section in your notebook for this phase of reading, you will save quite a bit of time when it comes to studying for exams. Draw a line down the center of your notebook page and write all of the questions from your section headings in the left-hand space. Write the answers opposite from the questions in the right-hand space.

If you take notes like this for every chapter of your textbook you will probably have many of the test questions and their answers. This material will already be organized. When it comes time to study for your exams, you will be prepared to sit down and learn the information.

A Reading in Psychology

A good memory comes in handy during midterm and final exam weeks. Read the article below to find out how we process information and what we can do to improve our ability to remember. Complete the vocabulary exercise first to learn the new terms and answer the comprehension questions that are interspersed throughout the reading. Finally, follow the directions in the Reading Between the Lines Box 11.3 on page 442 to complete the "Q" step in the PQ4R.

Vocabulary in Context

a. **precursor**—forerunner; thing that comes before

b. **impairment**—injury, damage, wound

c. **resilient**—elastic, bounces back from injury

d. **deterioration**—worsening, decline, weakening

e. **simultaneously**—at the same time; all together; at once

Use the above terms to complete the following sentences. The first one has been done for you.

_____c_____ **1.** About half of Alzheimer's patients remember the meanings of words; although much of their memory is damaged, their memory for words is _____.

_____ **2.** We can hold two types of information in our minds _____; we can read our mail while talking on the phone.

_____ **3.** When some people become forgetful, they worry that the forgetfulness is a _____ of Alzheimer's disease.

_____ **4.** A condition that affects memory as people become older is called age-associated memory _____. This condition indicates that simple aging damages the brain to a certain degree.

_____ **5.** One sign of serious mental _____ is when there is a loss of implicit memory, or how to do things such as walk or drive a car.

What We Now Know About Memory

[1]   The alarm finally goes off in your head around 3pm. Your face flushes and your hands plow through the papers on your desk. You have accidentally stood someone up for lunch. It gets worse. You can't remember who. And still worse: you can't recall where you left your glasses, so you can't look up the name in your appointment book.

[2]   Why does our memory betray us? Is this a **precursor** of Alzheimer's disease? Are there ways to make memory clear again?

[3]   First, reassurance: a momentary loss of memory is probably not a sign of Alzheimer's. People between 65 and 75 face only a 4–10 percent chance of Alzheimer's versus a 20–48 percent chance for those over 85. Yet

almost all of us will be tripped up by forgetfulness as we age. Memory may begin to get a little shaky even in our late 30s, but the decline is so gradual that we don't start to stumble until we're in our 50s.

[4]   In recent years some neuroscience researchers have begun to pay more attention to this condition, called age-associated memory **impairment** (AAMI). But because of the enormousness of the job, much about memory is still mysterious. The brain has billions of neurons (nerve cells), many with thousands of connections through which they can send signals to neighboring neurons. Even the most advanced super-computers would be unable to map the potential pathways.

_____c_____ **1.** What is the overall topic of the article?
> a. memory
> b. Alzheimer's disease
> c. neural pathways
> d. semantics

[5]   **Making Memories**. This much is known, however: neuron No. 28, say, fires an electrical signal, and in the synapse where one of 28's connectors touches a receiver of neuron No. 29, a chemical change triggers an electrical signal in 29. That signal gets passed on to neuron No. 30, and on and on. If the connection between 28 and 29 is made often enough, the bond between the two neurons grows stronger. This crucial marriage seems to be the stuff that memory is made of.

[6]   Many scientists believe new information is absorbed and then processed into memory in the hippocampus, a seahorse-shaped organ in the center of the brain. The memories are then stored in sometimes bizarre patterns in various parts of the brain. The names of natural things, such as plants and animals, are apparently lodged in one part of the brain; the names of chairs, machines and other man-made stuff are in another. Nouns seem to be separated from verbs.

_____ **2.** Memories are sometimes stored in bizarre patterns in:
> a. the same part of the brain.
> b. various parts of the brain.
> c. the hippocampus.
> d. the seahorse-shaped part of the brain.

[7]   While age affects our ability to remember, other factors also make a difference. Marilyn Albert, a researcher at Massachusetts General Hospital, notes that among elderly people she has been studying, those who are less educated, less active physically and less able to control their day-to-day lives tend to experience greater memory loss than those better educated, who regard themselves as more in control.

_____ 3. Elderly people tend to experience greater memory loss if they are all but:
   a. less educated.
   b. less physically active.
   c. less able to control their day-to-day lives.
   d. less controlled by others.

[8] **Five Types**. While most people distinguish between long-term and short-term memory, many scientists believe there are actually five types of memory, each with a different likelihood of decaying over time. In order of durability, they are as follows:

[9] *Semantic*. The memory of what words and symbols mean is highly **resilient**; about half of Alzheimer's patients retain much of their semantic memory. It's unlikely you'll forget what "prom" and "mess hall" mean, even though you haven't used the words in years. Nor do you forget religious symbols and corporate trademarks or what distinguishes a cat from a dog. You can add words to your semantic memory until death.

_____ 4. The memory for what words and symbols mean is called
   a. working.
   b. implicit.
   c. semantic.
   d. episodic.

[10] *Implicit*. Chances are, you will never forget how to ride a bike, swim, or drive a car—skills that depend on automatic recall of a series of motions. Conditioned responses, such as reaching for a handkerchief when you sense a sneeze, also aren't likely to disappear. Loss of implicit memory is a sure sign of serious mental **deterioration**.

_____ 5. Implicit memory is the type that:
   a. helps us remember facts.
   b. controls conditioned responses.
   c. helps us remember recent experiences.
   d. helps us remember information for a short period of time.

[11] *Remote*. This is the kind of memory that wins money on *Jeopardy*. It is data collected over the years from schools, magazines, movies, conversations, wherever. Remote memory appears to diminish with age in normal people, though the decline could be simply a retrieval problem. "It could be interference," says Johns Hopkins neurologist B. Gordon. "We have to keep sorting through the constant accumulation of information as we age."

[12] *Working*. Now we enter territory that erodes for most people. This is extremely short-term memory, lasting no more than a few seconds. It is the brain's boss, telling it what to cling to. In conversation, working

memory enables you to hang on to the first part of your wife's sentence while she gets to the end. It also lets you keep several things in mind **simultaneously**—to riffle through your mail, talk on the phone and catch the attention of a colleague walking by the door—all without losing your place.

[13]   Working memory in many people starts to slow down between ages 40 and 50. "Certain environments become more difficult, like the trading floor of a stock exchange, where you have to react very fast to a lot of information," says Richard Mohs, a psychiatry professor at Mount Sinai School of Medicine in New York City. Jet-fighter combat is out.

_____ **6.** The type of memory that allows us to do several things at one time but lasts only a few seconds is:
   a. working.
   b. episodic.
   c. remote.
   d. implicit.

[14]   *Episodic.* This is the memory of recent experience—everything from the movie you saw last week to where you put your glasses. It, too, dwindles over time, and its loss troubles many people. You remember how to drive your car, but you can't recall where you parked it.

[15]   Episodic memory could begin to dwindle in the late 30s, but the downward glide is so gentle that you probably won't notice it for a couple of decades. At 50, however, you are likely to feel a little anxiety as you watch the younger people in the office learn how to operate the new computer software more quickly than you do.

[16]   Several years ago a Massachusetts insurance company asked researchers to develop tests for identifying physicians at malpractice risk. Dean K. Whitla, a Harvard psychologist, and a team of researchers examined 1000 doctors, ages 30 to 80. In one test the subjects were asked to read stories crammed with details, such as street addresses. A few minutes later they took a multiple-choice test.

[17]   Ability declined steadily with age. Though some of the 80-year-olds were as good as the 30-year-olds, on average the 80s could remember only half as much as the 30s. There were also some 80s who couldn't match the patients they had seen that day with their complaints.

_____ **7.** All of the following are different types of memory except:
   a. working.
   b. semantic.
   c. implicit.
   d. synaptic.

[18]   **New Connections**. Unlike cells elsewhere in the body, neurons don't divide. They age, and some percentage of them shrink or die. By the time

someone reaches 65 or 70, neuron No. 28 and some of its neighbors may be dead, or so feeble they no longer transmit electrical charges efficiently. Still, there are billions more neurons remaining. And even though the brain cannot grow new ones, the neurons can probably sprout new synapses late into life and thereby form new connections with one another. William Greenough, a researcher at the University of Illinois, supplied certain lab rats with new toys daily and changed the chutes and tunnels in their cages. When he cut open their brains, he counted many more synapses than in rats that got no toys and no new décor.

_____ **8.** Unlike cells elsewhere in the body:
   a. neurons divide.
   b. neurons don't age.
   c. neurons don't divide.
   d. neurons never die.

[19]   It's a good guess that the human brain, too, grows more synapses when stimulated and challenged. So the brain—even while shrinking—may be able to blaze ever more trails for laying down memory. If neuron No. 28's path is no longer easily passable, the number of alternate routes may be virtually limitless. The trick is to force the brain to make them.

[20]   The habits of highly intelligent people offer a clue as to how to do that. "Memory depends on processing," says Daniel L. Schacter, a Harvard psychology professor. "Very smart people process information very deeply." Perhaps they relate a magazine article on memory to a book on artificial intelligence and a play about prison-camp survivors. Doing so, they could be laying networks of neuron highways that will make the recollection of the article, book or play accessible by multiple routes.

[21]   That might explain why some famous people have boasted extraordinary memories. Conductor Arturo Toscanini knew every note of more than 400 scores. Winston Churchill could recall so much Shakespeare that he would mouth the Bard's words from the audience during performances. Microsoft Chairman Bill Gates still remembers hundreds of lines of source code for his original Basic programming language.

[22]   Could some of these feats be explained by a photographic memory? No, because there's no such thing, say researchers. Though many people can recall lists of numbers or repeat conversations word for word, nobody, says Richard Mohs, "records in a raw, sensory form with the details a photograph does. Everybody's memory is selective."

_____ **9.** Relating a magazine article on memory to a book on artificial intelligence and a play about prison-camp survivors is an example of:
   a. processing information very deeply.
   b. using a mnemonic device.

c. acquiring age-associated memory impairment.

d. Alzheimer's disease.

[23]   **Tricks to Remember**. The good news is that, with effort, people who have average intellects can boost their memories substantially. For example, most people have trouble remembering numbers of more than seven digits or so, a limitation long recognized by telephone companies. But researchers at Carnegie Mellon University trained otherwise undistinguished undergraduates to memorize hundred-digit numbers. Focusing hard on that long string of digits, the students found patterns they could relate to meaningful number series, such as birthdays.

[24]   The forgetting of names bedevils many people, the more so as they age. But Harry Lorayne, 69, a memory coach and performer, can memorize the names of as many as 500 people in the audience. His technique is to look at and listen intently to everyone he encounters and then quickly invent a dramatic image to associate with that person's face and name. "I meet Mr. Bentavena, and I notice he has a big nose," Lorayne says. "So I think 'vane' like weather vane, a nose that's a bent weather vane."

[25]   College students may be superior at memorizing, not only because their neurons are young but also because they are in the habit of developing mnemonic devices to survive exams. That's an easy practice to resume. For example, memory is WIRES—working, implicit, remote, episodic and semantic.

[26]   Another way to improve your memory, according to many experts, is to exercise your brain. You might choose to hang out with challenging, fast-thinking company. Or you might take on a new field of study: accounting, zoology or a language.

[27]   Coming someday perhaps is a memory pill. Cortex Pharmacerticals, Inc., founded by three neuroscientists from the University of California at Irvine, claims to have developed a class of drugs that amplify the signals passed between weakened neurons. The company reports that laboratory tests with rats and preliminary clinical trials on humans in Germany have been encouraging. It hopes to test the drugs soon on Alzheimer's victims.

[28]   These or other drugs may eventually prove to be an effective way to help remember things. But why wait for drugs to be tested and approved? After all, you could be exercising your memory right now by learning Chinese. (L. Smith 98–102)

_____ **10.** All of the following are tricks that can help you remember information except:

a. inventing dramatic images.

b. using mnemonic devices.

c. having a photographic memory.

d. exercising your brain.

Reading Between the Lines Box 11.3

QUESTIONING

What We Now Know About Memory

The second step of the PQ4R method is to turn each of the headings and sub-headings of your chapter into questions and read to find out the answers. Apply the question step to the memory article and use the chart below to record your questions and answers. One example has been provided for you.

Questions and Answers

Questions from Headings	Answers
Making Memories: How are memories made?	1. New information is absorbed and processed into memory in the hippocampus.
	2. Different types of information is stored in different parts of the brain.
When is memory loss greater?	1. _____
	2. _____
	3. _____
Five Types:	1. _____
	2. _____
	3. _____
	4. _____
	5. _____
New Connections:	1. _____
Tricks to Remember:	1. _____
	2. _____
	3. _____
	4. _____
	5. _____

Read and Reflect (RR) During the read and reflect step of the PQ4R, you are, of course, looking for answers to the questions created in the Question step. However, you are also thinking over each sentence to be sure the meaning is clear. Oftentimes, concepts build upon previously discussed information, and so it is important to stop and deal with any information that you do not understand.

When you come to something you do not understand, there are many strategies you could use. You could go to an encyclopedia or dictionary for more information. You could reread the part that is troubling. Or, you could read ahead to see if your questions are answered at a later point in the passage. You may ask another student or even meet with your professor.

During the Reflect step of the PQ4R, we may reduce our reading speed for difficult paragraphs. We may even simply stop and think about what we are reading. There are many questions that we can ask ourselves that will help us process the information in a meaningful way, including the following:

- Can I give an example of this?
- What is the basic meaning of this?
- Can I sum this up into a generalization?
- What evidence supports this?
- How does this relate to the main topic?
- How would I explain this to someone else?
- How could I summarize this?
- How does this relate to my life?
- How does this relate to the professor's lecture or the information discussed in class?

A Reading in Sociology

In terms of relationships, how do we go about finding Mr. or Ms. Right? In the following article, psychologists say that we must *first* become Mr. or Ms. Right! Read the article to find out what we need to do to make a relationship work. (1) Before reading, complete the vocabulary exercise to learn the new terms. (2) Then follow the directions in the Reading Between the Lines Box 11.4 on page 445 to reflect on what you read. (3) After reading, complete the comprehension exercises to check your understanding.

Vocabulary in Context

a. **variable**—factor; issue point; consideration

b. **inevitably**—unavoidably; surely; positively; without a doubt; unquestionably

c. **aspirations**—ambitions; goals; objectives; wants; wishes

d. **clarify**—make clear; explain

e. **crucial**—vital; critical; most important

Use the above terms to complete the following sentences. The first one has been done for you.

_____b_____ 1. Intimate partnerships, without a doubt, _____ reflect a sense of personal adequacy.

_____ **2.** Their twenties are a _____ time in life for young people because they have to figure out where they want to live, who they will marry, and what type of career they would like.

_____ **3.** People who have figured out these three things (career, marriage, and religion) are better able to _____ what they want and make wiser choices when it comes to family matters.

_____ **4.** While choosing a lifetime partner, it is important to consider your _____, or ambitions and goals.

_____ **5.** One factor or _____ that should be considered when trying to achieve a successful marriage is that it is important to strive to become the right partner.

Self in Marriage

[1] Most people are surprised to learn that finding the "right" marriage partner is not the most significant **variable** in achieving a successful marriage; BECOMING the right marriage partner is. The first step in becoming a competent marriage partner is to learn as much as possible about yourself. You must clarify your sense of personal adequacy, which is **inevitably** reflected in intimate partnerships (Marks, 1986). Such self-evaluation is, at best, very unscientific, difficult, and complex, especially because most people see what they wish to see and believe what they wish to believe. While learning to know yourself fully—to understand your desires, **aspirations**, strengths, and weaknesses—is a continuous process, it should be well underway before you choose a lifetime partner. This is a two-fold process. First, your gender identity, your concept of self as feminine or masculine, must be crystallized. Second, your EGO BOUNDARIES, those psychological self-boundaries that differentiate you from others, must be maintained (Rubin, 1984). Persons who have accomplished these developmental tasks are better able to **clarify** their own needs, attitudes, and values and thus are able to make wiser, conscious choices concerning family matters.

[2] The study of marriage and family too often begins with the courtship process, thus ignoring the significance of previous life stages. Courtship in our culture normally bridges that span of time from adolescence to adulthood and progresses in perspective from individualism to couple bonding. A merging of these unfolding life patterns propels each person to seek a partner who will help to continue this process in the most desired direction (Marks, 1986). A person usually chooses a lifetime mate during what has been called the decade of decision, the ages 17 to 27. This period is a **crucial** time for young people to determine not only whether or whom to marry but also what profession or trade to enter and where to live. At

[3]the same time, they usually entertain serious political, religious, and ideological questions. Understanding this process of moving from singleness to pairing in a world of change may facilitate wiser decisions.

Even though marriage preparation most appropriately begins with self-assessment, learning how to assess potential partners objectively also increases the odds for long-term marriage success. Those who expect to eventually marry usually possess an imaginary list of qualities to seek in a lifetime partner. However, for various reasons and despite their best efforts, this list of qualities may fail the test of mate selection. One reason for this failure seems inherent in the very nature of the courting process: gamesmanship. According to the game theory, a framework of personal relationships, games are basically dishonest transactions whereby participants hide their true feelings (DeVito, 1986). Everyone is familiar with the courtship game in which each of the partners presents her/his best image while at the same time covering up more undesirable qualities. Another easily recognized culprit clouding objectivity during courtship is the lens through which a person views the relationship. Love may not be blind, but the rose-colored glasses of romance tend to distort reality and hinder the accurate assessment of partner compatibility (Moore, 1976). A less obvious but more significant issue is the hidden agenda which has lodged deep within the psyches of most persons by marriageable age. Without self-awareness, the process of mate selection is often motivated by this agenda, which seeks to fulfill unmet psychological needs, resulting in the selection of a partner who either seeks or allows a neurotic relationship. (Davidson and Moore 7–8)

Reading Between the Lines Box 11.4

READ AND REFLECT

After reading "Self in Marriage," shut your book and think about how you would explain these ideas to someone who has not read the passage. Write down three points that you felt were the most interesting. Then think about how this information applies to your life.

Interesting Points in "Self in Marriage"

Point 1: _____

_____

Point 2: _____

_____

Point 3: _____

_____

(continued on next page)

(continued from previous page)

How does "Self in Marriage" apply to you?

1. What are your aspirations with respect to career and family?
2. Do you perceive your personality to be masculine or feminine?
3. What makes you different or unique from others?
4. Where would you like to live?
5. What type of work would you like to do?
6. What type of person would you like to marry?
7. What are the three things that you value the most?
8. What are your political and religious beliefs?
9. What qualities would you like a lifetime partner to possess?
10. Have you ever been in a relationship in which someone hid their true feelings from you or vice versa?

Multiple-Choice Questions

_____ b _____ 1. According to the author, the most important variable in achieving a successful marriage is:
   a. finding the "right" marriage partner.
   b. learning about yourself.
   c. evaluating the other person's sense of personal adequacy.
   d. evaluating the other person's ego boundaries.

_____ 2. Before you choose a lifetime partner, your self-evaluation should include all of the following except:
   a. your aspirations.
   b. your strengths.
   c. your ability to cover up undesirable qualities.
   d. your weaknesses.

_____ 3. The "decade of decision" refers to people between the ages of:
   a. 18 and 21.
   b. 21 and 30.
   c. 15 and 25.
   d. 17 and 27.

_____ 4. Gamesmanship refers to:
   a. the process of mate selection.
   b. honest transactions whereby participants sincerely try to get to know each other.
   c. dishonest transactions whereby participants hide their true feelings.

   d. the process of making up imaginary lists of qualities to seek
      in a lifetime partner.

_____ **5.** Without self-awareness, the process of mate selection is often
      motivated by:
      a. gamesmanship.
      b. a hidden agenda.
      c. family requirements.
      d. dating rules.

Recite (R) *Reciting* is the most powerful study technique known to psychologists. During this step of the PQ4R, you should close your book and try to recite the main points and important subpoints, asking yourself, "What have I just read?" Then put these ideas into your own words.

It is wise to use VAK learning—which stands for visual/auditory/kinesthetic memory. As your eyes look at the print, you are using your *visual* memory. Saying the information out loud involves your *auditory* memory, or hearing memory. Writing the information down, typing notes, and drawing sketches and diagrams involves your *kinesthetic* or motor memory. You can increase your memory power by using all three modes of learning.

During the Recite step, you should think about the main points and write down what you want to remember. Choose about ten to fifteen facts. If, for example, a sociology exam will cover three chapters and there will be thirty questions on the exam, that leaves ten questions for each chapter. In this case, you should choose ten main points, write them down, and memorize them. Some chapters may have over 500 facts crowded into them. You cannot remember all of them, so you need to select the most important concepts and make an effort to understand and remember them.

A Reading in Ecology

Did you know that deserts have their own types of plants and wildlife? Read the following excerpt to find out how humans are destroying the natural environments of deserts. Before reading, complete the vocabulary exercise to learn the new terms. After reading, choose five important points made in this reading, write them down, and recite them aloud. Then complete the comprehension exercises to check your understanding.

Vocabulary in Context

   a. aridity—dryness; waterlessness; barrenness

   b. aborigines—ancient tribes of people

    c. irrigation—process of bringing water from a river, lake, or underground lake to a dry grassland or desert surface

    d. depleting—reducing; exhausting; diminishing

    e. degradation—withdrawal; removal

Use the above terms to complete the following statements. The first one has been done for you.

_____a_____ **1.** The _____ of a desert determines how much damage will result from human interaction. The driest deserts have had the least disturbances.

_____ **2.** Ancient peoples, such as the _____, were of hunting and gathering societies and thus did little damage to their environment.

_____ **3.** Today's societies radically change and pollute the desert regions through oil mining, _____ agriculture, and urban development.

_____ **4.** Irrigation projects are quickly _____ the fossil water supply.

_____ **5.** All-terrain vehicles are especially responsible for the massive _____ of the natural vegetation and life that it supports.

Deserts—Human Impact

[1]   In spite of their **aridity**, deserts have not been spared from human impact. Only extremely arid deserts have escaped significant disturbance. Ancient human intrusions were limited to food-gathering and hunting forays by **aborigines** or to grazing by nomadic pastoralists. In recent times most aborigines have vanished and many pastoralists have settled into agricultural communities. Today desert regions, particularly in the Middle East, have been invaded by the oil industry, radically changing and polluting the desert environment. In parts of the Middle East and in North America, urban development has expanded into the desert, complete with lawns and swimming pools. **Irrigation** agriculture also has turned some areas of desert green. These developments are **depleting** the fossil water supply. Deserts are also suffering massive **degradation** by unrestricted recreational use of all-terrain vehicles. Widespread collection of cacti of many species and sizes for the world plant trade in the deserts of the United States, Mexico, Peru, Chile, and Brazil is destroying the integrity of desert ecosystems and threatening some species with extinction in the wild. In the United States, the desert southwest has the greatest number of endangered species, many of which are endemic (common) to the desert region.

[2]   The greatest impact occurs on the semiarid edges of the natural deserts of the world, which support some agriculture and grazing. Their mismanagement of land has created new deserts. Virgin lands, even in dry climates, are able to support some vegetation. The roots of trees, shrubs, and grasses tap the deeper water supply and bind the soil. However, expanding populations and the periods of adequate rainfall encourage encroachment on marginal lands. Overcultivated and overgrazed, the land is exposed to wind and water erosion. Because these regions are subject to unpredictable droughts, the human population finds itself faced with devastating famines and increasing land degradation. Eventually the destruction is total. Vegetation and top soil are gone, dust storms become frequent, and sand dunes advance across the land. The land has reached a point of no return. The result is DESERTIFICATION—the creation of new deserts on the periphery of natural deserts in northern Africa, India, China, Argentina, Chile, Mexico, and the southwestern United States. Formation of new deserts has doubled over the past 100 years.

[3]   Supplied with water and managed well, many desert areas can be converted into productive agricultural land, but poor irrigation practices that allow the seepage of water from canals and over-watering of soil cause the water table to rise. As the moisture evaporates from the surface, it leaves behind a glistening surface layer of salt toxic to plants, and the land is abandoned to the wind. This salinization process has affected irrigated lands in India, Syria, Iraq, central Asia, California's San Joaquin Valley, and the Colorado River Basin. Because irrigation depends on "mined" fossil water beneath the desert and water drawn from rivers, irrigation severely affects the hydrology of deserts, further threatening the future of these regions. (Smith and Smith 417–18)

Five Important Points

1._____

_____

2._____

_____

3._____

_____

4._____

_____

5._____

_____

Multiple-Choice Questions

_____ a _____   **1.** Cacti in United States, Mexico, Peru, Chile, and Brazil are in danger of extinction because
    a. People are taking them out of the desert to sell.
    b. The cacti cannot take the desert heat.
    c. There is not enough water for them to grow.
    d. Irrigation has destroyed the cacti.

_____   **2.** The topic of this passage is:
    a. desertification
    b. human impact on deserts
    c. irrigation
    d. overcultivation

_____   **3.** The main idea of paragraph 2 is:
    a. Overcultivated and overgrazed, the land is exposed to wind and water erosion.
    b. Formation of new deserts has doubled over the past 100 years.
    c. Human impact on the semiarid edges of the natural deserts causes desertification.
    d. Eventually the destruction is total.

_____   **4.** The overall text pattern of this selection is:
    a. compare-contrast.
    b. problem-solution.
    c. cause-effect.
    d. narration.

_____   **5.** From the excerpt below, the implied meaning of the phrase "and the land is abandoned to the wind," the author is saying that:
    . . . poor irrigation practices that allow the seepage of water from canals and over-watering of soil cause the water table to rise. As the moisture evaporates from the surface, it leaves behind a glistening surface layer of salt toxic to plants, and the land is abandoned to the wind.
    a. The wind will sweep away the salt deposit, and the land will be productive again.
    b. The over-watering of soil will create windstorms.
    c. Seepage from water canals will create windstorms.
    d. The land can no longer support plant or animal life.

Visual Literacy Box 11.3 ● ▪ ▪ ▪ ▪ ▪ ▪ ▪ ▪ ▪ ▪ ▪ ▪ ▪ ●

CIRCLE DIAGRAMS: DESERTS—HUMAN IMPACT

Circle diagrams are used to show a cycle. Study the steps in the cycle below. Then find another cycle in the reading and create a similar diagram to show the steps in that cycle.

1 Land is overcultivated and overgrazed.

2 Exposure to wind and water erosion removes vegetation and topsoil.

3 Dust storms become frequent and sand dunes advance.

Review (R) When we finish reading a chapter in a textbook, our first instinct is to put the book away. We know we have read the assignment and believe we have understood it. However, if we took a test on that information a week later, we would probably fail it.

What happens to the material we just learned over the course of the week? A few things may occur: It is possible to understand something we have read but not remember it. It is also possible not to understand something we have read but still remember it. Finally, it is possible both to understand *and* remember what we have read. As critical readers, we should all strive to achieve the last scenario. Without reviewing the material immediately after, chances are that within two weeks we will lose 80 percent of it. Only 20 percent of what we first remembered will be retained. Putting aside time to review the materials we read will help us to retain 80 percent and lose only 20 percent.

Consider what happens if we type something on the computer and neglect to click on the Save button. Of course we would understand what we wrote, but because we did not save it, we cannot recall that information from the computer again—it is gone! Our brains function in a similar fashion. Even if we read information and understand it, we will lose what we have learned if we do not schedule immediate and spaced reviews. The forgetting curve drops after the first hour and then drops sharply after the first 24 hours. Therefore, it is important that we do not close the book after reading a chapter but instead immediately go back to the beginning of the chapter and quiz ourselves on what we just read.

Ideally, we should complete a broad review of the chapter. We do this by returning to the beginning of the chapter and trying to recite its broad organization and to recall the big thought patterns/divisions. Our goal is to look at the author's total picture or identify the major idea.

Next, we should check our memory and understanding of the important subpoints. We can do this by taking an index card and holding it over each paragraph, leaving only the headings and subheadings visible. Then we try to remember what is in each paragraph by looking at the headings and subheadings. If we cannot remember the information, then we should reread the parts we have forgotten. To aid our memories, we find the main points, say them out loud, and write down cue phrases as a memory aid.

Just as an actor memorizes lines well enough to deliver them without error, once we understand the material, we should memorize it until it becomes automatic. This memory technique is called **overlearning** and, in most cases, it will help us overcome test anxiety. For it is possible to understand information and not remember it, remember information that we do not understand, and understand and remember information. If we can both understand and remember the information on a test, our anxiety will diminish.

In addition to overlearning, we should use **spaced reviews**. This means that we will recite and review the information several times on different days to prepare for an exam. For example, if we read a psychology chapter on Sunday night for a Friday exam, we would do an immediate review after reading, and then another review on Tuesday. Again, we might review on Thursday evening and once again before the exam on Friday.

At first, this seems as though it is a lot of work. However, if we spend two to three hours reading a chapter and neglect to do a review, chances are that we will not pass the exam. Even if we remember 50 percent of the material, that is still not enough. Furthermore, as we have said, without a review we will probably only remember 20 percent of the material. If we take the time to complete the review step of the PQ4R and remember 80 percent of the information for an exam, it will then make the time we spent reading the textbook worthwhile.

Reading Between the Lines Box 11.5

APPLICATION
The PQ4R

What did you learn? Take the PQ4R quiz below to test your knowledge. Then apply what you have learned to one of your textbooks. Choose a chapter from one of your textbooks that your professor will soon be discussing in class. Go through all of the steps in the PQ4R. Then determine the following:

1. Did reading the textbook chapter before the class help you to understand the lecture?
2. Did the PQ4R help you recognize the main points of the lecture?
3. Did you find yourself participating more in the class discussion as a result of reading the chapter before the lecture?

PQ4R Quiz

1. List the five steps in skimming a chapter. _____
2. What is available in most textbook chapters that you can use to make up your own questions? _____
3. What does VAK stand for? _____
4. What percentage of the material will you retain if you use the review step? _____

A Reading in Computer Science

Use the PQ4R method to read and study the excerpt below. Answer the vocabulary questions first to become familiar with the new terms. Then answer the questions that pertain to the PQ4R Method.

Vocabulary in Context

   a. **protocol**—procedure
   b. **analogy**—comparison
   c. **cordial**—pleasant; warm and friendly
   d. **remote**—distant; far away
   e. **format**—arrangement; plan; setup; design

Use the above terms to complete the following sentences. The first one has been done for you.

_____a_____   **1.** A _____ is a chain of interactions or a procedure.

_____   **2.** A _____ server is one that is situated some distance away.

_____   **3.** The _____ refers to the arrangement or order of the messages that are exchanged between two or more parties.

_____   **4.** A friendly "Hello" in an email can be interpreted as a _____ message.

_____   **5.** A comparison between human messages and computer messages could be called an _____.

What Is a Protocol?

[1]   Now that we've got a bit of a feel for what the Internet is, let's consider another important buzzword in computer networking: **"protocol."** What is a PROTOCOL? What does a protocol do? How would you recognize a protocol if you met one?

A *Human* Analogy

[2]   It is probably easiest to understand the notion of a computer network protocol by first considering some human analogies, since we humans execute protocols all of the time. Consider what you do when you want to ask someone for the time of day. A typical exchange is shown in Figure 1.2. Human protocol (or good manners, at least) dictates that one first offers a greeting (the first "Hi" in Figure 1.2) to initiate communication with someone else. The typical response to a "Hi" message (at least outside of New York City) is a returned "Hi" message. Implicitly, one then takes a **cordial** "Hi" response as an indication that one can proceed ahead and ask for the time of day. A different response to the initial "Hi" (such as "Don't bother me!" or "I don't speak English," or an unprintable reply that one might receive in New York City) might indicate an unwillingness or inability to communicate. In this case, the human protocol would be to not ask for the time of day. Sometimes one gets no response at all to a question, in which case one typically gives up asking that person for the time. Note that in our human protocol: *There are specific messages we send, and specific actions we take in response to the received reply messages or other events (such as to reply within some given amount of time)*. Clearly, transmitted and received messages, and actions taken when these messages are sent or received or other events occur, play a central role in a human protocol. If people run different protocols (for example, if one person has manners but

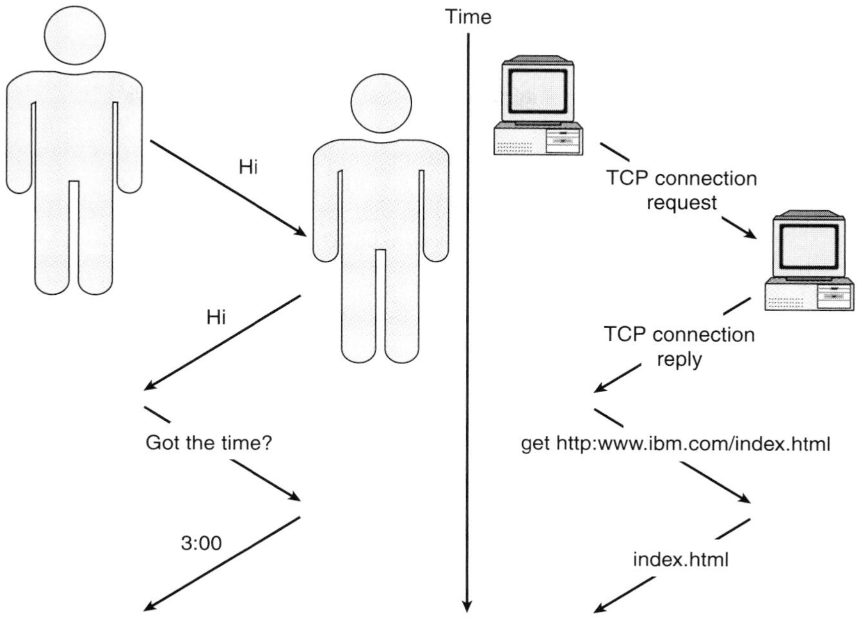

Figure 1.2   A human protocol and a computer network protocol.

the other does not, or if one understands the concept of time and the other does not) the protocols do not interoperate and no useful work can be accomplished. The same is true in networking—it takes two (or more) communicating entities running the same protocol in order to accomplish a task.

[3]   Let's consider a second human analogy. Suppose you're in a college class (a computer networking class, for example!). The teacher is droning on about protocols and you're confused. The teacher stops to ask, "Are there any questions?" (a message that is transmitted to, and received by, all students who are not sleeping). You raise your hand (transmitting an implicit message to the teacher). Your teacher acknowledges you with a smile, saying "Yes. . . ." (a transmitted message encouraging you to ask your question—teachers LOVE to be asked questions) and you then ask your question (that is, transmit your message to your teacher). Your teacher hears your question (receives your question message) and

Visual Literacy Box 11.4 ● ● ● ● ● ● ● ● ● ● ● ● ● ● ● ●

DIAGRAMS: WHAT IS A PROTOCOL?

Below is the protocol for the human analogy described in paragraph 3. Read the paragraph and finish the steps in the protocol below.

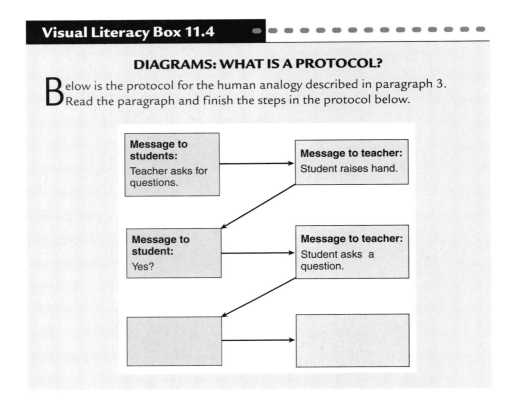

answers (transmits a reply to you). Once again, we see that the transmission and receipt of messages, and a set of conventional actions taken when these messages are sent and received, are at the heart of this question-and-answer protocol.

[4]   A network protocol is similar to a human protocol, except that the entities exchanging messages and taking actions are hardware or software components of a computer network. . . . All activity in the Internet that involves two or more communicating **remote** entities is governed by a protocol. Protocols in routers determine a packet's path from source to destination; hardware-implemented protocols in the network interface cards of two physically connected computers control the flow of bits on the "wire" between the two computers; a congestion control protocol controls the rate at which packets are transmitted between sender and receiver. Protocols are running everywhere in the Internet. . . .

[5]   As an example of a computer network protocol with which you are probably familiar, consider what happens when you make a request to a Web server, that is when you type in the URL of a Web page into your Web browser. The scenario is illustrated in the right half of Figure 1.2. First,

your computer will send a "connection request" message to the Web server and wait for a reply. The Web server will eventually receive your connection request message and return a "connection reply" message. Knowing that it is now OK to request the Web document, your computer then sends the name of the Web page it wants to fetch from that Web server in a "get" message. Finally, the Web server returns the contents of the Web document to your computer.

[6]   Given the human and the networking examples above, the exchange of messages and the actions taken when these messages are sent and received are the key defining elements of a protocol:

[7]   *A protocol defines the format and the order of messages exchanged between two or more communicating entities, as well as the actions taken on the transmission and/or receipt of a message or other event.*

[8]   The Internet, and computer networks in general, make extensive use of protocols. Different protocols are used to accomplish different communication tasks. . . . [S]ome protocols are simple and straightforward, while others are complex and intellectually deep. Mastering the field of computer networking is equivalent to understanding the what, why, and how of networking protocols. (Kurose and Ross 6–7)

Reading Between the Lines Box 11.6

PQ4R

"What Is a Protocol?"

I f you complete a review after reading you will remember 80 percent of what you read. Use the questions below to guide you through a review of the article "What Is a Protocol?"

PQ4R for "What Is a Protocol?"

1. What is the title?

2. What are the major headings?

3. What are the subheadings?

4. What questions can you create from the headings and subheadings?

5. What questions can you create from the topic sentences of each paragraph?

6. What ten facts or ideas do you think you would find on an exam?

7. What key words can you make up to help you remember these ideas or facts?

8. If you knew you were going to be tested on this material, when should you complete your first review?

9. How would you go about planning a spaced review?

10. How would you explain what a protocol is to someone who didn't know?

Comprehension Questions

_____d_____ **1.** The topic of this selection is:
  a. human nature.
  b. e-mail.
  c. the Internet.
  d. Internet protocols.

_____ **2.** The main idea of paragraph 2 is:
  a. If people run different protocols (for example, if one person has manners but the other does not, or if one understands the concept of time and the other does not), useful work can be accomplished.
  b. As with computer networking, it takes two (or more) people communicating with each other using the same type of protocol in order to accomplish a task.
  c. In networking, it takes two (or more) communicating entities running different protocols to accomplish a task.
  d. It takes only one person running a protocol to accomplish a task.

_____ **3.** The structure of paragraph 2 is:
  a. comparison.
  b. topic and list.
  c. description.
  d. time order.

_____ **4.** The overall text pattern for the selection is:
  a. chronological order.
  b. narration.
  c. process.
  d. problem-solution.

_____ **5.** From the human analogy, we can infer that
  a. Internet protocols imitate human interactions.
  b. Human interactions are very different from Internet protocols.
  c. The Internet hardly ever requires protocols.
  d. Computer networks rarely use protocols.

_____ **6.** In paragraph 4, the word **remote** means:
  a. entities.
  b. challenging.
  c. distant.
  d. rewarding.

_____ **7.** The author's purpose for writing this selection is:
  a. to argue a point.
  b. to persuade.

      c. to entertain.
      d. to inform.

_____ **8.** The tone of this selection is:
      a. formal.
      b. friendly.
      c. sympathetic.
      d. fearful.

_____ **9.** In Figure 1.2, human interactions are compared with
      a. computer networking.
      b. a Web server.
      c. a Web document.
      d. a Web page.

_____ **10.** The structure of paragraph 7 is:
      a. topic and list.
      b. description.
      c. narration.
      d. definition.

12

Ensuring College Success

- •

In this chapter, we practice three essential skills that increase our chances of success in college:

- listening to difficult material;
- note-taking from textbooks and lectures (marking, highlighting, annotating, and outlining);
- preparing for exams.

> INSTRUCTOR: What do you do when you go to a lecture? Do you take notes?
>
> LYNNETTE: Not really.
>
> INSTRUCTOR: Do you just go and listen and leave?
>
> LYNNETTE: Yes.
>
> ENRIQUE: It depends on what kind of mood I'm in. If I don't feel like listening, I just space out, draw stuff on my book, or read other chapters . . . sometimes . . . I don't listen at all . . . if a teacher is really boring, I'll space out totally.
>
> LUCY: So far, the teachers I have had here have not been very good note givers . . . . They will write a word on the board and then they will define it. The problem is, they define it just as quickly as I am speaking right now and expect you to write the definition down.
>
> INSTRUCTOR: What do you do when you go to a lecture? Do you take notes?
>
> NEIL: Anything that's written on the board, I write down, anything the teacher writes at all, I write down, anything that I think the teacher says is important, I take notes on . . . if it's a really important lecture, I'll bring a tape recorder with me.
>
> PREYA: Most of the time I try to write exactly what the professor says. When I write, I write in his own words; it's the best way.
>
> ROSHA: I take notes verbatim, every single word . . . people wonder why I write everything . . . It's just easier for me.

Among the six students quoted above, who do you think has the most success in college? Why?

LISTENING BETWEEN THE LINES

There are four obstacles to good listening: (1) lack of interest in the topic, (2) lack of knowledge about the topic, (3) lack of vocabulary knowledge, and (4) difficulty following the speaker's train of thought. How do we overcome these obstacles and become better listeners? We can find some sort of interest in the subject being discussed, increase our knowledge of the topic, increase our listening vocabulary, and identify the structure of the speaker's discussion or lecture.

Find an Interest

If you are interested in a topic, it is easier to stay focused on the speaker. Information will interest you when it affects your life directly or when you know a lot about the topic.

One way to make a lecture more interesting is to create **mental interactions** with the information:

■ Put yourself in the circumstances that you are hearing about. How can this information be applied to your life?

■ Think about how you can use this information. Can you use this information to have a conversation with others? to earn more money? to become more proficient at a certain type of work?

■ Think about how this information could benefit someone else. How could you explain this information to them?

■ Think about cases, situations, or examples in which this information has played a role in the lives of people you know. How were their lives affected? What would you do in similar circumstances?

Always remember, it is the *learner* who makes a subject interesting through *his* active involvement and use of the information.

Learn More About the Subject

To get the most out of a lecture you should prepare ahead. You should always read the textbook chapter before going to a class or read information on the topic if there is no assigned text. The more background information you have on a subject, the easier it is to understand and remember what you hear.

If you know in advance that the material to be covered during the lecture will be highly technical, difficult to understand, or completely unfamiliar to you, you should build your knowledge base before attending. One way to do this is to find books on the same subject that are less technical or written on a lower reading level. Another way to build background knowledge is to read newspaper and magazine articles that are written about the same topic. Speak with someone who is knowledgeable on the topic and ask questions based on news reporting: who? what? where? when? how? why? Finally, you could do an Internet search and begin reading about the topic from the information that you find.

For example, let's say the topic of your next history lecture listed in the syllabus is on the "Cold War" and you are not exactly sure what that means. After reading the explanation in your college text, you still feel confused about this event. You could then go to the library and check out an eighth grade history book and read about it in much simpler terms. Once you have this background knowledge, it is much easier to understand the higher-level text. Next, you could seek out a classmate or professor and ask questions about what you read. Finally, you could look up magazine and newspaper articles or go to the Internet to find more information on the cold war. By expanding your knowledge base, you will increase your ability to listen to new or difficult material.

Increase Your Listening Vocabulary

It can be very boring to listen to speakers who use a high level of vocabulary if you don't know what the terms mean. It takes effort and determination to bring yourself up to their level of communication. However, it can be very exciting to see yourself become more sophisticated in your speech. There are several ways to learn new vocabulary from lectures. As discussed above, reading the textbook and learning the new terms before the lecture provides a solid base for understanding words used in speech.

A second way to learn vocabulary from a lecture is to designate a portion of your notebook to new terms. During every lecture, write down all unfamiliar words along with the sentence or phrase in which they were used. After the class, look up these words in the dictionary and choose the meaning that makes sense with the given phrase or sentence in your notes. Write the meanings in your notes. Listen for these words to be used again in the following lectures. Try using these words in their proper context during class discussions.

Use "Thought Speed" to Your Advantage

Most speakers talk at a rate of about 150 words per minute. We can think at about four times that speed. Although we can be tempted to use class time to daydream, we can better use this **thought speed** to find the organization of the lecture and judge the content of the speaker's message. We can ask ourselves questions such as:

- What is the speaker's purpose for giving the lecture? Is it to inform, entertain, or persuade?

- What is the speaker's organizational pattern? Is it comparison-contrast? problem-solution? term, definition, and example? topic and a list?

- If directions are being given, what exactly are we required to do? What are the steps of the process, and in what order should we complete them?

- Is the speaker's information true to our own experiences? Will this new information change what I believe to be true?

- Does the speaker have good support for his statements and arguments? Is he giving us facts, statistics, or personal experiences? Is his support logical? Does his support contain any fallacies?

Reading Between the Lines Box 12.1

LISTENING TO DIFFICULT MATERIAL

Every evening, public television airs *The News Hour with Jim Lehrer*. During the first five to ten minutes, there is a summary of the day's news. After the news, two or three debates on current issues are presented.

1. Listen to one segment/debate and write down each speaker's main points. Then, go to the *News Hour's* website and read the transcripts (word-for-word printout) of that debate. Write in the main points that you missed while listening.

2. If you are unable to watch the *News Hour* on television, go to the website and choose one segment. Listen to the debate on real audio and then read the transcripts of the debate.

The News Hour Index (http://www.pbs.org/newshour/newshour_index.html)

Commentator's Questions	Speaker 1	Speaker 2	Speaker 3
Main Points	1.	1.	1.
	2.	2.	2.
	3.	3.	3.
	4.	4.	4.
	5.	5.	5.

NOTE-TAKING

Good listeners take notes. Therefore, be ready to listen for the speaker's outline or the organizational pattern of her lecture. Once you identify the topic, the main points (important main ideas), and the organization of the supporting details (information that explains the main ideas), you can easily make a written record of the information. You need to recognize if the speaker is providing a solution to a problem or comparing two things. You need to realize if he is presenting examples to support an idea or if he is presenting evidence to support an argument.

Many types of clues help you recognize the speaker's main points. The speaker may provide:

■ an outline of his lecture on a chalkboard, transparency, or PowerPoint presentation;

■ a summary of important points at the end of the lecture;

■ key words and phrases that introduce us to the main points or alert us to any changes in reasoning:

- The following are key words and phrases that help us recognize a main point:

Above all	The most important ideas are	This is the problem
The main point is	Statistics indicate	The solution to this is
The most important thing to remember is		

- Key words and phrases that help us recognize when supporting details fall into topic and list, sequence, or example patterns include:

Topic and List Pattern	Sequence Pattern	Example Pattern
first	the first step is	to illustrate
second	first	a demonstration
third	the process is	for example
also	next	
in addition	after that	
furthermore	finally	

- Key words and phrases that show us the speaker is changing direction or giving an opposite view are:

nevertheless	whereas	on the contrary
but	this is not always true	
however	different from this	

- Key words that indicate uncertainty or show that a statement has not been proved are:

perhaps	probable causes	sometimes
possible	may or may not	

■ A speaker's tone of voice and body language are other clues to his intended meaning. For example, the sentence "This is a good idea" could mean many things depending on the speaker's intonation and expressions.

This is a good idea! (excited, enthusiastically)
This is a good idea? (unsure, questioning)
This is a *goooood* idea. (sarcastic)

Finally, as we are listening to a speaker, we should try to make connections with what we are hearing to our own life experiences or to what we have read or heard about from other sources.

EXERCISE
12-1

Locating Clues to Organization

Key words provide clues to the organization of a presentation. Select the appropriate key words for the following actions. The first one has been done for you.

_____c_____ **1.** Which key word or phrase shows us the speaker is changing
direction or giving an opposite view?
  a. perhaps
  b. statistics indicate
  c. however
  d. after that

_____ **2.** Which key word or phrase helps us recognize when supporting
details fall into a topic and list pattern?
  a. to illustrate
  b. in addition
  c. a demonstration of this is
  d. for example

_____ **3.** Which key word or phrase helps us recognize a speaker's main point?
  a. sometimes
  b. on the contrary
  c. nevertheless
  d. above all

_____ **4.** Which key word or phrase helps us recognize when supporting
details fall into a sequence pattern?
  a. the process is
  b. to illustrate this
  c. for example
  d. the main point is

_____ **5.** Which key word or phrase helps us recognize when supporting
details fall into an example pattern?
  a. furthermore
  b. after that
  c. to illustrate this
  d. the first step is

Visual Literacy Box 12.1 ● ■ ● ● ● ● ● ● ● ● ● ● ● ■ ● ●

LISTENING FOR THE AUTHOR'S OUTLINE

Go to National Public Radio's homepage and choose a talk that is interesting to you. Listen to the real audio report and practice listening for the topic, the main points, and the supporting details. Listen to the audio report again and think about the speaker's outline.

1. Which organizational pattern does it follow?

2. Read the transcript of the talk and record the main points.

(continued on next page)

(continued from previous page)

3. Write down any key words that helped you identify the main points.

4. Record facts or details that are related to the main points.

5. Organize your main points and details into outline form.

National Public Radio (http://www.npr.org)

Topic: _____

Main Points: 1.
      2.

Key Words: 1.
      2.

Details related to the main points: 1.
      2.
      3.
      4.

Outline. (Your outline may vary from this format.):

      I.
        A.
          1.
          2.
        B.
          1.
          2.

      II.
        A.
          1.
          2.
        B.
          1.
          2.

Knowing how to take good notes is an essential skill needed to achieve as well as sustain college success. In the next section, you will learn how to take effective notes from your textbooks and class lectures. Let's take a look at the following textbook techniques first.

Marking

Marking is an extremely useful study technique. We mark the text for future reference. The purpose is so that later when we are reviewing the information, we will be able to see the main points and supporting information at a glance without having to read the entire page again. Also, when we mark the text, we can see exactly what to lift from the page and write into our notes.

It is best to read a paragraph to get a grasp of the main points before we mark it. It is also a good idea to mark with a pencil, so that we can erase if we find we have marked more than is necessary. Let's take a look at the way the following excerpt is marked:

As they develop this ability, at first children are able to take only the role of (significant others,) individuals who significantly influence their lives, such as **ex:** parents or siblings. By assuming their roles during play, such as by dressing up in their parents' clothing, children cultivate the ability to put themselves in the place of significant others. (Henslin 62)

The text pattern is term, definition, and example. Therefore, we drew a circle around the *term*, underlined the *definition*, and wrote the abbreviation *ex*: next to the phrase that gave an example of the term.

Visual Literacy Box 12.2

CHARTING COMPARISONS: STUDENT SUCCESS

Think of someone you know who has a high grade point average and think of someone else you know who has a low grade point average.

1. Make a list of all of the things that your high-GPA friend does that you believe make him or her successful. Then write them in the table below under "Behaviors of high-GPA friend."

2. Make a list of all of the things that your low-GPA friend does that you believe hold him or her behind academically. Then write them in the table below under "Behaviors of low-GPA friend."

3. What similarities do you see in their behaviors?

4. What differences can you see in their behaviors?

   Save this information for use in Reading Between the Lines Box 12.2 on page 468.

Behaviors of high-GPA friend	Behaviors of low-GPA friend
1.	1.
2.	2.
3.	3.
4.	4.
5.	5.
6.	6.

EXERCISE
12-2

Marking Practice

Read the following passage and mark the main points.

Many political scientists are critical of **investigative journalism**—the use of detective-like reporting methods to unearth scandals—which often pits reporters against political leaders. There is evidence that TV's fondness for investigative journalism has contributed to greater public cynicism and negativity about politics. Most analysts would agree that the most important change in media coverage of politics in recent years has been the much greater scrutiny to which politicians are now subjected.

Scholars distinguish between two kinds of media: the **print media**, which include newspapers and magazines, and the **broadcast media**, which include radio, television, and the Internet. Each has reshaped political communication at different points in American history. It is difficult to assess the likely impact of the Internet at this point, but there is at least some reason to believe that political communication is being reshaped once again. (Edwards, Wattenberg, and Lineberry 195)

Highlighting

Highlighting does the same thing as marking, but it is faster and easier. However, because it is fast and easy, we can end up highlighting too much. When this happens, all the information appears to be a main point and we are back at square one in trying to read almost all of the text when we review.

We can do two things to avoid highlighting too much. One is to mark the text in pencil first and then highlight only the main points. The other is to read the text first and carefully consider what to mark. In either case, it is wise to read the text before marking and/or highlighting. Let's take a look at the way the following excerpt is highlighted.

> The looking-glass self contains three elements: (1) We imagine how we appear to those around us. For example, we may think that others see us as witty or dull. (2) We interpret others' reactions. We come to conclusions about how others evaluate us. Do they like us for being witty? Do they dislike us for being dull? (3) We develop a self-concept. Based on our interpretations of how others react to us, we develop feelings and ideas about ourselves. A favorable reflection in this "social mirror" leads to a positive self-concept, a negative reflection to a negative self-concept. (Henslin 62)

The text pattern is "topic with a list." The "looking-glass self" is the topic, and the numbered items present a list of characteristics of the topic. Examples are also included. When highlighting, we would emphasize only the topic and main points. If we tried to highlight the examples or any additional information, we would end up highlighting the entire paragraph and thus defeat our purpose for making some information stand out.

Reading Between the Lines Box 12.2

WRITING INTRODUCTIONS

Student Success

Look at the chart that you created for the Visual Literacy Box 12.2. Use it to write an introduction to a comparison-contrast essay.

(continued on next page)

Step 1: Use the following questions in writing your topic sentence.

1. What is your topic?

2. Which two persons are you comparing?

3. How many things can you think of that help one person become more successful than the other?

Step 2: Now write this information into a complete sentence. For example: My friend Hanif has better grades than Olif for several reasons.

Step 3: Write three more sentences explaining what causes one person to be more successful than the other:

1. Who studies more?

2. Who goes to class more often?

3. Who is more prepared for class?

Step 4: Reread your introduction.

EXERCISE
12-3

Highlighting Practice

Read the following passage and highlight the main points.

> Another symbolic interactionist, George Herbert Mead (1863–1931), who taught at the University of Chicago, added that play is critical to the development of the self. In play, children learn to **take the role of the other**, that is, to put themselves in someone else's shoes—to understand how someone else feels and thinks and to anticipate how that person will act.
>
> Young children attain this ability only gradually (Mead, 1934; Coser, 1977). In a simple experiment, psychologist J. Flavel (1968) asked 8- and 14-year-olds to explain a board game to some children who were blindfolded and to others who were not. The 8-year-olds gave the same instructions to everyone, while the 14-year-olds gave more detailed instructions to those who were blindfolded. The younger children could not yet take the role of the other while the older children could. (Henslin 62)

Annotating

Once we mark a text and know the main points and support, we can take this information and write it in the margin of the page. We can later review the main points and supporting information at a glance without rereading the page or turning to other notebooks.

Let's take a look at the way the following excerpt is annotated.

significant others—
individ.s who sig.
influence our lives ex:
parents or siblings

As they develop this ability, at first children are able to take only the role of significant others, individuals who significantly influence their lives, such as **ex:** parents or siblings. By assuming their roles during play, such as by dressing up in their parents' clothing, children cultivate the ability to put themselves in the place of significant others. The looking-glass self contains three elements: (1) We imagine how we appear to those around us. For example, we may think that other see us as witty or dull. (2) We interpret others' reactions. We come to conclusions about how others evaluate us. Do they like us for being witty? Do they dislike us for being dull? (3) We develop a self-concept. Based on our interpretations of how others react to us, we develop feelings and ideas about ourselves. A favorable reflection in this "social mirror" leads to a positive self-concept, a negative reflection to a negative self-concept. (Henslin 62)

Looking-glass self:

We:

(1) imagine how we
appear to others.

(2) interpret others'
reactions.

(3) develop a self-concept.

EXERCISE
12-4

Annotating Practice

Read and annotate the following passage.

[Technological advances] altered the fundamental character of work. In general, we see three changes:

1. **From tangible products to ideas**. As we discussed in earlier chapters, the industrial era was defined by the production of goods; in the postindustrial era, work involves manipulating symbols. Computer programmers, writers, financial analysts, advertising executives, architects, editors, and all sorts of consultants make up the labor force of the information age.

2. **From mechanical skills to literacy skills**. The Industrial Revolution required mechanical skills, but the Information Revolution requires literacy skills: speaking and writing well and, or course, using computers. People able to communicate effectively enjoy new opportunities; people with limited literacy skills face declining prospects.

3. **From factories to almost anywhere**. Industrial technology drew workers into factories located near power sources, but computer technology allows workers to be almost anywhere. Laptop computers, cell phones, and portable fax machines now turn the home, car, or even an airplane into a "virtual office." New information technology blurs the line between work and home life. (Macionis 412)

Outlining

Outlining is important. The outline is a visual display of main ideas and supporting details. When we look at an outline, we can tell instantly which ideas are the main points and which ideas support them. Outlines also put information into categories and make recall much easier. For example, the list of words is the same in each column below. Which arrangement would you rather try to memorize?

starches	**I. Meat**
chicken	A. chicken
oranges	B. ham
meat	C. roast beef
lettuce	**II. Starches**
bread	A. bread
rice	B. rice
ham	C. potatoes
tomatoes	**III. Fruit**
cucumbers	A. oranges
bananas	B. apples
apples	C. bananas
roast beef	**IV. Vegetables**
potatoes	A. lettuce
vegetables	B. tomatoes
fruit	C. cucumbers

Most people would choose the arrangement on the right because it is organized into categories. Once you have looked over the list, it is easy to remember the four food groups and the types of food that belong to them. The arrangement on the left side is more taxing for our memory because it is presented as a list of random items and does not distinguish between the main points and subpoints or details.

EXERCISE
12-5

Outlining Practice

Create an outline for an essay that would compare the work of a homemaker with that of an office worker. Categorize the following items to show how the main points, subpoints, and details would fit together in outline form: vacuum cleaner, home, family members, computers, office tools, telephones, printers, coworkers, friends, office, home appliances.

Visual Literacy Box 12.3 ● ▬ ● ▬ ● ▬ ● ▬ ● ▬ ● ▬ ● ▬ ● ▬ ● ▬ ● ▬ ● ▬ ●

OUTLINING: STUDENT SUCCESS

Reread the introduction that you wrote about student success. Follow the steps below to create an outline for an essay to go with your introduction.

Step 1: Identify three reasons why one friend is successful. Write them in the outline below under roman numeral I. For each reason, find two things that you observed your friend say or do that made you think this has contributed to his or her success.

Step 2: Identify three reasons why one friend is unsuccessful. Write them in the outline below under roman numeral II. For each reason, find two things that you observed your friend say or do that made you think this has contributed to his or her lack of success.

I. Successful friend

   A. One reason for success _____

      1. What did he or she say or do that leads you to believe this is a good reason? _____

        _____

        _____

      2. What did he or she say or do that leads you to believe this is a good reason? _____

        _____

        _____

   B. One reason for success _____

     _____

      1. What did he or she say or do that leads you to believe this is a good reason? _____

        _____

        _____

      2. What did he or she say or do that leads you to believe this is a good reason? _____

        _____

        _____

(continued on next page)

C. One reason for success

_____

   1. What did he or she say or do that leads you to believe this
is a good reason? _____

_____

_____

   2. What did he or she say or do that leads you to believe this
is a good reason? _____

_____

_____

II. Unsuccessful friend

A. One reason for failure _____

   1. What did he or she say or do that leads you to believe this
is a good reason? _____

_____

_____

   2. What did she or he say or do that leads you to believe this
is a good reason? _____

_____

_____

B. One reason for failure_____

_____

   1. What did she or he say or do that leads you to believe this
is a good reason? _____

_____

_____

   2. What did she or he say or do that leads you to believe this
is a good reason? _____

_____

_____

(continued on next page)

(continued from previous page)

C. One reason for failure

_____

1. What did she or he say or do that leads you to believe this is a good reason? _____

_____

_____

2. What did she or he say or do that leads you to believe this is a good reason? _____

_____

_____

Paraphrasing and Summarizing

Paraphrasing involves finding the main ideas in a paragraph and putting them into our own words. We should mentally paraphrase every paragraph when reading information that we will be tested on. If we can put the information into our own words, then we know we understand it. Also, we will have a better chance of remembering it.

Example

The mass media are "the new parent," according to many observers. Average grade-school youngsters spend more time each week watching television than they spend at school. And television now displaces parents as the chief source of information as children get older.

Paraphrase

Television has become the authority figure for children, since they spend more time watching television than they do with their parents or in school.

Summarizing condenses or shortens the amount of text to one-third its length. We take only the main points and most important support and write it in paragraph form.

Example

Unfortunately, today's generation of young adults is significantly less likely to watch television news and read newspapers than their elders. A recent study attributed the relative lack of political knowledge of the youth of the 1990s to their media consumption, or more appropriately, to their lack of it. In 1965, Gallup found virtually no difference between age categories in frequency of following politics through the media. By the 1990s, a considerable gap had opened up, though, with older people paying the most attention to the news and young adults the least. If you have ever turned on the TV news and wondered why all the commercials seem to be for Geritol, laxatives, or denture cream, now you know why. (Edwards, Wattenberg, and Lineberry 169)

Summary

In 1965, both young adults and older people followed politics through the media. By the 1990s, a considerable gap had opened up: Older people pay the most attention to the news, while young adults today are less likely to watch television news and read newspapers.

Reading Between the Lines Box 12.3

SUMMARIZING/DRAWING CONCLUSIONS

Student Success

Complete the steps below to write an essay on student success. Finish the essay with a conclusion

1. Using your notes from the Visual Literacy Box 12.3, write the information from your outline in sentence form, with each roman numeral starting a new paragraph. **You should finish with six paragraphs altogether.**

2. Paraphrase the main points made in each of the six paragraphs.

Paragraph 1: _____

Paragraph 2: _____

Paragraph 3: _____

Paragraph 4: _____

Paragraph 5: _____

Paragraph 6: _____

3. Draw a conclusion. Explain in one sentence why one friend was more successful than the other. _____

| EXERCISE 12-6 | **Paraphrasing Practice** |

Read and paraphrase the following selection.

> Do you have your own personal definition of success? Regardless of the particular goals you have in mind, you need to think positively to attain them. Have you ever heard the saying, "It's all in your head"? People who say this believe that our mental attitudes have control over our body and our life and can, therefore, program our success or failure. Although many of our attitudes and beliefs come from early messages we received from our parents and teachers, as adults we can choose to keep or change these messages, depending on how helpful they are to us in achieving success and satisfaction in life. (Sukiennik, Bendat, and Raufman 21)

Paraphrase:

_____

_____

Taking Notes from Textbooks

Note-taking is just like annotating, except that we write the main points and support into a separate notebook instead of writing in the textbook. We also put this information into some type of organized form. There are many systems of note-taking. The Cornell System is very popular among college students. With this system, we divide our notebook page into three sections, as shown in the example below. In the right-hand column we write our main points and support in outline form. Then, we look at the information we have written in the right-hand column and ask ourselves what questions it answers. We write the questions in the left-hand column. (If the information consists mainly of terms and definitions, a simple question and answer format may work better than an outline format.) Finally, at the bottom of the page we write, in paragraph form, a summary of that page's notes. Let's look at an excerpt from a psychology text and the notes taken from it in Cornell form:

Locus of Control

The locus of control describes a person's belief as to the location of the cause for his success or failure. Julian Rotter (1966) presented locus of control as having two dimensions: external locus of control and internal locus.

An "external" person perceives the causes for events as located outside himself, thus external to the person. An external person believes that he has little control over the outcome and fails to perceive a cause-and-effect relationship between his actions and the consequences. Thus, Joan, who feels that she always fails the test because "the teacher hates her," is clearly placing the source for her success or failure onto the teacher. In contrast to such an external locus of control, the student who feels that she didn't do very well on the quiz because she really didn't study is placing the cause of the failure within herself and as such is demonstrating an internal locus of control. (Parsons, Hinson, and Sardo-Brown 299: *From* Educational Psychology *(non-Info Trac Version) 1st edition by Parsons/Hinson/Sardo-Brown. Copyright © 2001. Reprinted with permission of Wadsworth, a division of Thomson Learning: www.thomsonrights.com. Fax 800-730-2215.)*

Questions	Notes
What is the locus of control (LOC)?	belief as to the location of the cause for his success or failure
What is an external LOC?	person perceives the causes for events as located outside himself Ex.: Joan blames her teacher for her failure on the test
What is an internal LOC?	person believes the causes for events are located within Ex.: the student who feels that she didn't do very well on the quiz because she really didn't study

Summary: Locus of control refers to what a person believes causes his success or failure. If the person has an external locus of control, he believes the causes for events are located outside himself. He fails to perceive that his actions have consequences. If a person has an internal locus of control, he believes the causes for events are located within himself and understands that his actions have consequences.

EXERCISE 12-7

Note-taking with the Cornell Method

Read and take notes from the following excerpt using the Cornell System.

A *system* is defined as a set of concepts or parts that work together to perform a particular function. A system may comprise many subsystems. Transportation is an easily understood system, whether it be by plane, train, or car. Drive the freeways in a large city and see how they are designed as a system with subsystems such as interchanges and on- and off-ramps. All must work, or the system will start to break down. The five interconnected **reservoirs,** or subsystems, of the complete earth system are:

- The **solid earth**, which includes soil, the rocks beneath our feet, the **lithosphere** (the earth's rocky outer shell), and the very hot, mushy interior
- The **hydrosphere**, all water on and in the earth, including oceans, lakes, rivers, clouds, underground water, and glaciers
- The **biosphere**, all living and dead organic components of the planet. The **ecosphere** is a subsystem of the biosphere that includes the biosphere and its interactions with the other reservoirs.

- The **atmosphere**, the gaseous envelope surrounding the earth
- The **extraterrestrial**, which includes such things as energy from the sun, meteors, tides, back-radiation of energy from the earth to space, and the ozone layer. (Pipkin and Trent, Chapter 2)

Questions	Notes
Summary:	

TAKING NOTES FROM LECTURES

It is easier to read a textbook than it is to listen to a lecture for two reasons. Textbook information is more organized than speeches because the writer can write and rewrite the information until the meaning is very clear. Also, while we are reading a textbook we are able to stop at any point and think about the information or even re-read sections to gain an understanding of the author's organization and meaning.

We lose this advantage when listening to a lecture because the speaker has control of the pace and the words vanish into thin air as quickly as they are spoken. A speaker may forget a point and then later remember and mention it out of his planned sequence of ideas. Once spoken, a speaker cannot revise his words. A speaker may also drift away from his original outline or insert a long-winded example to further explain a point. Questions from the listeners may further drive the speaker from his intended organization. Therefore, our notes may end up a little jumbled at the end of the talk. There are a couple of things we can do to transform lecture information into organized notes.

First of all, never go to a lecture cold. Review your syllabus for what the instructor plans to discuss during your next class. Then read and take notes on the information in the textbook that corresponds to the lecture. This will help you become familiar with the new terms and their spellings and enable you to recognize them in the lecture. You will already be familiar with the concepts associated with the material and will be able to make the necessary connections when the speaker mentions them. It will also be easier for you to organize your notes because you will have seen the way this information was organized in your textbook.

Second, you should write down any questions that you may have from reading the textbook *and* questions you may have about anything you do not understand in a lecture. I*t is extremely important to ask* because it is much easier later to study notes that make sense than to try to memorize notes that you don't understand.

Finally, you should re-write your lecture notes immediately after the talk; you can rearrange jumbled parts and fill in any missing information before you forget it.

Setting Up a New Notebook

The best way to take notes from a class lecture is to buy a three-ring binder and to write only on one side of the page. Label each day's notes with the topic of the lecture and the date. This enables us to rewrite notes and place them in the best order. It is a good idea to read and take notes from the textbook chapter before the lecture. Leave the first page blank. The notes from the textbook chapter should start on the second page on the right-hand side of the notebook. This leaves the back of the first page to write lecture notes.

Once at the lecture, we can open to our first page of notes and compare them with the information provided by the speaker. If the information is already in our textbook notes—there is no need to write it a second time. If we have any gaps in our textbook notes, items that we did not understand or questions that were not answered by the text—we can quickly jot them down on spaces left blank in our notes or on the left-hand side under "lecture notes."

The information from the speaker may fill in the gaps that we have from our textbook reading. The speaker may also provide additional information that is not in our textbooks. By setting up our notebooks in this way, we are sure to get all of the information from both the lecture and the textbook without writing notes twice.

EXERCISE
12-8

Taking Lecture Notes with the Cornell Method

Apply the Cornell Method of taking notes to one of your lecture classes.

1. First, read the chapter(s) that the speaker will talk about.

2. Then, organize your notebook to include areas on each page for questions, notes, and summaries.

3. Take notes from the lecture.

4. Write questions in the margin and a summary of each page if you have time during the lecture or immediately after the lecture.

Creating a System

We should employ an overall note-taking technique, such as the Cornell Method, and use an outline, mapping, or chart format within that system to show the difference between the main points and supporting information. We also need to develop a system of abbreviations so we can write the information as quickly as possible. Since it takes so long to write entire sentences, our notes should include only the important points, supporting information, and examples. We can especially leave out words that carry little meaning, such as *the* and *a*.

Example: Abbreviations for note-taking

And	+
equals	=
number	#
therefore	∴

EXERCISE
12-9

Abbreviation Practice

Create your own system for abbreviating words for note-taking purposes. Practice abbreviating the following words. Then look at your abbreviations while covering the words. Can you tell what your abbreviation means? If not, choose another abbreviation that will quickly remind you of the word.

Word:	Abbreviation:	Word:	Abbreviation:
because		decreases	
the		for example	
without		biological	
increases		physiological	

Use a Key Word Technique

Once we have our notes in perfect order, we should use a study technique such as the recite-and-review step of the PQ4R to help us memorize our notes. At this point, we want to think up one key word to remind us of each main idea and its supporting details. Memorizing these key words will help us recall the information in our notes when we are taking an exam. We can number the key words and place them in the left-hand column across from the information they represent.

As in the review step of the PQ4R, we should quiz ourselves on the content of the notes by looking at the key word clues and reciting the corresponding information several times during the week before an exam. We can also use the key words to make up possible test questions. If we have trouble remembering the information that is connected with any of the key words, we need to study the information some more and quiz ourselves again on the weak areas.

Example of key word technique:

Associative learning is learning that a particular stimulus or a particular response is linked to a reward or punishment. If you keep a pet, you probably have observed one type of associative learning first-hand. A dog or cat will learn to associate a particular sound or word with some type of punishment or reward. Often times ducks in a pond will learn to associate the presence of people with handouts and will congregate rapidly whenever someone approaches the shoreline. This type of learning, in which an arbitrary stimulus is associated with a reward or a punishment, is called **classical conditioning**.

In natural settings, a much more common form of associative learning is trial-and-error learning. In this case, an animal learns to associate one of its own behavioral acts with a positive or negative effect. The animal then tends to repeat the response if it is rewarded or avoid the response if it is harmed. For example, a coyote that has obtained a face full of quills when attacking a porcupine learns to avoid attacking porcupines nose-first.

Another form of learning is **imitation**—learning by observing and mimicking the behavior of others. For example, jaguar cubs may develop a sense of which prey are easiest to kill partly by imitating their mother.

Innovation, sometimes called reasoning, is the ability to respond appropriately to a new situation without prior experience. Innovation involves an ability to analyze problems and to think of possible solutions to them. This type of learning is rare, and we see it mostly in primates. For example, if a chimpanzee is placed in a room with several boxes on the floor and a banana hung high above its head, the chimp will gradually "size up" the situation and then stack the boxes in order to reach the food. (Campbell, Mitchell, and Reece 744–45)

KEY WORDS AND CONCEPTS FOR NOTES

Types of Learning

Key Word	Term or concept	Definition	Example
Associative—dog	**Associative learning**	Stimulus/response is linked to reward or punishment.	Dog learns to associate a word with some type of reward.

(continued on next page)

Word	Term or concept	Definition	Example
Classical—duck	**Classical conditioning**	Arbitrary stimulus is associated with reward or punishment.	Ducks associate people with handouts and run up to them.
Imitation—cub	**Imitation**	Learning by observing and mimicking behavior of others.	Jaguar cubs develop sense of easiest prey to kill by imitating mother.
Innovation—chimp	**Innovation**	Appropriate response to new situations w/o experience. Analyze problems/think of solutions.	Chimpanzee stacks boxes to reach food.

EXERCISE
12-10

Creating Quiz Questions for Self-Study

Let's say that that you are in a biology course and that tomorrow's daily quiz will include the information from the passage above. Create three multiple-choice questions and three short-answer questions to use in studying for the quiz. Follow the example below:

Question: Define associative learning and give an example.

Answer: Associative learning is when either a stimulus or a response is linked to a punishment or a reward. For example, dogs and cats are able to associate certain words with either a punishment or a reward.

Question: The type of learning involved when a chimpanzee reasons that it can get a banana that is out of its reach by stacking boxes and climbing up them high enough to get the banana is called:

    a. associative learning

    b. classical learning

    c. imitation

    d. innovation

Short Answers

1. **Question:** _____

   Answer: _____

2. Question: _____

   Answer: _____

3. Question: _____

   Answer: _____

Multiple-Choice

1. Question: _____

   a. _____

   b. _____

   c. _____

   d. _____

2. Question: _____

   a. _____

   b. _____

   c. _____

   d. _____

3. Question: _____

   a. _____

   b. _____

   c. _____

   d. _____

TAKING NOTES FOR EXAM PREPARATION

Professors realize that we may not do well on the first exam of a course sim-ply because we did not know what to expect. Many of them keep old exams and copies of lecture notes on file in the library. This is so we can look over an exam similar to the one we will be taking and plan how to study for it. Therefore, it is a good idea to study the format of old exams. We should not confuse this advice with studying an old exam as a shortcut for learning the information from the textbook and lectures. *We will surely fail* if we take this shortcut. A three-page exam cannot possibly teach us how to understand all the information in a 600-page textbook or replace the forty-five hours of lecture/discussion that goes on in a classroom.

Recognizing possible test questions is not that difficult. There are not many places where test questions can come from. The instructor can test only on items that are covered in the assigned readings or class discussions/lectures. Therefore, we can try to guess the questions that will be on the exam, and we can also prepare the answers and memorize them before the exam.

The exam format will drive the way that we take and study our notes. For example, rereading a chapter is a good strategy for a multiple-choice exam. We read the chapter once through to gain an understanding of the information. Then, we read it a second time and create multiple-choice questions and distracters (incorrect choices) from the information as we read.

When we study for an essay exam, we should look for lists of items that can be defined, explained, or discussed. Because the grading of essay exams can be subjective, professors look for answers that contain lists of items that can be counted. In this way, they will be able to say that Susan's paper deserved an A because she included "all six types of love." However, Sam received a B because he left out one of the types in his explanation.

Guessing the test questions from lectures is not any more difficult. However, we must always be on our toes, or the clues could slip past us unnoticed. One thing we should notice are the questions the professor asks the class, writes on the board, includes on pop quizzes, or repeats in one or more lectures. If his questions are important enough to bring up in class, they will be important enough to include on an exam. We should also pay attention to questions that students ask the professor. Chances are that if they did not understand a point, we may not have understood it either. Other students may also bring up questions or problems that may have gone completely unnoticed to us. Finally, we should watch for class discussion of information from our reading assignments. If it is discussed in depth, then we know it will appear on the exam.

What do we do with all of these possible exam questions? We should be writing questions in the left-hand margin of our notebook and answers to these questions in the right-hand margin of our notebooks **after every textbook reading** *and* **after every lecture**. If we keep up with this system throughout the semester, we should have many of the test questions and answers to the test before we start to study. If we don't keep up with this question/answer system, we may end up using all of our study time to search for and organize information. We may even run out of time for memorizing and learning it.

EXERCISE 12-11

Creating Essay Questions for Self-Study

Choose one subject that you are studying and use the following key words to create essay questions for an upcoming exam. Use the information in your textbook and your lecture notes to predict the questions. After predicting the questions, choose one question and write out the answer. Use the information in your textbook and in your notes to formulate your answer.

1. **Discuss:** The term discuss asks you to examine and analyze. This means to write about any conflict and present the pros and cons regarding the conflict or problem involved. It also calls for you to compare and contrast elements if possible. This type of question calls for a complete and detailed answer.

2. **Define:** Provide the term, its definition or meaning, and an example that illustrates or shows the meaning in terms that people can relate to.

3. **Describe:** Write a detailed summary of events. Provide all characteristics, parts, or qualities of the object or subject.

4. **List/Enumerate:** Both terms direct you to mention one after another or present an itemized series of facts, reasons, ideas, events, etc. These items should be written in sentence and paragraph form—not numbered or bulleted.

5. **Compare:** Show both similarities (how they are alike) and differences of two or more concepts, persons, ideas, things, etc. Contrast means to only show the differences.

Reading Between the Lines Box 12.4

WRITING THE ESSAY

Student Success

Use the drafts that you created in previous boxes to answer the following essay question: *Why are some students successful in college while others fail?* Your essay should be eight paragraphs long:

1 paragraph

    a. **Introduction**—Use the paragraph that you wrote for Reading Between the Lines Box 12.2.

6 paragraphs

    b. **Body**—Use the six paragraphs that you wrote for Reading Between the Lines Box 12.3.

1 paragraph

    c. **Conclusion**—Use the sentences that you wrote for steps 2 and 3 in Reading Between the Lines Box 12.3 as your conclusion.

Integrating Text and Lecture

One way to make sure that we have not missed any information in the juggling of lecture notes and textbook notes is simply to combine them. Divide your notebook paper into three sections, as shown below. As stated earlier, you should always read the textbook before going to class so that you are already familiar with the new information. So, the first step is to attend the lecture and take notes in the middle column. The third step is to combine the information from the first two columns.

Textbook Notes	Lecture Notes	Combined Notes

Combine the information by looking for information that is common to both columns and write that in the third column. Then take the remaining information from the left column and write it in the third column. Finally, take any information remaining in the middle column and write that in the third column. If you find there is not enough space for taking notes when the paper is divided into thirds, then use one side of a piece of paper for taking notes from the textbook. Then take notes from the lecture on one side of a separate piece of paper. Then combine the notes from these two on a third piece of paper.

EXERCISE 12-12

Combining Textbook and Lecture Notes

Read and take notes from a textbook chapter that you will be discussing in class soon and will be tested on. Using the table above, take notes from the textbook in the left-hand column. When you attend the lecture on that topic, take notes in the middle column. After the lecture, combine the notes from the first two columns and write them in the third column.

A Reading in Political Science

Who owns and controls the information that we read in the newspapers everyday? Read the following passage about the print media to find out. Answer the vocabulary questions first to become familiar with the new terms. After reading, mark and annotate the passage. Then, answer the comprehension questions that follow.

Vocabulary in Context

a. proliferation—increase; rise

b. ratification—authorization; permission; approval

c. propensity—tendency

d. magnates—entrepreneurs; industrialists; capitalists; businesspersons

e. divested—parted from; disassociated from; separated from

Use the above terms to complete the following sentences. The first one has been done for you.

_____b_____ **1.** In 1791, the _____ of the First Amendment guaranteed American newspapers freedom to print whatever they saw fit.

_____ **2.** The American press has a _____ to put the government's faults on public display by reporting its mistakes.

_____ **3.** Businesspeople who earn tremendous wealth and power through their enterprises are often called _____.

_____ **4.** Winston Churchill accused American journalists of parting from the truth or being _____ of the truth.

_____ **5.** The _____ of the newspaper began in the mid-1800s, when technological advances made it affordable for everyone to be able to buy a daily paper.

The Print Media

[1]   The first American daily newspaper was printed in Philadelphia in 1783, but papers did not **proliferate** until the technological advances of the mid-nineteenth century. The **ratification** of the First Amendment in 1791, guaranteeing freedom of speech, gave even the earliest American newspapers freedom to print whatever they saw fit. This has given the media a unique ability to display the government's dirty linen, a **propensity** that continues to distinguish the American press today.

[2]   Rapid printing and cheap paper made possible the "penny press," which could be bought for a penny and read at home. In 1841, Horace Greeley's *New York Tribune* was founded, and in 1851 the *New York Times* began. By the 1840s, the telegraph permitted a primitive "Wire service," which relayed news stories from city to city faster than ever before. The Associated Press, founded in 1849, depended heavily on this new technology.

[3]   At the turn of the century, newspaper **magnates** Joseph Pulitzer and William Randolph Hearst ushered in the era of "yellow journalism." This sensational style of reporting focused on violence, corruption, wars, and gossip, often with a less than scrupulous regard for the truth. On a visit to the United States at that time, young Winston Churchill said that "The essence of American journalism is vulgarity **divested** of truth." In the midst of the Spanish-American conflict over Cuba, Hearst once boasted of his power over public opinion by telling a news artist, "You furnish the pictures and I'll furnish the war."

[4]   Newspapers consolidated into chains during the early part of the twentieth century. Today's massive media conglomerates (Gannett, Knight-Ridder, and Newhouse are the largest) control newspapers with 78 percent of the nation's daily circulation. Thus, three of four Americans now read a newspaper owned not by a fearless local editor but by a corporation headquartered elsewhere. Often these chains control television and radio stations as well. (Edwards, Wattenberg, and Lineberry 195).

Comprehension Questions

___d___ **1.** The topic of this selection is:
      a. yellow journalism.
      b. media conglomerates.
      c. the "penny press."
      d. the history of print media.

_____ **2.** The main idea of paragraph 4 is:
      a. Today's massive media conglomerates control newspapers with 78 percent of the nation's daily circulation.
      b. Newspapers consolidated into chains during the early part of the twentieth century.
      c. Three of four Americans now read a newspaper owned by a corporation located outside of their community.
      d. Corporate chains control television and radio stations as well as the print media.

_____ **3.** The overall text pattern of this passage is:
      a. comparison-contrast.
      b. topic and list.

c. description.
d. time order.

_____ **4.** One inference the author makes in paragraph 4 is:
   a. Today local editors have much control over what is printed as news.
   b. Massive corporations have little control over what is printed in local newspapers.
   c. In most cases, local editors can no longer report the news as they see fit.
   d. The information printed in most local papers is unique to those particular towns.

_____ **5.** The *New York Times* has been in circulation for:
   a. approximately one half-century.
   b. approximately one century.
   c. approximately one and a half centuries.
   d. approximately two centuries.

A Reading in Developmental Psychology

Developmental psychology deals with the various psychological phases that people experience throughout their lives. Researchers note trends that they see time and again. Read the passage below to gain an understanding of different views of the emotion "love." Answer the vocabulary questions first to become familiar with the new terms. After reading, answer the comprehension questions and follow the directions to complete an outline of the ideas presented in this selection.

Vocabulary in Context

   a. predominantly—mainly mostly; primarily

   b. physiological—about bodily processes

   c. manifestations—signs; symptoms

   d. palpitations—throbs; beats; pulsations

   e. idealization—glorification; idolization

Use the above terms to complete the following sentences. The first one has been done for you.

____a____ **1.** When people analyze their style of love, they _____ can be found to fit into one or two of the given categories.

_____ **2.** When some people fall in love, their heart races, or rather they experience _____ of the heart and trembling.

_____ 3. In romantic types of love relationships, _____ of the other person is common; people tend to overlook the other person's faults and idolize them.

_____ 4. The physical _____ of strong attraction can include trembling and breathlessness.

_____ 5. Developmental psychology is a combination of the psychological and _____ changes that people experience as they go the various stages of life.

Styles of Love

[1]   According to Lasswell and Lobsenz, lovers may blend any combination of the following styles of loving, but they tend to *predominantly* fit into one or two categories in most cases.

[2]   **Erotic love**: This is the romantic, erotic love that is portrayed in songs and movies. Characterized by strong emotion, intense attraction, it can arouse joy, ecstasy, and exhilaration. It can also arouse fear, jealousy, and depression if feelings are not mutual or are even so suspected. There are strong elements of sexual attraction, *physiological manifestations* like *palpitations* of the heart, trembling, breathlessness, and a certain amount of *idealization* of the love object.

[3]   **Friendly love**: This type of love is based on feelings of friendship. Ease of communication, similarity of interest, and a sense of compatibility contribute to feelings of respect and liking for the other person. Liking in a relationship brings a certain relaxation and comfort that affords security and dissolves tension.

[4]   **Playful love**: Playful love sees love as a game or challenge. There are probably elements of competitiveness in most persons that may surface in love relationships. Certainly the problem of getting one's needs met is more complex when there is another to think about, and playful love seeks to make sure one gets one's way through teasing, flirtation, game-playing. In modern American culture, this aspect is often seen as manipulative, but in other cultures it is often seen as a necessary means of keeping a relationship interesting, balanced, and satisfying to both partners. Playful lovers, however, tend to be more focused on the excitement and challenge of love, and find commitment difficult and uninteresting.

[5]   **Dependent love**: This type of love develops when one feels that one's needs are met by a particular person. In its simplest form, it is the kind of love a baby feels for the mother who feeds, clothes, and holds her. It is also the kind of love that develops between adults if they have intense needs that have been denied in the past. This may occur because the lover is a dependent type of personality or simply because their partner brings out a part of the personality they are not in touch with, as when a hard-working man

falls for a woman who recognizes his capacity to be a playful, uninhibited lover. Dependent lovers can be extremely possessive and jealous.

[6]   **Pragmatic love**: The pragmatic lover focuses on the practical aspects of a relationship, and on desired qualities of a prospective partner. Called "love with a shopping list," this type of love is very realistic, and people who love in this manner know exactly what type of person they want, and are willing to wait until they find him or her. Feelings fade, according to this type of lover, but if the relationship is based on a good match of desired qualities, stability is more likely.

[7]   **Altruistic love**: This is defined as an unselfish concern for the well-being of another, the investment of one's emotions and energies in caring for another individual and seeking what is best for them. By nurturing and doing all that one can to make the other happy, the lover finds meaning and fulfillment. This kind of love blends respect and caring for the person with voluntarily taking a responsibility to give to the other whenever one can. At its best, this style of love engenders no feelings of martyrdom or being put upon. Rather it seems to rest in a genuine belief in giving, and a deep reservoir of loving kindness. This kind of unselfish love occurs far less in real life than might be imagined. Few people have the emotional strength to be so giving, and even if they do they may have hidden agendas about some form of "repayment." Nowadays, some even may suspect that this form of loving is "co-dependent." Nevertheless, many people do have elements of this style in their own form of love. (Manis 88–89)

Comprehension Questions

____d____ **1.** The topic of this selection is:
  a. codependence.
  b. respect and caring.
  c. romance.
  d. types of love.

_____ **2.** The main point of the selection is:
  a. The pragmatic lover focuses on the practical aspects of a relationship.
  b. Lovers generally fit into one or two of the categories mentioned (styles of love).
  c. Many people have elements of altruistic love in their own style of loving.
  d. Erotic love can also arouse fear, jealousy, and depression if feelings are not mutual.

_____ **3.** This type of love focuses on getting one's needs met through manipulation and game-playing:
  a. erotic love.
  b. friendly love.

      c. playful love.

      d. dependent love.

_____ **4.** The overall text pattern for the selection is:

      a. chronological order.

      b. narration.

      c. process.

      d. topic with a list.

_____ **5.** This kind of love is characterized by respect, caring, and a genuine belief in giving:

      a. pragmatic love.

      b. altruistic love.

      c. dependent love.

      d. friendly love.

    Below is a partial outline of the "Styles of Love" passage. Reread the passage and fill in the missing details.

Styles of Love

    I. Erotic love

        A. characterized by

            1. strong emotion

            2. intense attraction

            3. joy an exhilaration

        B. If feelings are not mutual

            1. fear

            2. jealousy

            3. depression

    II. Friendly love

        A. Characterized by

            1.

            2.

            3.

        B. Liking brings

            1.

            2.

III. Playful love

    A. Getting needs met by

        1.

        2.

        3.

    B. More focus is placed on

        1.

        2.

    C. Commitment is seen as

        1.

        2.

IV. Dependent love

    A. This develops when

        1.

        2.

        3.

    B. Can be

        1.

        2.

V. Pragmatic love

    A. Focuses on

        1. caring for another individual

        2. doing what is best for him or her

    B. Stability happens when there is a good match of desired qualities.

VI. Altruistic love

    A. Characterized by

        1.

        2.

    B. Blends respect and caring with responsibility

C. Genuine beliefs in

1.

2.

Summary:

A Reading in Economics

Most people are very interested in making money. But what does money represent? Why do we need to have it? Read the following passage to find out how we came to use money. Complete the vocabulary exercise first to become familiar with the new terms and remember to answer the comprehension questions that follow the reading. Then, use the Cornell Method to take notes on this reading. Write your questions in the left-hand column and the answers to your questions in the right-hand column. Below, summarize the passage. Highlight only the main points in the summary.

Vocabulary in Context

a. **medium**—means; method; or way for accomplishing some task

b. **transaction**—business deal or contract

c. **monetary**—dealing with money

d. **commodity**—product service goods; article of trade

e. **currency**—money; coins; cash

Use the above terms to complete the following sentences. The first one has been done for you.

_____b_____ **1.** The use of money requires more than one _____ or business deal to buy something.

_____ **2.** *We use paper* _____ in our business exchanges because it is easily carried and stored.

_____ **3.** Examples of items that have served as money include cattle, olive oil, beer or wine, copper, iron, gold, silver, rings, diamonds, and cigarettes. We can refer to each of these items as a _____.

_____ **4.** Bartering is much more complicated than a _____ exchange in which currency is used instead of commodities.

_____ **5.** Anything that serves as a commonly accepted _____ of exchange can be called money.

The History of Money

[1]   What is money? *Money is anything that serves as a commonly accepted* **medium** *of exchange.* Because money has a long and fascinating history, we will begin with a description of money's evolution.

[2]   *Barter.* In an early textbook on money, when Stanley Jevons wanted to illustrate the tremendous leap forward that occurred as societies introduced money, he used the following experience:

> Some years since, Mademoiselle Zelie, a singer of the Theatre Lyrique at Paris, . . . gave a concert in the Society Islands. In exchange for an air from Norma and a few other songs, she was to receive a third part of the receipts. When counted, her share was found to consist of three pigs, twenty-three turkeys, forty-four chickens, five thousand cocoa-nuts, besides considerable quantities of bananas, lemons, and oranges . . . In Paris . . . this amount of live stock and vegetables might have brought four thousand francs, which would have been good remuneration for five songs. In the Society Islands, however, pieces of money were scarce; and as Mademoiselle could not consume any considerable portion of the receipts herself, it became necessary in the mean time to feed the pigs and poultry with the fruit.

[3]   This example describes barter, which consists of the exchange of goods for other goods. Exchange through barter contrasts with exchange through money because pigs, turkeys, and lemons are not generally acceptable monies that we or Mademoiselle Zelie can use for buying things. Although barter is better than no trade at all, it operates under grave disadvantages because an elaborate division of labor would be unthinkable without the introduction of the great social invention of money.

[4]   As economies develop, people no longer barter one good for another. Instead, they sell goods for money and then use money to buy other goods they wish to have. At first glance this seems to complicate rather than simplify matters, as it replaces one **transaction** with two. If you have apples and want nuts, would it not be simpler to trade one for the other rather than to sell the apples for money and then use the money to buy nuts?

[5]   Actually, the reverse it true: two **monetary** transactions are simpler than one barter transaction. For example, some people may want to buy apples, and some may want to sell nuts. But it would be a most unusual circumstance to find a person whose desires exactly complement your own—eager to sell nuts and buy apples. To use a classical economic phrase, instead of there being a "double coincidence of wants," there is likely to be a "want of coincidence." So, unless a hungry tailor happens to find an undraped farmer who has both food and a desire for a pair of pants, under barter neither can make a direct trade.

[6]   Societies that traded extensively simply could not overcome the overwhelming handicaps of barter. The use of a commonly accepted medium of exchange, money, permits the farmer to buy pants from the tailor, who buys shoes from the cobbler, who buys leather from the farmer.

[7]   *Commodity Money.* Money as a medium of exchange first came into human history in the form of commodities. A great variety of items have served as money at one time or another: cattle, olive oil, beer or wine, copper, iron, gold, silver, rings, diamonds, and cigarettes.

[8]   Each of the above has advantages and disadvantages. Cattle are not divisible into small change. Beer does not improve with keeping, although wine may. Olive oil provides a nice liquid currency that is as minutely divisible as one wishes, but it is a bit messy to handle. And so forth.

[9]   By the nineteenth century, commodity money was almost exclusively limited to metals like silver and gold. These forms of money had intrinsic value, meaning that they had use value in themselves. Because money had intrinsic value, there was no need for the government to guarantee its value, and the quantity of money was regulated by the market through the supply and demand for gold or silver. But metallic money has shortcomings because scarce resources are required to dig it out of the ground; moreover, it might become abundant simply because of accidental discoveries of ore deposits.

[10]   The advent of monetary control by central banks has led to a much more stable currency system. The intrinsic value of money is not the least important thing about it.

[11]   *Modern Money.* The age of commodity money gave way to the age of paper money. The essence of money is now laid bare. Money is wanted not for its own sake but for the things it will buy. We do not wish to consume money directly; rather, we use it by getting rid of it. Even when we choose to keep money, it is valuable only because we can spend it later on.

[12]   The use of paper currency has become widespread because it is a convenient medium of exchange. **Currency** is easily carried and stored. The value of money can be protected from counterfeiting by careful engraving. The fact that private individuals cannot legally create money keeps it scarce. Given this limitation on supply, currency has value. It can buy things. As long as people can pay their bills with currency, as long as it is accepted as a means of payment, it serves the function of money.

[13]   Most money today is bank money—checking deposits in a bank or other financial institution. Checks are accepted in place of cash payment for many goods and services. In fact, if we calculate the total dollar amount of transactions, nine-tenths take place by bank money, the rest by currency.

[14]   Today there is rapid innovation in developing different forms of money. For example, some financial institutions will now link a checking account to a savings account or even to a stock portfolio, allowing customers to write checks on the value of their stock. Firms are working on ways for people to use the Internet to pay all their bills electronically. (Samuelson and Nordhaus 165–67)

Comprehension Questions

___d___ **1.** The topic of this selection is:
   a. modern money.
   b. commodity money.
   c. bartering.
   d. the history of money.

_____ **2.** The main point of this selection is:
   a. Firms are working on ways for people to use the Internet to pay all their bills electronically.
   b. Money has taken on many forms in the past and is continuing to change.
   c. Money is anything that serves as a commonly accepted medium of exchange.
   d. Two monetary transactions are simpler than one barter transaction.

_____ **3.** The structure of paragraph 2 is:
   a. methods.
   b. topic and list.
   c. narration.
   d. time order.

_____ **4.** Text patterns that can be seen in this selection include:
   a. topic and list.
   b. term, definition, and example.
   c. process.
   d. all of the above.

_____ **5.** Today the most common form of exchange is:
   a. bartering.
   b. commodities.
   c. currency.
   d. bank money.

_____ **6.** In paragraph 5, the word *reverse* means:
   a. backward.
   b. setback.
   c. opposite.
   d. same.

_____ **7.** The author's purpose for writing this selection is:
   a. to argue a point.
   b. to persuade.
   c. to entertain.
   d. to inform.

_____ **8.** The tone of this selection is:
   a. formal.
   b. friendly.
   c. sympathetic.
   d. fearful.

_____ **9.** An exchange of soccer equipment for concert tickets would be an example of:
   a. bartering.
   b. commodity money.
   c. currency.
   d. bank money.

_____ **10.** Which of the following is not a problem with commodity exchanges?
   a. Monies with intrinsic value did not need government guarantees.
   b. It is difficult to mine metallic money.
   c. Accidental discoveries of ore deposits could make metallic money too common.
   d. It is difficult to get an even exchange.

Questions	**Notes**
Summary:	

Improving Your Reading Speed

In this chapter will learn:

■ how to adjust our reading rate according to our purpose;

■ how to skim and scan texts;

■ how to increase comprehension as well as reading speed.

On the first day of class you receive a reading list that seems a mile long, and you have only one semester to complete each text. What are you to do? The following article describes what one student, Aaron Hall, a Harvard undergraduate student and psychology major from Dunlap, California, class of 1999, did to ease himself into the demands of college reading:

> [Hall] signed up for the Harvard Course in Reading and Study Strategies, a seminar offered by the Bureau of Study Counsel that teaches students how to improve their reading and comprehension skills. He took the course in the fall of his freshman year, and in the following fall he was asked to assist the instructor.
>
> [Hall explains,] "I took the course for reading comprehension. The amount of reading [required] for a single class at Harvard is a lot more than anyone is used to [reading] in high school."
>
> The course, which started in the 1940s, was the precursor to the Evelyn Woods speed-reading course, according to Bureau Director Charles Ducey. The 14-day program, which draws about 200 to 300 students a year, introduces new ways of reading, such as deciding what needs to be read,

reading with a question in mind, discerning the implicit structure of expository text, and teaching oneself to keep one's eyes moving forward, not back, over a text. This is done, in part, through the use of new, upgraded teaching tools such as a computer-based videodisk text that mimics the experience of reading at varying speeds, from 180 words to more than 600 words per minute. The new technology will be debuting this fall.

The course, which is taught by the Bureau staff five times a year and is subsidized for students, can be frustrating, and some students become discouraged in their efforts to keep up with the films.

"Around day ten is the frustration point," Hall said. "It's very fast. There is a daily quiz, and my scores didn't go up—but my speed did. What they expect you to get out of the course is a different mindset about how to approach your work." *(Harvard University Gazette)*

SPEED READING

It's true. If you increase your reading speed, you can read more books in less time. For example, two students are enrolled in the same political science course. They are each required to read seven average-length books in twelve days. Linda reads at 150 words per minute (wpm), and Tony reads at 350 wpm. If Linda expects to complete all seven books, she will need to read for four hours each day. On the other hand, Tony will be able to complete all seven books by reading for only two hours each day. It seems that Tony has the advantage.

However, as we can see from the Harvard students' experiences, increasing speed without increasing comprehension can be very frustrating. Why does this happen?

Let's suppose that Tony has increased his speed to 350 wpm, but his comprehension level is at 50 percent. In other words, he has read seven books in twelve days but understood only half of what he read. He would like to get an A or a B on the next exam, and he feels confident that he will, since he was able to complete the entire reading assignment.

Linda, however, still reads everything slowly and carefully; nevertheless, she can understand 100 percent of everything she reads. That is, although Linda understands what she reads, it takes her twice as long to complete her assignments. She finds that each day she can only read half of the books before having to leave for soccer practice.

When the exams are returned, Tony is shocked to see a D– on the top of his exam, and Linda is relieved to see B appear on her paper. But, if we think about it logically, both students understood the same amount. Tony understood half of what he read, and Linda read half of the assignments. To earn an A, Tony needs to raise his comprehension level to 100 percent, and Linda needs to increase her reading speed to 100 percent of what she is assigned. The solution to frustrating experiences like this is to increase *both* reading speed and understanding.

A Reading in Interpersonal Communication

What is your reading speed and comprehension of college-level material? To find your reading rate, first record your starting time. Then read the passage below at a comfortable pace. In other words, read fast enough to stay interested in the passage, but at the same time read slowly enough to understand what you are reading. When you are finished, record your ending time. Then, answer the comprehension questions at the end of the passage. Finally, calculate your reading rate by using the formula described in Reading Between the Lines Box 13.1 on page 503.

Compliance-Resisting Strategies

[1]   Let's say that someone you know asks you to do something you don't want to do, for example, lend your term paper so this person can copy it and turn it in to another teacher. Research with college students shows that there are four principal ways of responding (McLaughlin, Cody, and Robey, 1980; O'Hair, Cody, and O'Hair, 1991).

[2]   In **identity management**, you resist by trying to manipulate the image of the person making the request. You might do this negatively or positively. In *negative identity management*, you might portray the person as unreasonable or unfair and say, for example, "That's really unfair of you to ask me to compromise my ethics." Or you might tell the person that it hurts that he or she would even think you would do such a thing.

[3]   You might also use *positive identity management*. Here you resist complying by making the other person feel good about himself or herself. For example, you might say, "You know this material much better than I do; you can easily do a much better paper yourself."

[4]   Another way to resist compliance is to use **non-negotiation**, a direct refusal to do as asked. You might simply say, "No, I don't lend my papers out."

[5]   In **negotiation**, you resist compliance by, for example, offering a compromise (I'll let you read my paper but not copy it") or by offering to help the person in some other way ("If you write a first draft, I'll go over it and try to make some comments). If the request is a romantic one—for example, a request to go away for a ski weekend—you might resist by discussing your feelings and proposing an alternative: for example, "Let's double date first."

[6]   Another way to resist compliance is through justification. Here you justify your refusal by citing possible consequences of compliance or non-compliance. For example, you might cite a negative consequence if you complied ("I'm afraid that I'd get caught, and then I'd fail the course"). Or

you might cite a positive consequence of your not complying ("You'll really enjoy writing this paper; it's a lot of fun").

[7]   Remember that compliance gaining and resisting—like all interpersonal communication—are transactional processes in which all elements are interdependent; each element influences each other. (DeVito 368)

Comprehension Questions

____d____ 1. The topic of this passage is:
   a. how to handle conflict.
   b. identity management.
   c. interpersonal relationships.
   d. strategies for resisting compliance.

_____ 2. The main idea of paragraph 1 is:
   a. There are four principal ways of responding to compliance demands.
   b. Someone you know asks you to do something you don't want to do.
   c. You should not lend your term papers to other students.
   d. There has been research on college students.

_____ 3. The author's purpose for writing this passage is to:
   a. inform.
   b. persuade.
   c. entertain.
   d. argue a point.

_____ 4. An example of a statement using the non-negotiation strategy is:
   a. "You'll really enjoy writing this paper; it's a lot of fun."
   b. "I'm afraid that I'd get caught, and then I'd fail the course."
   c. "No, I don't lend my papers out."
   d. "That's really unfair of you to ask me to compromise my ethics."

_____ 5. All of the following organizational patterns are used in this passage EXCEPT:
   a. compare-contrast.
   b. problem-solution.
   c. topic with a list.
   d. term, definition, and example.

_____ 6. The author's tone is:
   a. critical.
   b. doubtful.
   c. sarcastic.
   d. helpful.

_____ 7. From the information provided in the passage, we can infer that the author:
   a. Doesn't think these strategies are very effective.

      b. Thinks these strategies will work for some people, but not for everyone.

      c. Believes these strategies work well.

      d. Believes other methods work better than these strategies.

_____ **8.** The statement "You know this material much better than I do; you can easily do a much better paper yourself" is an example of:

      a. non-negotiation.

      b. negotiation.

      c. positive identity management.

      d. negative identity management.

_____ **9.** An example of a statement using the justification strategy is:

      a. "I'll let you read my paper but not copy it."

      b. "If you write a first draft, I'll go over it and try to make some comments."

      c. "You'll really enjoy writing this paper; it's a lot of fun."

      d. "I'm afraid that I'd get caught, and then I'd fail the course."

_____ **10.** The term *compliance* means:

      a. refusal.

      b. negotiation.

      c. justification.

      d. going along with.

Reading Between the Lines Box 13.1

CALCULATING YOUR READING COMPREHENSION SPEED

Calculating Your Reading Comprehension Speed

There are two scores that we are interested in calculating—your **reading speed** and your **comprehension speed**. To find your reading comprehension speed, use three simple math procedures: subtracting dividing, and multiplying.

Step 1:   Write down the time you begin reading the passage.

      Example: 10:00:00 (hour: minutes: seconds)

Step 2:   Write down the time you finish reading the passage.

      Example: 10:02:30 (hour: minutes: seconds)

Step 3:   Answer the comprehension questions at the end of the selection and correct your answers. There are ten questions, so each one is worth ten percentage points. For each question you miss, subtract ten percentage points. For example, if you miss one question, your score would be 90 percent. If you miss two questions, your score would be 80 percent, and so on.

(continued on next page)

Step 4:   Subtract your start time from your finish time. This gives you the number of minutes it took you to read the selection.

   Example: Finish   10:02:30

                    Start   − 10:00:00

                                          2:30 (2 minutes and 30 seconds)

Step 5:   Change your reading time into seconds.

   Example: If you read this passage in 2 minutes and 30 seconds, your reading rate would be calculated as follows.

   Multiply the number of minutes in which you read the passage by 60 (seconds) and add any remaining seconds.

   1 minute = 60 seconds

   2 minutes × 60 seconds = 120 + 30 seconds = 150 seconds

Step 6:   Then divide the 400 words from the passage by your time (150 seconds) and multiply that answer by 60 seconds to get your words per minute.

   400 / 150 seconds × 60 seconds = 160 wpm

Step 7:   Multiply your percentage correct on the comprehension questions times your words per minute.

   Example: If you missed one question, your percentage correct would be 90 percent or 0.90.

   0.90 × 160 = 144 wpm comprehension rate

So, in this case you would have read 160 words per minute but understood what you were reading at 144 words per minute. It's not necessary to do the final calculation because you can see by the percentage correct if you need to speed up your reading or slow it down.

READING RATE

How do you know what percentage reading rate is good? In other words, *how much* should you expect to understand and remember from what you read? This will vary according to your purpose for reading. We can answer these questions by taking a look at the various reading rates and the purposes they serve.

It is important to know your reading rate and to try to increase your reading speed and comprehension. However, you should not have one single rate but rather several different rates. Reading everything fast is a sign of a poor reader.

You should be able to shift from one rate to another according to your (1) purpose, (2) the difficulty level of the material, and (3) your familiarity with the topic.

For example, you should have varying reading rates to accomplish different tasks, and you should change your reading rate for different types of materials.

EXERCISE 13-1	**Identifying the Speed**

Look at each of the situations below and mark the speed with which you think each task should be approached. Use an *F* to indicate Fast, an *M* to indicate Moderate, and an *S* to indicate Slow. The first one has been done for you.

    S   **1.** studying for a biology exam

            2. reading a psychology chapter that has concepts and vocabulary that are new to you

            3. learning a new computer application by following printed directions

            4. finding the time and date of a particular event in a newspaper

            5. entertaining yourself with a light, easy novel

            6. reading a magazine article on a topic that you know well

            7. reading a history textbook that is structured much like a story

            8. reading the directions and examples for solving a math problem

            9. reading a novel to get a good understanding of the story

            10. skimming to find the organization of a book or chapter

We will come back to the answers to this survey, but first let's discuss the various reading rates. You may want to change some of your answers to the survey as we find out more about reading rate and purpose.

Reading Rates

Scanning—1500 wpm   Have you ever heard about people who can read at fantastic and unbelievable rates? Impressive as their claims may sound, they are probably not truly reading but rather **scanning** for bits and pieces of information that provide answers to particular questions they may have. Scanning is not a true reading rate; it involves merely glancing down the columns to find a single piece of information.

    There are three levels of scanning. At the *first level*, you're scanning for a piece of information that stands out easily, such as a name or a date. In this case, you know exactly what you are searching for and in which form it will appear. It could be a particular name, number, or word.

Example: *Question:* Did today's temperature in Houston reach **100**°?
Answer: yes, if you were able to locate the statistic **100**°
no, if you were unable to find the statistic **100**°

At the *second level* of scanning you look for an *answer that is worded exactly like a question*. In this case, you are expecting the fact to stand out from the rest of the page because you know the exact words you are looking for. Again, you do not actually read word for word, but rather look quickly over the pages, lists, or columns for this specific information.

Example: *Question:* What is **the average temperature in Houston during the summer months**?
Answer: **The average temperature in Houston during the summer months** is 100°.

At the *third level* of scanning, you are thinking about the concept. The wording may not be written exactly like the question even though the concept or idea is the same. Because the answer may be worded differently than the question, you must brainstorm words that are related to the concept. Then, you must hold them in memory while you look quickly over the pages for all possibilities.

Example: *Question:* What is the weather like in Houston during the summer months?

In this example, the word *weather* may not appear on the pages at all. Therefore, you must instead think of words or symbols that are associated with weather. You might therefore brainstorm and scan for words such as:

- temperature
- hot
- cold
- humid
- mild
- sub tropical
- temperate

Answer: Houston, with its **subtropical** tendencies, is so extremely **hot** and **humid** that employers provide hardship benefits to employees who are used to more **temperate** climates.

EXERCISE 13-2   Level I Scanning

Scan the table for the information given in the questions. Then use that information to answer the questions.

Median Annual Earnings by Education Attainment and Sex, 1998		
Education Level	Male	Female
Less than 9 years	$18,553	$14,132
9–12 (no diploma)	$23,438	$15,847
12 years (high school diploma)	$30,868	$21,963
Some college, no degree	$35,949	$26,024
Associate's degree	$38,483	$28,337
Bachelor's degree	$49,982	$35,408
Master's degree	$60,168	$42,002
Professional degree	$90,653	$55,460
Doctoral degree	$69,188	$52,167

Source: U.S. Bureau of the Census, Current Population Reports, P60-206 (Washington, D.C.: U.S. Government Printing Office, 1999). Cited in Bryjak and Soroka 149.

1. The average salary of a female with a high school diploma <u>$21,936</u>
2. The average salary of a male with a high school diploma _____
3. Which group makes $14,132 per year?_____
4. Which group makes $90,653 per year?_____
5. The average salary of a male with some college education, but no degree _____

A Reading in World Cultures

Scan the document below to find words or phrases that are used in the following questions. Then answer the Level II scanning questions that follow. Complete the vocabulary exercise before you begin.

Vocabulary in Context

- a. **injurious**—harmful; damaging
- b. **decree**—order; law; declaration
- c. **expedite**—speed up; hurry up; advance; accelerate
- d. **execute**—carry out; perform; accomplish; complete
- e. **summoned**—called for; sent for

Use the words above to complete the following sentences. The first one has been done for you.

___e___   **1.** He was _____ to court by order of the jury.

_____   **2.** Every citizen has the power to _____ his rights through legal action or litigation.

_____   **3.** Since the court system was backed up by months, the judge wanted to hear the old cases immediately and _____ the process.

_____   **4.** No one can be forced to take part in an action if there has been no _____.

_____   **5.** It is against the laws to take part in actions that are _____ or harmful to society.

The Declaration of the Rights of Man and Citizen

This moderate middle-class document of the French Revolution was inspired by the American Declaration of Independence. Notice, however, that it differs slightly in its precise mention of property rights. The National Assembly recognizes and declares, in the presence and under the auspices of the Supreme Being, the following rights of man and citizen.

1. Men are born and remain free and equal in rights. Social distinctions can be based only upon the common good.

2. The aim of every political association is the preservation of the natural and imprescriptible rights of man. These rights are liberty, property, security, and resistance to oppression.

3. Liberty consists in the power to do anything that does not injure others; accordingly, the exercise of the natural rights of each man has no limits except those that assure to the other members of society the enjoyment of these same rights. These limits can be determined only by law.

4. The law can forbid only such actions as are **injurious** to society. Nothing can be forbidden that is not forbidden by the law, and no one can be constrained to do that which it does not **decree**.

5. Law is the expression of the general will. All citizens have the right to take part personally, or by their representatives, in its enactment. It must be the same for all, whether it protects or punishes.

6. No man can be accused, or arrested, or detained, except in the cases determined by the law and according to the forms which it has prescribed. Those who call for, **expedite, execute**, or cause to be executed arbitrary orders should be punished; but every citizen **summoned or** seized by virtue of the law ought to obey instantly. . . .

7. The law ought to establish only punishments that are strictly and obviously necessary, and no one should be punished except by virtue of a law established and promulgated prior to the offense and legally applied.

8. Every man being presumed innocent until he has been declared guilty, if it is judged indispensable to arrest him, all severity that may not be necessary to secure his person ought to be severely suppressed by law.

9. No one should be disturbed on account of his opinions, even religious, provided their manifestation does not trouble the public order as established by law.

10. The free communication of thoughts and opinions is one of the most precious of the rights of man; every citizen can then speak, write, and print freely, save for the responsibility for the abuse of this liberty in the case determined by law.

11. The guarantee of the rights of man and citizen necessitates a public force; this force is then instituted for the advantage of all and not for the particular use of those to whom it is entrusted.

12. For the maintenance of the public force and for the expenses of administration a general tax is indispensable; it should be equally apportioned among all the citizens according to their means.

13. All citizens have the right to ascertain, by themselves or through their representatives, the necessary amount of public taxation, to consent to it freely, to follow the use of it, and to determine the quota, the assessment, the collection, and the duration of it.

14. Any society in which the guarantee of the rights is not assured, or the separation of powers not determined, has no constitution.

15. Property being a sacred and inviolable right, no one can be deprived of it, unless a legally established public necessity evidently requires it, under the condition of a just and prior indemnity. (Mosse et al. 591)

Level II Scanning Questions:

1. Upon what can social distinctions be based? _on the common good_
2. What is law an expression of? _____
3. According to this document, what is one of the most precious rights of man?_____
4. Although property is a sacred and inviolable right, under what conditions can someone be deprived of it?_____
5. What do the writers of this declaration call the power to do anything that does not injure others?_____

Comprehension Questions

___d___ **1.** The topic of this passage is:
  a. public forces.
  b. separation of powers.
  c. legal punishments.
  d. citizens' rights.

_____ **2.** "Liberty consists in the power to do anything that does not injure others" means
  a. People are free to do whatever they like as long as they do not hurt another person.
  b. There is no power in liberty.
  c. People have the liberty to do anything they wish.
  d. People are free to hurt other people.

_____ **3.** The author's purpose for writing this passage is to:
  a. argue a point.
  b. persuade.
  c. entertain.
  d. inform.

_____ **4.** The word *indemnity* means:
  a. condemnation.
  b. intimidation.
  c. guarantee.
  d. demand.

_____ **5.** The overall organizational pattern used in this passage is:
  a. compare-contrast.
  b. problem-solution.
  c. topic with a list.
  d. term, definition, and example.

A Reading in Psychology

The third level of scanning is looking for an answer to a question that is worded differently than the question. Instead of looking for one particular word, try to think of related words that you are most likely to find. Then, hold them in memory while you look quickly over the pages for all possibilities. Scan the following document to find the answer to the questions below. Before you begin, complete the vocabulary exercise to become familiar with the new terms.

Vocabulary in Context

a. **modest**—unexceptional; ordinary

b. **monetary**—financial; having to do with money

c. **inflation**—price increases; price rises

d. **randomly**—by coincidence accidentally by chance

e. **derived**—obtained; drew from

Use the words above to complete the following sentences. The first one has been done for you.

___a___ 1. Psychologists have proven that an increase to wealth from a _____ or ordinary income does not increase happiness.

_____ 2. In other words, _____ increases do not increase happiness, or money does not buy happiness.

_____ 3. During the last fifty years, people's salaries in the United States have doubled even when price increases or _____ is taken into account.

_____ 4. People were selected to participate in an experiment. The group was _____ selected to make sure that a variety of professions were represented.

_____ 5. People _____ pleasure from playing the lottery because it gave them a chance to daydream about being rich.

Does Money Buy Happiness?

[1]   We live in a culture that values money very highly, and most of us spend a great deal of time and effort trying to acquire it. One might imagine, therefore, that the amount of money a person has would be strongly related to how happy he or she is. It is also doubtlessly true that few extremely poor people are also extremely happy, although there is surprising little data on this point. What is clear, however, is that at least above some fairly **modest** income level, increase in **monetary** wealth is only weakly associated, if it is associated at all, with increased happiness.

[2]   Another way to look at money and happiness is to examine the degree to which levels of happiness have increased over time. National survey data are available back to the late 1950s, from which it is possible to determine the percentage of Americans who rate themselves as being "very happy." Between the late 1950s and the early 1990s, personal income in the United States, adjusted for **inflation**, has more than doubled. If there

were a strong link between income and happiness, one would expect to
see the percentage of "very happy" Americans increase as income has gone
up . . . and . . . it hasn't. . . .

[3]   Finally, and perhaps most strikingly, Brickman, Coates, and Janoff-
Bulman (1978) interviewed 22 people who had won major state lotter-
ies, the average amount won being almost $500,000. Among other
things, the lottery winners were asked to rate how happy they were
with their life in general before they had won, and how happy they were
at the interview, and how happy they expected to be in a couple of
years. A group of **randomly** selected control subjects were also interviewed and asked the same questions, except that they indicated how
happy they were six months before the interview. Here are the results
[based on a scale of 1 through 7, 1 indicating not very happy, and 7
indicating extremely happy].

	Past	Present	Future
Winners	3.77	4.00	4.20
Controls	3.32	3.82	4.14

[4]   The winners were slightly happier across the three time periods than
were the non-winners, but once again the effect of money is surprisingly
small. These are sobering data. Most of us have daydreamed about winning the lottery, imagining how happy we would be if we actually won.
Much of the pleasure **derived** from playing the lottery may lie in such
anticipatory daydreams; the reality being, perhaps less wonderful and
life-changing than we imagine. (Mynatt and Doherty 340–41)

Level III Scanning Questions

1. Does money greatly increase a person's happiness? No, monetary wealth
   is only weakly associated with increased happiness.

2. On a scale of 1 to 7, how much happier are people who win the lottery than
   people who don't win?_____

3. Given their increase in wealth, have Americans become happier since the
   mid-nineteenth century? _____

4. How do the authors account for the pleasure that people get from playing
   the lottery? _____

5. How did people who won the lottery compare to those who did not in terms
   of their beliefs of future happiness? _____

Comprehension Questions

_____d_____ **1.** The topic of this passage is:
a. happiness.
b. psychology experiments.
c. winning the lottery.
d. the effect of money on happiness.

_____ **2.** State lottery winners are
a. only slightly happier after winning the lottery than they were before.
b. much happier after winning the lottery than before.
c. less happy after winning the lottery than before.
d. terribly unhappy after winning the lottery than before.

_____ **3.** The author's purpose for writing this passage is to:
a. inform.
b. persuade.
c. entertain.
d. argue a point.

_____ **4.** Even though they usually lose, people enjoy playing the state lottery because:
a. They enjoy the competition.
b. They believe they are happier without money.
c. They enjoy the anticipation of winning.
d. They feel good about donating money to the state.

_____ **5.** The overall organizational pattern used in this passage is:
a. compare-contrast.
b. problem-solution.
c. cause-effect.
d. Term, definition, and example.

Skimming—800–1000 wpm Like scanning, **skimming** is not a true reading rate. It involves previewing or overviewing. You skim just to get the gist of an article, find the main points, or assess general content. You will not completely understand the details of the article, but you will know what the article is about.
You should skim:

■ chapters of textbooks before reading to find the author's outline

■ articles or books to find relevant information on a research topic

■ to decide if you are interested in reading a book or article

■ an editorial to learn an author's opinion on a particular topic

- as a review (assuming that you have already read the material at least once)
- to bypass irrelevant parts of a book or an article
- newspapers to get an overview of the day's events

Skim a chapter in a book by reading the:

- title
- introduction
- headings within the chapter
- first and last sentence of each paragraph for key ideas
- diagrams, pictures, charts, and graphs
- summary or concluding paragraphs

Skim a book by reading the:

- title
- print on the back or inside cover of the publisher's jacket
- preface and/or introduction
- table of contents
- first chapter
- first and last paragraphs of the other chapters
- last chapter

Skimming is an effective tool to use when trying to identify a selection's organizational pattern. Recognizing the author's outline helps you establish a framework for understanding the information. For example, if an author uses a problem-and-solution outline, you will know to look for the problem as you read and to pinpoint solutions that are given. If the pattern is one of comparison-contrast, you will begin to look for pros and cons instead of searching for solutions to a problem. If you do not recognize the author's organizational pattern, it will be more difficult for you to pick up on what you mentally need to do with the information in order for it to make sense.

Very Rapid Reading Rate—400 wpm The first true reading rate is approximately **400 wpm**. The average reading rate of most graduate students is about 300 wpm; thus, 400 wpm is truly a fast pace. You should read this fast when you:

- read light, easy, fast-moving fiction
- read only for entertainment
- read to get a general idea of what the material is about
- are very familiar with and interested in the material

Rapid Reading Rate—350 wpm A reading rate of 350 wpm is also very fast and should be used only when you want to get the main ideas and important

Reading Between the Lines Box 13.2

WHAT DOES SKIMMING LOOK LIKE?

When we skim, we are covering a large amount of material, but we are not reading every word. That is why we can claim such high reading rates.

1. Follow the diagram below to get an idea of what you should read and what you should skip when skimming. The marks ("""""") indicate what we would most likely skip.

2. Go to one of your textbooks and choose a passage. Skim it in the same way that you skimmed the example below. Write down the general idea of the passage. Next, read the entire passage. Turn over your paper and write your new understanding of the general idea. Compare it to what you wrote after skimming. Is it the same or different? If different, what changes did you make?

Read the Title

The title either spells out the topic in specific terms or provides clues to the topic. Then, *read the introduction*. The author explains his purpose and plan for the article in the introduction.

Read headings

Read the headings within the chapter. """"""""""""""""""""""""""" """"""""""""""""""""""""""

They show you the author's outline.

Read the first sentence and """""""""""""""""""""""""""""""" """"""""""""""""""""""""""""

the last sentence of each

paragraph for key ideas.

Read headings

Read the first sentence """"""""""""""""""""""""""""" """""""""""""and the last sentence.

Study any visual aids and read the captions, keys, or other information that is provided for their interpretation. """""""""""""""""""""""""""""""""" """"""""""""""""""""""""""""" """"""""""""""""""""""""""""" """""""""""""" Often it is easier to read the words that describe a concept once you have a visual image of it.

Read headings

Read the first sentence """""""""""""""""""""""""""""""

"""""""""""""""""""""""""""""""""" """"""""""""""""""""""""""""""" """""""""""""" and the last sentence.

The main idea is usually stated in the first sentence """""""""""""""""""""""""""""""" """"""""""""" while the last sentence provides a transition from paragraph to paragraph.

Summary
Read the summary or concluding paragraphs. Here the author pulls together all of the main points covered in the chapter.

details. At this rate, you are not stopping to reflect, paraphrase, or summarize what you have just read. You are only looking for the main points and the details that support them.

Read at this rate when you:

- want only important facts and ideas
- are very familiar with the topic
- have a good understanding of all of the vocabulary and terms used
- have a good understanding of all of the concepts discussed

Average Reading Rate—250 wpm   The average person speaks at a rate of about 150 wpm. The average reading rate is 250 wpm—clearly much faster. We generally read at an average rate when:

- reading newspaper or magazine articles to keep informed about what is happening in the news
- reading social studies or social science textbooks to gain an understanding of the topics discussed
- reading literary novels and short stories to prepare for class discussions
- reading articles and book chapters to gain background information for a research paper

Slow and Careful Reading Rate—50–250 wpm   This is the rate at which a lot of academic material should be read, especially if the subject is new or completely unfamiliar to you. You will need to stop and look up terms you do not know so that the passage will make sense. Even if new terms are introduced with definitions and examples, it takes time to read the definition, study the example, and then relate your understanding of it back to the term. When reading textbooks, you may need to reflect on the information in each paragraph and mentally summarize and digest it before going on to the next paragraph. Some situations in which it is beneficial to read slowly include:

- reading about concepts that are new to you
- reading about concepts that are difficult to understand
- reading about vocabulary that is new to you
- reading technical material, such as a computer science textbook
- reading to remember every detail
- reading when you are weighing the truth of difficult material (critical reading)
- reading to memorize classifications of systems (e.g., the Periodic Table in chemistry; classifications of plants in biology)
- reading for details

EXERCISE
13-3

Controlling Your Reading Speed

Remember that reading everything fast is a sign of a poor reader and that you should be able to shift from one rate to another according to your (1) purpose, (2) the difficulty of the material, and (3) your familiarity with the topic. Let's go back to the survey that you took at the beginning of the chapter. You looked at each of the situations below and marked the speed with which you thought each task should be approached. *F* was used to indicate Fast, *M* to indicate Moderate, and *S* to indicate Slow. Compare your answers with those provided below. Then take the reading rate quiz that follows.

_____S_____ **1.** studying for a biology exam

_____S_____ **2.** reading a psychology chapter that contains concepts and vocabulary that are new to you

_____S_____ **3.** learning a new computer application by following printed directions

_____F_____ **4.** finding the time and date of a particular event in a newspaper

_____F_____ **5.** entertaining yourself with a light, easy novel

_____F_____ **6.** reading a magazine article on a topic that you know well

_____M_____ **7.** reading a history textbook that is structured much like a story

_____S_____ **8.** reading the directions and examples for solving a math problem

_____M_____ **9.** reading a novel to get a good understanding of the story

_____F_____ **10.** skimming to find the organization of a book or chapter

Reading Between the Lines Box 13.3

READING RATE

Are you reading too fast or too slow? Take the reading rate quiz and analyze your approach to reading different materials.

Reading Rate Quiz

1. Name the three reasons you would shift from one reading rate to another.

_____

_____

_____

(continued on next page)

2. Describe the three levels of scanning.

_____

_____

_____

3. Name the six steps in skimming.

_____

_____

_____

_____

_____

_____

4. How fast should you read technical material?

_____

5. How fast should you read to get a general impression of an article/book?

_____

6. How fast should you read a social studies textbook?

_____

7. How fast should you read fiction novel for entertainment?

_____

8. How fast should you read to remember every detail?

_____

9. Magazine articles?

_____

10. To answer a question?

_____

INCREASING READING SPEED

Oftentimes, speed reading programs focus on reducing *subvocalization* (that is, suppressing the *inner voice*), increasing rapid eye movement, and reducing the number of fixations (how many times our eyes stop to look at words on the page). These techniques may increase the speed with which we look at the words on the page, but they do not increase our understanding of the words.

Modern research shows that our eyes actually focus on every word and that subvocalization supports comprehension (Rayner and Pollatsek 153–87). Reading is a complex process that cannot be reduced to just moving the eyes faster.

In fact, reading speed is closely connected with comprehension. That means we can only read as fast as we can think. If speed reading is *not* achieved by simply moving our eyes faster, then how can we learn to read faster?

The following are factors that support fast reading:

- knowledge of the vocabulary
- rapid word recognition
- an understanding of the author's purpose
- extensive knowledge of the topic (background knowledge)
- knowledge of organizational patterns or text structure

How to Increase Your Reading Speed

Before concentrating on rapid eye movements and timed readings, you need to establish habits for thinking faster. There are five types of exercises you can do to increase thinking speed and, in turn, increase reading speed. They include:

- building vocabulary
- building word recognition speed
- building thinking speed
- building background knowledge
- previewing/recognizing the author's outline

Building Rapid Word Recognition The ability to recognize words accurately is called **visual discrimination**. For example, let's say that you are reading the following sentence:

Jim took the interstate highway to a remote part of the country.

Let's suppose that while reading very quickly, you made a couple of mistakes in visual discrimination. At first glance, you read "intrastate" instead of "interstate" and "county" instead of "country." You are under the impression that the sentence reads:

Jim took the intrastate highway to a remote part of the county.

Since the word *interstate* suggests going through the states and the word *country* refers to the entire United States, we could imagine Jim starting in New York and ending up in some remote part of Georgia. However, given that the word *intrastate* means within a particular state and *county* is a geographic division within a state, the meaning has changed. In this case, we are looking for Jim to start in one particular state, let's say New York, and drive to a remote part of New York. If the story is about a truck driver whose route takes him down the coast, a mistake like this in visual discrimination would be very confusing. We would be wondering how Jim ended up in Georgia when we were not expecting him to cross the state line of New York.

The following exercise is designed to help you discriminate between similar words and, thus, increase rapid word recognition.

| EXERCISE 13-4 | **Matching the Words** |

The word in the left-hand column is repeated in the string of words on the right. Find and circle the word at the right that is exactly the same as the key word. Then go on to the next key word. Work as quickly as you are able to without making mistakes in visual discrimination.

1. Freud   fraud, Freud, friend, freed, fiend

2. essential   sentimental, essence, essay, essential, existential

3. penchant   penchant, pretend, chant, pension, penny

4. investigation   instigate, infestation, investigation, investing, stigma

5. interpersonal   personal, interpretation, personal, impersonal, interpersonal

6. attraction   attraction, attract, attracting, attack, traction

7. assumption   assume, consumption, assumption, assure, ascertain

8. evaluate   evolution, value, devalue, evaluate, equivalent

9. appreciate   apprehend, ample, apprehension, appreciation, appreciate

10. attachment   attach, apache, attachment, attack, adamant

11. intimacy   intimate, intimidate, interdict, intimacy, itinerate

12. emotional   emotional, emotion, motion, emote, emulate

13. dependence   depend, pension, dependable, depending, dependence

14. quality   quantity, quality, qualify, qualified, quantify

15. exclusive   exclude, executive, exclusive, execute, exclaim

16. absorption   abhor, absorb, absorption, abdomen, abstain

17. dominate   domain, dominion, dominate, dome, domination

18. measure   measure, measurable, meander, mean, measuring

19. fierce   fire, pierce, fiend, friend, fierce

20. possessive   positive, possess, recessive, position, possessive

21. possibilities   possibility, possible, posse, possibilities, positive

22. jealousy   jealous, lousy, jean, jalopy, jealousy

23. pain   pan, pane, planning, pain, plain

24. ecstasy   estimate, ecstatic, estuary, estate, ecstasy

25. passion   pass, pension, passion, passionate, press

        Time_____ Errors_____

Building Vocabulary Knowledge of vocabulary is absolutely essential to speed up comprehension. Sometimes not knowing the meaning of one word can stop you from understanding a sentence, a paragraph, or even a whole passage. While you are previewing a selection, highlight or underline all of the vocabulary that you are unfamiliar with. Then stop to read the sentence that contains each unknown word. If you can guess the word's meaning from the context, move on. If you cannot guess the meaning of the unknown word from the context or from its word parts, then look it up in the dictionary. Merrriam/Webster's electronic dictionary is especially quick and easy to use (http://www.m-w.com).

EXERCISE 13-5

Finding the Synonyms

The word in the left-hand column is defined within the string of words on the right. Find and circle the word at the right that is closest in meaning to the key word at the left. Then go on to the next key word. Look up the meanings of any words that you miss.

1. essential   sentimental, fundamental, consequential, vial, existential

2. penchant   inclination, pretend, chant, repent, aversion

3. assumption   supposition, consumption, requirement, assure, ascertain

4. evaluate   evolve, judge, devalue, evaluate, ascertain

5. intimacy   affection, intimidate, interdict, allocate, reiterate

6. exclusive   restrictive, execute, all-consuming, regenerative, affirm

7. absorption   reaction, preoccupation, activation, expulsion, assumption

8. dominate   dictate, consider, prescribe, distort, decline

9. possessive   jealous, positive, impolite, critical, prosperous

10. infatuation   apprehension, extension, crush, determination, infection

        Time_____ Errors_____

Building Thinking Speed   As we said earlier, you can read only as fast as you can think. If you read words without thinking, then you have only pronounced them either aloud or silently; you have not read them. Reading requires a certain amount of reflection on the meaning of the words and on the combination of words that make up a sentence or a paragraph. Questioning and searching for answers to our questions helps us think about the words we are looking at. Below is an exercise that will help you think about the words you are reading and to push yourself to think quickly.

EXERCISE
13-5   **Concrete or Abstract?**

No matter how fast you move your eyes, your speed of comprehension is dependent on your ability to understand one idea and to pass on to the next. As you look at the following phrases, ask yourself if any word in the phrase is concrete or abstract. Place a check in front of each group of words that is concrete. To determine if it is concrete, ask yourself if it can be perceived by the five senses. **Can you see it? taste it? feel it? hear it? or touch it?**

_____ **1.** commitment and intimacy

_____ **2.** love and work

_____ **3.** province of the poet

_____ **4.** evaluate them positively

_____ **5.** dominate your thoughts

_____ **6.** possibilities for jealousy

_____ **7.** Sternberg informs us

_____ **8.** triangular theory of love

_____ **9.** male-female relationship

_____ **10.** bring people closer

_____ **11.** decision-making process

_____ **12.** point of view

_____ **13.** people want to share

_____ **14.** children are gone

_____ **15.** consummate love

_____ **16.** pattern of development

_____ **17.** has passion but no commitment

_____ **18.** Erikson describes

_____ **19.** love is not static or unchanging

_____ **20.** passage of time

_____Time _____Errors

Building Background Knowledge The second type of exercise you can do to increase speed of comprehension is building background knowledge. The best way to do this is to read information on the same topic that has been written on a lower reading level. In other words, if you are reading a history assignment on the Bolshevik Revolution from a college textbook, you should go to the library and check out a junior high school history textbook and read the same information on an easier level first. You will be able to read with less effort and gain an understanding of the event. You will then be able to read the more detailed version from the college-level book with greater ease.

Reading Between the Lines Box 13.4

VISUAL DISCRIMINATION

The Psychology of Love

We can read faster if we can rapidly recognize the words with accuracy. Find and circle the word at the right that is exactly the same as the key word. Then go on to the next key word. Work as quickly as you are able to without making mistakes in visual discrimination.

1. Eskimos   ski, stamen, Eskimos, escalates, schemas

2. triangular   triangle, regular, triangular, trial, tribulation

3. subsides   subway, subsidy, subsystem, subsides, subsidiary

4. sustain   sustain, sustenance, Susan, maintain, retain

5. external   internal, external, extra, extreme, examine

6. constraints   constant, contain, restraints, constraints, constitution

7. economic   economy, ecology, nomadic, ecosystem, economic

8. disillusion   illusion, disillusion, division, disenchanted, illuminate

9. maintain   maintain, mainly, mountain, retain, matinee

10. irreplaceable   replaceable, irresponsible, irresistible, irreplaceable, unable

11. hormones   horses, harmonious, hormones, houses, homogeneous

12. diminish   dime, minus, mining, diminish, refinish

13. devoted   devalued, demoted, devoted, demolished, divorced

14. cultivates   culture, cultivates, culminates, culinary, culvert

15. evolves   evolution, elevate, revolves, evolves, evaluations

A Reading in Developmental Psychology

The following passage is on Sternberg's model of love. It is written in simpler terms and provides a more detailed account of the model than you will find in some other psychology books. The accounts that follow in later exercises (in this chapter) are more difficult to read because they assume that you are already familiar with this theory. Read the passage; then, answer the comprehension questions that follow.

Vocabulary in Context

    a. aspects—characteristics; features

    b. empathize—understand; relate to; identify with in a compassionate way

    c. gratifying—rewarding; satisfying; pleasing

    d. novelty—originality; newness; uniqueness; freshness

    e. fluctuate—vary; change; rise and fall

Use the words above to complete the following sentences. The first one has been done for you.

_____a_____ **1.** There are three _____ of love according to Sternberg: intimacy, passion, and commitment.

_____ **2.** Intimacy is a feeling of deep attachment, closeness, and warmth toward another person along with the ability to understand or _____ with him or her.

_____ **3.** The biological stimulators, or hormones, decrease as the _____ wears off a familiar relationship.

_____ **4.** A love relationship will end when the passion decreases if feelings of attachment, empathy, and understanding have not developed because there will be nothing _____ about the relationship.

_____ **5.** Commitment is an important part of lasting relationships because we cannot rely entirely on feelings, which tend to _____ under different conditions and circumstances.

Types of Love

[1]   The word "Love" has a lot to do. Generally, the more we talk about a certain idea, the more words we develop to describe it. It's said that Eskimos have some thirty or more words for snow. Not so with love. We use the same tired word to describe our intense passion for a lover as our

addiction to ice cream. We use the same word to describe our feelings for our lovers as our mothers and our pets. Perhaps it would be useful to know what we are talking about?

[2]   Psychologist Robert Sternberg has identified three components of love: intimacy, passion, and commitment. Each aspect involves different parts of the self, namely the emotional, biological, and mental. Depending on the presence and strength of each element in a particular relationship, we can describe the different kinds of love people feel.

Aspects of Love

[3]   *Intimacy* is described by Sternberg as a feeling of deep attachment, closeness and warmth toward another. We usually enjoy being with them, and understand and **empathize** with them, accepting their faults, and failures and appreciating the good qualities. We trust them. Feelings of intimacy generally take a long time to develop. They develop because we are able to feel vulnerable with the other, yet trust them not to hurt us.

[4]   *Passion* is a feeling of strong physical attraction, which is largely based on the biological drive for sex. Feelings of strong passion that are **gratifying** tend to decline in intensity because the **novelty** wears off, and because the biological stimulators, the hormones, decrease. A love relationship will end when the passion decreases if feelings of attachment, empathy and understanding have not developed.

[5]   *Commitment* is a conscious decision to maintain a relationship, whether for life or for a certain period of time. It is a key to stability in relationships, because feelings tend to **fluctuate**. Commitment may involve a dedication to the relationship simply because of the other aspects of love, or because of internal needs, values or morals or external constraints like social or economic pressures.

Types of Love

[6]   *Liking* is the basic feeling in friendship. It is based on warmth, closeness and even attachment, but there is no sexual attraction or long-term commitment. Close cross-sex friendships are not uncommon, but they can be sticky if attraction develops, or outsiders become suspicious.

[7]   *Romantic Love* is a combination of intimacy and passion. This type of love is common while in high school or college and has become more prevalent in other age groups as well. It, however, does not include commitment, either because one or more partners feels too young, or the partners feel too different, or even that one feels disillusioned with love in some way.

[8]   *Infatuation* is a kind of love characterized by intense physical attraction. It is "love at first sight" and tends to be obsessive, especially when it is not returned. The object of these feelings tends to be idealized, and shortcomings are minimized or even ignored. Because of its unrealistic

nature, infatuation does not include real intimacy or commitment. Getting to know the person better often diminishes the feelings, as reality sets in.

[9]   *Empty Love* relationships occur when people remain committed despite a lack of intimacy or passion for their partner. The major reason for continuing the relationship is duty, loyalty, dependence or gratitude. One common example is couples who remain together for the sake of their children. Another is in long-term relationships where the feelings have died, but the couple remains together for economic reasons. Still another may occur when one partner or both have developed romantic relationships outside the marriage.

[10]   *Companionate Love* relationships develop when passion is diminished, but the sense of attachment and commitment remain. It is often characteristic of elderly couples, but can occur when people marry for friendship or companionship. Most people in this kind of relationship report themselves as being quite satisfied. Some, however, stray looking for romance or lost youth.

[11]   *Fatuous Love* is a kind of love that involves both passion and commitment, without real intimacy. This can occur when people become involved very quickly, or when they lack the ability to develop empathy and understanding with each other. This can happen in rebound relationships, long-distance relationships or other situations where normal constraints do not occur to slow down and develop the relationship.

[12]   *Consummate Love* is a complete kind of love, characterized by all three components of love. The relationship tends to be secure and gratifying. Although passion may diminish with age, it does not disappear altogether. In fact, attachment and commitment often increase as the time and energy devoted to the relationship make it more and more irreplaceable.

[13]   Some experts feel that Sternberg's typology of love is simplistic. They point to a history of research that contains five or six different types of love that may be blended together in each person's feelings. (Manis 87)

Comprehension Questions

___d___ **1.** Which of the following is NOT one of the three components of love?
    a. intimacy
    b. passion
    c. commitment
    d. emotion

_____ **2.** A feeling of deep attachment, closeness and warmth toward another person is called:
    a. intimacy.   c. pasion.
    b. liking.   d. commitment.

_____ **3.** A conscious decision to maintain a relationship, whether for life or for a certain period, is called:
   a. passion.
   b. commitment.
   c. intimacy.
   d. non-love.

_____ **4.** A feeling of strong physical attraction, which is largely based on the biological drive for sex, is called:
   a. intimacy.
   b. infatuation.
   c. passion.
   d. commitment.

_____ **5.** A friendship that is based on feelings of warmth, closeness, and even attachment without sexual attraction or long-term commitment is called:
   a. liking.
   b. infatuation.
   c. romantic love.
   d. empty love.

_____ **6.** The type of love that is a combination of intimacy and passion is called:
   a. companionate love.
   b. fatuous love.
   c. consummate love.
   d. romantic love.

_____ **7.** The type of relationship that occurs when people remain committed despite a lack of intimacy or passion for their partners is called:
   a. infatuation.
   b. romantic love.
   c. empty love.
   d. liking.

_____ **8.** Infatuation is the kind of love that is:
   a. characterized by intense intimacy.
   b. characterized by long-lasting commitment.
   c. characterized by intense physical attraction.
   d. characterized by all three components of love.

_____ **9.** A kind of love that involves both passion and commitment without real intimacy is called:
   a. companionate love.
   b. consummate love.
   c. romantic love.
   d. fatuous love.

_____ **10.** The term *consummate love* refers to:
    a. a relationship that includes intimacy and commitment.
    b. a relationship that includes passion and commitment.
    c. a relationship that includes intimacy and passion.
    d. a relationship that includes intimacy, passion, and commitment.

Previewing In order to think quickly, you need to know what to expect. You would never go to a social function without first asking what type of gathering you will be attending. You would want to know the type of gathering, the length of time it would last, how many people would be there, what type of food would be available, and what you would need to bring with you. For example, you would prepare differently for a football game than you would for a formal wedding dinner or a ski trip. If you were not prepared, you would not have essential accessories with you such as a suitcase and ski equipment for a ski trip or a warm coat and hat for sitting outside watching a football game.

It is the same with reading. In order to read more efficiently, you must prepare to read. We do this by previewing the topic, the vocabulary, and the author's outline. You use the same steps for previewing as you do when you skim a chapter.

- Read the title.
- Read the introduction.
- Read headings within the chapter.
- Read the first and last sentence of each paragraph for key ideas.
- Read the diagrams, pictures, charts, graphs.
- Read the summary or concluding paragraphs.

However, be sure to look for the author's outline or the organizational pattern of the text. Is the paragraph comparison-contrast? problem-solution? topic with a list? etc.

Once you know the author's outline, you know how the main ideas are arranged. In other words, you know what the author's main ideas are and where they are. Once you know this, you can read much faster.

A Reading in Developmental Psychology

The following article is also on Sternberg's model of love. It is a little more difficult to read because the author assumes that you already have an understanding of this model. First, complete the vocabulary exercise to become familiar with the new terms. Then, preview the selection by completing the outline at the end of the reading. Then, answer the comprehension questions.

Vocabulary in Context

   a. essential—necessary, important, vital

   b. province—realm, area of interest

   c. penchant—desire, preference, partiality

   d. assumption—belief, idea, notion

   e. interdependent—codependent, mutually reliant

Use the words above to complete the following sentences. The first one has been done for you.

_____c_____ **1.** Psychologists have a _____ or preference for scientific investigation and have thus tried to explain what love is in logical ways.

_____ **2.** Love is based on the _____ or belief that two people care about each other and feel an attachment to each other.

_____ **3.** Statistics is the mathematician's _____ or area of interest just as love is the realm of the poet.

_____ **4.** As love grows, two people become _____; they can rely on each other.

_____ **5.** According to Freud, love and work are absolutely necessary, or _____, for adults to feel healthy.

Love

[1]   Freud (1935) put it very simply: There are two things that are **essential** to be a healthy adult: love and work.

[2]   Love was the **province** of the poet long before science turned to claim her. And even now, science may have less to say about love itself than the poets do.

[3]   Still, science with its **penchant** for measurement and investigation provides us with ways of measuring, if not of completely understanding, love. Rubin's (1970) *Loving and Liking Scales* attempt to provide a way of separating interpersonal attraction into two categories. The scales are based on the **assumption** that when we like people, we sense that we have things in common with them, we evaluate them positively, we appreciate their company. But loving is not simply more of liking, according to Rubin. Loving involves three components: caring, attachment, and intimacy. It also implies a degree of emotional **interdependence**, a quality of exclusiveness

Visual Literacy Box 13.1 ● ● ● ● ● ● ● ● ● ● ● ● ●

DIAGRAMS: MODEL OF LOVE

Diagrams can help us see information from a different perspective than we would have if we looked at a chart. Study the different types of relationships in the chart below. The checks indicate which elements are found in the various types of relationships. Rearrange this information to fit into the diagram beneath the chart.

Relationship	Passion	Commitment	Intimacy
Nonlove			
Infatuation	✓		
Liking			✓
Romantic love	✓		✓
Companionate love		✓	✓
Fatuous love	✓	✓	
Empty love		✓	
Consummate love	✓	✓	✓

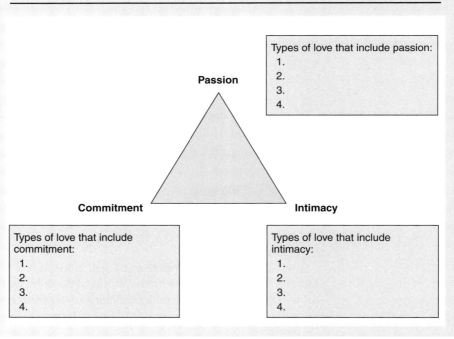

Types of love that include passion:
1.
2.
3.
4.

Passion

Commitment   **Intimacy**

Types of love that include commitment:
1.
2.
3.
4.

Types of love that include intimacy:
1.
2.
3.
4.

and absorption. If you simply like someone, that person does not dominate your thoughts and your dreams; nor are you concerned that someone else might also like the same person. Love, on the other hand, often brings with it a measure of fierce possessiveness and possibilities for jealousy and pain—perhaps possibilities for ecstasy as well.

A Model of Love

[4]   But there is more to interpersonal attraction than simply liking or loving, Sternberg (1986) informs us. There are at least eight varieties of this thing, including nonlove, romantic love, liking, fatuous love, infatuation, companionship, empty love, and consummate love. What differentiates these states from one another is the combination of *intimacy, passion,* and *commitment* involved in each. Accordingly, Sternberg, who . . . has given us a *triangular* theory of love. But the triangle in this theory is not the classical male-male-female or female-female-male love triangle. It is the intimacy-passion-commitment triangle.

[5]   In this model, intimacy refers to emotions that bring people closer together—emotions such as respect, affection, and support. Feelings of intimacy are what lead two people to want to share things, perhaps to disclose personal, private things.

[6]   Passion is defined as a strong, sometimes almost overwhelming, desire to be with another person. Passion is often, although not always, sexual. Sternberg suggests that passion is a feeling that builds rapidly, but then gradually subsides.

[7]   Commitment implies a decision-making process, and may involve either a short-term or a long-term decision. On a short-term basis, commitment requires making the decision that one is in love. From a long-term point of view, commitment involves deciding to cultivate and maintain the loving relationship. In practice, this most often implies a decision to share living arrangements and perhaps the raising of a family, either in marriage or otherwise.

[8]   Sternberg's theory of love holds that it is the particular combination of these three components—intimacy, passion, and commitment—that determines the nature of the relationship. . . . For example, *empty love* involves commitment but is devoid of passion or intimacy ("By $%#, we'll stay together until the children are gone. Then *adios!*") *Consummate love,* on the other hand, has all three components.

[9]   There is a pattern to the development of many relationships, Sternberg suggests. Thus, two individuals might begin with *nonlove*—no passion, commitment, or intimacy. In time, as intimacy grows, nonlove might give way to infatuation, which has passion but no commitment or intimacy—or perhaps to romantic love, which now adds intimacy but is still short of commitment. Eventually, consummate love might evolve as commitment is brought into the relationship. And perhaps the end result will be marriage or some other long-term commitment. . . .

[10]   But even consummate love is not a static, unchanging thing. Sternberg points out that passion is usually very high early in a consummate

relationship. But with the passage of time, it diminishes; at the same time, however, commitment and intimacy might increase. Sternberg reports that intimacy and commitment are generally seen as being more important for a lasting love relationship than is passion. (Lefrancois 538–41)

Previewing Exercise

I. Introduction

II. The three components of love

    A. _____

    B. _____

    C. _____

III. A model of love

    A. Eight varieties of love and their components

        1. _____

        2. _____

        3. _____

        4. _____

        5. _____

        6. _____

        7. _____

        8. _____

IV. Triangular theory of love

    A. Definition of Intimacy

        1. _____

        2. _____

     3. _____

  B. Definition of passion

     1. _____

     2. _____

     3. _____

  C. Definition of commitment

     1. _____

     2. _____

V. Relationships that have the best chance for lasting

  A. _____

  B. _____

Comprehension Questions

_____d_____ **1.** According to Freud, healthy adults need:
    a. intimacy and love.
    b. passion and commitment.
    c. commitment and intimacy.
    d. love and work.

_____ **2.** Sternberg's triangular theory of love involves the following three components:
    a. intimacy, passion, and commitment.
    b. liking, romantic love, and companionship.
    c. passion, infatuation, and companionship.
    d. commitment, consummate love, and infatuation.

_____ **3.** Sternberg reports that the two necessary components for a long lasting relationship are intimacy and commitment, are:
    a. passion and commitment.
    b. commitment and intimacy.
    c. intimacy and passion.
    d. passion and infatuation.

_____ **4.** Empty love has only
  a. intimacy.
  b. passion.
  c. commitment.
  d. infatuation.

_____ **5.** Sternberg terms the condition of *no* passion, intimacy, or commitment as
  a. nonlove.
  b. consummate love.
  c. romantic love.
  d. empty love.

A Reading in Psychology

Now that you are familiar with the topic "the psychology of love," test your speed of comprehension by reading yet another article on this same topic. By reading the two previous articles, you have built vocabulary and background knowledge on this topic and are at the point where you can begin to push yourself to read faster. Calculate your reading rate and your comprehension rate according to the directions given earlier in this chapter. Your reading rate is computed by dividing the number of words in the article (300) by your reading time. Your comprehension rate is computed by multiplying your reading rate by your percentage correct on the multiple-choice questions. Take 30 seconds to preview the article before you start your timed reading.

Vocabulary in Context

  a. components—parts

  b. reciprocate—to give in return; to give back

  c. cognitive—having to do with intellectual thought; thinking

  d. declines—weakens; falls off; drops

  e. leisure—free time; spare time; vacation

Use the words above to complete the following sentences. The first one has been done for you.

____d____ **1.** As a relationship grows, affection and care-giving increase and passion weakens or _____.

_____ **2.** Unlike passion, commitment is the part of love that is based on intellectual or _____ thinking.

_____ **3.** Sternberg's theory of love is based on three _____: intimacy, passion, and commitment.

_____ **4.** Love involves being concerned for the other person's well-being and wanting that person to _____, or return, these feelings and concerns.

_____ **5.** At the beginning of a relationship, couples have more time for fun and _____ activities, whereas later in the relationship they spend more time doing household chores.

The Components of Love

[1]   What feelings and behaviors tell us that we are in love? According to one well-known theory, love has three **components**: intimacy, passion, and commitment. Intimacy is the emotional component. It involves warm, tender communication, expressions of concern about the other's well-being, and a desire for the partner to **reciprocate**. Passion, the desire for sexual activity and romance, is the physical and psychological arousal component. Commitment is the **cognitive** component. It leads partners to decide that they are in love and to maintain that love. (Sternberg, 1987, 1988).

[2]   The balance among these components changes as romantic relationships develop. At the beginning, passionate love—intense sexual attraction—is strong. Gradually, passion **declines** in favor of intimacy and commitment, which form the basis for companionate love—warm, trusting affection and care-giving (Fehr, 1994; Hatfield, 1988). Each aspect of love, however, helps sustain modern relationships. Early passionate love is a strong predictor of whether partners stay together. But without the quiet intimacy, predictability, and shared attitudes and values of companionate love, most romances eventually break up (Hendrick & Hendrick, 1992).

[3]   An ongoing relationship with a mate requires effort from both partners, as a study of newlyweds' feelings and behavior over the first year of marriage reveals. Husbands and wives gradually felt less "in love" and pleased with married life. A variety of factors contributed to this change. A sharp drop in time spent talking to one another and in doing things that brought each other pleasure (for example, saying "I love you" or making the other person laugh) occurred. In addition, although couples engaged in just as many joint activities at the beginning and end of the year, **leisure** pursuits gave way to household tasks and chores. Less pleasurable activities may have contributed to the decline in satisfaction. (Berk 461)

Reading rate (based on 300 words) _____

Reading comprehension rate _____

Comprehension Questions

_____d_____ **1.** At the beginning of a relationship, which of the following components of love is strong?
    a. intimacy.
    b. well-being.
    c. commitment.
    d. passion.

_____ **2.** The emotional component of love is called:
    a. intimacy.
    b. liking.
    c. passion.
    d. commitment.

_____ **3.** The desire for sexual activity and romance is called:
    a. passion.
    b. commitment.
    c. intimacy.
    d. nonlove.

_____ **4.** The cognitive component of love is called:
    a. intimacy.
    b. infatuation.
    c. passion.
    d. commitment.

_____ **5.** Romances eventually break up if they do not have:
    a. companionate love.
    b. infatuation.
    c. romantic love.
    d. empty love.

Multiply the number correct by 20 to find your percentage score. For example, if you missed one question, you would multiply 4 correct by 20 to get 80 percent or 0.80.

References

INTRODUCTION

Merriam-Webster's New Collegiate Dictionary, 9th ed. ©1989. Merriam-Webster, Inc.

U.S. Bureau of the Census, *Current Population Reports*, P20-513. Washington, D.C.: U.S. Government Printing Office, 1998.

CHAPTER 1

Anderson, Richard C., Ralph E. Reynolds, Diane L. Schallert, and Ernest T. Goetz. "Frame-works for Comprehending Discourse." *American Educational Research Journal* 14 (1977): 367–81.

Bartlett, Frederick C. *Remembering*. Cambridge: Cambridge University Press, 1932.

Berk, Laura E. *Development through the Lifespan*. 2nd ed. Boston: Allyn and Bacon, 2001.

Davidson, J. Kenneth, Sr., and Nelwyn B. Moore. *Marriage and Family: Change and Continuity*. Boston: Allyn and Bacon, 1996.

Garraty, John A., and Mark C. Carnes. *The American Nation: A History of the United States*. 10th ed. New York: Addison Wesley Longman, 2000.

Goetz, Ernest T., Diane L. Schallert, Ralph E. Reynolds, and Dean I. Radin. "Reading in Perspective: What Real Cops and Pretend Burglars Look for in a Story." *Journal of Educational Psychology* 75 (1983): 500–10.

Lefrancois, Guy R. *The Lifespan*. 3rd ed. Belmont, CA: Wadsworth, 1990.

Savage, John. "The Getaway." *Saturday Evening Post* 10 (1966).

Zunker, Vernon G. *Career Counseling: Applied Concepts of Life Planning*. 6th ed. Pacific Grove: Wadsworth Group, 2002.

CHAPTER 2

Berk, Laura E. *Development through the Lifespan*. 2nd ed. Boston: Allyn and Bacon, 2001.

Campbell, Neil A., Lawrence G. Mitchell, and Jane B. Reece. *Biology: Concepts and Connections*. 3rd ed. San Francisco: Benjamin/Cummings, 2000.

Edwards, George C. III, Martin P. Wattenberg, and Robert L. Lineberry. *Government in America: People, Politics, and Policy*. 9th ed. New York, Addison Wesley Longman, 2000.

Hewitt, Paul G., John Suchocki, and Leslie A. Hewitt. *Conceptual Physical Science*. 2nd ed. New York: Addison Wesley Longman, 1999.

Etymologically Speaking. http://www.westegg.com/etymology/.

Merriam-Webster's Collegiate Dictionary. http://www.m-w.com.

CHAPTER 3

Barker, Larry L., and Deborah Roach Gaut. *Communication*. 8th ed. Boston: Allyn and Bacon, 2002.

Bryjak, George J., and Michael P. Soroka. *Sociology: Changing Societies in a Diverse World*. 4th ed. Boston: Allyn and Bacon, 2001.

Campbell, Neil A., Lawrence G. Mitchell, and Jane B. Reece. *Biology: Concepts and Connections*. 3rd ed. San Francisco: Benjamin/Cummings, 2000.

Davidson, J. Kenneth, Sr., and Nelwyn B. Moore. *Marriage and Family: Change and Continuity*. Boston: Allyn and Bacon, 1996.

DeVito, Joseph A. *Essentials of Human Communication*. 3rd ed. New York: Addison Wesley Longman, 1999.

Edwards, George C. III, Martin P. Wattenberg, and Robert L. Lineberry. *Government in America: People, Politics, and Policy*. 9th ed. New York: Addison Wesley Longman, 2000.

Hewitt, Paul G., John Suchocki, and Leslie A. Hewitt. *Conceptual Physical Science*. 2nd ed. New York: Addison Wesley Longman, 1999.

Manis, Robert. *The Marriage and Family Workbook.* Boston: Allyn and Bacon, 2001.

O'Connor, Karen, and Larry J. Sabato. *American Government: Continuity and Change.* Alternate 2000 Edition. New York: Addison Wesley Longman, 2000.

Tischler, Henry L. *Introduction to Sociology.* 5th ed. Fort Worth: Harcourt Brace College, 1996.

Yaworski, JoAnn. "Why Students Succeed or Fail: Theories of Underachieving Affluent College Students." Diss. State University of New York Albany, 1996.

CHAPTER 4

Barker, Larry L., and Deborah Roach Gaut. *Communication.* 8th ed. Boston: Allyn and Bacon, 2002.

Campbell, Neil A., Lawrence G. Mitchell, and Jane B. Reece. *Biology: Concepts and Connections.* 3rd ed. San Francisco: Benjamin/Cummings, 2000.

DeVito, Joseph A. *Essentials of Human Communication.* 3rd ed. New York: Addison Wesley Longman, 1999.

Halegood, Rog. "The Anatomy of Drink I, II." *Future Magazine.* Lincolnwood, IL: Jamestown Publishers, 1989.

Hughes, Langston. "Tain't So." *Short Stories.* New York: Hill and Wang, 1996.

Manis, Robert. *The Marriage and Family Workbook.* Boston: Allyn and Bacon, 2001.

Yaworski, JoAnn. "Why Students Succeed or Fail: Theories of Underachieving Affluent College Students." Diss. State University of New York Albany, 1996.

CHAPTER 5

Barker, Larry L., and Deborah Roach Gaut. *Communication.* 8th ed. Boston: Allyn and Bacon, 2002.

Benedetti, Robert. *The Actor in You.* Boston: Allyn and Bacon, 1999.

———. "The Actor's State of Mind." *The Actor in You: Sixteen Steps to Understanding the Art Of Acting.* Boston: Allyn and Bacon, 1999.

Bennett, Jeffrey, Megan Donahue, Nicholas Schneider, and Mark Voit. *The Cosmic Perspective.* Menlo Park, CA: Addison Wesley Longman, 1999.

Berk, Laura E. *Development through the Lifespan.* 2nd ed. Boston: Allyn and Bacon, 2001.

Brummett, Palmira, Robert B. Edgar, Neil J. Hackett, George F. Jewsbury, Alastair M. Taylor, Nels M. Bailkey, Clyde J. Lewis, and T. Walter Wallbank (Late). *Civilization: Past and Present.* 9th ed. New York, Addison Wesley, 2000.

Bryjak, George J., and Michael P. Soroka. *Sociology: Changing Societies in a Diverse World.* 4th ed. Boston: Allyn and Bacon, 2001.

Campbell, Neil A., Lawrence G. Mitchell, and Jane B. Reece. *Biology: Concepts and Connections.* 3rd ed. San Francisco: Benjamin/Cummings, 2000.

Danziger, James N. *Understanding the Political World.* 5th ed. New York: Addison Wesley Longman, 2002.

DeVito, Joseph A. *Essentials of Human Communication.* 3rd ed. New York: Addison Wesley Longman, 1999.

———. *The Interpersonal Communication Book.* New York: Addison Wesley Longman, 1998

Edwards, George C. III, Martin P. Wattenberg, and Robert L. Lineberry. *Government in America: People, Politics, and Policy.* 9th ed. New York, Addison Wesley Longman, 2000.

Fischer, Joannie. "The First Clone." *U.S. News and World Report* 3 December 2001: 57.

Garraty, John A., and Mark C. Carnes. *The American Nation: A History of the United States.* 10th ed. New York: Addison Wesley Longman, 2000.

Manis, Robert. *The Marriage and Family Workbook.* Boston: Allyn and Bacon, 2001.

Maxwell, Russell. "Criminal Procedure." Lecture. Green Mountain College, Poultney, Vermont. 1995.

———. "Three Elements of a Crime." Lecture. Green Mountain College, Poultney, Vermont. 1995.

Parkay, Forrest W., and Beverly Hardcastle Stanford. *Becoming a Teacher.* 5th ed. Boston: Allyn and Bacon, 2001.

Stanley, Thomas J., and William D. Danko. *The Millionaire Next Door.* Atlanta: Longstreet. 1996

Yaworski, JoAnn. "How to Create and Use Power-Point Presentations to Teach Reading Skills." *Journal of College Reading and Learning* 32.1 (fall 2001): 14–21.

———. "Why Students Succeed or Fail: Theories of Underachieving Affluent College Students." Diss. State University of New York Albany, 1996.

CHAPTER 6

Barker, Larry L., and Deborah Roach Gaut. *Communication*. 8th ed. Boston: Allyn and Bacon, 2002.

Bennett, Jeffrey, Megan Donahue, Nicholas Schneider, and Mark Voit. *The Cosmic Perspective*. Menlo Park, CA: Addison Wesley Longman, 1999.

Berk, Laura E. *Development through the Lifespan*. 2nd ed. Boston: Allyn and Bacon, 2001.

Bryjak, George J., and Michael P. Soroka. *Sociology: Changing Societies in a Diverse World*. 4th ed. Boston: Allyn and Bacon, 2001.

Campbell, Neil A., Lawrence G. Mitchell, and Jane B. Reece. *Biology: Concepts and Connections*. 3rd ed. San Francisco: Benjamin/Cummings, 2000.

Davidson, J. Kenneth, Sr., and Nelwyn B. Moore. *Marriage and Family: Change and Continuity*. Boston: Allyn and Bacon, 1996.

DeVito, Joseph A. *Essentials of Human Communication*. 3rd ed. New York: Addison Wesley Longman, 1999.

———. *The Interpersonal Communication Book*. 8th ed. New York: Addison Wesley Longman, 1998.

Farr, Grant, and Corie Hammers. *Global Societies to Accompany Sociology: Changing Societies in a Diverse World*. 4th ed. Boston: Allyn and Bacon, 2001.

Finney, Jack. "Contents of a Dead Man's Pocket." Ohio: Crowell-Collier Publishing Company, 1956.

Garraty, John A., and Mark C. Carnes. *The American Nation: A History of the United States*. 10th ed. New York: Addison Wesley Longman, 2000.

Lakoff, George. *Women, Fire, and Dangerous Things*. Chicago: University of Chicago, 1990.

Macionis, John J. *Sociology*. 6th ed. Upper Saddle River, NJ: Prentice Hall, 1997.

Marieb, Elaine N. *Human Anatomy and Physiology*. 3rd ed. Redwood City, CA: Benjamin/Cummings, 1995.

Maxwell, Russell. "Business Law." Lecture. Green Mountain College, Poultney, Vermont. 1994.

O'Connor, Karen, and Larry J. Sabato. *American Government: Continuity and Change*. New York: Addison Wesley Longman, 2000.

Smith, Robert L., and Thomas M. Smith. "Time to Rethink the Lawn," *Elements of Ecology*. 4th ed. San Francisco: Addison Wesley Longman, 2000. V-C.

Tischler, Henry L. *Introduction to Sociology*. 5th ed. Fort Worth: Harcourt Brace College, 1996.

CHAPTER 7

DeVito, Joseph A. *Essentials of Human Communication*. 3rd ed. New York: Addison Wesley Longman, 1999.

Farr, Grant, and Corie Hammers. *Global Societies to Accompany Sociology: Changing Societies in a Diverse World*. 4th ed. Boston: Allyn and Bacon, 2001.

Finney, Jack. "Contents of a Dead Man's Pocket." Ohio: Crowell-Collier Publishing Company, 1956.

Garraty, John A., and Mark C. Carnes. *The American Nation: A History of the United States*. 10th ed. New York: Addison Wesley Longman, 2000.

Janaro, Richard Paul, and Thelma C. Altshuler. *The Art of Being Human: Humanities for the 21st Century*. New York: Addison Wesley Longman, 2000.

King, Martin Luther, Jr. Address. The March on Washington for Jobs and Freedom. 28 Aug. 1963.

Rodman, George. *Making Sense of Media: An Introduction to Mass Communication*. Boston: Allyn and Bacon, 2001.

CHAPTER 8

Associated Press. "Lawn Chair Pilot Says One Flight Is Enough." *Lancaster Sunday News*, July 4, 1982.

Bennett, Jeffrey, Megan Donahue, Nicholas Schneider, and Mark Voit. *The Cosmic Perspective*. 2nd ed. San Francisco: Pearson Education, 2002.

Colby, Michael. "Osama ConAgra: Anatomy of a Recall." *Wild Matters* (Sept. 2002): 14.

DeVito, Joseph A. *Essentials of Human Communication*. 3rd ed. New York: Addison Wesley Longman, 1999.

Gaines, Larry K., Michael Kaune, and Roger LeRoy Miller. *Criminal Justice in Action*. Belmont, CA: Wadsworth/Thomson Learning, 2001.

Hewitt, Paul G., John Suchocki, and Leslie A. Hewitt. *Conceptual Physical Science* 2nd ed. New York: Addison Wesley Longman, 1999.

Jordan, Barbara, and Shelby Hearon. *A Self-Portrait by Barbara Jordan*. Doubleday & Co., Inc., 1979.

Manis, Robert. *The Marriage and Family Workbook*. Boston: Allyn and Bacon, 2001.

Miller, LeRoy, Daniel K. Benjamin, and Douglass C. North. *The Economics of Public Issues*. 12th ed. New York: Addison Wesley Longman, 2001.

Nash, Gary B., Julie Roy Jeffrey, John R. Howe, Peter J. Frederick, Allen F. Davis, and Allan M. Winkler. *The American People: Creating a Nation and a Society*. New York: Addison Wesley, 2000.

Naylor, Gloria. *The Women of Brewster Place*. New York: Viking Penguin, 1982.

Reagan, Ronald. "A Lesson for Living." *Plus: The Magazine of Positive Thinking* (Feb. 1990). The Foundation for Christian Living, P.O. Box FCL, Pawling, NY 12564.

Rodman, George. *Making Sense of Media: An Introduction to Mass Communication*. Boston: Allyn and Bacon, 2001.

Smith, Robert Leo, and Thomas M. Smith. *Elements of Ecology*. 4th ed. New York: Addison Wesley Longman, 2000.

Vacca, JoAnne L., Richard T. Vacca, and Mary K. Grove. *Reading and Learning to Read*. 4th ed. New York: Addison Wesley Longman, 2000.

CHAPTER 9

Douglass, Frederick. *The Life of Frederick Douglass*. New York: Penguin Putnam, 1997.

Eidson, Stacey. "Got rBGH?" *Metropolitan Spirit* 9.8 (1998): 15–17.

Hayden, Torey L. *One Child*. New York: Avon, 1981.

Parkay, Forrest W., and Beverly Hardcastle Stanford. *Becoming a Teacher*. 5th ed. Boston: Allyn and Bacon, 2001.

"Researcher Says Teacher Shortage Is 'Misdiagnosed.'" *Express Times* (Easton, PA). 12 Dec. 2001: B-9.

Wlodkowski, Raymond J., and Judith H. Jaynes. *Eager to Learn: Helping Children Become Motivated and Love Learning*. San Francisco: Jossey-Bass, 1990.

CHAPTER 10

Berk, Laura E. *Development through the Lifespan*. Boston: Allyn and Bacon, 2001.

Canfora, Alan. *1970 Events Summary*. http://alancanfora.com/.

Garraty, John A., and Mark C. Carnes. *The American Nation: A History of the United States*. 10th ed. New York: Addison Wesley Longman, 2000.

Miller, Roger LeRoy Miller, Daniel K. Benjamin, and Douglass C. North. "Slave Redemption in Sudan," *The Economics of Public Issues*. 12th ed. New York: Addison Wesley Longman, 2001.

Mynatt, Clifford R., and Michael E. Doherty. *Understanding Human Behavior*. Boston: Allyn and Bacon, 1999.

Nash, Gary B., Julie Roy Jeffrey, John R. Howe, Peter J. Frederick, Allen F. Davis, and Allan M. Winkler. *The American People: Creating a Nation and a Society*. New York: Addison Wesley Longman, 2000.

Seppa, N. "Secondary Smoke Carries High Price." *Science News Online*. 17 Jan. 1998. http://www.sciencenews.org/sn_arc98/1_17_98/fob1.htm.

Wendell, Barbara. "Can Untenured Faculty Members Stop Grade Inflation?" *The Chronicle: Daily News*. 13 Dec. 2001. http://chronicle.com/jobs/2001/12/2001121301c.htm.

CHAPTER 11

Bransford, John D., and Marcia K. Johnson, "Contextual Prerequisites for Understanding: Some Investigations of Comprehension and Recall." *Journal of Verbal Learning and Verbal Behavior* 11 (1972): 722.

Davidson, J. Kenneth, Sr., and Nelwyn B. Moore. *Marriage and Family: Change and Continuity*. Boston: Allyn and Bacon, 1996.

Halegood, Rog. "The Anatomy of Drink I, II." *Future*. Lincolnwood, IL: Jamestown Publishing Company, 1989

Kurose, James F., and Keith W. Ross. *Computer Networking: A Top-Down Approach Featuring the Internet*. New York: Addison Wesley Longman, 2000.

Moore, E. E. "An Experiment in Teaching College Students How to Study." *School and Society* 2. 17 July 1915.

Smith, Lee. "What We Now Know About Memory." *Fortune*. 17 April 1995: 98–102.

Smith, Robert Leo, and Thomas M. Smith. *Elements of Ecology*. 4th ed. San Francisco: Addison Wesley Longman, 2000.

CHAPTER 12

Campbell, Neil A., Lawrence G. Mitchell, and Jane B. Reece. *Biology: Concepts and Connections*. 3rd ed. San Francisco: Benjamin Cummings, 2000.

Edwards, George C. III, Martin P. Wattenberg, and Robert L. Lineberry. *Government in America: People, Politics, and Policy*. 6th ed. New York: Addison-Wesley Educational Publishers, 2002.

Henslin, James M. *Essentials of Sociology: A Down-to-Earth Approach*. 4th ed. Boston: Allyn and Bacon, 2002.

Macionis, John J. *Sociology*. 9th ed. Upper Saddle River, NJ: Prentice Hall, 2003.

Manis, Robert. *The Marriage and Family Workbook: An Interactive Reader, Text, and Workbook*. Boston: Allyn and Bacon, 2001.

Parsons, Richard D., Stephanie Lewis Hinson, and Deborah Sardo-Brown. *Educational Psychology: A Practitioner-Researcher Model of Teaching*. Belmont, CA: Wadsworth/Thomson Learning, 2001.

Pipkin, Bernard W., and D. D. Trent. *Geology and the Environment*. Pacific Grove, CA: Brooks/Cole: A Division of Thomson Learning, 2001.

Samuelson, Paul A., and William D. Nordhaus. *Macroeconomics*. 17th ed. (New York: McGraw-Hill, 2001.

Sukiennik, Diane, William Bendat, and Lisa Raufman. *The Career Fitness Program*. 6th ed. Upper Saddle River, NJ: Prentice Hall, 2001.

CHAPTER 13

Berk, Laura E. *Development through the Lifespan*. Boston: Allyn and Bacon, 2001.

Brummett, Palmira, Robert B. Edgar, Neil J. Hackett, George F. Jewsbruy, Alastair M. Taylor, Nels M. Bailkey, Clyde J. Lewis, and T. Walter Wallbank (Late). *Civilization: Past and Present*. 9th ed. New York, Addison Wesley, 2000.

Bryjak, George J., and Michael P. Soroka. *Sociology: Changing Societies in a Diverse World*. 4th ed. Boston: Allyn and Bacon, 2001.

DeVito, Joseph A. *The Interpersonal Communication Book*. 8th ed. New York: Addison Wesley Longman, 1998.

Harvard University Gazette. 2 Oct. 1997. "Reading Better, Thinking Better." http://www.news.harvard.edu/gazette/1997/10.02/Readingbetterth.html.

Lefrancois, Guy R. *The Lifespan*. 3rd ed. Belmont, CA: Wadsworth, 1990.

Manis, Robert. *The Marriage and Family Workbook: An Interactive Reader, Text, and Workbook*. Boston: Allyn and Bacon, 2001.

Mynatt, Clifford R., and Michael E. Doherty. *Understanding Human Behavior*. Boston: Allyn and Bacon, 1999.

Index